P9-CLE-621

JUDITH MILLER

A TOUCHSTONE BOOK
Published by Simon & Schuster
New York London Toronto
Sydney Tokyo Singapore

One, by One, by One

FACING THE HOLOCAUST

TOUCHSTONE
Simon & Schuster Building
Rockefeller Center
1230 Avenue of the Americas
New York, New York 10020

First Touchstone Edition 1991
TOUCHSTONE and colophon are registered trademarks
of Simon & Schuster Inc.
Designed by Nina D'Amario/Levavi & Levavi
Manufactured in the United States of America

10 9 8 7 6 5 4 3 2

10 9 8 7 6 5 4 3 2 Pbk.

Library of Congress Cataloging in Publication Data
Miller, Judith, date.
One, by one, by one: facing the Holocaust/Judith Miller.
p. cm.
Includes bibliographical references.
1. Holocaust, Jewish (1939-1945)—Public opinion. 2. Holocaust, Jewish (1939-1945)—Historiography. I. Title.
D804.3.M55 1990
940.53'18—dc20 90-30091
CIP

ISBN 0-671-64472-6
ISBN 0-671-74034-2 Pbk.

To my parents and for Masha

Contents

PREFACE, 9
GERMANY, 13
AUSTRIA, 61
THE NETHERLANDS, 93
FRANCE, 112
THE SOVIET UNION, 158
THE UNITED STATES, 220
CONCLUSIONS, 277
NOTES, 288
ACKNOWLEDGMENTS, 304
INDEX, 307

Preface

This book is not about the Holocaust but about how it is remembered.

It is about memories of an event so horrible that scholars disagree to this day about what it should be called. The term Holocaust—a Greek word that originally meant a sacrifice wholly consumed by fire—is obviously a misnomer. The Nazi genocide was not an offering to God; nor were the Jews and Gypsies and others who were slaughtered willing victims. The word Holocaust, rather, is a palatable way of alluding to man's descent into almost indescribable cruelty, not during ancient times but in this century. For sometimes, words fail us. The term genocide or massacre does not convey the enormity of what happened. So for want of a more accurate term, the word Holocaust has come to symbolize the evils that were perpetrated by the Germans and their accomplices. Today, even uttering the word makes people deeply uncomfortable.

This book is about that discomfort, about the struggle within each of us between the very human desire to repress memories of that era and the need not to forget it. I have tried to explore the way different people have tried to distort, to justify, to erase memories of the Holocaust, and how some have tried to use them to rationalize the past.

This book is also about the obligations of memory, about what we owe those who survived and those who did not. Survivors, Jews especially, want us all to remember the Holocaust and to pass the memories on to all our heirs. But how can this be done most effectively and honestly? If the Holocaust was unique, as I believe it was, how can it be compared to other catastrophes? If it may not be compared, how is it relevant?

I asked these questions in six countries. All, except the Soviet Union, are democracies today. All share European roots and heritage.

Germany, of course. Though the Germans do not use the word "Holocaust" (they prefer "Final Solution" and other ambiguous terms devised by the Nazis), the event was a German inspiration. Young Germans today know this; despite attempts at evasion, many are deeply ashamed of the past. The name of the town of Dachau was not changed after the concentration camp nearby was destroyed, but pregnant women frequently go to hospitals in neighboring towns so that their children's birth certificates will not bear its name.

The ways in which the Holocaust has been remembered and taught are very different in the two parts of Germany. I concentrated on the Federal Republic, because, unlike East Germany under its Communist domination, it has not argued that the Holocaust was something perpetrated by the "other" Germany.

Austria, too. The Austrians elected as their president Kurt Waldheim, a former Nazi soldier who declared that he had only done his "duty" in serving with the Waffen SS during the war. Why do they call themselves Hitler's first victims when they were his first enthusiastic allies?

The Netherlands. Holland is the home of Anne Frank, the Holocaust's most famous victim. Its citizens are among those most frequently honored by Israel. Few countries enjoy such a sterling reputation; few have so high an opinion of themselves and their wartime conduct. And rarely is the gap between perception and history so glaring.

France, the post-revolutionary home of liberty, equality, and fraternity, had a well established Jewish community. Under German occupation, it betrayed many of its Jewish citizens with little prodding or regret. Even so, seventy-five percent of French Jews were saved, or some would say, saved themselves. The French, absorbed by their civilization, are deeply troubled by this chapter.

The Soviet Union lost the greatest number of people during the war. By the war's end, only 20 percent of men born in 1923 were alive. But this nation that lost so much has been unable and unwilling to recognize that its Jews suffered disproportionately because of their Jewishness. The historical record has been officially distorted.

Finally, the United States. The majority of Jewish survivors came here. They found a democratic, tolerant culture in which they and their children prospered. Americans are far removed, morally and geographically, from the scene of the genocide. While this distance has enabled many American Jews to confront the Holocaust, for many it has become an obsession. It is they who have been most enraged by the efforts to erase or alter the memory of what happened. They have led the campaign against President Reagan's commemoration at the cemetery at Bitburg, against Kurt Waldheim, and against the presence of Polish Carmelite nuns at Auschwitz. They have a practical stake in keeping memory of the Holocaust alive, as a way of maintaining American support for Israel, and as a talisman in fighting discrimination against themselves and other minorities.

As I traveled in Europe and America, I heard different people describe different Holocausts. There did not seem to be a "collective memory" in any country I visited. The war bitterly divided people already split by class, religion, and political ideology. Jews, however, do seem to have something resembling collective memory. For them, memory is almost religion. As Saul Friedlander, the Israeli Holocaust historian, has noted, Judaism is partly the retelling of a story; remembrance is the essential component of Jewish tradition.

In each of the six countries, I found many signs of Holocaust revisionism. Facts have been recrafted, through false comparisons and analyses of peripheral rather than the core events of the Holocaust. There is what the Germans call "Schlusstrich," (the creation of historical dividing lines) and inversion of guilt, blaming the victims.

Only a tiny group of malevolent cranks contends that the Holocaust did not take place, but the more subtle forms of revisionism are evident in battles over how history should be taught, in jokes, in literature, and in the popular culture, in television and films.

I am a journalist. So I tried to let people describe the Holocaust they remembered in their own words. What I have written are their memories of the past. Some of what they said was true, some distorted. But I wanted the clashes of memory to emerge through the voices of those who endured those years and those struggling today to understand or rationalize the inexplicable.

Through their stories, I have come to a few conclusions about the prospects for coming to grips with the Holocaust. Some of them are troubling.

Judith Miller
New York
January 1990

Germany

A tiny gap in history was closed in May 1987 when Henny Oppenheimer returned to Fulda, a picture-postcard West German town near the border with East Germany.

Mrs. Oppenheimer, née Henny Lump, one of eleven Lump children, was born in 1918. She had fled Nazi terror in 1939 for safety in England, and later in America. At age sixty-eight, she had come back, along with nineteen members of her own family and some three hundred former residents, at the invitation and expense of the town council, for a reunion of Holocaust survivors from Fulda.

In 1933, when the town had 30,000 residents, Jews had numbered 1,200. In 1987, the population was 60,000; there were 36 Jews.

The day before the ceremony, the "Jewish guests," as the former residents were called, visited the Jewish cemetery in Edelzell, a tranquil suburb where townsfolk picnic on sunny spring weekends, like the one that May.

As Henny stood at the foot of her mother's gray tombstone, badly eroded by fifty years of harsh German winters and other seasons of neglect, she studied a map of the cemetery that her hosts had distributed. Five years ago, the town council had funded a project to identify the individuals buried in the Jewish cemetery to preserve some memory of the Jewish community that had once flourished here.[1]

Henny noticed that the grave on the map immediately beyond her mother's was designated, as were several others, "unidentified."

"But I know who is buried here," she murmured to her daughter. "I know who is here," she repeated, her tiny frame trembling with recognition, her voice rising in pitch and volume. "It's Hugo," she exclaimed. "Hugo Plaut!"

She went to find a Fulda official with whom she could share her discovery. Hugo Plaut's grave was not the one marked on the cemetery map, she said. A mistake had been made.

Hugo, she told the tall young city official, had been her boyfriend, one of many before the war. Henny, by many accounts, was the most beautiful of the Lump children, indeed, one of the most alluring young women in all of Fulda. Hugo had been arrested before she had fled Germany. He had been sent to a camp somewhere. They had lost contact.

In England friends had told her that Hugo had died in the camp in 1939 on the day he was to have been released—how they did not know. His body had been returned to Fulda, a rarity in those times. Because Hugo had always adored Henny's mother, they recounted, he had been buried next to her grave.

The young official listened intently and wrote down in a notebook the letters "P-L-A-U-T," while Henny talked on, unconsciously tugging on his sleeve in her excitement. As details of Hugo's brief life poured forth, a young man seemed to take shape: a slender, love-smitten young Jew, with dark hair, black eyes, a somewhat shy youth who lived near her house, who was gifted in sports but loved poetry, who had a "musical voice."

He is buried right "there," Henny insisted, pointing to the unmarked grave just beyond her mother's.

Now, there is one less misplaced Jewish grave. Thanks to her memory, one more member of Fulda's once-thriving Jewish community has regained an identity of sorts, if only in death.

This was but one of the many gaps in Fulda's past that were filled last spring as a result of the town's largest reunion of Holocaust survivors.

In the past few years, there have been many such reunions in West Germany. Holocaust exhibitions and commemorations have become so common that they are virtually a cottage industry in the Bundesrepublic.[2]

The phenomenon has been most pronounced in Germany. Though Poland, Austria, Belgium, and France lost thousands of Jews in the Holocaust, none has invited survivors back in such large numbers for commemoration ceremonies. Why the belated German interest in renewing contacts with the Jews who were forced to flee their native land? Why now?

"Because we sense their loss more deeply with every passing year," said Wolfgang Hamberger, Fulda's Lord Mayor, a Christian Democrat in his fifties, a staunch Catholic, who began trying to reestablish contacts with Fulda's Jews more than eighteen years ago.[3]

The rash of commemorations and Holocaust reunions in Germany suggests that for survivors, too, the time for remembrance has finally come.

"I thought of coming back before now, but my heart didn't allow it," said Lisa Wallach Levy, who returned to Fulda last May for the first time in forty-five years. "I lost a sister here, my parents, my cousins, a beautiful family. Both my children had come to visit; they encouraged me to come back. But I couldn't do it before now."

Hermann G., a participant who asked not to be identified, said he had returned because "I wanted to see Fulda just once more before I die." Now in his late seventies, he knew, he said matter-of-factly, "The end is near. So I wanted to visit my parents' graves, the school I attended. I wanted to see even one familiar face from my childhood. Would they know what had happened to me all these years? And I wanted my grandson to see it, to know what happened here."

"I needed to show them that I had survived," declared Johanna Lump Weiss, another survivor. "I came to show the Germans, but I guess I needed to prove it to myself as well."

Many students of the Holocaust believe that reunions like the one in Fulda could not have taken place much before now. "Only a generation more distant from the immediate catastrophe could dare to approach it," observed Michael Berenbaum, the project director of the U.S. Holocaust Memorial Museum. "As the story of Lot's wife illustrates, a person cannot afford to look back while fleeing."[4]

The commemorations have been occurring not one but two generations after the war. This, according to Berenbaum, was also predictable. Many Holocaust survivors were psychologically unable to discuss their experiences with their own children; it was their grandchildren's curiosity that sparked a response, a resurgence of memory.

The commemoration in Fulda, an extraordinary gathering, underscored the benefits, as well as the limitations of such events. It provided clues to the motivations of Germans who have sponsored such events, and of the Jews who have chosen to return and participate in them. It showed why commemorations like this one can, under certain circumstances, for certain people, be an effective transmitter of memory, a means of overcoming man's natural instinct to forget or suppress. Commemoration can also be an excellent mechanism for reconciliation—with one's past, with one's former enemies, between children of former enemies.

But like war-crimes trials or political tests of strength, commemorations are complex phenomena. And the gathering in Fulda was emotionally wrenching for most of the survivors, and, often, even more so for their children and grandchildren. For some, it proved only how elusive the goal of reconciliation with oneself and one's former enemies remains.

Fulda is something of an anomaly. Founded in 744 by the Benedictine monk Sturmius, better known as St. Boniface, the city is a Catholic enclave in the predominantly Protestant region of Hesse. More than 70 percent of its inhabitants are Roman Catholics. St. Boniface is buried in St. Michael's Cathedral, and German Catholic bishops have been convening their annual conferences here since 1867. In 1949, Fulda also became the seat of the presidial office of the German Protestant church organization.

It is a fiercely conservative town, "black as the night," say its inhabitants, a reference to the dominance of Germany's conservative Christian Democratic Union party, whose color is black and which in 1986 controlled an absolute majority on the fifty-seven-member town council.

A glossy tourist brochure distributed to the Holocaust survivors contains a "brief historical information" section that omits any reference to the years of National Socialism. Between 1927, when Fulda became an "independent municipality" and 1944, which, according to the brochure, was marked by a "heavy air raid on the city," there are no entries.

As in many German towns, its officials appear somewhat defensive about its wartime record. Anton Schmidt, editor of the local newspaper, *Fuldaer Zeitung,* and president of the city's chamber of commerce, argued that because of the residents' deeply ingrained Catholicism, National Socialism in the 1930s had far less appeal in Fulda than in other parts of Hesse and in Germany as a whole.[5]

In 1933, for example, Fulda's last prewar democratic town council election, the conservative, heavily Catholic Zentrum party, the historical predecessor of the Christian Democrats, won 51.6 percent of the votes cast; the National Socialists won 26.9 percent, or eight of the thirty-two seats on the town council.[6]

Having come to power at the national level, however, "the National Socialists were relentless in putting in motion the machinery of uniformity and, in Fulda, too, they hindered the existence of our elected town council," recounted Paul Gwosdz, Fulda's chief town councillor. "After several elected representatives had been forbidden to take up their council seats, the majority—the center—resigned their seats under pressure by the National Socialists." The places were filled on October 13, 1933, by National Socialists, the "death certificate of democracy in Fulda," he said.

What officials here did not mention is that while a German Catholic bishops conference would later condemn the Nazis, it was here in Fulda in 1938 that the bishops overwhelmingly approved a resolution congratulating Hitler for his invasion of Czechoslovakia and the liberation of the oppressed Germanic peoples of the Sudetenland.[7]

Nor did town officials volunteer that no Jewish adult was hidden successfully during the war in this God-fearing town.

"There was a priest, Heinrich Huhn, my teacher in school," recalled Herbert Naftali Sonn, a Fulda-born historian who has written two books on the town. "The priest saved two Jewish children by hiding them in his home. He sent them to America after the war," said Professor Sonn, who now lives in Israel.

"But where were all the other Catholics? Yes, it was a religious town, but it was a silent crowd."[8]

Mayor Hamberger did not disagree. Although there had been some "courageous examples of self-sacrificing assistance" to the community's Jews, he said, "there was also a lack of steadfastness, loyalty and prayer, a lack of faith and love." The majority had simply "surrendered to the suggestion of authority of the totalitarian Nazi state."[9]

The ceremony in Fulda in May 1987 was among the largest of its kind ever held in Germany. The guests included 130 Jews from Israel, 97 from the United States, and 70 from more than 20 other countries.

"We invited everybody because we did not want to select guests," Mayor Hamberger explained in May 1987 at his office in the stately Stadtschloss, the baroque town hall. "The word itself—'select'—has terrible connotations for us," he said. "It's a bad word, a bad concept. So we decided to invite everybody.

"Much to our surprise," he continued, "nearly everybody came."

Despite the fact that Fulda had expected one hundred guests and received more than three hundred, including spouses and children, the week-long commemoration ran smoothly, "like clockwork," one survivor observed, an ironic nod to legendary German efficiency. Buses shuttled participants back and forth to hotels and events with near-perfect punctuality; hotel rooms and restaurants offered crisp, efficient service to the city's guests; the college students hired by the town's tourist office to help out were models of decorum and spared no effort to ensure that the former residents' many needs and conflicting requests were satisfied; townspeople were warm, helpful, and hospitable. The organization was, in brief, impeccable.

The German hosts paid special attention to the guests' sensitivities. City officials and residents seemed to understand that their every word, every gesture, in a restaurant or shop or hotel, would be scrutinized. For many of the guests, any German would be judged automatically guilty until proven innocent—guilty of anti-Semitism, intolerance, aloofness, and insensitivity. So Lufthansa, the German national airline, which had flown participants to Frankfurt from around the globe, made certain that flights with Fulda's Jews as passengers had an ample supply of kosher food on board. The town's largest bookstore featured a window display of Holocaust and Jewish literature in German. Security in town was tight but discreet. The Mayor had ordered that no uniforms be worn by guards who had been specially hired to provide security for public events. The Mayor and other city officials donned yarmulkes for appropriate occasions.

The most important events—and the most emotionally taxing for the Jews—were the visit to the cemetery, the dinner meeting with residents of Fulda, and the dedication of the former Jewish school, which so many in the group had attended, as Fulda's Jewish cultural center. Thanks to the town council's ambitious program of city and museum tours, walks, concerts, lunches, dinners, and lectures, every minute of the day was filled.[10]

Martin Steinberger, of London, found the reunion a little too efficient. "Everything was organized to the last detail. It reminded me of the Nazi period and the deportations—how well they managed everything."

"It is almost as if they didn't want us to have too much time to think—to dwell on what happened here," mused Bert Wallace, an inventor from New York who was making his first trip back to Fulda since his family fled to the United States in 1938.

But for most the return to Fulda was a journey not only into the past but into themselves—a time to evaluate what had happened to them in this city and since. While reactions, predictably, varied sharply, most of those who participated expressed enthusiasm and described the trip, especially after they returned home, as an extremely positive experience. They said they had been unprepared for, and pleasantly surprised by, the warmth of their reception in the city they had fled.[11]

Countless memories returned: the evil, sad, and bitter, long repressed; but also pleasant and uplifting ones, of people who had helped them, of comfort and humor, of sympathy and support.

Bert Wallace recounted how Fulda's police chief, a "good man" named Berenson, had warned the Wallace family to leave their house on four or five occasions when the Nazis were conducting raids. Berenson had long since died, but Wallace was delighted to encounter his son at the reunion dinner.

Frank Feist Schuster, a physician, who had left Fulda with his parents when he was nine months old, met an elderly German woman in a neighboring town where his grandparents and an aunt are buried. She had known his relatives, she told him. During what she characterized as "those bad times," her parents used to bake challah for the Friday-night Sabbath dinner; they would leave it for the Schusters under a bridge so that they could enjoy the forbidden ritual bread.

Several of the participants said that they felt more "German" after the trip, for better or worse. "It's very strong, this sense of German identity," said Lisa Wallach Levy.

"I hadn't spoken German for years but it all came back," said

Doris Fingerhood, a member of the Lump family. "I not only got to know my own family better here, I was once again steeped in Fulda's history and culture. I love the sense of history here."

For some, this discovery of their "Germanness" was a bit of a shock. "You can suddenly see how it could have happened," said Yaakov Hain, of Danville, Virginia, whose father came from Fulda. "They don't walk when the stoplight is red, even if there isn't a car in sight. Stores close one minute after 2 P.M. Restaurants won't serve you after the appointed hour. They're so structured and regimented, to this day!"

"There remains a tremendous compulsion to follow orders, to do everything thoroughly," said Bert Wallace. "I keep thinking: a little bit of anarchy is good for the soul."

At breakfast one morning at the Hotel Lenz, Else Baum Reiter, who had come from Fulda, and her American-born son, Ron, were discussing the visit when Mrs. Reiter began chiding a non-German guest at their table for her manners. The guest had failed to deposit the wrappers of the butter slices in the bowl in the middle of the table marked "Für den Sauberen Tisch," or "For a Clear Table."

"My mother," said Ron, sipping his coffee, bemused, "is a German Jew."

The most rewarding part of the visit for most of the participants was finding old friends and people they had known and cared about among the survivors.

Lee Stern, who was born in Fulda and now resides in New Jersey, was walking out of a restaurant when she heard someone call her name. "I turned around and there was my kindergarten teacher!" said Mrs. Stern. "I thought she had been killed in a concentration camp, but there she was, large as life, and like me, enjoying life in the United States."

"I found a school chum who had dropped out of the gymnasium in 1934 before graduating because the Nazis had doubled the fees for Jewish students," Mr. Wallace said. "I thought he had died at Auschwitz, but Hermann Wiesenberg and his brother had survived five years at Buchenwald and were living in New York. Imagine my joy at finding him alive!"

Nancy Campus, a psychologist whose mother was born in Fulda, said that the large numbers of visitors were "critical" to the success of the reunion because the event was intended to "connect people with people" and because "the crowd provided a sense of camaraderie and support."[12]

"Knowing and dealing with painful realities in isolation is too much for the human spirit to endure," Ms. Campus observed. "So there was a healing that emerged from sharing and a strength in numbers."

The Lump family, in many respects, was a microcosm of the group of returnees. Their reactions mirrored the intensity and variety of what many of the participants experienced. For some of the survivors, it was their first trip back to Fulda since the war; for some of their children, it was their first visit to Germany. Several could "forgive" young Germans for what had happened here; others said that the trip had not changed the way they felt about Germany or older Germans. Some had resisted the trip; but one said that she had been more afraid of not going. "If you don't return, the fantasies get stronger. They overwhelm you."

Berta Salomon, Henny Lump's older sister, said she had not wanted to come back and would not have but for the encouragement of her family. "I wanted to wipe this out," she said. Her reluctance was reinforced by a previous trip here for two days in 1972 to visit her mother's grave.

"It was terrible," she recounted. "All the Jewish stores had disappeared, all the people I had known. I had no contact with people in the town and didn't particularly want any," she said. "But I decided that since the whole family was going, this trip would have some meaning. We have three generations at the reunion. And I've seen lots of people I know. And I'm glad I came."

Nancy Campus, who is Berta's daughter, said it was not true, as many of the participants maintained, that they had returned only because of "family pressure or encouragement."

"I sensed that they themselves needed to revisit their past," Ms. Campus wrote soon after the trip.[13] They needed questions answered: "What happened to my best friend in school? Is my house still there? Who is living in it? They needed to share memories with others who understood. Some came to reconnect with Germans who had been friends or who had helped them escape, for almost every survivor I spoke with had been aided by a *goy*. In short, for those who came, the need to know overshadowed all the other considerations."

Berta's positive feeling about the trip was the result of her own confrontation with the past, of the discovery of answers to many of the questions her daughter had articulated for her, and the fact that she was able to share her very mixed memories and feelings with former school friends and her family.

"It was like a dam breaking. We heard stories about our family I had never heard before," said Steven Fingerhood, the grandson of Rosie Lump, Henny and Berta's sister, who was killed at Auschwitz. "The trip brought us much closer together. It was a mass catharsis."

The Lumps had been well known throughout the town because of the size of their family, large even by German standards, and because most of the Lump boys were active in sports—excellent soccer players. Like most of the Jews in Fulda, they were orthodox. Bernard, the head of the family, had been a cattle trader. His wife, Regina, the mother of eleven, had been known as a kind, gentle woman who was never too busy to help a friend. They had lived in a four-story house with a red tile roof, typical of the town, at 23 Petersberger Strasse.

The family had prospered in Fulda. Ludwig, the eldest son, was a prominent lawyer. Leopold, another son, was a pharmacist who patented a much-used drug. Berta had married Hans Salomon, who lived in Celle, four hours north of Fulda. Hans's family had relatives in the United States, but there was an eighteen-month wait until their names were scheduled to come up on the quota list. Rather than stay in Germany, where conditions for Jews had been deteriorating rapidly, especially after Kristallnacht, the November 1938 Nazi-orchestrated pogrom against the Jews, Hans and Berta moved to Shanghai to wait.[14]

She remembered her attempt to persuade her mother and father to go with them. "They told us that it was better to die in Germany," said Berta.

"The conditions in Shanghai were horrible," she said. "And many did die there. But we believed it was better than taking a chance of staying in Germany."

Until they got permission to immigrate to the United States, Hans and Berta lived off savings. Other family members were not as lucky. Ludwig, the eldest, was sent briefly to a concentration camp. He was released and fled Germany to Shanghai to join Berta and Hans. Depressed and weakened from his camp incarceration, he died of typhus in 1939.

Leopold, the pharmacist, had moved to Belgium before the Nazis took power in Germany. When the Wehrmacht invaded Belgium, he fled to France. By that time, Berta had arrived in America, and desperately tried to get Leopold the papers he needed to enter the United States. Bureaucratic snafus ensued. The American consulate in Marseilles sent Leopold's documents back three times for what Berta called "petty bureaucratic reasons."

Finally a visa to the United States was granted. But Leopold was arrested by the police en route to his boat to America. He was sent to a concentration camp "somewhere in the East," she said. There he died.

A similar fate awaited Rosie Lump, Berta's sister and Steve Fingerhood's grandmother, who had "married up" in status to Leo Cohen, a wealthy Jew in Berlin. Rosie and her husband sent their two daughters to England in a special children's transport. But they could not leave Berlin and were hidden by a Christian family in the capital. Six months before the liberation of Berlin by the Allies, they were betrayed by a Jewish informer, Steven said. Rosie and her husband both died in the camps. Steven did not know what had happened to their Christian protectors.

On a walking tour of the town, Henny was startled when she saw the convent to which she had run for help one night in 1939 when her mother was critically ill. Under Nazi law, non-Jewish doctors and nurses could not treat Jewish patients, but there was no Jewish physician available to see Regina during a particularly brutal bout of cancer-induced pain.

Henny recalled running down the cobblestone road to the massive wooden doors of the convent. She had banged on the door with her fists, sobbing. A nun, whom she remembered as Sister Theresa, had accompanied her to their home and given her mother injections to ease her pain. She had stayed with Henny and her mother through the night. In the morning, Henny touched her mother's toes. They were ice cold, so she started making a hot-water bottle to warm them.

"It's no use," Sister Theresa said, placing her hand gently on Henny's shoulder. "Your mother is with God now."

Regina was buried at 5 A.M. in a secret Jewish ceremony at the cemetery so that the Nazis wouldn't interfere.

At the convent some forty years later, Henny and Berta found a contemporary of the nun who had helped their mother. The sister said that the nun was a nurse named Ilona, not Theresa. She, too, was with God now, they were told.

"There were a good number of gentiles here in Fulda who had helped us whom we had forgotten," said Mrs. Wallace. "This trip has made us remember them, all the good people who helped."

But with the surfacing of good memories came the bad and the ambivalent. One day, for example, some of the Lumps mustered the courage to visit their former home. It had been occupied for years by a woman, now very old, whose husband had probably bought it at auction from the Nazis.

"She let us enter in stages," said Doris Fingerhood, Rosie's daughter, who had left Germany for England when she was eleven years old. "The house looked physically much as I remembered it, only much smaller. I kept thinking: where did my parents put eleven children?

"But I had remembered the house as full of character. Now it was peculiarly devoid of any. The woman who owned it was eighty. She kept saying that she had lived there for twenty years, but knew nothing about how her husband, who was dead, had acquired it. She was crusty, and very formal, typically German. I didn't know what to believe, and that made me uncomfortable.

"She complained about her health, about the cost of keeping up the house. It was so expensive to maintain that she couldn't travel," Doris said.

"Finally she looked at Steven and me—at our blondish hair and blue eyes—and she said: 'You don't look like the Lumps.' "

There was a final shock awaiting them. Regina's bedroom was virtually unchanged from the day she had died there, with one exception. Over what had been the Lump family's old double bed hung a large wooden cross.

"I'm glad my mother could not see it," Doris said softly.

Other returnees received similar mini-shocks during the visit. Yoram Adler, an Israeli whose parents came from Fulda, recalled that Isfried Adler and Willi, Yoram's father, had a grocery business in town. "It was right there," said Yoram, a computer specialist who pointed to where the store had been. The Adlers had given credit to many of their clients. But one man in the neighboring village of Langebieber had accumulated so much debt that Isfried decided to remind him that payment was long overdue. The customer replied that he did not have to pay because he was a Nazi party member. Isfried told him that his party and Adolf Hitler could "kiss his ass," Yoram recounted.

On April 23, 1933, soon after Hitler came to power, the Adler grocery received a letter from Langebieber.

"M. Isfried Adler," the letter began. "I will denounce you to the county leaders. Do you still remember when you said that Adolf Hitler could kiss your ass?"

Signed: "Respectfully, F. J. Goldbach."

The precise script of the handwritten letter, now tattered and yellowed with age, probably helped save their lives: it prompted Willi's departure for Palestine in 1934, and Isfried's in 1936. All of Yoram's father's family got out of Fulda, but his mother's mother was sent to the East and died at Theresienstadt.

Israeli Professor Sonn's family had been in Fulda for hundreds of years. His father and grandfather had taught in the Jewish school, and he had been a student there. He and his sister had fled Germany to Israel, but his father refused to leave.

"He told us that nothing would happen, that Germans were civilized people," Professor Sonn recounted. "He was very naïve. He did not know the Germans."

After he immigrated to Israel, Sonn concentrated on the history of Fulda and its Jewish community. That history, he said, had begun and ended with slaughter. The first reference to the presence of Jews in Fulda was in 1236, when thirty-six Jews, accused of using Christian blood in Jewish rituals, were locked in the city's *Stockhaus,* which was set on fire and burned to the ground.

The Jewish community here was small, but it flourished over the centuries. There was even a celebrated yeshiva here in the seventeenth century. Most of the community were not assimilated. But like Sonn's father, they felt very German.

After the Nazis came to power, many Jews from neighboring villages sought safety in Fulda, swelling the city's Jewish population from 1,200 to 1,700 in 1936. About half of Fulda's Jews managed to get out of the country before the deportations to concentration camps began. The first deportation, in 1941, consisted of people under fifty. The second, in 1942, included mostly old people.

Professor Sonn's father was among the latter group, which was sent first to Theresienstadt, and finally to Auschwitz. The thirty-six Jews in Fulda today were not born in the city, he said. They were

East Europeans who had nowhere to go after they were released from camps, and settled here. For all practical purposes, Sonn said, the Jewish community of Fulda was dead.

Although Mayor Wolfgang Hamberger has learned much about the suffering of Fulda's Jews, he was not born in this city. He was born in 1931 in Bensheim, a small town near Heidelberg. And he had his own memories of the war.

"You cannot compare our suffering to those people's pain," he said. "We started the war. But for us, too, the war was horrible."

His father, he said, "was a real Catholic, not just a Catholic on paper."

Wolfgang was seven years old during Kristallnacht. Before that he had had Jewish neighbors and friends in school. After that, they left Germany or disappeared. "I couldn't understand it at the time," he recalled.

His father, who was not a Nazi party member, was a postal worker. He was taken to Russia for a time to work. Wolfgang's older brother, Willie, and he both joined the Hitler Youth. "It was required," the Mayor explained.

Their meetings were on Sundays. But their father insisted that they attend mass first. "If there was a choice, it would always be mass," he said.

Willie's frequent absences from youth meetings "got him into trouble." When he was sixteen, he was taken with his squad to France, where they built barricades and defenses against the impending American invasion. Soon after their arrival, half of his unit of sixteen-year-olds were killed in a bombing raid. Willie ran away and returned home one Sunday night. His father took him to a town in Bavaria, where the family was not known, and put him in a postman's uniform so that he did not have to return to the front.

One day when Wolfgang was visiting relatives in Mainz, he was caught in a bombing raid. "Bombs were falling like rain," he recalled. "It happened too fast for me to find a shelter. If it hadn't been for the soldiers on the street directing me where to go, I would have been killed. I remember one day in particular, when I saw a bridge one hundred meters away from me collapse into the Rhine. For a young boy, it was terrifying."

After the war was over, his father became an official in the new government. Wolfgang went to work in the private sector in Mannheim, but his religious beliefs propelled him toward public service. He came to Fulda in the mid-1960s and was elected mayor in 1969.

From the beginning of his tenure, he took a strong interest in the fate of Fulda's Jews. "I felt we had to pay back the Jewish community for what they had contributed to the traditions and culture of this town. I also felt that now, with a younger generation in Germany, there was a chance for Christians and Jews to lay the groundwork here and elsewhere for future understanding. Finally, I thought that young people in this town, who had no experience with Jews and Jewish culture, needed to learn more about them."

So in 1970 the Mayor started locating the city's former residents and sending city newsletters to them. In 1976, he organized the collection to build a house—the Fulda House—for foreign students in Jerusalem. In connection with the fund-raising project, Fulda's high school students studied what had happened to Fulda's Jews between 1933 and 1945 and collected information about particular families who had lived in the city.

A few years ago, the Jewish school—the last Jewish remnant in the community—was scheduled to be torn down. The Mayor encouraged the city council to save and restore it at a cost of one million German marks, then over $500,000.

"We decided that we would give it to our small Jewish community as a place for activities and prayer, and in memory of the former Jewish community," the Mayor said.

Among those who attended the dedication of the school that May was Alan Bloom, a thirty-one-year-old staff sergeant in the United States Army who was stationed in Fulda. Until the dedication of the school as a synagogue–cultural center, Bloom said, Jewish servicemen who wanted to attend synagogue had to travel to Frankfurt. "From now on, we'll have a place to go right here in Fulda."

But Fulda still had no rabbi, so apart from the twenty or so American-Jewish soldiers in the region, who would use the cultural center? Since the thirty-six Jews in Fulda were elderly and there were no young Jews in town, who was the center really for?

The Mayor demurred. "Now Jews will have a home here and I hope that the small plant will grow. But," he added, "I suppose it is also partly for us. For some of the high school students who attended the commemoration, it was the first time they had ever met a Jew. The younger generation cannot be guilty for things they did not do. But younger Germans are responsible, not guilty, but historically responsible for what happened.

"The more we can make them understand that distinction, the better the chances of opening their minds and hearts to tolerance and humanism. That's the main purpose of an event like this: to perform this reconciliation, to lay the groundwork for future co-operation between faiths. And for reconciliation, we really need the Jews. We hope they will come again. We're really asking for their forgiveness and their help in order to prevent another war and build a better world."

Virtually all of the participants said they believed that the Mayor was sincere, that he had made a genuine effort to make amends for what had happened in his adopted city. Some said they would hold out their hands to him and other Germans who felt as he did. But a few were unrelenting.

Yoram Adler, the Israeli, was among them. "He wanted us to have a good time, to make us feel good about the experience and about them, to be grateful to them, and to forgive them. But it won't work," said Yoram. "They want too much." His attitude, he admitted, was paradoxical. "The Jews have always had enemies," he said. "The Germans were our worst enemies—the most efficient. But they were the only enemy ever to pay reparations, money for forgiveness. But just as it is German to make the offer, it is Jewish to accept the money but not really to reconcile."

Suspicion of their German hosts was particularly pronounced among the second generation—the children of those who had suffered. Jeffrey S. Adler, Yoram's younger American-born cousin, concluded that the benefits of the reunion outweighed whatever reservations the visitors might have had about the hosts. But he had reservations.

"I could never quite escape the feeling that they were doing this as much for themselves as for us," Jeffrey wrote in his diary. "It often seemed to me that it was their way of paying tribute to the Jewish community of Fulda or trying to do something to bring that community back together. Undoubtedly, there are some people who had sincere motives and intentions in putting this project together, but one could never escape the feeling that many of the people were just going through the motions and had no real interest in this program except to get it over with."

Steven Fingerhood had similar misgivings. Everyone had treated the family exceedingly politely and warmly, he acknowledged. "I seemed equanimous, but every night during the trip I woke up in a cold sweat, my tee-shirt soaked through. The nightmares grew worse after the visit to our old house," said Steven. "The longer I stayed in Fulda, the more Jewish, the more self-conscious I felt . . . something like Woody Allen in the movie *Annie Hall.*

"In Fulda," he continued, " 'the Holocaust' was no longer an abstraction. Suddenly, I was at the scene of the crime, the place where my grandfather was murdered."

Steven, a soft-spoken, sensitive student at Stanford, was aware that part of his reaction was, as he put it, irrational. He had not encountered anyone anti-Semitic. And the one alleged incident of it turned out to be a misunderstanding. But it was revealing.

The incident involved a dispute over a dry-cleaning bill at the Hotel Lenz. The young boyfriend of Steven's cousin Dana had been overcharged, he asserted. When he challenged the concierge about the bill, he thought he heard her reply in German: "So that's it. I guess we will always have to pay for you Jews."

One of Steven's relatives was so disturbed by the story that she asked the concierge exactly what she had said. The concierge seemed perplexed by the query. What she had said, she told Steven's cousin, was: "I guess we will always have to pay for you young people." In German, the words "Jews"—"Juden"—and "youth"—or "Jugend"—sound very similar.

"Now I ask myself: was I seeing my own projection, or what was actually out there?" asked Steven, reflecting on the incident. "That's the real problem for Jews of my age: separating out real anti-Semitism from our hypersensitivity to it."

While the vast majority of survivors believed that young Germans were truly different from their parents, young Germans in Fulda seemed less interested in the event than their parents. "If you ask most young people about the Jews visiting us here," said Mr. Schmidt, the newspaper editor, "they will say, What does this have to do with me? It was my grandfather."

"I don't feel at all guilty, but as a German I do feel a sense of shame about what happened," said Martin Steinhage, twenty-five, a college graduate who came from Berlin in 1986 to work at Radio Fulda. "It has created quite a complex for young Germans. But I guess it's better for us to have a complex now, which will gradually disappear, than to do what our parents did in the fifties and suppress the whole experience."

As Martin reflected over a Weizen *hefe* beer, young Germans poured into the City Guards Pub, one of the few young people's hangouts in town.

They did not talk about the reunion, or the past. Younger Germans seemed more concerned, understandably, about the absence of nightlife or possibilities for job advancement in their city than about an event that was ancient history to many of them. Fulda's economy was not doing badly. But there was no university here, so young people seeking higher education had to go elsewhere. As a result, there were relatively fewer younger Germans in Fulda than in other towns of its size. Its young people found the town, in Martin's words, "boring." "Berlin represents sex and crime to the people of Fulda," Martin said. "Here there is no crime because it's a relatively small town; and there is no sex because it's a staunchly Catholic town."

A young salesgirl in a store on Fulda's main street seemed confused by the sudden appearance of three hundred persons, many of the men wearing yarmulkes and most nattering away in German. "It's been good for business," she said cheerfully. "Are they from Rome?" she asked me. "They are wearing caps like the bishops."

An aide to the Mayor, a young man with two earrings in his right ear and a small, neatly clipped beard, had temporarily left his chemistry studies at the university in a neighboring city to help the tourist office cope with the influx of politically sensitive visitors.

What did the Fulda commemoration mean to him?

He was silent for a moment. "It's very important for the older people here to see that people they knew came back, that they are still alive," he said. "But it's not so important for the younger people. It doesn't really affect us in the same way."

He probably did not know as much about the Holocaust as he should have, he said. When he was in school, his teachers had taught them almost nothing about what had happened. "Now it's much better," he added. "There is more being discussed, more books and films about it, so young people tend to know. But a trip like this still has less meaning for us."

Hans, age nineteen agreed. He had made money running Fulda residents between their homes and the school in his taxi. The memorial, he volunteered, was "a good thing."

"Every religion and every culture has its buildings," he said. "So why not the Jews?"

For Hans, the Jews were just another group, another culture entitled to their own special place. Did he know what the school represented? He shrugged his shoulders. "I came from another town recently, so I don't know what has gone on here."

During the Fulda reunion, many of the Jews wanted to visit the border area, only eight miles away. So the mayor organized a trip to the border town of Tann. Given the region's topography—a low-slung valley area with neither rivers nor other natural boundaries—military strategists had long considered this the most likely setting for a potential East Bloc invasion. For years, the so-called "Fulda gap" had triggered anxiety among defense planners and a generation of Germans who had known the ravages of war.

As a result, the area around Fulda was among the most heavily armed slices of real estate in West Germany. Older residents of Fulda had grown accustomed to the perpetual military exercises and maneuvers, the 580,000 low-level NATO flights a year over their country, the 3,000 American soldiers who were headquartered in Fulda alone.

But young Germans did not see things that way. To them, the division of their country was of far greater importance than the events that had produced it.[15]

As the buses ambled through the small towns that dot the border, the Jews sang German folk songs from their childhood and pointed out spots where their families used to picnic or go for tea on weekend excursions.

The tour guide on our bus, Klaus, age twenty, was born in Fulda and knew the area well. His expression clouded as we reached the border. "Each year someone dies trying to come across," he said. "You can see little crosses that mark the spots."

The Jews got off the bus and stared in silence into the garrison state just across the field. But Klaus stayed behind. The contrast between the police dogs and machine guns and barbed wire that marked the other side and his own part of Germany did not seem to disturb him as it did his visitors. He was troubled by something else.

"This is the worst spot in my country," he said softly. "This is where families and friends are divided . . . where cousins and brothers and sisters have been separated by a line that politicians drew through our nation decades ago. This is Germany's true shame. I can think of nothing worse. We call it the line of inhumanity. And one day, it will be gone."

Perhaps no country has explored its past as intensively as the Federal Republic of Germany. It was, of course, not entirely voluntary. "Unlike the Austrians or the French, we were forced to do so," said Hans Mommsen, a professor of history at the University of Bochum, near Düsseldorf.[16]

On the surface, Germans seemed to have "mastered the past," to use their controversial expression for confronting their history.[17] Since the end of the war, Germany has become economically powerful, militarily sound, firmly anchored in the North Atlantic Treaty Alliance, and politically a thoroughgoing democracy, much to the approval and relief of its Western allies.

But the superficial tranquillity of the Federal Republic was deceptive. Sensitive observers of the German scene detected even before the momentous revolts in the East Bloc what Fritz Stern, a German-born Jewish scholar, called a new "restlessness" among Germans.[18] "The German future," he says, "has suddenly become a new national focus at the very time when a new revisionism would like to end or moderate German self-laceration about the past. Germans are tired of their 'special' guilt; they point to the historic sins of others.

"Many Germans are growing impatient with their own—relative—impotence, with the limits on their autonomy, even if these limits are the result of Germany's last, desperate, criminal bid for world power. They still live with the consequences of their past, and in recent years many of them have felt an even greater political and psychological need to deal with the past; some wish to understand it, others to banish or trivialize it," Stern wrote. "The German past has assumed a new portentous present."[19] A subtle, and sometimes not so subtle, desire to distance themselves from their history has taken root. It is growing stronger.

Germany, of course, has its historical revisionists—ultra-conservatives and ultra-left-wing writers in Western Europe and the United States—who deny the existence of gas chambers and the Nazis' extermination of millions of Europeans, six million of them Jewish. But they are a tiny isolated minority; they have no weight in Germany or anywhere else in Europe. Nevertheless, by taking an outrageous position, they have made the arguments of other, more moderate revisionists, or conservative historians, as they prefer to be called, seem less extreme.

"Each day brings new evidence that the thresholds are being lowered," said Jürgen Habermas, a professor of philosophy at the University of Frankfurt. "There is a new lack of constraints. Things are being written and spoken in official and ordinary conversations which were morally and politically unacceptable only a decade ago."[20]

The Federal Republic's confrontation with its Nazi history has had several stages, in political-popular culture and in historiography, which have both affected and reflected each other.

West German historians in the late '40s and '50s were initially "uneasy" about Nazism, observed Saul Friedlander, the Israeli scholar of the Holocaust.[21] While they acknowledged National Socialism as a "German catastrophe," the worst Nazi crimes, in particular the extermination of the Jews, were left unexplored. In the most superficial histories of that phase, Nazism was portrayed as a kind of accident, whose sources could be traced only to 1933.

A second phase of historical scrutiny began toward the end of the 1950s. A new generation of German historians, such as K. D. Bracher, began emphasizing sociostructural conditions that had prompted the rise of Hitler, such as the critical role of the German bureaucracy.[22] Emulating to a certain extent the more ambitious work of academics in other countries, German historians explored in depth major aspects of Nazi ideology and policies, including the regime's anti-Jewish laws and regulations.

By the 1970s, significant research had expanded into delicate topics, such as the criminal complicity of the Wehrmacht in implementing Hitler's policies. Prior to this period, the Wehrmacht tended to be portrayed as a traditional military organization fighting for its homeland. But sensitivity about the Holocaust remained. Not until 1983 did international historians meet in Stuttgart specifically to explore the Final Solution, the Nazi program to exterminate the Jews.

While some German historians began exploring this psychologically treacherous terrain, however, others began focusing on what Friedlander called the "soothing aspects of life in the Third Reich," the normality of everyday life for the average German.[23] Many of these studies by both conservative and liberal historians gave rise to a subtle form of historical revisionism, whose effect through concentration on topics like the normal aspects of the Third Reich was to soften the hard edges of Hitler's unprecedented mobilization of sadism in the name of nationalism.

The softening trend, reinforced by political events, culminated in the '80s in what became known as the "historians' debate." Some prominent German academics, dubbed neo-conservatives by their critics, were making an effort to alleviate national guilt by "relativizing" Hitler's crimes and portraying them as by no means historically unique.[24]

The "historians' debate" was not confined to historians. It was a political and ideological confrontation over how history of the Nazi period should be presented and what kind of new German identity could evolve from such a history. It was not about the past; it was a fight for the future.

The tempest began in April 1986 with the publication of a slender book, *Two Kinds of Destruction: The Shattering of the German Reich and the End of European Jewry,* by Andreas Hillgruber, then a historian at Cologne University and a renowned authority on National Socialism.[25]

In his hundred-page book, Hillgruber focused primarily on the "catastrophe" of the fall of the eastern front in Germany to the Soviet Army during the winter of 1944–45. To the core of the book he added a twenty-two-page essay on the Holocaust, almost as an afterthought. Hillgruber, a native of East Prussia, who was then sixty-one years old and who died in 1989, described in dramatic prose the murders, rapes, and other forms of "barbarian" behavior of Soviet troops, who caused millions of Germans to flee from their homes, and caused two million deaths. The German people, Hillgruber maintained, should "identify" with the valiant German soldiers who defended their countrymen and the Reich's eastern territories.

Hillgruber's brief second chapter on the annihilation of the Jews seemed to pale after the emotional appeal of "identification" with the heroic Wehrmacht, battling against hopeless odds to protect the fatherland (without any mention of its massacres of Red Army prisoners).

The book concluded that although May 8, 1945, the day Germany surrendered unconditionally, was a day of "liberation" for concentration-camp victims, it was "not appropriate to apply [that term] to the fate of the nation as a whole." Moreover, Europe had lost "Prussia's and the German Reich's role as mediator." Thus, he argued, "all of Europe was the loser in the catastrophe of 1945."

"Hillgruber's is not exactly an evil book," Charles S. Maier, the American historian, concluded charitably. But it was, to say the least, "badly balanced; and its particular imbalance opens the way to apologia."[26]

The apologia was not long in coming. In June 1986, Frankfurt's conservative-centrist daily newspaper, the *Frankfurter Allgemeine Zeitung,* published a commentary entitled "The Past That Will Not Pass Away." Its author was Ernst Nolte, a brilliant but brooding philosopher of history who had written earlier a penetrating study of fascism in three countries. In the article and in another essay in a book published in 1985[27] in London, Nolte argued that National Socialism must be seen as a reaction against what he termed the "Bolshevik actions of annihilation" in the 1930s in the Soviet Union. Every Nazi atrocity, with the possible exception of poison gas, he contended, had been committed by the Bolsheviks in the early 1920s.

"Did the Nazis carry out, did Hitler carry out, an 'Asiatic' deed [the term that one of Hitler's advisers supposedly used to describe the 1915 massacres of Armenians by Ottoman Turks] perhaps only because they regarded themselves and their ilk as the potential or real victims of an 'Asiatic' deed? Wasn't the Gulag Archipelago more an original than Auschwitz? Wasn't class murder on the part of the Bolsheviks logically and actually prior to racial murder on the part of the Nazis?" Nolte wrote.

Germans, he complained, remained unduly preoccupied with their Nazi past. Was there not cause for stopping this obsessive reexamination? Was the harping on the "guilt of the Germans" not reminiscent of Nazi charges about "the guilt of the Jews"?

He asserted that the history of the period must be reexamined, or "revised," because it had been written largely by the victors, and hence had been transformed into what he termed a "negative" and "state-supporting mythology."

"We need only imagine, for example," he wrote, "what would happen if the Palestine Liberation Organization, assisted by its allies, succeeded in annihilating the state of Israel."

Hitler, Nolte argued further, had reason to believe that the Jews wished to "annihilate" him. As proof, he cited a "declaration of war" proclaimed by Chaim Weizmann on behalf of the World Jewish Congress in September 1939. Weizmann, a leading Zionist who helped found the state of Israel, had called upon Jews everywhere to fight on the side of England. His appeal came after Germany had passed its law "on the protection of German blood and German honor," after Kristallnacht in 1938, and after the Nazis had already deported or forced hundreds of thousands of German Jews into exile. But Nolte did not mention these developments.

True, Chaim Weizmann and the World Jewish Congress had no standing in international law and, therefore, no authority to declare war on Nazi Germany, he acknowledged; it had no army with which to engage in a war against Hitler. But Nolte stated nonetheless that he had to "reproach" himself for not having known of the Jewish leader's statement when he wrote his previous work on National Socialism. It might have served to "justify the consequential thesis that Hitler was allowed to treat the German Jews as prisoners of war and by this means to intern them," he wrote.

In an interview in Munich after his article appeared, Nolte agreed that "interning" Jews was something of an understatement. And he acknowledged that even if Weizmann's declaration constituted a Jewish declaration of war against Hitler, "no one is justified in killing interned prisoners of war."[28]

But he displayed no misgivings about his reference to Weizmann or about any of the other assertions in the newspaper article and the essay. "Facts are facts, even if they appear in the political tracts of the extreme right," he said. "They must be examined critically and fairly. Moralistic treatment is not enough. Facts must prompt a 'normal' reaction. This part of history must be explored as other parts of our history," he declared. "Normalization of the past is not to say that the past was normal."

The Hillgruber book and Nolte essay were too much for Jürgen Habermas. "Outraged to the core," he explained in an interview at his university office, he denounced what he termed the "grossly apologetic tendencies" of Hillgruber and Nolte in a July article in the widely read liberal weekly *Die Zeit.* His impassioned essay accused the historians of having a political motive: they, along with aides to Chancellor Helmut Kohl, were attempting to rewrite history to help fashion a new, patriotic German identity.[29]

"The only patriotism that does not alienate us from the West is a constitutional patriotism," warned Habermas. "Anyone who tries to summon the Germans back to a conventional form of their national identity is trying to destroy the only reliable basis for our bond to the West."

Another prominent historian, Eberhard Jackel, tore Nolte's arguments apart in the pages of *Die Zeit.* It was true, he observed, that the twentieth century was one of mass murder. Yet the Holocaust remained unique because "never before had a State . . . decided and so declared that a certain group of people—including the old, women, children, and babies—were to be killed in toto if possible, while executing that decision with all the means available to a State."[30]

Hitler had explained why the Jews had to be eliminated, or as Himmler declared, made to "vanish from the earth." Hitler's reasoning, Jackel concluded, constituted a "complex and coherent structure of thought." The disappearance of the Jews was to be total, from history and memory. After the race had been eradicated, Hitler had planned to build a museum in Prague to the extinct Jewish race. The last phase in their extermination was to be the calculated reconstruction of Jewish identity through the lens of National Socialism.[31]

By contrast, Communists in the Soviet Union did, indeed, speak of the "liquidation" of the bourgeois and ruling classes, but few historians had concluded that their intention was literal. And yes, Stalin probably did kill as many people as Hitler. But Stalin's terror lay in its randomness, rather than its thoroughness.

As the debate intensified, other historians and social critics joined in. Scholars engaged in intellectual combat on television and in the pages of newspapers with such high-minded insults as "establishment historian," "demagogue," "Nazi constitutionalist," and "Himmler apologist."[32]

By 1988, Germany had wearied of the debate. In the fall of that year, President Richard von Weizsäcker declared an end to it, arguing that Germans now understood that the crimes of the Third Reich could not be compared with genocides elsewhere, but that the debate had raised important questions for the society to ponder.[33] But despite Weizsäcker's desire to put the debate behind Germany, it has continued, perhaps not as intensively among historians, but among politicians contemplating Germany's future.

The historical literature on the Holocaust and National Socialism has grown dramatically in Germany and elsewhere in the West. One recent select bibliography listed close to two thousand book entries in many languages and cited over ten thousand publications on Auschwitz alone.[34]

The proliferation of work on the Holocaust and the Nazis has not comforted Saul Friedlander. The image of Nazi Germany presented by German and foreign historians was now so diversified and complex that it had become "somewhat blurred," he argued. The sheer magnitude of studies on the minutest details of the era tended to "erase the sharp outlines of certain central issues," he wrote. The very momentum of historiography, he argued, might well serve to "neutralize the past."[35]

Attitudes toward the past within popular and political West German culture have also evolved in stages. In the immediate postwar years, the Allies supervised Germany's reconstruction—overseeing the rewriting of German history textbooks and the drafting of laws and a new constitution designed to prevent the emergence of a Fourth Reich.

The Allies also conducted the Nuremberg war-crimes trials, which not only created a legal definition of "crimes against humanity," but also documented for posterity many of the Third Reich's most heinous crimes. Nuremberg today symbolizes the triumph of civilized judicial proceedings over uncivilized, institutionalized criminality. But the months of public testimony and hundreds of thousands of pages of appalling descriptions of German atrocities resulted in relatively few convictions.

A second phase began with the onset of the Cold War and the election of Chancellor Konrad Adenauer in 1949. Because of growing East-West tensions, Germany deemphasized events of the past and the Allies let it do so. De-Nazification, which the Allies began and the Germans were supposed to continue themselves, was quietly shelved. Germans with questionable backgrounds began showing up in Adenauer's government.

"In failing to ensure that the German government engaged in extensive de-Nazification," said Mommsen, "we lost an important opportunity to clarify the historical burden. This was especially true because Germans weren't really participants in the Nuremberg trials, except as defendants. This lack of participation helped foster the myth that somehow, National Socialism had been imposed externally. Germans began to see themselves as having been 'occupied' by National Socialists."

Germany was busy rebuilding, economically and militarily. At the end of the war, millions of Germans were dead; one-fifth were prisoners of war or homeless refugees; one-fifth of the housing stock was totally destroyed; the daily food ration was 1,500 calories; a third of the country had been taken over by the Soviet Union and Poland; the country itself was divided. But the Germans went back to work. And the German army, dismantled in 1945, was reborn in the early 1950s. The personnel files of World War II German officers, located with captured document collections in the Federal Records Center in Alexandria, Virginia, were returned to Germany.[36]

The Federal Republic needed to be counted among the states opposed to the totalitarianism of the East Bloc. An implicit concord was reached between the German right and American anti-Communists. All NATO members had an interest in overlooking recent history.

This "latent" period of memory, or suspension of it, was replaced by a third phase: the leftist rebellions of the late 1960s. In Germany, and especially in France, the student riots were a protest about, among other things, what has been called the "silence of the fathers."

"French and German students and other young West Europeans discovered that they had a formidable weapon to wield in what amounted to a generational war," said Robert Paxton, an American historian and highly respected expert on Vichy France. "They turned on their parents with a vengeance and condemned them with a question: 'And what did you do in the war, daddy?' "[37]

"In the United States, anti-war protestors could appeal to the democratic traditions of their fathers, who had after all, waged war against Hitler. In Germany, we could only voice our protest by taking a stand against our fathers," wrote novelist Peter Schneider. "From the beginning, we were burdened with the historical urge—to not be like our fathers. On an emotional level, the protest in Germany was specifically addressed to the general responsibility for Nazism."[38]

In Germany, many young people discovered the horrors of the Holocaust as if it were new. Historians differ about what triggered this angry reckoning with the past. But many commentators credit part of the resurgence of memory to a delayed reaction to Israel's trial in 1963 of Adolf Eichmann.[39] The gruesome protracted testimony of the witnesses was covered intensively not only by international newspapers but for the first time by television.

The exploration of Germany's Nazi past by a new generation also gave rise to some of the first instances of what liberal historians call the "marginalization" and "externalization" of the Holocaust. Young leftists, outraged by a past they felt had been kept from them, turned on their society and elders. But they were still terribly naïve and unself-conscious in their anti-Nazism. Germany continued to be ruled by "fascists," they charged. The Americans were committing "genocide" against the Vietnamese. Israelis were acting "like Nazis" toward the Palestinians. Such evil had to be confronted—with violence, if necessary. To resist passively was to succumb, as had Germany during the war, to fascism and authoritarianism.

The student rebellion was not the first instance, of course, in which Germans sought to peddle a kind of equivalence between the fascism of the '30s and American imperialism. In the early 1950s, *Stern* magazine, along with other German publications, carried spurious accounts of American "atrocities" in the Korean War; some German papers published reports spread by Communist-front organizations that American forces were using biological warfare in Korea. *Stern* implicitly compared the two wars by juxtaposing photos of the devastation in Korea and of Nazi-generated destruction in Poland and the Soviet Union.

What was most striking in the '60s was the students' use of language.

"The fast and loose use of 'fascist' had grotesque results," argued Peter Schneider, who was a protester at the time. "We thought we could detect traces of fascism in every corner of West German society. After 'fascism' had become a generalized term of opprobrium in Germany it served hardly at all to refer to the twelve years that gave it its concrete meaning."

There were costs incurred by the abuse of the term "fascism," he wrote. "They can be felt most obviously in the generally unconscious attempt by younger Germans to project their fathers' guilt onto parties who are 'guilty' today. How else does one account for the not-insignificant segment of the sixties generation that identified unreservedly with the Palestine Liberation Organization? It is the hounded Palestinian's business if he chooses to call his occupiers the 'new Nazis'; a German's self-consciousness ought to keep him from joining in such accusations."

It was "obvious," Schneider maintained, that the "Nazis' sons and daughters went shopping in Al Fatah headgear to prove they were free of historical inhibitions," that many identified with the PLO so that they would not appear as inhibited as their fathers, who now identified with Israel.

"But I'm afraid that my generation and those younger than us ... will truly have the right to talk freely about Israeli politics only when we have admitted our very real historical inhibitions," he concluded.

Thus, his generation's "anti-fascism" was motivated by what he called "an unconscious desire for exculpation." It was an anti-fascism that had not been worked through, "either historically or emotionally."[40]

Developments in the '80s have shown that a thorough reckoning with the past has still not taken place. Revisionism and ugly, more subtle attempts to fashion a more "acceptable" past have continued. The historian Friedlander has argued that at least four categories of distortion of fact and history are prevalent in West Germany.

Among the most frequent is revisionism through comparison, which cuts across the German political spectrum. As one is reminded by Nolte's work, Stalin may have killed more people than Hitler. Or, as the Greens and other leftists in Germany are so fond of noting, the United States dropped atomic bombs on Japan. The Pol Pot regime committed "genocide" in Cambodia, the argument goes.

Therefore, it follows, Germany's wrongdoing was not a unique horror, but just another manifestation of man's inhumanity to man. 
The specificity of the Holocaust—in magnitude, in method, and in intention—is buried in comparison.

A second strategy of distortion is describing the periphery instead of the core of fascism. A case in point is the impressive fifteen-hour series by Edgar Reitz, entitled *Heimat.* The series, which premiered in the fall of 1984, drew record audiences.

Heimat is an almost untranslatable word, which means home, native place, homeland, a mystical place from which one comes and to which one can therefore return. The series is the saga of the inhabitants of a fictional tranquil village of Schabbach before and after the war. It is not unlike the Rhineland village of Morbach, in which Reitz was born in 1932, its director said. Heimat's citizens are basically decent folk, who live through the brutal Nazi era, in most cases without changing significantly.

There is a jarring omission in the emotionally powerful program, however: there are hardly any Nazis in Schabbach. The Mayor of the town, who is a party member, is portrayed as a kindly, but bumbling opportunist. The second Nazi is a self-important fool. The third is a detestable S.S. officer, who executes one wounded British pilot and goes around scolding the good women of Schabbach for feeding French prisoners.

In *Heimat,* James Markham of *The New York Times* observed, "many Germans could for the first time see the Nazi era as part of a continuum—not a brutal parenthesis. The message is a reassuring one of normality, of continuity at the level of the village despite great upheaval in the barely glimpsed world outside."[41]

Critics see the film as revisionist precisely because it emphasizes "normality" in a highly abnormal period. "By emphasizing the normalcy of daily life under the Third Reich," Hans Mommsen maintained, "you tend to lose touch with the essentials of the regime."[42] The absence of Nazis in *Heimat* also enabled ordinary Germans to see themselves as decent, ordinary citizens, even as victims.

The unmistakable message, Mommsen observed, was that "this terrible thing, National Socialism, was done to us by a few brutes called the Nazis, a tiny minority who seized power and disrupted the peaceful life of ordinary German people." Evil occurs in the script, but it is almost incidental.

The third device of revision is inversion—the portrayal of perpetrators as victims and victims as witting or unwitting perpetrators of their own misfortune. Within the field of history, Nolte's citation of Weizmann's declaration of war against Hitler is a prime example. But a far more striking case is found in popular culture, in the five-part television series *The War of the Bombers,* which was first broadcast in Germany in January 1985. The series focused on the devastation of German cities during World War II. The title itself suggested a lack of connection between the world war that Hitler initiated and the Allied response. The series featured the saturation bombing of poorly defended German cities, images that reinforced a sense of German helplessness. No mention was made of the Luftwaffe's bombings of London in 1940, or of the fact that it was the German Condor Legion that first experimented in 1937 with saturation bombing over Guernica, Spain.

The last installment, "The Fearful Finale," recounted the Allied firebombing of Dresden, in which thousands of Germans were killed. The legion of other bombed-out cities includes Cologne, Hamburg, Düsseldorf, and of course, Berlin. "By the end of the war, most big cities looked like Dresden," the announcer solemnly intoned. "The bombing war claimed 600,000 lives in

Germany. Seven and a half million people were homeless. Almost two million tons of bombs fell on the territory of the German Reich."

The program touched viewers, especially younger ones, because Germans have not really been permitted to mourn their dead. "We started the war," said one German student in Fulda. "So it's as if we deserved whatever we got. We had it coming. But my grandmother didn't start the war; she didn't even like Hitler, but she was killed in the bombing of Hamburg."

Just as the Germans have felt a deep-seated but long-repressed need to mourn their own country's losses, they have felt an intense longing for heroes. Western commentators have frequently remarked on the country's intense pride in any athlete, artist, academician, or person who excels in his field and the high standards to which such individuals are held. The tennis champion Boris Becker told Western reporters that he sometimes felt he had to conduct himself better than the other players "because I am German." And when the objects of such reverence disappoint, the nation practically goes into mourning. One need only think back to Becker's dejection after he failed to capture the world tennis championship at Wimbledon in 1986.

"It's only a tennis match," he said graciously. "There was not a war; no one died; I lost a tennis match."

The craving for heroes was also evident in Germany's fascination with *Das Boot,* the five-hour television film that was broadcast in early 1985, an extended version of the highly successful movie about a German submarine crew during the war. An estimated twenty-four million West Germans, 40 percent of the country's population, sat transfixed in front of their television sets. The saga of fifty German sailors struggling to survive a series of harrowing attacks by the British and Allied forces, dodging depth charges, evading Sonar listing devices, overcoming internal leaks and surface attacks had a larger audience than any program since *Holocaust,* which had attracted fourteen million German viewers when it was broadcast in 1979.

The sailors fight valiantly against the odds. While it is true that the German Navy was known as an élite force, and many of its aristocratic officers were contemptuous of the "little housepainter," there is little historical justification for the film's portrayal of virtually every man on the U-boat, with the exception of one nasty

Nazi officer, whom most of the crew dislikes, as slightly hostile to or deeply skeptical of Hitler's war.

The U-boat's captain, an appealing, charismatic leader, speaks reverentially of his "good men" and the difference they make; at another point in the film, he refers, only half jokingly, to his "real German heroes." And in case the viewer missed the point, the audience is told that of the forty thousand U-boat men in World War II, thirty thousand did not come home.

The movie and the five-part series were based on a novel by Lothar-Gunthar Bucheim, himself a U-boat veteran. James Markham noted in his coverage of the film that it "turned the traditional, glorified view of German submarine warfare on its head. Instead of the hunter, U-96 is the hunted."[43]

At the culmination of the film, the submarine returns to occupied France after its men have saved the boat from destruction countless times and becomes a casualty of the war. It is blown up in port by a British fighter-bomber.

The filmmaker who directed the series, Wolfgang Petersen, was born in the port city of Emden in the second year of the war. He described himself as an "absolute pacifist." Markham noted that he seemed "troubled" by the suggestion that the film might have reinforced German feelings that they, too, were victims of the war.

"The idea is that everyone who took part in the war—everyone —was a victim," he told Markham. "I wanted to concentrate on tormented and martyred men, the simple small man."

Friedlander argues that these devices of revision and deflection reflect an impulse for "exorcism," a desire to "normalize" an abnormal past, if possible to "externalize" it. He wrote of revisionist historians and artists who ostensibly attempt to explore the horrific past with a fresh eye. And he spoke of a "confrontation that at the same time remains an evasion; of a neutralization of the past, of concealment, voluntary or not, of what in this case has made the past unbearable."[44]

A fourth strategy for distorting the past is what the Germans call *Schlusstrich*, that is, drawing a line at the bottom of an account, or in this case, an era. In historical terms, it means putting the Third Reich behind Germany, as Chancellor Kohl and other politicians have said.

In the arts, Schlusstrich meant a fierce debate at the end of 1985 over whether Rainer Werner Fassbinder's play *Trash, the City and*

Death was anti-Semitic and should be staged at the city-financed theater in Frankfurt. The play was shut down, but the dispute over free speech versus sensitivity to anti-Semitism was protracted and divisive.

In politics, Schlusstrich was symbolized by the Bitburg affair. Chancellor Kohl's effort to draw such a historical line resulted in a telling example of what one diplomat called Kohl's "shoot yourself in the foot" diplomacy. But Bitburg also produced, as Helmut Sonnenfeldt, the German-born U.S. foreign policy expert, pointed out, sterling examples of "incredible hypocrisy" in both West Germany and the United States.[45]

Kohl had long held the view that the time for Schlusstrich had come. Friends and diplomats knew that he had always counted himself among the staunchest supporters of America. His first suit had come to him after the war when he was thirteen years old—courtesy of an American "care" package.[46]

Though he had been in the Hitler Youth, he had claimed innocence for his generation when he spoke in 1984—in Israel—of the "grace of having been late born." By billing himself as the first "postwar" chancellor, ostensibly spared by luck of birth from guilt over the past, he could neither comprehend nor accept young Germany's muted patriotism, its lack of enthusiasm for the society his generation had created from "the year zero," the end of the war, May 8, 1945. Kohl often said that he wanted young West Germans to be proud of their country, that he did not understand why they did not sing their national anthem with gusto and conviction, why they were hesitant to stand up and take their rightful place in the struggle for Western freedom and democratic values.

The sentiments of the young were partly a response to the politics of the time. The late '70s and early '80s had witnessed the rise of the Greens and other leftist groups, which partook, more than they would acknowledge, in the delusions and reckless romanticism that have made Germany such an unstable nation. The student rebels of the 1960s had grown up; they had evolved into a new generation of politicians who showed blatant disrespect for the society that Kohl and his generation had built. They had for the most part abandoned the language of comparison that had characterized their student revolt for a more sophisticated form of relativization.

"The Greens were comparing their own country's Nazi past with the putative future," said Sonnenfeldt. "Yes, their argument goes, Germans had committed the Holocaust; but the Americans were preparing a holocaust for Germany and the entire world through plans for using nuclear weapons."

In the early 1980s, the Greens waged an intense campaign to prevent NATO's installation of Pershing and ground-launched cruise missiles in response to a massive Soviet buildup of SS-20 nuclear missiles capable of decimating all of Europe.

Although Kohl was too clumsy a politician to articulate his concerns persuasively, he and many of his advisers perceived that the threat to democratic values in the Bundesrepublik came not from the right, but from this growing leftist tendency. They believed that many on the left, especially the Greens, had little sense that their miraculous democracy was worth defending. The result was what Pierre Hassner, a French historian, called a debilitating "leftist neutralism" that made these ecologically minded young romantics unwilling to see much difference between the United States and the Soviet Union.[47]

It took foreign observers, like John Vinocur, writing in *The New York Times,* to point out that this fervent neutralism was also a form of suppressed nationalism. The Berlin Wall, then the world's most infamous example of Communist architecture, did not remind these young Germans of the profound political and moral differences between the two republics. Instead, it served as a constant reminder of the division of their nation into two artificial states. Fearing that the German Democratic Republic would not tear down the actual and metaphorical walls between them, young leftists, sometimes unconsciously, cloaked their nationalism in neutralism as a means of securing eventual reunification, or at the very least, stronger economic and political ties and reduced tension between East and West. If West Germany was shorn from NATO, if it was studiously neutral, it *would* pose no threat to the Soviet Union and could be joined with its fraternal eastern half once more.

It was against this political backdrop that Michael Stürmer, a first-class historian and an adviser to and occasional speechwriter for Chancellor Kohl, decided along with others in the center-right coalition that ways had to be found to reinforce a more positive sense of national identity among young Germans.[48] There was an identity vacuum in West Germany, he maintained. And it was going to be filled by something. Kohl's forces had to produce a "safe" overt nationalism, an alternative to the anti-NATO, anti-

Western left. Having a U.S. President visit a German war cemetery in Bitburg was seen as part of that solution.

The controversy over Bitburg dates back to June 1984, according to several serious observers of German politics, when the Allies celebrated the fortieth anniversary of the D-Day landings on the beaches at Normandy without the West German Chancellor.[49]

Kohl, who saw himself destined to lead his country out of the psychological isolation it had endured since the war's end, was deeply stung by his exclusion. Forty years of standing on the sidelines of such commemorations of the Allies' triumphs were enough, he and his advisers complained to other West Europeans and Americans. He was determined to have the Bundesrepublic included among the Allies in the fight against Communism, and through that, to help fashion a positive national identity for Germans.

As a consolation, French President Mitterrand invited him later that year to a commemoration at the military cemetery at Verdun, where the two leaders were photographed holding hands as they honored the death of German and French soldiers during World War I. But Kohl wanted a more powerful symbol of German redemption—a ceremony on German soil commemorating Germany's suffering during World War II. That, indeed, would be a Schlusstrich.

Eager to bolster the political standing of their friend and staunch ally, wary of offending Kohl who was leading the fight to install the medium-range missiles in Western Europe, the Reagan Administration accepted the invitation to visit a German military cemetery just before V-E Day in Germany, May 8. In February 1985, German and American staff teams surveyed and privately approved a visit by President Reagan to the Kolmeshohe military cemetery at Bitburg in May. The White House announcement of the presidential visit to Bitburg "in a spirit of reconciliation, in a spirit of 40 years of peace, in a spirit of economic and military compatibility," aroused immediate protests from Jewish and veterans' organizations. The White House announcement was made on the last day of the Jewish holiday of Passover, and three days before the beginning of nationwide "Days of Remembrance" of the Holocaust in the United States. One week later, opposition to the trip exploded after it was disclosed that among the two thousand German soldiers' graves were more than thirty members of the Waffen S.S.

Helmut Sonnenfeldt, for one, found the reaction of many Americans, including the Jewish community, problematic. "It was the United States that had encouraged the Germans not to separate the Waffen S.S. unit members' graves from others in the military," Sonnenfeldt said. "We had urged intermingling because we were afraid that if the S.S. units were singled out for burial at separate locations, these sites might become shrines for unreconstructed and neo-Nazis. It would have been hard to find a cemetery in West Germany that did not have Waffen S.S. unit graves, and most sophisticated observers of the German scene knew that."

Moreover, Kolmeshohe had long been recognized by the United States as an official German military cemetery. Every year since the Kennedy Administration the commander of the U.S. air base at Bitburg had attended an annual German Veterans Day ceremony there.

Despite the furor in America, or perhaps because of it, Chancellor Kohl dug in. He refused to withdraw the invitation or to change the site of the commemoration. The Bundestag rejected a motion by members of the Greens asking Kohl to eliminate the visit to Bitburg 398 to 24. "Reconciliation is when we are capable of grieving over people without caring what nationality they are," Kohl asserted heatedly during the debate.

The wreath-laying ceremony took place at Bitburg on May 5, as German policemen barred more than a thousand Jewish and Christian protesters from the site. There was no clasping of hands between Reagan and Kohl, as there had been between Kohl and Mitterrand. The American President was silent, reserving his remarks for soldiers at the U.S. air base near Bitburg.

The unfortunate outcome of Bitburg for the Germans was that Kohl's attempt at "reconciliation" pitted Germany's need to mourn its war dead publicly and in concert with its Allies—a psychologically desirable objective—against the world's abhorrence of any commemoration that appeared to diminish Nazi Germany's responsibility for the deaths of almost 6 million Jews, 600,000 Gypsies and millions of non-Jewish victims of Hitler's Reich.

There was no way to reconcile these conflicting objectives. Just as American Jews were starting to remember in earnest, Germans were eager to forget. And in the end the image of everyone connected with the Bitburg commemoration suffered. But that was not its only effect. "The Battle of the Historians was surely launched among the graves of Bitburg on 8 May, 1985," concluded journalist

Joseph Joffe. "If the past could not be laid to rest, it had to be reconstructed." Or, as Michael Stürmer had aptly put it: "Whoever supplies memory, shapes concepts, and interprets the past . . . will win the future."

The Bitburg affair did produce a clear articulation of the philosophies for confronting or, as Stürmer would have it, "supplying" the past. Kohl's position at least before the nasty Bitburg controversy, was that Schlusstrich was long overdue: Germany had literally and figuratively paid its debt to the Jews and the civilized international community. The war had been over for more than forty years. Germans must stop wallowing in guilt and move on.

The leftist model of remembrance relied on a set of mostly unarticulated hypotheses. Germany would never be able to wash the stain of the Holocaust from its hands. Germans, therefore, had to be on guard constantly against future putative holocausts. Any transgression of human rights by any country—by any Allied nation, in particular—had to be combatted. The United States had committed grave violations of human rights—in Korea, in Vietnam, in Nicaragua. The U.S. military strategy could produce a nuclear holocaust for future generations. Given this record, the United States had no moral right to sit in judgment of Germany. The Germans must find their own path to redemption.

Bitburg proved that both models were flawed. The left understood that Germany's postwar challenge was to integrate the lessons of the Holocaust in individual and national political behavior. But its tendency to see holocausts everywhere, to equate American motives and power with those of the Third Reich, and its sympathy for the lofty rhetoric of communism resulted in faulty political translations of those lessons.

The right, too, was in error. It saw the past not as something that had to be absorbed and learned from, but as an obstacle to Germany's aspirations. "The right has sought to promote its own form of nationalism to counter that of the left," Hassner argued. "But they did so by portraying Germany as an ordinary nation, no better or worse than any other. There is a quest for normalcy from the right, as well as the left. But given Germany's history, this was not an appropriate response to left-wing nationalism."

Anxious about the neutralist new left, eager to establish a strong, pro-Western, pro-NATO Germany, the Reagan Administration supported Chancellor Kohl's model of remembrance. America's implicit decision to overlook unpleasant parts of Germany's Nazi past, in order to help shore up young Germany's fragile political identity and its identification with Western political values placed American policy firmly in Helmut Kohl's camp.

For American officials after Bitburg, there was no longer a "year zero" in German history. In a speech in May 1986, twelve months after Bitburg, Ambassador Burt argued—in Nuremberg—that democracy could not have succeeded in postwar Germany had there not been "a long tradition of German experiences with democracy."[50]

He cited as examples of democratic experiments the German Hanseatic League, the constitution written by the Frankfurt Parliament, which he admitted was "stillborn," and even the Weimar Republic, the pathetically weak government that handed over power to Hitler. That republic, Burt asserted, "deserves a better historical verdict than it has been given." Although he acknowledged that key sectors of German society, including the intelligentsia, harbored anti-democratic attitudes that served to cripple Weimar, Burt asserted that had it not been for the Great Depression of 1929 the Weimar Republic "could probably have consolidated itself further."

Ambassador Burt's rosy interpretation of German history provoked a strong reaction, even among some of those who agreed that young Germans must become more self-confident. Habermas, Mommsen, and others argued that Germany's positive new identity must not be built on a false reconstruction of history. It must be based, they maintained, on acceptance of the past. It must rest, in effect, on a paradox: namely, that Germans should be proud of their political and economic postwar miracle precisely because it was created on the ashes of National Socialism and because there was so little historical precedent for Germany's impressive, vibrant modern democracy. Any effort to rewrite history, to deny the past, to gloss over the horrible and embarrassing and focus selectively on positive events and developments in German history was crafting a positive German identity on a myth.

"Germany is not America," cautioned Mommsen. "This positive new identity that you Americans and Chancellor Kohl want so much to nurture can backfire dangerously here if you begin making a habit of rewriting the past, or encouraging Germans to do it in the name of patriotism. Haven't you learned by now that you can't play around with nationalism in Germany?"

Fortunately, Germans themselves produced yet a third model of remembrance, one which seems to have forged something of a compromise between leftist and rightist visions and which has gained widespread acceptance in the wake of Bitburg. It was articulated by President Weizsäcker, a member of Chancellor Kohl's ruling Christian Democratic Union, in a remarkable address before the West German Bundestag on May 8, a few days after the Bitburg commemoration. Since then, the themes of his address have turned up in the speeches of many prominent politicians, among them Helmut Kohl.

Weizsäcker said that, while "hardly any country has in its history always remained free from blame for war or violence," the Nazi genocide of the Jews was "unparalleled in history." Yes, other individuals and states had engaged in genocide, but the Germans had given mass murder a very special character that did, indeed, make it unique in history. He spoke out eloquently against forgetting and of the futility of "mastering" the past. There was no such thing as guilt or innocence of an entire nation, he said. Guilt, like innocence, is not collective, but personal.

"The vast majority of today's population were either children then or had not been born. They cannot profess a guilt of their own for crimes that they did not commit. . . . But their forefathers have left them a grave legacy. All of us," he stressed, "must accept the past. We are all affected by its consequences and liable for it. . . . It is not a case of coming to terms with the past. That is not possible. It cannot be subsequently modified or made not to have happened.

"However, anyone who closes his eyes to the past is blind to the present. Whoever refuses to remember the inhumanity is prone to risks of new infection."

Weizsäcker noted that the "Jewish nation" remembered and would always remember; remembrance was part of the Jewish faith. So, because Germans were seeking reconciliation, "we have to understand that there can be no reconciliation without remembrance."

Weizsäcker's words did not end the historians' debate or the larger battle over who would control the future through the formulation of the past. But in his statements Germany found a compromise formula for confronting its history. The crisis sparked by Bitburg was, for the moment, over.

On November 10, 1988, the ghosts of the past temporarily shattered Germany's mood of euphoria. The perpetrator was Philipp Jenninger, a well-intentioned but hapless Christian Democrat who was President of the West German Parliament.

At the prodding of the Greens and the Social Democrats and over the initial objections of his own ruling party, Jenninger had organized a memorial session in Parliament to commemorate Kristallnacht. He spent three weeks in the archives researching and preparing what he hoped would be hailed as a milestone of candor and humility, the kind of praise lavished on Weizsäcker's Bitburg speech before the Parliament in 1985.

Jenninger's speech was a history lesson of sorts. He attempted to explain to young Germans how the vast majority of their parents' generation had been "blinded and seduced" into supporting Hitler's policies or remaining indifferent to them. He conjured up from the past a Germany humiliated since World War I that became euphoric over Hitler's achievements: the annexation of Austria, the Munich agreement, the elimination of mass unemployment and soaring inflation. Noting that these successes were achieved at the cost of the destruction of the Weimar democracy and the society's freedoms, he recalled the giddy nationalism that rationalized the demise of Germany's civic culture. "Did not Hitler make into reality what was only a promise under Wilhelm II, that is, to bring wonderful times to the Germans? Was not Hitler someone selected by Providence, a leader who was given to a people once in a thousand years?

"And as for the Jews," he continued, echoing what many Germans had said in the 1930s, "hadn't they in the past, after all, sought a position that was not their place? Mustn't they now accept a bit of curbing? Hadn't they, in fact, earned being put in their place? And, above all, apart from the wild exaggerations which were not to be taken seriously, did not basic points of the propoganda reflect one's own speculation and convictions?"

It was clear to those reading the speech that Jenninger neither shared nor condoned such sentiments, that he was merely quoting what Germans had said at the time. But that, apparently, was not clear to those listening to it in the Parliament. About fifty Parliamentarians—Greens, Social Democrats, and Free Democrats—walked out in protest.

Based on misleading news accounts of what he had said, Israeli officials, prominent Jewish leaders, and members of the opposition demanded his resignation. Twenty-four hours later, crushed by the outcry, he resigned at the request of his own party.

Michael Fürst, deputy head of the Central Council of Jews, resigned too after having defended Jenninger as a staunch opponent of anti-Semitism and friend of Israel.

After the resignation, a debate raged over his speech and the official reaction to it. In an interview in early 1989, Jenninger said that of the ten thousand letters he had received, only forty or fifty had failed to understand his intent. He was heartened by such expressions of support, he said. Young people, in particular, had understood his message. "Young Germans no longer ask are we really responsible, or how can we atone. They ask their grandfathers: how could it have happened?"

Much of the criticism of his speech was politically motivated, he said. But, he added, many of those listening had neither expected nor wanted to hear the type of speech he delivered. "They wanted a funeral oration, a eulogy," said Jenninger. "But I gave them a history lesson. Many did not want that; they wanted to excuse themselves."[51]

Simon Wiesenthal, the celebrated Austrian Nazi hunter, called Jenninger's ouster "a tragedy," asserting that he was a "good and honest man."

"It is strange that in our state it takes months or years to get a corrupt or unsuitable politician out of office, but there's no problem to strip an honest and engaged man of his office and reputation because of some misguided passages and clumsiness," wrote Peter Ehlers of Süderbrarup.

Many politicians and commentators, however, defended the campaign against Jenninger. "He had no sense of occasion," said Sebastian Haffner, a prominent publicist who has written extensively about German history and identity. "He said true things at the wrong moment. The 10th of November is not the right moment to think of fascination with Hitler, which certainly existed. If a man has been murdered, one doesn't speak at his funeral about the interesting personality of the murderer."

Dietrich Stobbe, the former Mayor of West Berlin and head of the Social Democrats' foreign-policy committee in the Bundestag, did not walk out of the Parliament as did many of his party members. But he was deeply offended by the speech. It was clumsily written, and delivered like a university lecture, Stobbe asserted in an interview.[52]

"He not only gave the impression that he was speaking on behalf of those who did nothing to stop Hitler, he avoided defining moral lessons. He did not note how dangerous the crime of moral apathy can be, the crime of inaction, the crime of looking away," said Stobbe. "He had a unique opportunity to tell our nation's young people how we can live with that terrible history. Such an occasion demanded a discussion of values that would help future generations not look away again. There was no moral component to his speech, no effort to teach a moral lesson, and that was a shame, given the demands of our history and the occasion."

The silver lining of the debacle, Stobbe said, was that Germany had the "moral strength" to oust him.

Others were not so sure. The explanations did not account for the intensity of the uproar. "He was hounded out of office by cynical political operatives because he broke all the taboos," said Sonnenfeldt. "He said some very unpalatable things, perhaps badly, that unfortunately were true. He told Germans something that they still didn't feel comfortable hearing."

Lily Gardner Feldman, a political scientist at Tufts and fellow at the congressionally funded United States Institute for Peace, argued that the hysterical reaction to the Jenninger speech showed that, while West Germany had achieved what she has called "external reconciliation" with its past, "internal reconciliation" still eluded Germans.

Bitburg could only have happened because Germans had not faced the past sufficiently, she maintained. "In order to be a 'normal' country, Germany needs internal reconciliation." Instead, she argued, the past forty years had focused largely on making amends—to German Jews outside of Germany and especially to Israel.[53] "Now, as in the past, the external process of reconciliation *(Versöhnung)* with former enemies is emphasized over the internal process of confrontation with the past."

An example was the dispute in late 1986 and 1987 over a proposal by the Greens and the Social Democrats for compensating victims of Nazism—Gypsies, homosexuals, and the victims of Mengele's experiments on Jewish twins, one-third of whom live in Israel. In the report on the proposal, the government referred to the "so-called Mengele twins" and denied that the activities had amounted to pseudo-medical experiments that had permanently wounded and crippled many of the victims.[54]

Gypsies, homosexuals, and other non-Jewish victims of the Nazis were awarded nothing. West Germany, once again reflecting its traditional preference for "external reconciliation," for historical fence mending, concluded a compensation agreement in 1987 with the Mengele Twins organization, based in Tel Aviv.

West Germany has genuinely attempted "internal reconciliation" through several primary vehicles of memory: commemorations, war crimes trials and judicial proceedings, political tests of will, and public education. But each of these has been problematic. The commemoration at Fulda, for example, demonstrated that commemorations often fail to engage emotionally and intellectually the younger generation, who have not experienced what is being commemorated. Commemorations may, indeed, be wasted on the young.

On the judicial front, Germany has conducted substantial investigations of Nazi war criminals. Between May 8, 1945, and September 1988, there were some 90,000 investigations for war crimes. Of these, about 6,480 individuals were convicted, 12 of whom were sentenced to death before the death penalty was abolished, 170 to life imprisonment.

But at a conference in September 1988 marking the thirtieth anniversary of the founding of West Germany's Central Office for the Investigation of Nazi Crimes, Neal Sher, director of the American counterpart office, the Justice Department's Office of Special Investigations, argued that German restrictions on the disclosure of material from the archives were hampering prosecutions. And Henry Friedlander, an American historian and former concentration-camp inmate, complained that many of the German sentences were too lenient.[55]

Political tests of will in the 1980s, including the Bitburg affair, succeeded in reviving painful memories, but they did not prompt reconciliation. Quite the contrary. Chancellor Kohl persuaded President Reagan to visit Bitburg. But his victory, while cheered by many in his country, deeply embarrassed others in Germany and abroad.

Germans have done much in the sphere of public education. Walter F. Renn, a history professor at Wheeling College in West Virginia, who surveyed textbooks in several countries, has noted a vast improvement in the content of history books dealing with

National Socialism and the Holocaust.[56] The textbooks available in the 1980s, paradoxically, have been far more thorough and sensitive than those written under Allied supervision immediately after the war. But there were still significant gaps, particularly in efforts to draw moral lessons from the period, he concluded. While none of the fifty West German texts he surveyed displayed any trace of anti-Semitism, students did not learn from them how the Holocaust could have come about. Moreover, the religious roots of anti-Semitism in Christianity were only briefly mentioned. Nor did students learn much from the texts about the Jewish people or their heritage.

Most textbooks, moreover, exhibited "scant interest in the broader circles of complicity involved in murdering millions of men, women, and children. The German people are conspicuously disassociated from mention in any connection with the perpetration of the Holocaust," Renn observed.[57]

Other questions about the degree of internal reconciliation have been raised. Why, for example, was it not until 1979 that West Germans decided that there should be no statute of limitations on war crimes? And why in a 1980s law making it a crime to deny the existence of the Holocaust did they add language that included all other "acts of despotism," which served to dilute the Holocaust's specificity? Why, asked Moritz Neumann, director of the Regional Association of Jewish Communities in Hesse, had it taken forty years for Fulda and towns and cities throughout Germany to begin building cultural centers and other memorials to the Jews of Germany?

The Jenninger affair was not the first example of insensitivity stemming from a lack of internal reconciliation. In 1971, Germans decided to inaugurate the first German Culture Week in Israel on the anniversary of Kristallnacht. They disclosed plans to sell weapons to Saudi Arabia—plans that were eventually shelved—on the eve of Chaim Herzog's visit to Germany, the first visit ever by an Israeli head of state.

Most vividly, it was reflected in the decision in 1988 to destroy the ruins of the Frankfurt Jewish ghetto to build a municipal center. The fight over the Frankfurt ghetto, which received little coverage in the American media, began in mid-1987, when the Frankfurt City Council voted to raze the remains of what had been Germany's second-largest Jewish community. Protests from archeologists, prominent Jews around the world, and opposition politicians mounted, to no avail.

"The true outrage was not what Jenninger was trying to say in

Bonn," said Sybil Milton, a research curator at the U.S. Holocaust Memorial Museum. "It was that Chancellor Kohl and Mayor Wolfram Bruck and others who had condoned the destruction of the last remnants of traditional Jewish life in that city had the audacity to deliver Kristallnacht commemoration speeches in a Frankfurt synagogue as the bulldozers rolled."

"For all their effort to make amends," said Feldman, the Germans were simply incapable at times of empathizing sufficiently with the victims "because they haven't dealt psychologically and morally with their own history. So many of them go on thinking that they can 'resolve' the past." Many want, in their own words, to "master" it; others simply want it to go away.

The new generation of Germans may be the first that has the distance necessary to confront the past. But this challenge comes as Germany—indeed, all of Europe—is at a political crossroads. A new era has begun in Europe. The Cold War that dominated the last forty years is over.

The emergence of Mikhail Gorbachev has meant, if not harmony, surely less tension in East-West relations than at any time since the war. The Gorbachev era has in turn shattered what Theo Sommer, the prominent commentator of the liberal weekly *Die Zeit* called the three fundamental "givens" of postwar Europe: the political, economic, and military dominance of the United States; the USSR as the implacable enemy of the West; and the division of Germany and Europe into two hermetically sealed zones of "East" and "West."

For no country in Western Europe has Gorbachev been as important as he has been for Germany.

In October 1989, a new government took control in East Germany, with Gorbachev's encouragement. Less than a month later, that government did what a succession of American presidents had dared the East Germans to do, all the while believing that no East German government would ever take the dare: it opened the Berlin wall and permitted its citizens to travel to the once forbidden West without passports or visas.

Within twenty-four hours, more than two million East Germans crossed into West Berlin to sample West German democracy and to test the limits of their own. They shopped, drank champagne, and revelled in the streets with their West German brethren.

Riveted to their televisions, people in the West watched as East Germans flooded over the wall—the Cold War's most vivid symbol. At first there was disbelief, then breathless joy. After twenty-eight years and ninety-one days, the wall that had divided the German nation into two states was no more. "Only today is the war really over," proclaimed an improvised poster attached to the wall.[58]

Only slowly did the implications of East Germany's actions become clear—if the Cold War was ending, the structures created in the immediate postwar environment to ensure that Germany would never again be in a position to disrupt world order would undoubtedly be torn asunder.

The "German question," as it has been known after the war, was answered by the division of Germany and Europe, and the creation of NATO, the Warsaw Pact, the European Community and COMECON. But at the week's end, European analysts realized that the old, relatively stable order was crumbling just as surely as the wall itself. Quite suddenly, a new set of "German questions" was being posed. Wasn't economic, and later political, reunification of Germany inevitable? Until then, was some kind of "confederation" or "reassociation" not likely? If Germany was reunited, what kind of nation would it be? Democratic? Capitalistic? Committed to Western values of freedom, tolerance and human rights? Anchored in the West? If the NATO alliance and Warsaw Pact continued to outlive the existence of an obvious Soviet military threat, would Germany be a member of either? Wouldn't Germany automatically become the dominant force in the European Community? In Europe?

Or would Germany become a semi-socialist state, an amalgam of capitalist markets and socialist social welfare structures? A neutralist, demilitarized country, without NATO and Warsaw Pact forces and American and Soviet weapons?

Of even greater import, could a united Germany—eighty million people strong, the world's fourth largest country, with Europe's strongest economy—turn its turbulent history around? If unleashed from the military alliances of both East and West, would it not seek to rebuild independent military capabilities and develop its own nuclear force? Armed with massive economic power and what would be significantly enhanced political clout, would Germany be able to resist the temptation to reclaim territory taken away after the war and intervene in its neighbors' affairs? Would it shun its traditional desire to be a "third force" between East and West?

Despite the euphoria about the prospect of more freedom and democracy for the eighteen million people of East Germany, long memories of two world wars—and aggression long before them—have made these new German questions deeply troubling for Europeans and even for some Americans. On at least three occasions —1870, 1914, and 1933—a united Germany has meant instability or chaos for Europe.

East and West Germans alike are well aware of their neighbors' qualms. So many Germans on both sides of the wall and of varied political stripes have taken pains to deny that reunification is either probable or desirable. Timothy Garton Ash noted soon after the wall crumbled that East Germans were outwardly resisting the notion of political reunification for two interlinked reasons. First, he argued, many East Germans who had suffered under the repressive regime of Eric Honecker did not wish to acknowledge that their suffering had been in vain. "If you go for reunification—that is, incorporation in a West Germany—you are in effect saying that the last forty years have just been one big mistake." Second, Ash observed, there is still a fairly widespread belief among intellectuals in both Germanies that West Germany is not the best of all possible Germanies. In other words, some Germans still hope for a "third way," a German brand of "socialism with a human face" or capitalism with a more humane and less exploitative set of values.[59]

Nevertheless, Ash concluded, as have many seasoned observers of the German scene, "the logic of events may begin to pull both halves together at remarkable speed."

This viewpoint is apparently shared by Willy Brandt, one of the relatively few Germans who actively resisted Hitler and fled Germany, the father of *Ostpolitik,* its policy toward East Germany or, literally, its "Eastern policy." Brandt sought to assuage Europeans' fears by urging them to look at the happy, innocent East German and West German youth cavorting at Potsdamer Platz near the wall. Watching the blond, blue-eyed teenagers embrace and dance and drink together, listening to their expressions of devotion to freedom and democracy, Brandt asked: Could anyone really be afraid of them?

Yet despite such words of assurance, memories of the war, of the Holocaust in particular, have made the prospect of German reunification disquieting to many of Germany's former enemies.

For Europe, the prospect of reunification and the collapse of the Cold War structures have important implications for memory. For while it is impossible to have confidence in predictions about Eastern Europe, this much is clear: The prospect of German reunification has placed an unprecedented premium on forgetfulness.

Germans who want to unify their two states will want more than ever before to forget the past, to erase the memories of six million Jewish victims and fifty million casualties of World War II. They will want Europeans to put all that behind them, to consign the Third Reich to history. Or if it is to be remembered, they will want the world to believe that such a thing could never again happen in a Fourth Reich.

Only if the four powers who control the fate of Berlin, and in effect all of Germany, forget the past, or decide that what occurred cannot be repeated, can the prospect of German reunification be tolerable. For Germans to become one nation state again, the Soviet Union must bury its memories of its twenty million war dead and what must be an intense fear of a united, unfettered Germany. America, France, and Britain will also have to push aside the memories of their people's suffering and losses. Even Soviet and Allied memory-fueled opposition might in the long run prove unable to prevent a determined Germany from reasserting its nationalism once more and re-exerting its influence. But the trend toward economic and political reunification is likely to be abetted either by a sustained bout of historical amnesia among Germany's neighbors or a growing conviction that a reunited Germany would be free, democratic, and stable and, hence, that the world has nothing to fear from such a country.

Therein lies something of a paradox. Only if the world persuades itself that a Fourth Reich cannot become the Third Reich, or if it forgets the past, can it comfortably accept a reunified Germany. But that confidence can come only if the Germans themselves demonstrate more convincingly than they have to date that they remember the very past they wish the world to forget. Only if the Germans fully confront their past can their neighbors come to believe that history will not repeat itself.

Austria

The most memorable scene in *The Sound of Music* is the songfest competition. Christopher Plummer, who in the movie plays Baron Von Trapp, defies Nazi Germany by daring to sing "Edelweiss."

As Von Trapp, an aristocrat and ardent nationalist, Plummer becomes so choked up that his voice fails him. Julie Andrews, as the ever-patient, wholesome helpmate, rushes to his side, as do his innumerable children. They pick up the chorus. Hearing the words of the beloved ballad, the audience leap to their feet, passionately singing the refrain, "Bless my homeland forever!" He cries; she cries; the audience explodes in patriotic applause. The Nazis are furious.

Had the film been historically accurate, the audience might have been singing with conviction, but they would have been singing a different song—something like "Deutschland Über Alles." For history, as opposed to Hollywood, tells us that the overwhelming majority of Austrians preferred the German national anthem to their own.

According to crowd estimates of the day, some 250,000 people filled Vienna's Heldenplatz, or Hero's Square, to greet Hitler on March 15, 1938. Half a million more lined Vienna's imperial Ringstrasse to cheer him a month later after he decreed the absorption of his native Austria by the Third Reich.[1] Since the population of Vienna in 1938 was 1.8 million, almost one-third of the Viennese had turned out to manifest support for the Austrian born Führer.

"In the days that followed," reported Gordon A. Craig, the historian, "mobs in all of the country's principal cities continued the celebratory mood by looting their Jewish fellow citizens, going about their job as the German S.S. paper 'Schwarzer Korps' wrote admiringly, 'with honest joy,' and managing 'to do in a fortnight what we have failed to achieve in this slow-moving ponderous north up to this day.' "[2]

This was the reality in Austria before the war. But until recently it was not Austria's image. Most Americans were not aware of Austria's love affair with Nazi Germany or of its vicious persecution of the Jews. American impressions of Austria were those of *The Sound of Music.* So many Americans saw the 1965 movie, which celebrated purity, courage, and the fight against fascism, that *The Sound of Money,* as it came to be called in the industry, broke all existing box-office records.

To Americans, Austria once conjured up images, in the writer Paul Hofmann's words, as frothy and sweet as the dollops of whipped cream that float atop their coffee. Austria was the land of *Gemütlichkeit,* of opera balls and coffeehouses, of hand kissing and waltzes, of *Lederhosen* and Lipizzaner stallions, of the Vienna Boys Choir and Salzburg.

Today, Austria has become synonymous with a different set of images. It has become the country of Kurt Waldheim, the former United Nations Secretary General who lied about his past for forty years, and who told Austrians that he, and by implication they, had only done their duty in yielding so willingly to the Third Reich. It has become the land of men and women who blame others for their misfortunes and crimes, who see themselves as history's victims, and who by a 54 percent margin chose as their President, a largely ceremonial post, a man who had come to symbolize for many in the West unrepentant political cowardice, pragmatic anti-Semitism, and evasion of responsibility for the past.

No matter how history ultimately judges his service with the Wehrmacht, Waldheim can claim one undeniable accomplishment: he has succeeded as have few individuals in changing the way his country is seen by outsiders.

But there is less evidence that he has changed Austria or Austrians or how they see themselves. Israel Singer, secretary general of the World Jewish Congress, which led the fight against Waldheim, and other opponents asserted that Waldheim was "a very effective tool of memory." "He woke them up," Singer maintained in an interview in late 1988.

Many Austrians are not so sure. They are skeptical about sweeping assertions that Austrians can live more easily with the dark shadows of their Nazi past because of the wrenching struggle over Waldheim. Some maintain that the presidential election, this political test of strength, which some analysts consider an essential vehicle of memory, might have made it even more difficult for Austrians to examine their past objectively or to draw appropriate conclusions.

While the long-term effects of the bitter internal struggle over Waldheim cannot yet be known, it seems in the short run to have made political anti-Semitism respectable again in Austria. It has also shown that politically self-serving myths resist being discarded, even when repeatedly confronted by contradictory information. Finally, the acrimonious contest has made it clearer to some Austrians, and particularly to other Europeans, that Austria, the home of forced gaiety and faded splendor, has become more adept than most Western countries at living with illusions.

In his perceptive book on Austria, Paul Hofmann, a native Viennese, asserted that the country was riddled with "pleasant lies," that "Viennese charm" and "merry Vienna" were both true and false. The Blue Danube, he noted, was hardly ever blue; most of the time it was a dull gray. The proud city that had produced some of the turn of the century's most celebrated writers, artists, and philosophers was also the home of the psychoanalyst Alfred Adler, who while walking Vienna's streets found a name for a common syndrome, the "inferiority complex." The city that was once the capital of the multinational Hapsburg empire and home to Hungarians, Czechs, Poles, Croatians, and Slovenians for hundreds of years was also a place of intense xenophobia. The capital, whose reputation for creativity and progressiveness came largely from its once-thriving Jewish population, was also intensely anti-Semitic. And the city that had inspired Mozart, Beethoven, and Schubert has long had one of the world's highest suicide rates.[3]

Austria's problems with its history did not begin with Kurt

Waldheim. Sipping what the Viennese call "a little brown one" in one of the fake Art Nouveau coffeehouses in the city center, Gerold Christian, a spokesman for Waldheim, said that Austria had been historically demoralized since the early part of the century. "It has been a bad history since 1918, ever since we lost our empire," said Christian, who had come to say that Waldheim would not agree to an interview.[4]

The decline of an empire is never easy. But Austrians took it harder than most. For seven hundred years, the Hapsburgs had ruled much of central Europe. Since the fifteenth century, the head of the house of Hapsburg had also been accustomed to being elected German King and Holy Roman Emperor. Under Frederick III and Maximilian I, the empire's holdings had expanded dramatically through a series of astute marriages. "Let others wage war; thou, happy Austria, marry," the empire's motto became. Although he was repeatedly humbled by Napoleon I, Hapsburg Emperor Francis managed to emerge, in part through skillful diplomacy, as one of the strongest monarchs at the Congress of Vienna in 1815. Austria gave up the Netherlands, but regained Dalmatia, Istria, and Tyrol. It was also given Salzburg and much of what is modern-day Italy.[5]

The empire's fortunes only began to decline irrevocably with the rise of Bismarck and after the revolution of 1848, during which Francis's son Ferdinand abdicated in favor of his nephew Francis Joseph. But by 1900, Austria's reach still included a multitude of peoples and lands and nine official languages. It was a hub of international intrigue, gossip, and fashion. It was, in many respects, the intellectual, artistic, and political center of Europe.

World War I was catastrophic for the Hapsburg empire, which had fared better through diplomacy and marriage than war. In October and November of 1918, bitter military defeats and cold, hunger, and influenza killed thousands at the front and at home. The decisiveness of their defeat and the dissolution of the country later that year was a bitter blow for people accustomed to thinking of themselves as politically indispensable.

To this day, an almost obsessive nostalgia for lost empire is palpable in Vienna. This imperial ghost city, built to rule one of the most powerful and creative empires of Europe, has become a gigantic swollen head on a shrunken body of a nation, roughly the size of New York State. It has been reduced to a provincial Alpine republic of 7.5 million people, fewer than Belgium. Once the second home of fashion, awash in elegant cafés, sophisticated theater, opera, and ballet, Vienna has taken on an almost rustic style. Much of the city's haute couture has been replaced by Tyrolean hats, *Lederhosen,* and other accouterments of the rural style.

"Since 1945, the city has looked like a permanent folklore festival," Hofmann wrote.[6]

That *Anschluss,* or absorption by Hitler in a new Germanic empire, should have appealed to German-speaking people with such a heritage and historical longing was not surprising, said Oliver Rathkolb, a young Austrian historian and specialist on the postwar period.[7]

Another basic feature of Austria's political landscape that made it particularly vulnerable to the allure of National Socialism was its anti-Semitism. "Ours is very old, Christian anti-Semitism, as old as the empire," said Ruth Beckerman, a young Jewish filmmaker who worked against Waldheim's election. "A cross hangs in every classroom. Prayers are said in school. In Austria, even the Jews are anti-Semitic."

Jews and Christians had lived together in Vienna since Roman times, as legend would have it. But the oldest documents referring to Jews in Vienna date from the twelfth century. In the centuries that followed, periods of persecution alternated with what Hofmann called "spells of reluctant and relative tolerance." This changed dramatically in 1781, when Emperor Josef II issued his Edict of Toleration. Outward signs of discrimination were banned, and Jews were admitted to schools and other public institutions.[8]

The legal change reflected the growing dependence of the Hapsburgs on Jewish financiers, the "court Jews," as they were called—Samson Wertheimer and the Rothschilds, for example. Another set of legal changes followed the revolution of 1848, which swept Western Europe. Jews were granted legal equality with the Christian majority. After that, they reveled in their new and privileged position "in maintaining the fame of Viennese culture in its old splendor," wrote Stefan Zweig.[9]

But as Viennese Jews were making an impressive contribution to the cultural life of the empire, anti-Semitism among the lower middle class of artisans, small shopkeepers, and bureaucrats was undergoing a resurgence. Jews, the killers of Christ, were becoming too visible, too prominent, too invaluable in the country's life, some Austrians argued. Although Jews never comprised more than 8 percent of Vienna's population, those Christians deeply resented what they viewed as the Jews' disproportionate influence.[10]

Outside of sophisticated Vienna, religious anti-Semitism continued to flourish. In Rinn, the old capital of folkloric Tyrol, residents had long commemorated the ritual murder of "little Anderl," the only son of the widow of a day laborer. As legend had it, Anderl was murdered on July 12, 1462, by a band of traveling Jewish merchants who wanted to use his blood in a religious ceremony. For centuries, Tyroleans made pilgrimages to the rock upon which little Anderl was allegedly bludgeoned to death and said prayers at the church next to it. The murder was commemorated inside the church in a series of fifteenth-century frescos. In 1961, Vatican II banned all references in Catholic theology and teaching to alleged ritual murder by Jews. But the Bishop of Innsbruck did not close the church to the annual processions in honor of Anderl von Rinn until the mid-1980s. And to this day little Anderl's tragic end at the hands of the Jews is still recounted in books of Tyrolean folktales kept in some town libraries.[11]

A third factor that made National Socialism attractive to so many Austrians was the chaos and discord of the period between the two world wars. Between the end of the First World War and Hitler's annexation, Austria's weak federal government was deeply divided. The economy was in shambles; unemployment was high; it had virtually no parliamentary tradition. In such a context, civil war was all but inevitable. On February 12, 1934, twenty thousand underground members of left-wing militias that the government had dissolved battled government forces and eventually army units. Almost a thousand Austrians died, many in "Red Vienna," before Austria succumbed to what Robert Knight, the British historian, called "clerico-fascist" authoritarianism and repression.[12]

When Anschluss finally came, those who were not supporters were at least relieved that the civil strife had ended. On April 10, 1938, 99.7 percent of the Austrians voted in a plebiscite in favor of their country's union with Germany.

There was little resistance in Austria. Radomir Luza, who was active in the resistance in Czechoslovakia, has estimated that about 100,000 Austrians were involved in all forms of political resistance to Nazism.[13] But some historians believe that the figure is too large. Efforts by the Allies to establish underground networks almost always ended in betrayal and failure.

Austria played a major role in the Holocaust. The country's Jews, the vast majority of whom lived in their beloved Vienna, were slaughtered. As soon as the Anschluss took effect, Jews were paraded through the streets of the capital and forced to scrub away with lye, using their own shirts and coats and bare hands, the anti-Nazi political slogans that were scrawled across sidewalks and buildings, toilets and gutters.

The campaign was even more vicious outside Vienna. In Hitler's hometown of Linz, a pogrom preceded Hitler's arrival in the city in March. Gordon Craig observed that the "cleansing" that was carried out was so thorough that on Kristallnacht, eight months later, local storm troopers were unable to find any Jewish property that had not already been looted or expropriated. The only remaining Jewish structure was the synagogue, emptied of its congregation, most of whom had fled; they nevertheless burned it to the ground. The remaining three hundred Jews of Linz were then subjected to daily humiliation, until they were deported in 1942 to concentration camps in Poland, where virtually all died.[14]

According to Simon Wiesenthal, Austria's celebrated Nazi hunter, little Austria, whose population hovered around 7 million before the war, compared with Germany's roughly 65 million people at the time, supplied nearly 75 percent of the staff of the Nazi concentration camps. About 80 percent of the entourage of Adolf Eichmann, in charge of transporting European Jews to the death camps, were Austrian.[15] And Austria had a higher percentage of Nazi party members than did Germany.

Some 120,000 of Austria's 200,000 Jews fled the country after annexation. An estimated 65,000 were killed in death camps, many at Mauthausen, the largest Nazi concentration camp in Austria, near the town of the same name, eighty miles west of Vienna on the Danube near Linz.

"For non-Jewish Viennese, the departure of the Jews was a God-send," said Ruth Beckerman. "It completely solved Vienna's housing shortage by adding seventy thousand Jewish apartments to the city's housing stock virtually overnight."

Until the furor over Waldheim began, few young Austrians seemed aware of these facts. The war years were little discussed in Austria. Many young people did not seem to know that their country had played a significant role in the Holocaust.

While ignorance of the war years is not confined to Austria, several Austrian historians and political scientists see their country as a case study of how not to deal with the past. "Austria was not forced to do what the Germans did after the war. They never accepted a historical and moral responsibility for what happened here," said Rathkolb. "Everything was the fault of the Germans plus a few horrid Austrian Nazis."

Austria did not come to this conclusion alone, of course. The lie it had been living since 1945 was partly created by the Allies. In October 1943, the Foreign Ministers of Great Britain and the Soviet Union and the American Secretary of State met in Moscow to discuss, among other pressing topics, the future of Austria. They agreed upon a formulation: "Austria, the first free country to fall victim to Hitlerite aggression, shall be liberated from German domination."

Initially, the Foreign Ministers added that Austria had "a responsibility which she cannot evade for participation in the war on the side of Hitlerite Germany, and that in the final settlement account will inevitably be taken of her own contribution to her liberation."[16]

But by the time the four Allies were ready to leave the country to its neutralized fate in 1955, Austria's image as the "proto-martyrs of Europe," as one British diplomat put it, was well established. For reasons that historians have been debating ever since, the 1955 settlement was termed a "state treaty," in which Austria was deemed not to have been a belligerent. To emphasize the point, the day before they signed the treaty the Allies deleted the reference to Austria's "responsibility" for participation in the war.[17]

John Bunzl, of the Austrian Institute for International Affairs, has argued that the Allies' decision to create what he calls a "founding myth" of the Second Republic by enshrining Austria as Hitler's first victim was deliberate.[18] A new national identity was essential because Austria had no political tradition to fall back on, he argues. The Allies understood the extent of the continuing loyalty to the Third Reich in the country they were occupying. They knew that the majority of Austrians did not feel that National Socialism was a "reign of foreign terror," or that they had been "liberated" from a foreign yoke by Germany's defeat.

"In the Moscow Declaration of 1943, the Allies used the formulation of Austria being the 'first victim' of Hitler's aggression for strategic reasons and in order to stimulate Austrian resistance against the Third Reich," Bunzl maintained.[19]

Rathkolb and others have argued that the Americans, in particular, were motivated partly by the Cold War. Austria was being wooed by both the Soviets and the United States; neither wanted to displease its potential friend by making it confront its role in the war. A neutral Austria, therefore, served the interests of the West and of the Soviet Union. "You gave us a historical out, and we grabbed it," Rathkolb said.

Austria was not required to pay reparations to victims. Karl Gruber, who was then Austria's Foreign Minister, had opposed the inclusion in the Austrian state treaty of any compensation provision for Jews. Such measures, he warned, presented a "danger of arousing afresh the embers of anti-Semitism in Austria, while it would also appear unfair that those Austrian Jews who had escaped should receive better terms than those who had remained and been placed in concentration camps."[20]

Austria's de-Nazification program was problematic from its inception and far less effective than its counterpart in Germany. Sympathetic juries convicted only 13,600 of the 123,000 Austrians tried for war crimes between 1945 and 1955. The head of the Vienna Gestapo, the chief of the Nazi euthanasia program, and the Gauleiter of Tyrol were all living quietly in Austria in April 1988.[21] History textbooks that were inaccurate were not changed after the war as they were in West Germany. No reeducation program was implemented. As East-West tensions grew in the late 1940s, the de-Nazification program, always overly formal and perfunctory, was further truncated. People's wartime records were quietly buried. Rathkolb cites letters and memoranda from American State Department and intelligence officers, some of which have not been published in the United States. The correspondence reflected their discomfort with the Austrian reconstruction and the de-Nazification programs.[22]

These tensions were evident in the letters of Paul R. Sweet, now a professor emeritus of history in East Lansing, Michigan, who served in Austria as an intelligence officer for the State Department in 1945. Sweet was responsible for the regeneration of the Steyr-Daimler-Puch Works, a major Austrian industrial concern, part of which was in the Russian zone. Always a large firm by Austrian standards, Steyr had expanded under the Third Reich and employed at its peak between forty-five and fifty thousand workers, many of them forced labor. From a humble Austrian automobile producer, Steyr had become one of the leading armaments manufacturers for Nazi Germany.

Sweet wrote of his difficulties in recruiting top managers for Steyr. Both Oskar Hacker, a chief engineer, and Karl Rossner, in charge of administration, "have been with the Steyr concern for many years," he wrote in a lengthy report in July 1945. "Like anyone who has held an important managerial position in a Nazi war industry continuously during the last seven years, they were necessarily accomplices in a brutal labor system. . . . In general, however, they give the impression of being about the best types one may expect to find among collaborationist industrialists."[23]

The situation was even worse in Linz, home of Hitler's former Hermann Goering Works, which were not badly damaged during the war. Sweet estimated that 75 percent production could be attained "without difficulty" once new management was in place. However, he added, "the situation with respect to the provincial government and the Goering works stinks so that I am almost afraid to touch either."[24] In a letter to a friend on July 3, 1945, Sweet noted that an American colleague had introduced him to a "big industrialist," an Austrian who was a candidate for a senior post in new management at the Goering plants. "In my opinion the fellow ought to be in jail," Sweet observed. At dinner, the industrialist "got quite excited" because the Germans claimed that a "big tank was produced at Nuernberg, whereas he said 'we are the only ones who could have produced it.' "[25]

"It is rather idle to attempt to clean out a Nazi-nest like the Goering works," Sweet noted two weeks later. "We got some good leads today; it may take some running around to track them down, however," he wrote, his frustration mounting.[26]

By August 1945, "Austrianization" at the Goering Works, which had employed 4,000 "white-collars" workers in Linz at the time of the German military collapse, was well under way. Hans Malzacher, called by Sweet the "Nazi industrialist," had been appointed the new general-director. "Although the Goering Works is a clear-cut example of a war industry built by German capital and, in the better positions, largely staffed by German personnel," he wrote, "the local Austrians regard it now as a valuable Austrian asset which they hope to salvage for their own benefit. Even Austrian workers and employees whose political position is well to the left indicate that they prefer a 'good' Austrian Nazi to a Piefke [German] of any political variety, and they condone keeping and putting Austrians in leading positions, even when their records as Nazis are well known."[27]

So it went throughout Austria. As at the Goering Works, the Nazi issue was largely evaded for two reasons. "Because of the number and influence of the Germans at the plant, the problem of a purge has presented itself to the local Austrians more as a German than as a specifically Nazi issue," Sweet concluded. "Second, the top direction has successfully opposed any efforts made to inject the Nazi issue into the personnel problem, since they are fully cognizant of the increased vulnerability of their own positions once political factors come into consideration."[28]

The conspiracy to bury history was not confined to industrialists. In sharp contrast to Germany, Austria's political class immediately rewrote history after the war. Although Austria's 500,000 Nazi party members were not permitted to vote in the 1945 elections, Austrian parties were actively competing for their support, roughly 10 percent of the country, by 1949.

Bruno Kreisky, or "Emperor Bruno," as he later was called in Vienna, leader of the Socialist party, Austria's first postwar Socialist Chancellor, and a Jew, was among the key competitors for the Nazi vote.

"Bruno Kreisky, of all people, should have understood the price of burying or misconstruing the past," said Peter Michael Lingens, who was editor of *Profil,* the weekly magazine, when it disclosed information about Waldheim's past. "He is guilty of a monumental historical failure. Kreisky was in a position to exert a positive influence on Austrians because he was a Jew. But he did not."

The descendant of a Jewish, upper-middle-class family in the textile business, Kreisky had been active in the Social Democratic party's underground organization after the 1934 civil war, had been arrested and served time in prison, and had fled to Sweden during the war.

When Kreisky was elected in 1970, he brought former fascists back into Austrian politics. There were four former Nazis and one S.S. officer in senior ranks of his first government. In the 1970s, he sought to solidify his political hold by building a coalition with the Freedom party, which was composed of numerous former Nazis and their sons. The Freedom party's mission was to protect the "Germanness" of Austrian life from Slavic influences. Kreisky's pragmatist strategy was so successful that the Socialists were able to govern for a time without the conservative People's party which was ultimately to back Waldheim.

Kreisky remained unrepentant about the political course he had chosen. Yes, he admitted in an interview at his home in Vienna in September 1986, he had brought the Freedom party into the mainstream of Austrian political life. "The time for an end to purges and recriminations had come," he said. "Besides," he added, "there were roughly 250,000 Austrians alive then who had been members of the Nazi party. With whom should we have rebuilt the country?"

Embraced by the country's politicians and its industrialists, the "first victim" myth had genuine resonance among ordinary Austrians. Those old enough to remember the war saw themselves as victims, first of Germany's Third Reich, and later of the occupying Allies, particularly the Russians. The Red Army's lack of discipline, in the sector they controlled resulted in pillage, rape, and terror that are remembered by Viennese still.

Peter Sichrovsky, an Austrian Jewish writer who has explored the attitudes of both children of Jewish survivors and of Nazis in Germany and Austria, said that this perception was still common among the postwar generation. "They remember the hunger, their cities being bombed by Allied planes, the loss of fathers and uncles in the war, and they cannot understand why their suffering is not appreciated, why it doesn't count," Sichrovsky said. "They don't want to look at how and why the war started."

Austria Today, a government-supported English-language quarterly, published an article on Austrian de-Nazification just before the Waldheim controversy erupted. The article listed the "guilty" and the "victims." Included in the latter category were 65,000 Austrian Jews who were killed in extermination camps; 32,600 Austrian opponents of the Nazi regime who died in camps or prisons without formal charges; 2,700 Austrians who were convicted and executed for resistance to the Nazis; 70,000 Austrians imprisoned for listening to "enemy" radio or for other anti-Nazi activities; 30,000 Austrians who were sentenced to prison for "undermining morale," refusing military service, or desertion; and 271,300 Austrians, including 24,300 civilians, who "met their deaths in Hitler's war machine." The remaining number, one presumes, died fighting alongside the Wehrmacht.

The implicit equation of Jewish deaths with those who died

helping defend the regime that was killing them is breathtaking. But another unstated conclusion of the "victims" list illustrates Austria's "victimization" psychosis: 65,000 Jews died in death camps; but altogether, 400,000 non-Jewish Austrians were victims. Austrian suffering, the argument would seem, was more than four times as great as that of the Jews.

Perhaps a clash between the founding myth of the Second Republic and history was inevitable. Before the Waldheim scandal began, Austria had endured a few isolated pinpricks to their memory. The first centered on the man whom Kreisky backed in 1983 as President of the Austrian Parliament, Friedrich Peter.

Simon Wiesenthal began investigating Peter's background in 1975. He discovered that he had been a lieutenant for two years in the First S.S. Infantry Brigade, a German unit that had killed 10,000 civilians, 8,000 of them Jews, in the Ukraine. The disclosures, published that same year in *Profil,* prompted widespread protest. More than 2,000 people signed petitions demanding his withdrawal from the election campaign.

Peter denied any wrongdoing, asserting that he had only done his duty. The Freedom party called for Wiesenthal's expulsion from the country on grounds that he had "defamed" Austria. Both themes were later echoed by Waldheim supporters. But Peter ultimately withdrew his nomination.

"In 1986, Peter retired and began receiving his pension," said Peter Lingens, the *Profil* editor who had published Wiesenthal's research. "He had not become President of the Parliament, but he had remained a member. And when he retired, he received a standing ovation from members of all three parties."

In 1985, Defense Minister Friedhelm Frischenschleger, also a Freedom party member, created a scandal by going to Graz airport to greet Walter Reder, an Austrian-born former S.S. major who was being returned to Austria by Italy. Reder had been released from Gaeta prison in Italy after having served forty years of a life sentence for his part in the mass killing of civilians in 1944. The warm high-level welcome for Reder infuriated members of the World Jewish Congress, which was holding its annual meeting in Vienna for the first time since the war.

Such incidents prompted debate, and temporarily broke through the amnesia that enveloped Austria since the war's end. But the case of Kurt Waldheim put squarely before the world and before

Austrians the issue of their own and Austria's moral responsibility for the war and the Final Solution.

"And this, understandably," said Rathkolb, "was an enormously unpopular and divisive issue in a conservative country that since the war has deplored differences and adored consensus."

At least two Austrians—Hubertus Czernin, who worked for *Profil,* and Georg Tidl, a local historian—had been working on Waldheim's background for months by the time the World Jewish Congress began its inquiry in January of 1986. The first article about Waldheim's hidden record with the Wehrmacht was published on March 3, 1986, in *Profil.* No one paid attention. The next day, *The New York Times* published a detailed, front-page article about Waldheim's hidden wartime service with the Wehrmacht. The article was based in large part on material supplied by the World Jewish Congress. Waldheim had confirmed in an interview with *The Times* that he had been in the units in question, but he insisted that he had played a minor role and knew of no war crimes or atrocities ascribed to those units.[29] The article caused an instant sensation. Members of the World Jewish Congress said at the time that Waldheim would be forced to withdraw his nomination within a week.[30] A succession of stories revealed new details of Waldheim's activities with Nazi units from 1941 to 1944, when, according to his invented autobiography, he was back in Vienna working on his doctoral dissertation.

By the time of the critical presidential runoff election in June 1986, Austrians had been told much about the candidate and former Secretary-General of the United Nations.[31] As a young man, he had been an admirer of Engelbert Dollfuss, the Catholic fascist who ended Austria's embattled parliamentary democracy and was himself shot by the Nazis in 1934. Waldheim's father had lost his job when the Nazis took over. Waldheim had stood on a street corner in Vienna handing out leaflets that said: "VOTE AUSTRIA, NOT NAZI." After the Anschluss, he joined a cavalry unit in the Sturmabteilung, or S.A., as it was called. Waldheim, when pressed over the years, has spoken vaguely of his membership in a riding club where young men on the way up mingled and made useful contacts. He married a young woman, Elisabeth Ritschel, who was a staunch member of the Hitler Youth and who became a party member as soon as she turned eighteen.

After the war began, he served with the senior staff of a German army unit, translating and transmitting orders to combat groups, interrogating prisoners, and gathering intelligence and analysis. From March to November 1942, he was attached to the command staffs of the Bader Combat Group and the West Bosnian Combat Group that succeeded it, both in Yugoslavia. During his service there, 68,000 people were deported to concentration camps, and Waldheim won a service medal from the puppet government that the Nazis had installed. Between March and July 1943, he was a member of the staff of General Alexander Loumiauthr in Arsakli, Greece, and in Podgorica, Yugoslavia. During this time, more than 40,000 Jews of Salonika, about one-fifth of the population, were deported to Auschwitz. In Podgorica, photographs show Waldheim attending staff strategy sessions for "Operation Black," a savage, highly effective action against the partisans of Montenegro. Between July and October of 1943, he was Loumiauthr's liaison officer with the Italian Eleventh Army in Athens. A report prepared by the World Jewish Congress revealed that part of Waldheim's responsibilities from July through August 1943 was the keeping of the daily war journal. Waldheim had dutifully recorded the orders for the murder and deportation of partisans captured in battle, both of which are war crimes under the Nuremberg Tribunal's charter.[32] From the end of that year through December 1944, he was at the Army Group E's headquarters at Arsakli once more.

General Loumiauthr, who was also an Austrian, was hanged as a war criminal by Yugoslavia in 1947.

Austrian voters also knew by June 1986 that the Yugoslav War Crimes Commission had declared Waldheim a war criminal in 1947 and that the United States had placed him on a list of suspected war criminals in 1948. They did not know, nor is it known today, whether his wartime record was taken into account by the USSR, which like the United States supported Waldheim's candidacy for the top UN post in 1971.

Waldheim had a simple, consistent response to the questions and charges about his wartime activities. He initially denied that the allegations were true. When confronted with proof during the presidential election, he conceded that war crimes had probably taken place, but that he had neither participated in nor known about them.

Campaigning throughout Austria, Waldheim maintained that he had only done his duty as a soldier in the war, a theme that was well received by Austrians. But Waldheim and his supporters soon found a more powerful defense mechanism, one that aroused both popular anti-Semitism and xenophobia. The World Jewish Congress was the target. In reality, the World Jewish Congress, based in New York, was until then among the smallest and least influential in American politics of the Jewish mass organizations. But its name encouraged Austrians to complain that Waldheim and their country were being slandered in a vendetta that was both "worldwide" and "Jewish."

Once again, Austria fell back on its status as first victim. If it had been victimized by the Germans and then by the Allies, little Austria was now the target of an international Jewish conspiracy. The country was under attack by "some Americans living on the East Coast," one of the favorite euphemisms for Jews used in the campaign. Some officials and newspapers even dispensed with circumlocution. "Jews Accuse Waldheim of War Crimes," screamed the headline of one of the prominent dailies. Almost all of the newspapers, irrespective of their political slant, sided with Waldheim. *Neue Kronen Zeitung,* for example, the largest daily in Austria, with a circulation of roughly one million, was owned by a friend of Waldheim's and defended him throughout the campaign. In the end, only *Profil* and one newspaper, the *Salzburger Nachrichten,* which is read by 2.9 percent of Austrians, opposed his candidacy.

The Socialists realized in May, after Waldheim came close to winning a majority vote in the first round of voting, that every attack on him was translating as a vote for him. So the Socialist party candidate, Kurt Steyrer, a doctor and by all accounts not a charismatic campaigner, tried to avoid raising Waldheim's war record as an issue. Socialist party functionaries justified their silence by saying that attacks on Waldheim's war record would have violated the rules of consensus politics that had kept the Second Republic functioning since the war. The unofficial agreement of the "grand coalition" that has governed Austria, they said, required the exclusion of certain topics from public debate—such as the anti-Semitism that runs particularly deep within the Catholic-influenced conservative parties, or the Social Democrats' flirtation with German nationalism and with Moscow. To dredge up Waldheim's role in the war was one of those taboo issues of the past that was unfair and potentially divisive, the argument went.

Only once in the bitter campaign did a senior Socialist official let slip a truly biting comment. Asked what he thought about the

People's party's contention that Waldheim's membership in the Storm Troopers' riding unit did not make him a Nazi, Chancellor Fred Sinowatz replied: "Waldheim wasn't a Nazi; only his horse was."[33]

A group of about four hundred writers, artists, and intellectuals who banded together under the name "New Austria" tried to rally broader opposition against Waldheim in irreverent, witty ways. After Sinowatz's "horse" remark, for example, they began carrying giant papier-mâché horses to rallies. But apart from the solidarity they achieved among themselves, their appeals to Austrians to reject Waldheim and stop negating the past did not sway Austria's 4.7 million voters.

On June 8, 1986, Waldheim was elected President by 53.9 percent of the Austrian voters. Two voting trends were noteworthy. First, the abstention rate, particularly among the young, was the highest in Austrian postwar history. Clearly, many young Austrians were uncomfortable with the choice they were being asked to make. Second, young Austrians voted for Waldheim in far greater numbers than did their elders.[34]

Political scientists argued that this was not because younger Austrians were particularly xenophobic or anti-Semitic (opinion polls have shown that they tend to be less so, particularly the highly educated). Rather, they simply seemed less interested in the issue of Waldheim's past and more determined to end the forty-year rule by the Socialists.

"Unfortunately," Kreisky conceded, "the Socialists were very unpopular, especially among young people. They didn't like Waldheim, but they disliked my party more." Waldheim, he ventured, probably would have won with 60 percent of the vote had it not been for the scandal about his past.

Younger Austrians appeared fed up with the legacy of their country's leftist government: a whopping 40 billion schilling debt in the Socialists' nationalized industries; a succession of scandals involving corruption and favoritism; a bloated, rigid bureaucracy in which patronage was all-important and in which there were few opportunities for advancement on merit. They chafed at having to be members of one political party or another in order to teach in the schools, work in government, or hold a variety of desirable jobs that the parties controlled. There was, indeed, much to reject in 1986 in the Socialists' record.

Academics debate why Austrians voted the way they did. Public-opinion surveys offer conflicting explanations, and some of the polls, especially those conducted by the political parties, must be viewed with skepticism. What we know from one published in 1986 by the *Journal of Social Studies,* a scholarly Austrian publication, is that only 7 percent of Austrians said that their votes were affected by the issue of Waldheim's past.[35] About 4 percent of Waldheim's voters cited "anti-Semitism" as a reason for voting for Waldheim. But 4 percent of Steyrer's voters said they had supported him because of his "anti-fascist" views. Hence, according to the poll, anti-Semitism and anti-fascism tended to cancel each other out in the popular vote.

While most political scientists and students of Austrian society believe that the poll understated the impact of anti-Semitism in the Waldheim vote, the *Journal* poll and another exit survey sponsored by Waldheim's People's party both showed that the vast majority of Austrian voters cited Waldheim's experience as a "statesman" as the principal reason for their support.[36]

In the exit poll on May 4, 1986, sponsored by the People's party, for example, 81 percent of those who had voted for Waldheim said they had supported him because of his "international experience as a diplomat." But 49 percent said they had done so because "unjustified accusations have been raised against him"; and 31 percent said they had voted for him because "foreign circles have attempted to influence the Austrian election outcome."

There is no doubt that Waldheim's stature as a former United Nations chief was critical to his success. As Jane Kramer argued in a thoughtful article in *The New Yorker,* Austrians' support for Waldheim probably had less to do than many thought with Nazi stirrings or anti-Semitism, or even stubbornness. Austrians supported Waldheim because he was "prominent."[37]

"They long for prominence," Kramer wrote in her June 20 letter from Vienna. "Waldheim was Secretary-General of the United Nations from 1972 until 1982, and Austrians—nearly fifty-four percent of them, anyway—do not much care that he was a terrible Secretary-General for every one of those years, that he was greedy and cowardly and vain and laughably ambitious, or that he wanted to stay and was defeated, or that he tried to leave New York with the residence furniture and did, in fact, manage to leave with the silver. At home, he has let it be known that he ran the world from his United Nations suite, and by and large the people at home believe him. How he ran the world is not important. What is important," she concluded, "is that the world was run by an Austrian."

Although the polls do not reflect the ferocity of the anti-Semitism and xenophobia that also contributed to Waldheim's victory, it was impossible to visit Vienna during the political campaign and not feel the resentment so many Austrians harbored toward Jews and other "outsiders."

Leon Zelman, a Polish Jew who survived three and a half years at Mauthausen, Auschwitz, and other camps, was stunned by the outpouring of vitriol. He had settled in Vienna, a city he dearly loved, to rebuild a life after the war. For many years, he has headed the Jewish Welcome Service in Vienna. The city's shrinking Jewish community of six thousand has been his pride and joy.

Zelman also helped found one of the most innovative educational programs about the Holocaust in all of Europe. Launched by the Socialist Minister of Education in 1977, the program sends Austrian concentration-camp survivors into high schools throughout the country to discuss their wartime experiences with students. Zelman had visited 120 schools by the time the furor over Waldheim began.

Usually, he recalled in an interview in Vienna shortly after Waldheim's victory, "the kids knew almost nothing about the Holocaust, about Austria's role during the war. But at least," he said, "they had open minds and a genuine sense of shock and outrage about what we told them had happened."

The atmosphere changed dramatically, however, when he visited a school during the Waldheim campaign. "The kids were aggressive and hostile," he said. "For the first time I heard children saying 'you Jews.' They said that Waldheim had only been a soldier, like their grandfathers. He had only done his duty, echoing Waldheim's words. I was so upset that I almost had to leave the schoolroom," he said.

Zelman stopped participating in the program, and vowed not to go into the schools anymore. "It was too painful," he explained.

He and others were shocked not only by the depth of the anti-Semitism that surfaced, but also by the lack of reaction from the Austrian Jewish community. "It was normal for non-Jews to want to forget the war," Zelman said. "But the Jews here wanted to forget it too. I suppose that Jews who wanted to live in Vienna always knew they would have to pay a price. And I suppose many of them were tired and very afraid. Most of them were furious at the World Jewish Congress. They said: 'We just want to be left alone.' "

Defacements of synagogues and other acts of anti-Semitic vandalism soared during the campaign. Hate mail poured into Zelman's office and those of other Jewish representatives. Ivan Hacker-Lederer, a retired lawyer who served in 1986 as spokesman for the Jewish community, said that his office got between sixty and seventy letters a day, some addressed "To the Jewish Community, Division Swines."[38] Some Jews were afraid to send their children to school.

Even many of Waldheim's opponents maintained that the tactics of the World Jewish Congress were counterproductive here psychologically and politically. Elan Steinberg, executive director of the WJC, defended its actions. He said that the scandal over Waldheim had "exposed Austria's true colors" to all the world, and thus had proven educational. But, he conceded, "if we made any mistake at all it was in thinking that Austria was America. It is not."

"The Waldheim affair managed to undo years of our work," lamented Peter Lingens, then the *Profil* editor.[39] "For decades, we had been trying to prompt Austrians to explore their past, to make them understand that there were different degrees of guilt in the war and to distinguish between them. Those who worked in concentration camps, for example, had a different level of guilt from Nazi party members in Austria, or from simple soldiers who agreed to fight in a Nazi uniform.

"What the Waldheim affair did was to mix them all up in people's minds. Waldheim is a liar, not a war criminal, and it was wrong to destroy the difference between these two charges," he said. "It made it harder to deal with the past, not easier. Waldheim's victory was all of Austria's exoneration. So nobody wants to talk about collective responsibility or to examine individual guilt anymore," he said.

"The World Jewish Congress was stupid and arrogant," Ruth Beckerman agreed. The campaign was weak because "the information was weak," she argued. "It was enough to say that he had lied about his past. They should have known that calling him a war criminal because he was a staff officer for a Nazi war criminal would be interpreted here as an attack on all Austrians who wore

German uniforms. But they had no idea about how Austrians reacted to things, and they did not take the time or effort to find out."

"My life's work has been hunting Nazi war criminals," said Wiesenthal in an interview. "Waldheim covered up his past, but there is no proof that he personally committed war crimes." In making this assertion, Wiesenthal was arguing that true war criminals are those who initiated orders that killed Jews or acted personally against them in camps or in prisons. Waldheim had merely passed orders along. No one had actually seen him murder a prisoner or partisan himself.

There has always been much debate about Wiesenthal's Nazi-hunting activities and now his defense of Waldheim. Some of his detractors argued that he defended Waldheim because he was embarrassed by the fact that he had failed to uncover the truth about Waldheim's past, an assertion he has denied vehemently. While he has long been close to the People's party, Wiesenthal's position seems to have been dictated more by his strong belief that, as he once put it, "Jews need allies." Separating Jews from their country's mainstream was dangerous, he warned.

Moreover, the Waldheim affair was destined, he feared correctly, to shatter the "brotherhood of victims"—Jews, Gypsies, Russians, Poles, Czechs, even Austrians—he was trying to build and which he believed was needed to defend humanity against the next Hitler.

"You cannot punish Austria collectively for Waldheim," he declared. "We do not need Austria as the enemy of the Jewish people."[40]

Kreisky accused the World Jewish Congress of "monumental stupidity." "No one likes meddling in their internal affairs," he said. "And that's exactly what the World Jewish Congress was perceived as doing. Even if this country did not have an anti-Semitic tradition, voters would select the candidate whom the World Jewish Congress had opposed."

Singer and other WJC representatives have rejected criticism that their organization inflamed Austrian anti-Semitism. "Semites do not create anti-Semitism. Anti-Semites do," said Singer. The reaction of the Austrian Jews to the disclosures was "cowardly" and particularly disappointing, he said. "Jews everywhere should know by now that if they don't stand up for themselves, no one else will."

Besides, he and others argued, the Austrians had distorted the issue. The WJC did not specifically assert that Waldheim had been a war criminal, though virtually all their members believed it, said Elan Steinberg in an interview long after the election. "What we said, and what we proved, was that he had lied about his past, that he had served in the Wehrmacht, and that he had recorded, interpreted, and transmitted orders that the Nuremberg Tribunal were later to classify as war crimes."[41] The distinction, Steinberg conceded, might well have been lost in the highly charged political atmosphere of the Austrian presidential elections, but WJC representatives insist that they always took the position that only the courts could make a legal determination about Waldheim's guilt or innocence of war crimes.

The WJC's assertions were endorsed by the Reagan Administration when it barred Waldheim from visiting the United States in April 1987 by placing him on a so-called "watch" list. The forty thousand individuals on this list are suspected of having taken part in wartime "persecutions based on race, religion, national origin, or political opinion."

The administration's action was based on a report and a recommendation from the Justice Department's Office of Special Investigations, its Nazi-hunting unit. Neal Sher, the head of OSI, said at the time, and reiterated his view again in an interview in early 1989, that although only an international tribunal had legal authority to determine whether Waldheim had committed war crimes, "I would have had no trouble as a prosecutor bringing war crimes charges against him."[42]

Waldheim's election in June 1986 stunned Austria's tiny, traumatized Jewish community. For the first time, anti-Semitism had been successfully used in a campaign. It had helped propel Waldheim to victory. "A new threshold had been crossed," said Beckerman.

Ten percent of traditionally Socialist voters had cast ballots for Waldheim in the second round in June; two-thirds of the environmental vote, the Austrian equivalent of the German Greens, had supported him after their candidate was eliminated in the first round in May.

"I kept thinking during those months that things had to improve; they simply could not have gotten worse," said Zelman. "It was a terrible time."

The political mood in Austria remained ugly. In May 1987, Ronald S. Lauder, the former executive vice president of Estée Lauder, Inc., the cosmetics company, and then American Ambassador to Austria, received a letter from Carl Hoedl, the Deputy Mayor of Linz. It was a copy of one addressed to Bronfman, the World Jewish Congress president.

"I'm still incredulous when I think about it," said Lauder in an interview in New York.[43] "It said, and I'm quoting verbatim: 'You Jews got Christ, but you're not going to get our Waldheim in the same way.' "

Lauder said he had wanted to protest the letter immediately, but officials at the embassy warned against doing so. It would only backfire, they said. Once the letter's existence became known in Vienna, the Austrian people would react, they predicted.

So Lauder kept quiet. The letter was widely circulated by the WJC; everyone in political circles knew of it. No one protested. "Never once did any Austrian official come and tell me that he was really very embarrassed by it. They said nothing," Lauder reported.

Finally, Lauder made the letter's existence known by discussing it in an interview with *The New York Times* as he was leaving his ambassadorial post.[44] In November 1987, one month later, Deputy Mayor Hoedl resigned at the request of his party. So did Michael Graff, the general secretary of the Austrian People's party, who had told the French news weekly *L'Express* that "so long as it is not proved that he [Waldheim] strangled six Jews with his own hands," Waldheim would be able to stay in office.

Eventually, the Austrian public, which had been whipped into a frenzy by the June runoff elections, calmed down. Two significant events—a report by a panel of independent historians and a year of commemorations and remembrance—prompted a less-publicized but more profound reflection. Some maintain that a period of calm is essential to a less-charged debate that might change public opinion on Waldheim and enable Austria to confront its past.

For reasons that have long been a source of speculation in Austria, Waldheim agreed soon after his election to the formation of a panel of historians from several countries to investigate his war record. In February 1988, the six-man panel completed its report. The 202-page document, which the Austrian government has not yet translated or published in full, stated that the panel could not make a determination about whether Waldheim was a war criminal because it was not a panel of jurists. However, the report also concluded that he must have known of the atrocities committed by the army unit with which he served in the Balkans, that he had done nothing to stop them, and that he had then lied about his service there.

The findings triggered protests. On the Sunday after the historians released their report, five thousand people gathered in the main square in front of St. Stephen's Church in Vienna to demand that Waldheim step down. *Profil* published a three-page advertisement in which fifteen hundred of Austria's most prominent intellectuals, actors, writers, and professionals reiterated the demand. The atmosphere was further inflamed when the Austrian and foreign press published reports quoting Waldheim as having said that he was not surprised that the panel had criticized him because three of the historians were Jewish. (Only two of the six members were Jewish. The third supposed Jew was Hagen Fleischer, who has both German and Greek nationality.)[45]

The Austrian government denied that Waldheim had made such a statement, but the political cognoscenti in Vienna continued to gossip that the story was true. Those who had not opposed Waldheim openly now called for his resignation: Bruno Kreisky, Simon Wiesenthal, and two members of the historians' panel—Yehuda L. Wallach of Israel and Manfred Messerschmidt of West Germany.

By mid-February 1988, the clamor had become so intense that Chancellor Franz Vranitzky, a Socialist and the senior partner in a governing coalition with the People's party, warned that he might have to resign. Vranitzky complained that since coming to power in January 1987, about 60 percent of his time had been spent on the Waldheim affair; he could no longer deal with Austria's other problems. But he did not do what some of his advisers had urged: he did not trigger a political confrontation by vowing to resign unless Waldheim left office.

The outcry following the historians' report might have comforted those who predicted that the revelations would eventually force Austrians to examine the past and press for Waldheim's ouster or resignation. But little evidence has emerged to suggest that belated moral indignation over Waldheim's Nazi past was responsible for the growing sentiment that he should resign.

Rather, many Austrians have simply grown tired of the scandal that has refused to die. By 1988, they realized that the uproar in

Western Europe and in the United States would not subside; that governments would continue to shun contact with him; that Israel would not send an ambassador back to Vienna. In short, they realized that Waldheim, once the symbol both of prominence and of the "simple soldier," the "man in the street," had become a national embarrassment. He was no longer merely prominent; he was notorious. As Heinrich Keller, secretary of the Socialist party, put it, Waldheim would "continue to be an unbelievable burden for our country."[46]

Vranitzky, ultimately, did not resign, and Waldheim dug in. In a press conference, Waldheim continued to portray himself as a victim of "manipulations, lies and forgeries" by enemies at home and abroad. Wrapping himself more tightly in the cloak of patriotism and his oft-cited "duty," he showed no sign of remorse. The affair had come to an impasse.

Waldheim's visit at the Vatican did not grant him political absolution. Only two heads of state visited Austria in 1987—those of the Soviet Union and Liechtenstein. He received only two invitations that year from foreign leaders to visit them: King Hussein of Jordan and Hosni Mubarak of Egypt. One of the few leaders to congratulate him after his election was Libyan leader Muammar Quaddafi, who said in a telex that his victory was an "act against international zionism."

Meanwhile, Bronfman and other senior WJC representatives continued to press not only for the exclusion of Waldheim from diplomatic forums, but also for the exclusion of Austria, even from the European Community, as long as Waldheim was President.

Austrians, even Jews and others who favor Waldheim's departure, reacted just as they did during the initial furor. They warned that such tactics were bound to misfire politically by drawing the country together again. The WJC approach failed to recognize that Austria had become deeply divided by the Waldheim affair, and that some Austrians had finally, painfully, been forced to confront their nation's past. A few of them, at least, had even drawn appropriate conclusions. It would not help them or Austria to put them on the moral defensive once again, the argument went.

Some of the soul searching that took place after the election was prompted by the designation of 1988, the fiftieth anniversary of the Anschluss, as the "Year of Reflection." For an entire year, intellectuals and scholars explored the country's Nazi past in panel discussions in universities, in schools, in television debates, in articles and editorials in the newspapers. In a decided rebuff to Waldheim, the Austrian Parliament, for the first time, voted not to allow him to address the chamber on the anniversary in March of Austria's annexation to Germany, the centerpeice of the year's events.

Barred from addressing the Parliament, Waldheim delivered a nationally televised speech the night before the fiftieth anniversary and "apologized" on behalf of his country for Nazi war crimes committed by Austrians. Characteristically, he made no reference to the dispute over his own actions in the German Army as he urged his fellow countrymen to "wrestle with the shadows of the past." Many Austrians, he reiterated, had been "victims" of the war.

The next day, ten thousand Viennese gathered outside the City Hall to demand his resignation, again to no avail.

Austrians continue to differ about whether the protracted and often bitter debate over Waldheim has helped the country reexamine its wartime past and whether it has changed public opinion about their President.

Leon Zelman, who said that the Waldheim controversy was the most painful event in his life other than his years in Nazi death camps, concluded that on balance the episode was beneficial for Austria.

"We didn't change a lot of people's minds," he said in an interview in early 1989. "But the intelligentsia were forced for the first time to confront the past. They had not done it before. They had been sleeping."

What began as a vitriolic confrontation had evolved into a positive debate, he said. Waldheim had become a symbol. "He's a symbol of yesterday. Many of us have decided that it is time to give Austria a new symbol, of hope for the future."

Zelman has remained strongly opposed to the political and diplomatic boycott of Austria favored by the World Jewish Congress. "Now is not the time to lump all Austrians together and say we are all terrible people," he said. "Now is the time to reach out to those young Austrians—to actors, journalists, writers, and other intellectuals—who are looking for help in changing their society. What we need is not a boycott, but a partnership."

He has resumed his work in the schools. "Those of us with

numbers on our arms are dying," he said. "So we are now videotaping our meetings with the children, so that one day, when we are gone, other children will be able to learn of our experiences from us directly."

In December 1988, at Zelman's behest, the Austrian government sponsored and financed a week-long trip to Israel by 165 non-Jewish Austrian students, aged sixteen to eighteen. The students visited Yad Vashem, Israel's Holocaust memorial, toured Jerusalem to learn more about ancient Jewish culture, and talked in schools with Israelis who were children and grandchildren of survivors. It was the first exchange of its kind, and Zelman was encouraged by the results.

"Some of the Austrian children were shocked when their Israeli counterparts asked them how they could live in a country with a liar as President," he said. "They talked a lot about it during the trip and when they got home. Most of them had never met Jewish children their own age before. Most of them had known nothing about Judaism. So the visit made a strong impression on them."

Since more members of Austria's Jewish community are over eighty-five than under five, Zelman said, the opportunity to mix with Jewish children, to see that "they did not have horns," was extremely positive.

"We must keep searching for new ways to transmit the experience of the Holocaust," he said. "The children of today have been born in a democracy, in a time of peace, in loving and stable families. How can we expect them to understand about gas chambers and crematoriums?"

He had concluded from the Waldheim affair that his countrymen had grown defensive and xenophobic when they were made to face their past in the context of a highly charged political test of strength, such as an election. "I now know a little more about what does not work," said Zelman, "but we need to know more about what does." Children talking to children was one new approach, he said, but Zelman, an optimist, remained persuaded there were others.

His optimism is not shared by many Austrian analysts, however. Poll after poll has shown the resilience of what the analyst Bunzl has called two pronounced Austrian proclivities: "a refusal to take responsibility" and "a continuing high degree of anti-Semitic tendencies compared with other countries."[47]

In 1973, when asked whether Austrians should feel a special degree of responsibility toward the Jews, 67 percent said no, 13 percent were undecided, 15 percent agreed partly, and 5 percent completely. In 1976, 83 percent wanted an end to war-crimes trials, while 16 percent were opposed. Later polls showed that sentiment has not markedly shifted.[48]

A 1987 publication by the Austrian government, *The Truth About Austria,* continued to list as Austrian "victims" of the war the 247,000 soldiers of Austrian origin who "lost their lives in the front line or were reported missing."[49]

A Gallup survey in July 1986 showed that the percentage of Austrians who thought the Jews had an aversion to hard work had risen from 32 percent in 1980 to 39 percent after Waldheim's election. The proportion of those who thought that Jews had too much economic and political influence rose from 33 percent in 1980 to 48 percent in 1986. Sixteen percent of those polled in 1986 said they believed it would be better for Austria to have no Jews; 38 percent said they believed Jews were partly responsible for their own frequent persecution in the past.[50]

A survey of 458 articles that appeared in 1987 in Austria's four largest daily newspapers, two weekly magazines, and press releases of the three biggest political parties, showed that anti-Semitic remarks appeared in more than 20 percent of the articles about Waldheim, according to the Anti-Defamation League of B'nai B'rith. *Neue Kronen Zeitung,* the daily with the largest circulation, which is bought by more than 40 percent of all Austrian newspaper readers, made anti-Semitic remarks in more than a third of its stories about Waldheim. Newspaper readers could frequently learn about what the press called "Jewish greediness," "Jewish impertinence," "Jewish wirepullers," and the "Jewish manhunt" for Waldheim.[51]

Long after the ADL's survey, examples of vicious anti-Semitism appeared in the leading Austrian dailies. In December 1988, Richard Nimmerrichter, a columnist for *Neue Kronen Zeitung,* attacked A. M. Rosenthal, *The New York Times* columnist, for having criticized Austria. Rosenthal had written a series of columns about Austria after attending an interfaith conference in Vienna devoted to "Jewish-Christian dialogue." He had written that although Vienna was lovely, "there are too many memories of the fact that Austrians produced Nazis as villainous as those from the Fatherland."[52]

This statement of the obvious, or what should have been so by the end of 1988, infuriated Nimmerrichter, who referred to Rosenthal on second reference as "Rosenbaum," and on the third, as "Rosenberg." The paper deleted the variations on the surname in its later editions, but Nimmerrichter had made his point.

One of the most disturbing indications of the effect of the Waldheim controversy can be found in the survey conducted in January 1989 by the Vienna-based Institute for Conflict Resolution, a nonpartisan research center. In January 1989, the center posed nine questions about attitudes toward Jews in a telephone poll of 710 Austrians throughout the country.[53]

They found what researcher Christian Haerfer described as "hard-core anti-Semitism" in 10.2 percent of those polled. Twenty-seven percent showed what he termed "latent anti-Semitism," that is, those who professed to be neutral toward Jews but spoke in anti-Semitic stereotypes. Thus, Haerfer concluded, 37 percent of the Austrians could probably be mobilized in an anti-Semitic campaign if the political environment fostered it.

Comparing responses to similar questions over the years, Haerfer found that anti-Semitism and racism had increased dramatically since the Waldheim affair. In previous years, 8 percent of Austrians had admitted that they felt "revulsion" when asked to shake hands with a Jew. In 1988, following the "Year of Reflection" during which the Waldheim case was debated, only 4 percent had acknowledged such a reaction. But in 1989 more than 14 percent said they felt revulsion about physical contact with Jews.

The same surge was evident in responses to the question: "Would you like there to be no Jews in Austria?" In the 1970s, long before the Waldheim controversy erupted, 13 percent had replied yes. In 1988, 9 percent had responded in the affirmative. But in the new poll the desire to make Austria *Judenrein* rose again to 13 percent.

"What we see from this survey is that expressing these thoughts —which was unacceptable only last year—has become politically respectable again," said Haerfer.[54] "It seems clear that the Waldheim affair has had at least the temporary effect of destroying more than a decade of political education and acculturation."[55]

Moreover, he said, the levels of anti-Semitism in young Austrians, who had traditionally been the least racist, were converging with those of the oldest compatriots, historically the most anti-Semitic.

"What these figures show is that the phenomenon is not dying out," said Haerfer. "There are powerful transmissions of stereotypes from generation to generation, and this will not change unless something is done."

Erwin Ringel, a psychiatrist at Vienna University and author of a book called *The Austrian Soul,* agreed that "unfortunately, nothing has changed."[56]

"We've talked a lot. But it seems that only people who had already thought about the issues raised by Waldheim bothered to listen. The country was divided; it has remained divided. About 40 percent want him to go; about 40 percent want him to stay. Twenty percent do not know or are indifferent. The main difference before and after Waldheim is that now it is clear where people stand."

Ringel, who worked for the Catholic Church before the war and was arrested by the Gestapo for anti-Nazi activities, agreed with the polls that anti-Semitism was as firmly entrenched as ever in Austria. "It was hidden before. Now it is overt, and I suppose on balance it is better that anti-Semitism be declared than latent or suppressed. But the level and intensity have not changed very much."

The tone of Austria's public pronouncements has not evolved because the Ministry of Foreign Affairs has been controlled since 1987 by the People's party. The Minister, Alois Mock, the head of the party, has been one of Waldheim's much ardent defenders. So much of what the world has heard on behalf of the Austrian government has reflected the most insensitive, hard-line sentiments of Waldheim supporters.

In October 1987, Mock attempted to improve his country's image abroad by announcing that Austria had quietly been helping thousands of Jews to leave Iran by granting them temporary visas until they immigrated to Israel or the United States. At a luncheon for reporters at the United Nations, Mock said that since 1983, 5,100 of the Jews had come through Austria. The policy was consistent with what he characterized as Austria's deep commitment to the values of freedom and human rights. Since the end of 1945, Mock noted, more than 2 million refugees or emigrants had passed through Austria, including 272,000 Soviet Jews and 115,000 Jews from Eastern Europe, he said.

Israeli officials at the United Nations confirmed Mock's disclosure about the Iranian Jewish emigration, and they acknowledged that Austria's policy of facilitating the flow of refugees from Eastern Europe to Israel and the West had helped enable thousands of Jews to escape Communist tyranny. But they were also deeply chagrined by Mock's statements. Disclosure of the emigration flow might serve to embarrass Iran and prompt it to shut off Jewish emigration. The Israelis had not been warned that Austria was going to make the program public.[57]

In March 1988, Austria took another step to polish up its human rights credentials. More than forty years after the war's end, the Parliament voted in March 1988 to pay $4 million in reparations to victims of Nazis. But WJC officials noted that the sum was minuscule compared to the billions that West Germany had spent in compensation. A survivor, or his family, under the Austrian program, would be eligible to receive between $220 and $440 in reparations. "This paltry sum makes my face red with shame," said Freda Meissner-Blau, the head of the Austrian Greens.[58]

In each of these actions, Austria was motivated more by a sense of public relations than chagrin over its moral standing emanating from a confrontation with its past. Time and time again, unpleasant Austrian habits have resurfaced: the country's penchant for self-pity; its claim to be an innocent victim of world affairs it no longer controls; its continuing desire to blame others for its own failures; its crass opportunism wrapped in noble sentiments and self-exonerating explanations; its deeply entrenched xenophobia and anti-Semitism.

"Austria has learned to live with certain facts," said Paul Grosz, President of the Austrian Jewish community. "Some intellectuals have been trying to keep the debate about Waldheim alive, but most of the country is resigned to the fact that he is going to be here. So they have stopped talking about it altogether.

"Some even expressed a sense of relief that 1988, the 'Year of Reflection,' was over. Much about the past was unpleasant to hear, so many preferred not to listen.

"In order to make people accept certain facts," said Grosz, who was one of six hundred Jews who managed to survive the war by hiding in Vienna, "you have to make them sensitive to emotions. You have to make them feel it. Otherwise, they will not digest the information. We have not been able to make them do that. There has simply been no fundamental change yet."

If anything, he added, Jews had an obligation to err on the side of pessimism about change in Austria. "On February 26, 1938, less than three weeks before Hitler marched into Austria, the head of the Jewish community told his fellow Jews in a nationwide broadcast: 'There is no reason for panic.' That broadcast probably cost ten thousand Austrian Jews their lives."

Austrian Jews were probably the only group to have benefited from the Waldheim affair, he maintained. "It was painful and very alarming for many young Austrian Jews," said Grosz. "But it caused them to be more aware of the facts, more attuned to possible danger. And it has led many of them to wonder, some for the first time, if they would spend their lives in Austria."

His own children were not likely to remain, said Grosz, who spent a decade in Buffalo, New York, after the war, but returned to the city he loved and had missed intensely. His daughter would probably marry an Italian and move there. His son, who kept kosher, wanted to live in Israel.

Grosz was depressed about surveys which showed that anti-Semitism in Austria had remained constant, despite the furor over Waldheim. But one element in particular puzzled him, he said. Polls always showed that younger, better educated Austrians tended to be less anti-Semitic than older, less educated citizens. That was not surprising, he noted. But this trend had been recorded for decades. Hence, if the figures were accurate, the more tolerant, less anti-Semitic twenty-year-olds eventually became the less tolerant more anti-Semitic fifty-year-olds.

"It seems that the longer they live in this environment, the more anti-Semitic they become, even now that there are few Jews left," said Grosz. "Anti-Semitism must slowly seep into them through a kind of social osmosis. It is pervasive here. And I am forced to wonder: will all of this ever change?"

The Netherlands

Florentine van Tonningen lives about an hour from Amsterdam in a small town called Velp on a quiet street whose name in Dutch means "the one who dwells alone."

The description is apt.

None of her three sons or nine grandchildren comes to visit the "black widow," as she is called.

During Germany's occupation of the Netherlands from May 14, 1940, to May 5, 1945, she was married to Meinoudt Rost van Tonningen, the deputy chief of the Dutch Nazi party, the head of the Bank of Holland, and by all accounts one of the country's most ardent and outspoken proponents of National Socialism. He died in prison after the war shortly before his trial for treason was to start. His death was called a suicide, but Mrs. van Tonningen, several Dutch historians, and other students of the war say that he was murdered by fellow prisoners.

Her status as the widow of one of the most notorious Dutch Nazis would automatically make her an isolated figure in Dutch society. But she has made herself even more a pariah by continuing to defend her husband and his political credo.

In the fall of 1986, a court in Arnhem gave the then seventy-two-year-old widow a four-week jail sentence, suspended, the judge said, only because of her age.[1] She had been convicted of violating Dutch bans on distributing literature aimed at inciting religious and ethnic hatred. Yet, despite repeated warnings from Dutch officials, she has continued to travel and speak out.

Her activities have deeply embarrassed many in the Netherlands partly because Dutch taxpayers are indirectly financing her neo-fascist campaign. As the wife of a former member of Parliament, Mrs. Rost van Tonningen has received a monthly pension since the early 1950s that now totals about $11,000 a year.

Many politicians, veterans groups, leftists, and liberals have called upon the Dutch government to take away her pension, which they claim she uses to help finance neo-Nazi activities in the Netherlands and elsewhere in Europe. Members of Parliament have even introduced legislation that would remove her from the pension list. Yet the Dutch Cabinet—a coalition of Christian Democrats and Liberals—decided in 1986 not to eliminate her stipend, and the Parliament has not been able to muster sufficient support to overrule it.

Some opponents of the measure have argued that it would only call more attention to her. But the majority of those who oppose a cutoff, expressing the pragmatism for which the country is celebrated, maintain that meddling with the Dutch pension system to end her stipend might open it up to far more radical cutbacks and changes, all to eliminate payments to one silly old woman with virtually no base of political support.

Those who favor severance cite another reason for the impasse: they say softly that there are those who fear such an action might trigger an inquiry into other pensioners with National Socialist backgrounds. And there are some who worry that a protracted debate over Mrs. van Tonningen would undoubtedly conjure up uncomfortable memories of the country's lack of resistance during the occupation. No one likes to be reminded that he was no hero. And in this country, that includes the overwhelming majority of the country, who did not collaborate with the Nazis, but simply obeyed orders and went along.

Seated primly in a wing-back chair in the living room of her suburban house, a German shepherd sleeping fitfully at her feet, Mrs. van Tonningen seemed bemused by the government's predicament and well aware of the psychological threat she posed. "This is a very small country; we all know one another," she said demurely. "During the war we were all pro-German. My husband was murdered in prison because he knew ninety-nine of the hundred people in the Netherlands who had worked most closely with the Germans. I know those people too. Some are still around, a few in very high places. The Dutch like to think of themselves as healthy people in a democratic society. But deep down, they are not."[2]

The discomfiture over the black widow's pension rights is but one indication of the persistent sensitivity about the war years in the Netherlands, and, in particular, about the country's role in the Holocaust. In 1988, the Dutch government voted, following an impassioned twenty-four-hour debate in Parliament, to release two German war criminals from the prison in Breda where they had been held since the war. Supporters of their release argued that the men were old, that they had paid a sufficient price for their crimes, and that they should be permitted to die at home in Germany. The government's decision in that case effectively ended a protracted debate and laid a painful war-related issue to rest. But a resolution of the dispute is not possible in the case of Mrs. Van Tonningen.

Because of the government's paralysis, the impasse over her pension seems likely to be resolved only by her death. Her ultimate weapon is a bevy of accusations against individuals, which, true or not, would stir up inconvenient memories of a time many of the Dutch have put behind them.

The Netherlands, in fact, has gone to great lengths, sometimes consciously, often not, to create and preserve a positive wartime image. By and large, it has succeeded remarkably, mainly through the astute use of national symbols.

If Waldheim has come to symbolize Austria, Holland's self-ascribed national symbol is not Mrs. Rost van Tonningen, known to few outside of this country. It is Anne Frank, Holland's unofficial patron saint.

Thanks to the country's careful cultivation of the memory of Anne Frank and to the world-wide dissemination of the poignant journal of the little girl who was hidden by a Dutch family for two years before being discovered and sent to her death at Bergen-Belsen, Holland has achieved in the West a near universal reputation for moral steadfastness, political courage, and resistance that can only be envied by Austrians and others.

The Anne Frank Museum, located in downtown Amsterdam in the building in which her family hid, is one of Holland's most popular tourist sites, outranked only by the Rijksmuseum and the Van Gogh Museum, according to Dutch tourism officials. Dutch schoolchildren throughout the country are taken to visit the house. In 1988, some 564,000 people paid a modest entry fee to peer into the attic in which Anne's family struggled to stay alive.[3] The Anne Frank Foundation, which operates the museum and sponsors research and activities aimed at fighting racism and preserving the memory of the Holocaust, is tax exempt. It has an office in New York, a staff of seventy part-time employees, and an annual budget of 5 to 6 million guilders, about $2.5 to $3 million. Dutch journalists say that the foundation, created in 1957, receives funding both from the federal government and the Amsterdam city council, and operates without independent scrutiny, a luxury in a country in which financial transactions of all sorts are closely monitored.

"The independence of the foundation reflects the reverence that so many in this country feel for Anne Frank," said Abner Katzman, who has headed the Associated Press bureau in Amsterdam since 1982. "She has been canonized by the Dutch."[4]

This sanctification, of course, is convenient and self-serving. "It enables the Dutch to alleviate their guilt and blame the Nazis for having decimated their Jewish population," said Katzman. "The Anne Frank lore says to the world: Look, we Dutch hid her; the terrible Germans killed her. They were evil and we were virtuous."

The reality, of course, is more complicated. Most Dutch citizens volunteer that Yad Vashem in Israel has honored more of their countrymen than any other European nationality for saving Jews from the Germans, and that resistance to the Nazis in this small, cramped country was earlier and more fervent than anywhere else on the continent. It was, in fact, the Germans' seizure of four hundred Jews in February 1941 that helped trigger the celebrated general strike throughout Holland later that month, for which the Dutch were severely punished. Yet Holland's record during the war is in many other respects appalling. And in no Western European nation has there been as large and enduring a gap between popular image and historical reality.

These are the facts. Before the war, the NSB, the National Socialist party in Holland, had more than 100,000 members in a population that then totaled about 8 million, the largest indigenous

National Socialist party in Europe, save perhaps Austria's.[5] More than 30,000 Dutch volunteered after the Germans invaded to serve with the Nazis and their Waffen S.S., again one of the highest percentages in Europe. The Germans ruled Holland through a brutally efficient civilian occupation of barely one thousand men and women, administration that would have been impossible without the active cooperation of thousands of Dutch civil servants from the country's well-disciplined bureaucracy. Westerbork and the other Dutch concentration camps were run mainly by the Dutch S.S., not by Germans. And the brutality of the indigenous Dutch S.S. was such that at Amersfoort Camp, for example, the German-sponsored Dutch Jewish Council once officially protested to the Germans the ill-treatment of Jews by Dutch Gestapo.[6]

But the important figure to note is the Jewish death toll: of the 140,000 Jews in Holland at the outbreak of the war, 35,000 survived, only 25 percent. The Dutch Jewish death rate was the highest in Western Europe. In the East, only Poland had a higher kill ratio.[7]

Because the Dutch and Germans kept meticulous records, we know that approximately 110,000 Jews were deported from the Netherlands, and that a total of 5,450 people (2,361 men and 3,089 women) returned, less than 5 percent.[8] Some 1,150 of the 60,000 sent to Auschwitz survived; fewer than 20 of the 34,313 sent to Sobibor; 2,000 of the 5,000 sent to Theresienstadt; about half of the 4,000 deported to Bergen-Belsen; and of the 1,750 Jews deported to Mauthausen, there is one recorded survivor.[9]

Jacob Presser, the late Dutch historian and a Jew, noted in his exhaustively researched book on the extermination of Holland's Jewish community that even these staggering figures do not fully reflect the enormity of the loss. Within the country itself, almost all Jews over fifty years of age and under sixteen were destroyed. So Jews who returned to the Netherlands from the camps often had no alternative after the war but to marry non-Jews and assimilate, "not only because so many Jewish had been butchered, but also because quite a few of those who had survived preferred to emigrate."[10]

A. Harry Paape, of the government-sponsored Netherlands State Institute for War Documentation, estimates that in 1987 there were only 10,000 to 20,000 Jews in a country of 14 million.[11] Awraham Soetendorp, the chief liberal rabbi of the Netherlands, put the estimate as high as 30,000 Jews, but added that fewer than half were members of a congregation and identified themselves as Jewish.[12]

Many analysts share Presser's view that, because of the wartime devastation, those Jews who lived in Holland after the war did not constitute a community as such. "Can we really call it that?" Presser wrote in the late 1960s. "The writer himself prefers to speak of a group. A group pieced together after the Liberation, from a host of fragments; a few thousand men and women married to gentiles and spared for that reason, a few thousand who emerged from hiding, the survivors of Westerbork, the very small number who returned from Theresienstadt and the other camps. Among them is to be found every conceivable kind of misfortune: parents without children, children without parents . . . and all too many who are left with no one in the world. . . . The working class, so strong before 1940, has been almost completely exterminated. A large number of family names has completely disappeared; the Jewish communities in the provincial towns have been broken up; only a handful of Jews have returned to retail trading; many artists and intellectuals have been massacred. . . . All we can try to do here is to convey a vague idea of the enormity that struck down Dutch Jewry."[13]

The Dutch are fond of pointing out that 25,000 Jews were hidden by 20,000 Dutch gentiles in the resistance during the war.[14] "It's not too bad a record really, if you consider the difficulty of shielding people from the Germans and from informers in cramped quarters in such a small country," Dr. Paape asserted.

But about one-third of those who hid—more than 8,000—were captured and sent off to camps. And the Germans and Dutch special police often found those in hiding, including young Anne Frank and her family, through the assistance of Dutch informers. Professor Louis de Jong, Holland's official historian, estimates that about 16,000 Jews of the 25,000 Jews in hiding managed to survive the war.

The record, widely known within the Netherlands but less so in other parts of Europe, has weighed heavily on the Dutch. "To understand Dutch attitudes toward the war years, you must know that these people are overwhelmed by guilt, intense Calvinist guilt," said Katzman, of the Associated Press. "They've beaten the issue to the ground so many times that they almost always overreact in order to prove that they are decent folk, to polish up their anti-fascist credentials."

So the pension issue, said Katzman, had touched the core of this guilt and their sensibilities, triggering charges and counter-charges about the meaning of the government's inaction. "She's served as a rallying point for what is left of the anti-Semitic right wing in this country, which isn't much."

But the government's unwillingness to sever her pension had also prompted charges that some members of Parliament were acquiescing to her views, he added. "No one in the Netherlands wants to start pointing fingers at who was and who wasn't a collaborator," Katzman said.

The intensely conflicted feelings about the war years, the country's collective sense of shame over the destruction of its Jews, and its long and mixed history have ensured that memories of the war have endured in the Netherlands in ways not immediately discernible to outsiders.

"In no other country in Europe, except Germany, is the war as alive as it is here," de Jong declared. One indicator of the power of wartime memories is the number of World War II monuments and memorials. There are more than eight hundred of them in a country the size of New Jersey.

While the war was traumatic for all countries occupied by the Germans, it was especially so in Holland, which had not known war on its soil since Napoleon.

"While war ravaged the rest of Europe, Holland for the most part escaped it on our soil from 1814 to 1945," said Paape. "Even during World War I, Holland was neutral."

Neutrality kept the Germans from invading Holland in 1914. It was one of the few European states to be so blessed. Neighboring Belgium was not as fortunate. Belgium resisted heroically, and its army defended the southwestern corner of Flanders until the war's end. But as a result, "the Belgians suffered famine, poverty, and the ruin of their economy," wrote Luigi Barzini.[15] The Germans "killed and deported thousands of civilians, set fire to the priceless library of Louvain, incited the rebellion of the Flemings against the French-speaking Walloons in order to break up the people's solidarity, exploited mines and industries, and starved the population."

The Dutch, by contrast, were not only spared, they flourished. But their prosperity, Barzini noted, was enjoyed "in humiliating vassalage" to the Germans, and "they hated themselves for it."

Self-contempt, however, did not persuade them to abandon their centuries-old attachment to the avoidance of war through treaties and neutralism. As Hitler acquired power in Germany and became increasingly belligerent, the Dutch were convinced that neutrality would once again save them.

"Somehow, we believed that as long as you behaved like a neutral nation, others would respect that neutrality," recalled Paape. "The sudden German attack on our soil without even a proper declaration of war was a true shock for the Dutch."

On May 10, 1940, the Germans invaded. On May 13, Queen Wilhelmina and the Dutch government arrived in England. One day later Holland fell under German occupation, or as Presser notes the Germans preferred to call it, "administrative control."[16]

The shock of the invasion resulted in paralysis. "For the first year of occupation, people simply did not know how to behave or what to do," said Paape. "There was still a strong conviction that the Germans would win the war, so that the only sane course was to get along with them under occupation as well as possible."

There were other reasons for the widespread passivity. Holland's location left it physically isolated—surrounded by occupied countries and the Atlantic Ocean, "To escape, you had two frontiers to cross: Belgium and France," said Paape. In addition, Holland, unlike Belgium, where the German military ruled, was administered with Dutch help by the German civil service, which was filled with ardent Nazi party members and placed a higher priority than the military on the extermination of the Jews.

Resistance grew slowly, as did the campaign against the Jews of Holland. German records indicate that the Nazis implemented their anti-Jewish measures cautiously, unsure of how the Dutch would react. Jewish history in Holland provided ample reason for German concern. Holland's Jewish community traced its roots to the sixteenth century, when vast numbers fled Spain, Portugal, and Belgium during the Inquisition. The pragmatism of Dutch mercantile society provided a home and hospitality to the largely skilled, but poor Spanish Jews. A century later, another substantial immigration occurred, this time from Poland, Russia, and Germany.

Dutch Jews rapidly became, if not assimilated, a fixture in Dutch life. There was no history of pogroms in the Netherlands. "My family had come here three hundred years ago from Spain," said Eva Furth, a spokesman for the Auschwitz Committee, which represents Jewish survivors of that camp in Holland.[17] "We felt Dutch; we spoke Dutch; none of us even knew Yiddish. And like most of our friends, my family was very secular, not at all religious. We were diamond cutters. And we had lived more or less without problems here, quietly and freely.

"Some Jews were actually prominent in Amsterdam," she said. "But most were not rich, unlike German Jews. We Dutch Jews were mostly proletariat, working class. Trade unions were very important for us, and my family, like so many, were Social Democrats."

For centuries, more than half of the Dutch Jewish community had lived in Amsterdam. At the outbreak of the war, Jews constituted about 10 percent of Amsterdam's population, and their cultural influence was deeply felt and for the most part, if not actively appreciated, accepted.

"When I think back," said Mrs. Furth, "I really cannot recall much anti-Semitism. We lived separately, but together as Dutch citizens."

"Jews as a group were not very important, or even very interesting here," said Louis M. Tas, a Dutch Jew who survived Bergen-Belsen. "We lived fairly ordinary lives, with substantial intermarriage compared to other countries. There was a tolerance toward us that bordered on indifference."[18]

Given this history, the Nazis were eager not to incur the displeasure of the Dutch by ordering the immediate isolation of Jews from public life. "The Jewish question must be treated with great care," a German official wrote in July 1940.[19] "The main task remains. . . . Am expecting orders soon. . . . Then we shall pounce on them."

The Germans waited some months. Presser reports that less than a month after German occupation the Burgomaster of Amsterdam, Dr. W. de Vlugt, summoned a number of Jewish dignitaries to the Town Hall to inform them of the assurances he had received from the German military commander that Dutch Jews would not be molested.

The first direct action against Jews came in July 1940 with their expulsion from the Dutch voluntary fire-fighting brigades. Many non-Jews resigned in protest. On July 20, 1940, Simon de la Bella, vice president of the Dutch Federation of Trade Unions, was arrested just after he managed to transfer five million guilders of union funds to England. The Germans said that he had been arrested for his resistance and trade-union activities, not because he was a Jew. And Dutch Jews and gentiles alike wanted to believe that.

The succeeding months brought further isolation and repression —the exclusion of Jews from the country's civil service, from university teaching posts, and finally, the beginning of the end, the ordering of a special registration of all people with Jewish blood.

Presser and other historians repeatedly note that each anti-Jewish measure prompted opposition, resignations, and other forms of protest from Dutch gentiles. When Jewish teachers were barred from Dutch universities, for example, the Germans were forced to close the universities of Delft and Leyden because of student and teacher demonstrations.

"There is no doubt that the anti-Jewish measures contributed to the growth of the Dutch resistance movement by fueling anti-German sentiment," said Cyp de Grout, who helped organize and run a resistance group in Amsterdam. "There was a saying in the Netherlands during the war: 'Take your dirty hands off of our dirty Jews,' " he recalled. "In Dutch, the word for 'dirty' Jews was a term of endearment; for the Germans, the Dutch word was an insult."[20]

But despite the resistance of many gentiles, the measures were implemented with increasing rigidity and determination.

Many historians regard the October 1940 German announcement of a special registration of all Jewish-owned or Jewish-operated businesses and individuals with Jewish blood as the turning point in the Nazis' war against the Dutch Jews. The event also revealed what has proven to be a recurring characteristic of Dutch national character—the preference for a disciplined, well-ordered society.

Article 4 of the German decree, now infamous in the Netherlands, called for the registration of full Jews as "J," half, or "bastard Jews" as "B," a bastard Jew with two Jewish grandparents as "B I" and bastard Jews with one Jewish grandparent as "B II."

Dutch burgomasters were instructed to check the information supplied against identity cards or police registers, wrote Presser. The registration forms, he noted, were in quintuplicate—in white, blue, violet, dark and light green with carbon papers interleaved.[21]

Records of the Census Bureau indicate that by the deadline a total of 160,820 people had registered: 140,552 Jews, 14,549 half Jews (BI), and 5,719 quarter Jews (B II).[22]

"The registration meant that Jews were identifying themselves and, in effect, signing their own death warrants. But not more than 20 Jews in the entire country refused to do so," said de Jong.

Not only did they register, they did it with the thoroughness and efficiency in which their Germanic society had long taken pride. Jews throughout the country praised the Dutch Census Office for keeping registration offices open night and day so that everyone could comply with the decree. A delay did occur in the town of Apeldoorn due to the "difficulty in registering the inmates of the local Jewish Insane Asylum," according to a report in the Government Gazette.[23] But, the article was quick to add, "there was no reason to think that the Dutch were in any way sabotaging the measure."

Presser asserts that the registration was aided enormously by the Dutch-run Census Bureau. He quotes a Census Bureau document, dated January 15, 1941, expressing satisfaction with the process, adding that, thanks to the German measure, there had been "an untold administrative simplification and a saving of tens of thousands [of guilders] for the country."

Why did the Dutch Jews register so faithfully and assist in their own extermination? A. J. Hertzberg, in *Chronicle of the Persecution of the Jews,* maintains that ethnic pride and an element of defiance through compliance were partly responsible. Many Jews who had never been members of a Jewish congregation decided to label themselves Jews as a matter of principle and solidarity with their identifiably Jewish peers.[24]

But survivors cited other reasons. "It never occurred to us not to register," said Mrs. Furth. "If you didn't and were caught, you were subject to five years imprisonment, the confiscation of your property, and a stiff fine."

In 1940 and 1941, few could imagine the fate that awaited European Jewry. What was known at the time was that Jews who did not comply would most likely be punished. Fear of fine, punishment, and possibly even deportation were sufficient to induce compliance.

Louis Tas, however, offered another explanation. "We did it because we were Dutch," said Tas. "Our lives had always been full of index cards and registers. We were accustomed to living in a well-regulated society in which regulation had never threatened us."

The same tragic belief in the virtue of a law-abiding, well-disciplined society permeated the ranks of the German-initiated Dutch Jewish Council—prominent rabbis, merchants, and leaders of the Jewish community, whose cooperation with the Nazis remains a source of shame and bitter controversy in Holland. The Germans had ordered the formation of the council to preserve order in the Amsterdam Jewish quarter, which the Germans had sealed off, transforming it into a ghetto. Among the council's first acts was a meeting with some five thousand residents of the Jewish quarter in the Diamond Exchange in February 1941. A. Ascher, the council's president and before that the head of the Council of the Great Dutch Synagogue, announced the council's mandate, and ordered those present to hand over to the Dutch police all firearms, clubs, knives, and other weapons by noon the next day. "There were no incidents," a German officer wrote in his report of the gathering.[25]

Members of the Dutch Jewish Council assisted in the waves of deportations of Dutch Jews, each time hoping that if they cooperated, additional roundups could be avoided. About 650 members of their own families and prominent friends were protected for most of the war at a castle in Barneveld. Near the war's end, these privileged Jews were deported to concentration camps, most of them to Theresienstadt; the vast majority survived. In May 1943, the two presidents of the council gave the Germans as they had demanded another list of seven thousand Jews who could be deported—without the names of themselves or their families.[26]

After the war ended, a special "Jewish Court of Honor" appointed by the Jewish Co-ordination Committee in the Netherlands issued a report on the role of the Jewish Council during the war. The court concluded in December 1947 that it was "dishonorable" to have formed an Amsterdam Jewish Council on German orders; that it was "dishonorable" to have continued publishing a Jewish paper when it became clear that this would only serve German rather than Jewish interests, that it was "dishonorable" to have lent support to anti-Jewish measures, such as the issuance of Jewish stars and the herding of Jews into Westerbork camp; and that the council's leadership had acted "dishonorably" by cooperating in the selection of deportees."[27]

A decade later, the judgment was even harsher. Professor P. S. Gerbrandy, a Jew and former Dutch Prime Minister and Minister of Justice, in a sworn declaration to a Parliamentary Commission of Inquiry, concluded: "The Jewish Council let itself be used for the liquidation of Dutch Jewry. They collaborated with the Germans by compiling registers [of deportees] and in many other ways, all of which facilitated the final murder of the Jews."[28]

Given the fate of the Dutch Jews, it is understandable that those Jews old enough to remember the war have remained traumatized by it. But that trauma in Holland has not been confined to Jews. The war years have left deep scars even on those who are regarded today as heroes—non-Jewish members of the Dutch resistance. A case in point is the Dekking family.

A. F. Dekking, "Flopp" as he is known to family and friends, was a medical student in Amsterdam when the Nazis invaded. He was neither a Jew nor political, he said, but he joined the resistance after watching a German officer beat up a Jewish student. Dekking was caught months later forging identification cards and deported to a series of concentration camps, including Dachau. But since he was trained as a doctor, his skills were needed. "So I had a relatively easy time," he acknowledged.[29]

Maryanne van Raamstonk, an artist whom he met at Vught concentration camp in Holland and married after the war, fared less well. She, too, had been arrested for her work in the resistance. "I carried messages in the hem of my red skirt," she recalled. At Vught camp, she worked for Philips, then under German direction, making radio components, a war-related occupation that probably saved her life. When her work camp closed down, she and 1,900 other women prisoners were sent to Ravensbrück. "I am one of the 150 who came back," she said.

As shy as her husband is gregarious, she had, at the urging of her daughter, tape-recorded her memories of her camp experience. But in 1987 she still could not bring herself to tell a stranger what she had seen and felt there.

When their three children were born, Flopp discouraged her from discussing their wartime experiences. But sometimes, said her daughter, Yara, a psychologist, memories or "associations" just seemed to slip out.

"My father talked only in anecdotes," said Yara, who was born in 1947 and has no memory of the war. "It happened only a few times when I was growing up, and the stories were almost always humorous."

For her mother, the associations were obviously painful, "so we never asked her. No one told us not to. We just instinctively knew that something terrible had happened and that we shouldn't ask."

One warm summer night when Yara was quite young, her father was barbecuing chicken in their backyard. Her mother emerged from the kitchen and stared silently for some time at the grill. "Then, all of a sudden, my mother said to no one in particular that the smell reminded her of something . . . ah, the crematorium. It was the same smell as bodies in the crematorium," Yara recounted. "She uttered those words without emotion. For her it was a simple statement of fact. And that made it all the harder for me to bear."

On another occasion when she was about eight, Yara was picking fleas out of her cat's fur and crushing them between her nails. "My mother saw me and said that she had once done more or less the same thing. She, too, had picked lice off her clothing and hair every night in the camp. If a prisoner stopped doing that, it was a sign that he would soon die, that he had become a *Musselman,* someone who had given up all hope of living."

Yara said that she never discussed these incidents in school. "For a long time I thought that this kind of past was normal, since both my parents had experienced it. Only much later, when my father gave me a book to read about the Holocaust, did I understand that most of my friends and colleagues had no idea what people like my parents and the Jews must have gone through."

Only once did she remember hearing about the camps in school. In gym class, one day, a student was raising a set of iron rings when her gym teacher asked her to stop. The chains, the teacher said, made a noise that reminded her of the squeaking of chains in prison. "Her tone was just like my mother's. Maybe that was why I recognized it."

No one ever taught her in school about the camps and the Jews and the Holocaust. "They taught us about the war. And once in May my class visited a war memorial. But I never made the link between the war and the Holocaust. The story of the war is one thing in Holland. You learn about the war. But the camps are another. You don't learn about that."

But not a day passes, she said, that she does not think about it. "When no one around you talks about it, not even in your own family, you begin to fantasize, which is often worse than having experienced something. I suppose it is one reason that I was attracted to psychology. I needed in a very immediate, personal way to understand man's descent into this kind of inhumanity—to understand the incomprehensible. What happened here in this well-ordered society is probably partly responsible for my decision not to have children," she said. "Until I understand it, how can I bring children into a seemingly civilized world in which such things can happen?"

When Flopp Dekking retired as a professor of virology from the university in 1980, he gave a speech that was supposed to focus on science and his work. Instead, without warning, he launched into a monologue about his deportation and life in the camps.

"I remember sitting in the audience with my mother and brothers, totally unprepared," said Yara. "Suddenly, there was my father, telling every Tom, Dick, and Harry about things, truly awful and personal things, that he had never been able to tell us. First I was astonished. Then I became angry. And I became even more furious when I looked at my poor mother, sitting there, unable at that time even to think about what had happened to her and her friends."

Dekking said that, in retrospect, he should have told his family of his plans, that he was sorry he had shocked them. But the university speech was cathartic for him. Soon after retiring, he turned his speech into a book called *The Memoirs of Ivo Pannekoek,* which sold well in Holland.

Meanwhile, Yara went on encouraging her mother to apply for the resistance pension to which she was entitled and to secure for her the Distinguished Cross that her father had received from the Queen for his wartime activities.

"I lobbied and lobbied and made quite a pest out of myself," Yara recalled. "It was the first time I realized that even discussing this period with officials made them deeply uncomfortable. Very nervous. I didn't understand why at the time. But I kept on pressing. And finally I succeeded. She applied for and received the pension, and eventually, they sent her a cross.

De Jong confirmed that many Jews and non-Jewish resistance fighters alike were loath at first to apply for benefits to which they were entitled. Initially, the Dutch government offered little assistance to war victims. In the early 1950s, it offered aid only to war widows and orphans. In the late '50s and early '60s, the payments were expanded to include individuals who were unable to work or who needed medical assistance or psychological counseling because of war-related activities and illnesses. In the first year that such expanded pensions were offered, only a handful applied and only seven were granted. In 1966, 234 people applied; in 1969, 410 requests were received; in 1977, there were 1,321. By 1985, he said, pensions were given to 6,000 Jews and former resistance members and to 4,000 of their widows.

"Immediately after the war people wanted to put their experiences behind them and get on with their lives," said de Jong, who spent the war with the government-in-exile in London. "Only thirty years after the war did people really begin to crack up."

Moreover, as time passed, people were no longer ashamed to present themselves to the society at large as victims. "Many were simply too embarrassed to do so early on."

As in other European countries, interest in the war in Holland grew very slowly after a period of sustained repression of memory. There was for so many so much to forget. Soon after the war, the Dutch government launched a series of trials of Dutch collaborators that lasted till the early 1950s; their children were often stigmatized. "There is no doubt that many former Nazis and their families were treated harshly," de Jong observed.

"For the first two decades after the war, all people, especially non-Jews, wanted to forget what had happened," said Harry Paape. "We were busy rebuilding the country and ourselves. No one wanted to think back on those horrible memories, or to confront the questions raised by our behavior as a society during and immediately after the war."

It was during this period, for example, that Otto Frank searched in vain for a publisher for his daughter's diary. Four of the leading Dutch publishing houses rejected the manuscript, along with ten American publishing houses. Few publishers saw commercial possibilities in the memoir of a period so many wanted to forget. A small Dutch house finally agreed to print a tiny number of copies of the book, news of which spread largely by word-of-mouth.

Eva Furth recalls the years immediately after the war with almost as much bitterness as her experiences at Auschwitz. "I remember the day I returned home," she said. "I had lost my whole family, everyone except one cousin. I had come back to nothing. To nobody. To no aunts and uncles and grandparents. I no longer had a home. And what did I get from the Dutch when I arrived at the railroad station in Amsterdam? They gave me ten guilders and a pat on the back. That was it," she said.

Maryanne Dekking also remembered the loneliness. "People were so suspicious of those of us who had resisted. After all, the word, in Dutch, could be translated as 'illegality.' There was a slightly perjorative cast to it. Our survival seemed to make those who hadn't resisted all the more uncomfortable. All I wanted was to get a job and feel like a normal person again. But for more than a year nobody would hire me."

Presser reported in his book that many Dutch gentiles tried after the war to minimize the important role that Jews had played in the resistance. So many ordinary Dutch citizens, in fact, were hostile to the returning Jews that there were calls in the summer of 1945 for a special study group to assess the prevalence of anti-Semitism in the Netherlands. A study group was formed, he notes, but for reasons that are still unclear it disbanded before it could publish its results. "Possibly they reached the conclusion that this question was best left alone," Presser observed.[30]

Paape cited the early 1960s as a turning point in the country's collective amnesia. "A survey of high school students by a group of historians indicated that they knew next to nothing about World War II or the Holocaust," said Paape. "So Dutch television put together a series of programs on the war years which were narrated by Louis de Jong. They shocked many in the country."

Since then, he said, interest in World War II and the Holocaust has steadily increased. At his Institute for War Documentation, for example, curiosity is reflected in the number of requests received each year for material on these subjects. In 1960, the institute received less than 1,000 inquires, "virtually none at all," said Paape. In 1981, 6,022 people asked for information; by 1985, the figure had risen to 9,625.

A similar trend has occurred in scholarship at Dutch universities. Whereas in 1965 Presser's book on the destruction of Holland's Jews was one of a handful of books available in Dutch on the Final Solution, twenty-five doctoral theses on this subject were completed in 1985 as well as eighty research papers, the level just below a thesis. That same year, more than three hundred books about World War II or the Holocaust were published in Dutch.[31]

Between 1979 and 1985, World War II history received high priority in Dutch schools, with mandatory examinations at the academic year's end.

"I believe that we are now approaching the peak of interest in this period," said Paape. "I doubt, given the age of our population, that it will be sustained," said Paape.

That so many Dutch people are now interested in the war years is of little comfort to Yara Dekking, some of whose patients include other children of resistance and Holocaust survivors. "Yes, people are interested now," she said. "They scream about the black widow's pension. But the screaming and demands often are a way of coping with shame. The uproar, I think, is a way of masking our inability to examine and analyze these shameful events in our past. Even Jews who yell 'never again' are engaging in a form of self-defense. They are not really confronting the fact that it did happen, and that it happened here, and that it could happen again. Perhaps not in the same way or perhaps not to them, but to others.

"I feel lonely because I am haunted by experiences that I cannot recall," she continued. "But many of those old enough to remember in this country do not seem to want to recall, even now. They take refuge in campaigns and demands and uproar."

On the surface, said Yara Dekking, "my country is neat and orderly. We are good hosts, enormously civilized, and tolerant. And we think of ourselves in that way. But I believe that it is misleading to have too high an opinion of ourselves, dangerous not to look at what lies below the surface.

"I look at my countrymen and sometimes I am afraid," she said. "My fear is: they would do it again."

The Dutch have, at least on the surface, gone to extraordinary lengths to prove that they would not do it again. Their intense commitment to airing different points of political view has resulted in no fewer than twenty-six political parties. The country's anti-racist credentials are impeccable: it is illegal in the Netherlands to bar someone from an apartment, a job, or even a club on the basis of race or religion. Even when immigrant Moluccans burned down their own stores and poor housing in the early 1970s to protest conditions in Holland, the government did not punish them severely.

In foreign policy, the country opposed doing business with racist South Africa, whose whites are of Dutch origin, long before other nations jumped on the anti-apartheid bandwagon. More than a million Dutch citizens signed petitions in 1982 calling for free emigration of Soviet Jews. The country's relations with Israel have remained strong and close, despite a growing chorus of citizens' protests over Israel's fierce suppression of the Palestinian uprising on the occupied West Bank and Gaza Strip.

Dutch diplomats since the war have been disproportionately represented in most international peacekeeping groups and conflict-resolving missions.

"We have become moral to a fault. We have continued to be the most insufferably moral people on the face of the earth," said Mark Blaisse, a journalist who used to teach history. "And as a result, we have remained the most insufferably smug Europeans."

Therein lies the problem, some analysts like Blaisse believe. Many of the Dutch seem to have drawn some curious lessons from their experience in the Holocaust. Taking pride in one's culture as essentially disciplined and law-abiding and, above all, peace-loving and morally right, the Dutch have not engaged in the collective soul searching that would prompt greater true tolerance and independence of spirit. "Instead, we prefer to blame the Germans," said Blaisse. "We say to ourselves that it was all their fault; even young people who have no memory of the war do so. It amazes me how much the young dislike their German counterparts, who had nothing to do with the war and the Holocaust.

"Most Dutch like to buy the Anne Frank lore about ourselves. We were basically O.K. during the war. But *even* those who concluded that we were bad then seem to be intent on proving that, as a nation, we will never again be bad," said Blaisse.

By and large, the Dutch have not concluded that more anarchy in their neatly clipped, well-manicured society would be good for the country's soul.

"The young squatters who took over abandoned buildings in the '70s were reviled for being disorderly," Blaisse noted. "They were violating Dutch rules regarding property. No one talked much about their motives, only their tactics."

Similarly, Holland has not concluded that neutralism is no way to stop evil men from implementing evil designs, despite its wartime experiences. "Yes," he said. "We're members of NATO. And yes, we agreed to deploy nuclear missiles on our soil. But nowhere else in Europe are neutralism, pacifism, and anti-nuclear movements as strong as here."

Yara Dekking agreed. "We think of ourselves now as new people who have examined the past, faced bitter memories and experiences, and learned from them," she said. "But my mother once told me that I would never know the smell of an oven, or understand the tyranny that she endured. I might imagine it, but I would never be able to know it as she does.

"When I see the way we react to things in this country today, I fear she is right. Most don't want to try to remember or even imagine. So I wonder whether we would not react just as we did before."

France

History is mythology recreated by each generation.
—Voltaire

The conversation over dinner at the Élysée Palace had been typically Parisian—an hors d'oeuvre of political gossip followed by animated discussion of the city's new plays, films, music, mini-crises in foreign policy, the French domestic scene, and the latest *affaire,* or scandal, which had gripped the capital for at least a week.

During the salad course, one of the guests mentioned the impending trial of Klaus Barbie. The infamous "Butcher of Lyons," chief of the Gestapo in occupied Lyons from 1942 to 1944, had been languishing in a French jail for four years while French courts sorted out whether he could stand trial and for which crimes he could be charged. At the mention of his name, the clinking of wine glasses and silverware, the laughter, the chatter all stopped; it seemed as if the guests had forgotten to breathe.

"It's going to be quite a spectacle, isn't it? It'll be a grand show for entertaining the masses. More than five hundred journalists from one hundred countries descending on Lyons, booking up all the best three-star restaurants at night after consuming atrocities in court during the day," said Pierre Lefèvre, one of France's most prominent television journalists. "I don't like trials of the street; I do not approve of the justice of the sidewalks."

Another pause.

"But you made a remarkable contribution to the show," replied Blandine Kriegel, a striking blond woman seated across from him. "You gave Vergès quite a forum for spreading his filthy lies, his rationalizations for his client's crimes. Why did you interview Klaus Barbie's attorney on your show?"

"You know why, Blandine," Pierre responded quickly. "Freedom of expression required it. If we silence Vergès, we'll silence Jean-Marie Le Pen next," he said, referring to the extreme-right-wing politician who had garnered more than 10 percent of the French vote during the 1986 election campaign. "If we silence Le Pen, then we'll silence President Mitterrand. Who will be next? Where will it end?"

Everyone knew that the trial had almost nothing to do with justice, argued Jean-Marie Bourguburgu, a lawyer and the hostess's husband. By permitting Barbie's crimes against members of the French Resistance to be heard in the same trial with his deportation and other crimes against the Jews, the French lower courts had hopelessly blurred the traditional distinction in France between "war crimes"—or crimes against combatants—and "crimes against humanity"—those committed against civilians for reasons of race, religion, or political views. "The trial now has far more to do with morality, with history, than with justice," he asserted.

"And what will happen," Pierre agreed, "when some old Resistance hero steps forth to testify against Barbie, and Barbie turns to him in court and says: 'Ah, but wasn't it you who betrayed the leader of the Resistance to save your own skin?' Think of the headlines! The honor of the Resistance destroyed!" he said sarcastically. "The journalists will be salivating for scoops, another sensational headline that will impugn the honor of our country's fighters!"

"Are you really saying that the trial should not take place?" said Blandine, her voice wavering in barely controlled anger. "We need this trial. France needs this trial. Look at the sudden revival of Céline and other fascist writers. Oh, the public is ever so fascinated with them once again."

A friend of Pierre's chimed in. "But, Blandine, you know that there were many worse than Barbie in Germany, and even in France. Must we name names here in the President's house?"

Our hostess, Danielle Bourguburgu, who worked for President Mitterrand and had organized the dinner for friends in the press while she was on call one weekend at the Élysée, sighed. Here at her dinner table, the two Frances had become visible once more. Political battalions were forming around the exquisite porcelain china and the Baccarat wineglasses. Skirmishing over the past was under way again. But Pierre and his allies had to be cautious. Blandine, born in 1943, was, unlike most at the table, a true child of the Resistance. Her entire family had been Communists who had fought the Nazis and the Vichy government during the war. At birth, a Resistance doctor had registered her under a false name to protect her.

Danielle made several deft attempts to change the subject of conversation. But the debate raged on, over dessert, over coffee, over cognac and cigars.

What began as a *dîner intime,* with nine guests, at the Élysée Palace—the French equivalent of the White House, only more so —had turned into a fascinating glimpse at the profound divisions within the *classe politique.* The disagreement in this family quarrel was ostensibly over whether Klaus Barbie should be brought to trial in France forty years after he had committed his crimes. But the cleavages that night were more profound. For France has yet to decide where it stands on a variety of fundamental historical questions. How should the Vichy government that ruled during the war be viewed: as collaborationist or as the vehicle that helped preserve the country? Did France's deportation of thousands of Jews to concentration camps stem from circumstances of the war or from the country's deep-seated anti-Semitism? Was the Resistance riddled with spies and informers who betrayed one another for sometimes petty reasons, or was it closer to the glorious fighting force whose image was carefully crafted by Charles de Gaulle after the war? Could France, a country that reveled in its rich and often glorious history, face at last the implications and the moral lessons of this particular period of shame?

It was not surprising that the French were divided over this period of history. France has been deeply split along left-right lines since the 1789 Revolution, which solidified the modern nation-state.

At the same time, France has prided itself on having one of the strongest senses of national identity and prerogative in Europe. Surveys have consistently shown that the French are more nationalistic than other Europeans, more chauvinistic, more united on their country's right to project military force to defend its interests, more insistent on their independence of policy and spirit.

The French, far more than other Europeans, are also deeply interested in their country's history. In 1986, more than 800,000 copies of historical journals and publications were published each month, the highest per capita rate in the world, roughly eight times the production of Britain, which rivals France's attachment to its past.

Because the Barbie trial was likely to sharpen national focus on the fundamental issues that had divided France so painfully and which the French would have preferred to ignore, the impending trial was more problematic for the French than almost any judicial proceeding in the country's postwar history. The trial threatened to force France to examine its very soul.

Barbie might never have come to justice in France had it not been for Serge and Beate Klarsfeld, the renowned Nazi hunters. They tracked him down in Bolivia in 1971. In May 1981, a Socialist President dedicated to the memory of the Resistance was elected in France, and in 1983 the newly elected leftist government in La Paz deported to François Mitterrand's government the twice-convicted war criminal. The deal brought to an end more than thirty-eight years of impudent freedom for Klaus Barbie, who had been living as a businessman under the alias Klaus Altmann. Robert Badinter, then the Minister of Justice, played a key role in arranging the transfer. Badinter's father had been deported by Barbie in 1943.

With great fanfare, Barbie, an ashen-gray old man, was shown on television news in February 1983 being unloaded from a French police van into the Montluc military prison, where he and his Gestapo had kept and tortured prisoners. Montluc's most celebrated occupant and Barbie's most prominent victim was Jean Moulin, the martyred hero of the French Resistance, General de Gaulle's personal representative in France, and more than any other, the symbol of French courage and valor.

In 1952 and 1954, Barbie had been tried in absentia in France, convicted, and sentenced to death for "war crimes," including the torture and murder of Jean Moulin. But such crimes were covered by a statute of limitations. Therefore, they could not be included in a new trial in France. And because the statute of limitations had expired and the Socialist government had abolished the death penalty, the previous sentences could not be carried out.

A succession of French courts pondered how and for which crimes Barbie could be tried. The delays were so systematic, the process so protracted, that many began to wonder whether their unstated goal was to ensure that Barbie, who was then seventy-three and in poor health, would die before he could ever be brought to trial.

In December 1985, France's highest appeals court broke through the last legal impediment to a wide-ranging trial. It overturned a lower court decision and ruled that the murders of Resistance members could be considered not just as "war crimes," but as "crimes against humanity," for which there was no statute of limitations in France. Since the conventions established for the Nuremberg war crime trials in 1945, "crimes against humanity" were acts committed against civilians because of race, religion, or opinion.

As a result of the ruling, the charge against Barbie of "crimes against humanity," which until then had been reserved in France for crimes against Jews and other civilians, would include his torture and slaughter of Resistance leaders.

The ruling prompted an outcry from many French intellectuals. Simone Veil, a survivor of Auschwitz, the former President of the European Parliament, and among the most distinguished conservative politicians in France, called the decision "shocking."[1]

The ruling, she argued, had broadened, and hence blurred, the very specific definition of what constituted a crime against humanity. It weakened the distinction between genocide against the Jews and other wartime atrocities, such as the murder of Resistance members. "This was a terrible banalization of the Holocaust, a denial of its specificity," she argued before the trial.

Another danger concerned her. Jacques Vergès, a radical leftist who had defended Arab terrorists and other opponents of the French political system, had promised that he would question French behavior not only during World War II but in the country's protracted battle against Algerian independence. He would argue that Barbie was no worse than the French who tortured Algerians, or the Americans who dropped atomic bombs on the Japanese, or the Pol Pot government, which murdered more than a million fellow Cambodians.

"The tactic is designed to show that every war-related death—the Nazi genocide, Hiroshima, Algeria, Vietnam, Cambodia, and the like—is the same. If everyone is guilty, then no one is guilty. And certainly not Barbie," she said.

But there were far deeper reasons for anxiety. Some were shared by Mme. Veil, her critics charged, though she vehemently denied it. Vergès had long hinted that Barbie would tarnish the image of the Resistance, and of France itself, by focusing on its treacheries. Would Barbie reveal the identity of the people who betrayed Jean Moulin? Would those informers turn out to be rightists who had done so because they believed Moulin was a Communist or a dangerous Socialist? Would he expose the many others who had collaborated with the Nazis and denounced fellow Frenchmen?

And Alain Finkielkraut, a prominent, provocative writer about Jews and French intellectual history, voiced another concern. "The great risk of such a trial is that a judicial proceeding will somehow be turned into a circus, a new kind of World Cup soccer match." Sensationalized history was "the antechamber of forgetfulness," he warned.[2]

The trial might also prompt a resurgence of anti-Semitism, but in a new form. "It could enhance the competition among Jews and Resistance groups for preeminence as victims. This competition among the victims has become more of a problem than the issue of collaboration with the Nazis," he said, shaking his head sadly. "All of a sudden, as memory of this terrible period has returned, everyone wants to get into the victim act. Why do the Jews want to monopolize the status of victim? people say. This is their new greed, they say. This has become one of the modern faces of anti-Semitism in France, indeed, in Europe today."

Fear of banalization of the Holocaust, of sensationalized history, and of revived anti-Semitism were not as strong, however, as the country's quiet fear—articulated so vividly at the Élysée Palace dinner that night—that France would once again be torn apart internally, and hence become less effective externally, by the rekindling of old divisions and hatreds. France had interests and a future to protect. This was no time for self-flagellation, a revival of hatred and suspicion toward Germany, France's most important partner in defense, or questioning the state of the national soul. This would divert the country's attention from the pressing needs of the present. In such a world as this, France could not afford to dwell on the past, because the present required strength. France would never be conquered again.

France's worst fears about the Barbie trial were never realized. One of the trial's many ironies is that the controversy over whether it should take place generated almost as much debate as the proceeding itself or its aftermath. At the end of the two-month trial, the French shrugged their shoulders and wondered: what was all the fuss about? The blasé reaction raised troubling questions. What purpose had the trial served? Justice, surely. But history? Memory?

The trial had evoked painful memories of the war for those who had experienced it. But what had it taught young French people about their fathers and grandfathers? About the Holocaust and France's role in it? About Vichy and the shame that so many of the French harbored? Did it help transmit to those too young to have lived through those years of confusion any moral or even political lessons? Had it educated them about their society, its strengths, and above all, its weaknesses?

Tentative answers to these questions are not reassuring.

Fortunately, the Barbie trial did not become "justice of the streets," despite some unavoidable elements of the "circus." Changes were made to accommodate the unusual public and international interest in the trial. A vast ornate hall in the Palais de Justice was renovated at a cost of more than $2 million to hold the more than nine hundred reporters, one hundred witnesses, their forty lawyers, and throngs of spectators who would not have fit into a standard Lyons courtroom. Given the size of the hall, witnesses were compelled to speak to the panel of three judges and nine-member jury through a microphone. But the Barbie trial itself did not turn into the show that so many of the French had dreaded.

On the contrary, France's first trial for crimes against humanity, given the months of intense polemics and soul-searching that had preceded it, struck many who attended as something of an anticlimax, often as dramatic as a high school history lesson. There were moments of incredible passion and unfathomable pain in the testimony of those who had suffered at Barbie's hands. But the language of the courtroom was dry and much of the judicial procedure tedious.

Some old enough to remember the Eichmann trial in Israel said that the trial in Lyons lacked the drama or impact of that trial twenty-six years before. The Eichmann trial had been the first to focus specifically on the Holocaust; and Eichmann, unlike Barbie, who was a relatively small cog in the Nazi killing machine, was one of the master planners of the extermination industry.

There was another difference as well: in Lyons, there was no villain in the glass box. Klaus Barbie left the courtroom on the third day of the trial. Asserting that he had been kidnapped from Bolivia against his will and, therefore, had been brought to court illegally, the self-proclaimed "victim" of French justice chose not to participate in the trial or to testify in his own defense. Except for his sentencing on the last day of the trial, he was forced to return to the courtroom briefly only twice.

His absence was a relief to some in Lyons. Because he left the trial, not a single Frenchman was denounced by him as having betrayed a member of the Resistance, as many had feared. And despite the threats from Vergès, the reputation of no one in the Resistance was sullied.

At the same time, however, Barbie's absence meant that almost none of the witnesses was able to confront his tormentor publicly. Almost no one was able to stare into the face of the man who had tortured and humiliated him forty years before and say before his peers, Yes, it was you. Yes, it did happen. Instead, the survivors stood before the judge and the jury, their backs to the audience, describing in detail the horror they had endured at the hands of the man who wasn't there. The voices of history echoed hollowly through the massive hall.

By removing himself, Barbie made sure that Frenchmen would not be able to search his eyes for a tinge of hatred for Jews (he said that he had none). They would not be able to watch the men and women he had tortured and humiliated confront him with their survival. They would not be able to look for any sign of revulsion about the crimes he had committed so long ago, or for any sense of remorse.

It was almost as if Barbie had never been brought back from Bolivia, as if he were being tried and convicted in absentia, as he had been in 1952 and 1954.

I arrived in Lyons the day after Barbie left the courtroom. In keeping with the national preoccupation with form, the French were in an uproar over the judge's decision to permit Barbie to leave. "They should have dragged him back and chained him to the chair and made him listen," said Lise Lesèvre, one of the trial's star witnesses, a genuine French heroine, a non-Jewish Resistance member who had not cracked under Barbie's torture.[3]

Many of my French colleagues in the press and many witnesses agreed. They were furious that the judge had acceded to Barbie's request. Michel Thomas, who was born in Poland and grew up in France, where he had joined the Resistance, was particularly outraged. Thomas, who now runs a language school in New York, said he had been recruiting for the Resistance at the General Union of French Jews, or UGIF in France, the only Jewish social-service organization permitted to operate in occupied Lyons, when the Gestapo had raided the group to round up Jews on February 9, 1943. He told the court that he spent an hour and a half at the tiny office on the Rue Ste. Catherine in front of a Gestapo leader whom he identified as Barbie, passing himself off as an itinerant painter looking for work. Barbie had released him and he had been spared.

Like most of the witnesses, Thomas had confronted Barbie in prison in 1985 when the French government was preparing its case. Had he recognized Barbie, the old man who now resembled an aging pharmacist rather than the sadistic torturer of Lyons? Yes, he declared over coffee. "I recognized him immediately. You could never forget those eyes: the eyes of a rat; or the unmistakable asymmetry of his ears, and a peculiar, almost effeminate way of holding his pinky finger aloft, so that it was separated slightly from the rest of his hand."

Several witnesses had mentioned the little finger and the strange alignment of Barbie's small, slightly protruding ears, and above all the eyes. Those terrifying eyes. But Thomas was the only witness to have placed Klaus Barbie at the scene of the infamous Jewish roundup at No. 12 Rue Ste. Catherine.

Stanislas DeHoyos, an investigative reporter, a rarity in France, had tracked Barbie, with Serge Klarsfeld's help, to Bolivia in 1971 and had interviewed "Klaus Altmann" that year in La Paz.

"Klaus Altmann told me that the crimes of this fellow Barbie, wherever he was, were no worse than what France had done in Algeria, or what the United States had done in Vietnam," said DeHoyos, recounting the interview, which later became part of his book on Barbie. "He also said that if ever Barbie were apprehended, it would be a very bad day for France. All of the old stories of collaboration and betrayal would resurface."

"Now the French press is blaming his lawyer, Vergès, for Barbie's defense strategy. They say it's Vergès's idea to try to blackmail France into dropping charges by threatening to name names and reveal embarrassing secrets of our past, by relativizing his crimes," he said. "But that is not only Vergès; that is vintage Barbie. That is the kind of man with whom we are dealing."

According to DeHoyos, the Barbie trial was wrenching for France because it involved three separate confrontations. First, there was the confrontation with history seen through Barbie's reign of efficient cruelty in Lyons. That included reopening the old wounds between those who had collaborated with the Germans and those who had resisted them. "Today, it translates as those who want to continue covering things up and those who want to know what happened in this city and in France," he said. For him, this was the most important function of the trial. When the victim-witnesses had returned from the camps, no one wanted to listen to their stories. Now their experiences would be told and recorded indelibly.

Second, the Barbie trial was to some extent the scene for the settling of accounts between the Resistance and the Jews. It had aired some long-standing bitterness within the Jewish community over the Resistance's paltry efforts to save them. As Klarsfeld had noted, the Resistance never attempted to stop a single deportation train.

Finally, the trial was a judgment of Barbie's crimes, which DeHoyos described as almost an "annex" of the trial. For this, however, witnesses needed to confront the accused. Barbie would, of course, be found guilty. There was never any doubt about that. But for ultimate justice to be served, the victims were entitled to a long-delayed catharsis—the right to demand justice for those who did not return with them from the camps, the right to denounce the Nazi war criminal directly and in public.

Finkielkraut understood this need on the part of the witnesses. France, he argued, knew what had happened during the occupation. The country did not require another history lesson. But a public confrontation between Barbie and his former victims would have forced people to think about the specificity of his crimes and those of the Nazis. Barbie would no longer be merely a symbol of an abstraction called "crimes against humanity," but a man who had once cradled a cat in his arms and gently stroked it between delivering savage blows to the head of thirteen-year-old Simone Lagrange. "A public confrontation would make people think about what kind of man he is and the kind of things he did to earn the title 'Butcher of Lyons.' That, to me, is critical," Finkielkraut said.

However, he was troubled by the intensity of the outcry over Barbie's departure from the courtroom. There was, he suspected, an element of voyeurism involved in the disappointment. "There is a strong desire in Lyons, in France, for a grand spectacle. They mask the desire for a good show with intellectual justifications. If Barbie is present, the argument goes, the trial is a moment of history. If he's not, it's worth nothing."

Despite the dismay over Barbie's disappearance from his own trial, the French press continued to provide detailed coverage of each day's testimony. Not all the journalists remained after Barbie left, of course. Some reporters, particularly the foreigners, took advantage of the trial's slow days to cover a more pleasant French spectacle, the fortieth annual Cannes international film festival, only a few hours away on the Mediterranean coast. Even Vergès was said to have dined in Cannes and mingled with the stars the weekend after the trial began.

But those who did not abandon Lyons could not totally escape the film festival either. The evening newscast gave new meaning to what the French call "mediaization"—in this case, the blurring of specific instances of horror and joy and shock and boredom into one indistinct image by linking them sequentially in a television news program. First, there was the most powerful image of the day from Lyons: tiny, frail Lise Lesèvre, supported by a cane, describing how Barbie had tortured her for nineteen days, how he had stripped her naked, how he had beaten her, submerged her head in water, and starved her until he was persuaded that she would not talk. Highlights of her testimony were followed by a tearful but smiling blonde *starlette,* a word the French invented and still adore, whispering huskily that this was the night she would never forget, how thrilled she was that the Cannes jury had voted her best comedienne of the year.

The amount of daily trial coverage was staggering. The irreverent French newspaper known in French slang as *Libé,* for *Libération,* had set up an entire production facility in Lyons and produced a special "daily supplement" on the trial and the city in which it was being held.

Every French magazine or newspaper sent correspondents, analysts, artists, photographers. The city of Lyons distributed to reporters registered for the trial a reinforced plastic press kit marked "RENDEZ-VOUS IN LYONS." The case contained, among other items, a city map, pamphlets about tourist sights in the city, two restaurant guides, biographies of key players in the city and the trial, and a guide to the location of various news organizations' temporary headquarters for the trial. Lyons's restaurateurs made a concession to the trial schedule. Since the court hearings opened at 1:30 P.M. each day—right at lunchtime—they quickly announced that an early lunch would be served at 11 A.M. They were filled to capacity every day.

Young French legal analysts were on hand to enlighten foreign journalists about the intricacies of the criminal-justice system. Since the twenty-year statute of limitations on his convictions in 1952 and 1954 of war crimes had expired, Barbie had been charged with four other major crimes committed against Jews and Resistance members to avoid double jeopardy. One was the arrest and deportation of 49 Jews and Resistance members. The second was the Gestapo raid on the UGIF, the Jewish group on the Rue Ste. Catherine. Third, he was accused of ordering the last deportation train from Lyons in 1944, in which 650 prisoners, including Jews and Resistance members, were sent to camps in Germany and Poland. Finally, he was charged with what became the centerpiece of the trial, the raid on a farmhouse in the nearby village of Izieu in which 44 Jewish children were hidden. All were deported. All died at Auschwitz.

The descriptions of Barbie's zeal in his work were harrowing. "He kicked heads and hung almost lifeless people upside down from ceiling hooks while he took a break from business to play a little love song on the piano. " 'Parlez-moi d'amour' was one of his favorites," wrote Erna Paris, in her account of Barbie's crimes. "Women were always tortured naked, to the deep enjoyment of the torturers. Barbie kept two German shepherd dogs. One was trained to lunge and bite. The other was trained to mount naked women who had first been ordered on their hands and knees, a humiliation that could cut deeper than the whip, than having one's fingernails pulled out, or one's nipples burned with cigarettes. He threatened the lives of his victims' families, sometimes presenting them in person, or pretending they were just downstairs about to be tortured."[4]

Simone Lagrange told the court that Barbie had shown her bloodied and broken body to her mother, saying: "This is what you have done to your daughter." She had been arrested with her mother and father on June 6, 1944, after they were denounced to Barbie's office by a neighbor. She was beaten for refusing to tell

Barbie where her brother and sister were living in the country. There had been all this fuss over two more Jewish children, she told the court. He had hit and beaten her till she lay on the ground, swollen and semiconscious. Then he had turned her over "with the tip of his boot," she recalled.

At one point in her testimony, Lagrange paused, flashed a worried glance out into the audience, and gripped the white rail of the witness box more tightly. What she was about to tell the court would pain her brother, who was in the courtroom but who obviously had never heard the story she was about to recount. During one of her final days at Auschwitz, she happened to spot her father by chance among a group of prisoners. They were all being evacuated by the Germans ahead of the advancing Soviet troops. The war was almost over.

One of the camp guards allowed her to approach her father. She had not seen him for two years. As she rushed to embrace him, the guard abruptly stopped her father, forced him to kneel, and shot him in the head. "It was not Barbie who put bullets into our heads," she said, "but it was he who sent us into that hell. He is the first to be responsible."

Lise Lesèvre testified that she knew when Barbie was approaching her cell for another torture session by the sound of his swagger stick tapping against his boots. He loved to carry the stick and tap when he wasn't using it to beat a prisoner. Lesèvre, who is not Jewish, was arrested on March 13, 1943, while carrying a letter addressed to "Didier," the false name of a young liaison officer in the Resistance. Barbie was intent on discovering Didier's identity. So he tortured Lesèvre for nineteen days. She was almost drowned in a bathtub, hung by her wrists until she was unconscious, beaten, as she lay across a chair, with the back of a copper ball into which bristles had been imbedded. Finally, when she still refused to talk, she was deported to Ravensbrück. Her husband, who was also deported, died at Dachau; her son was killed in a detention center in Neuengamme. He was sixteen years old.

Michel Cojot-Goldberg was only four years old when his father, a Polish Jew who had immigrated to France before the war, was rounded up by Barbie on the Rue Ste. Catherine and deported to his death. Thirty years later, when Goldberg was married and the father of three children, he heard on the news that Bolivia had rejected France's request for the extradition of Klaus Barbie. "I felt a frustration, an anger that is difficult to describe to you," he told the court.

Goldberg decided to kill Barbie. Klaus Barbie, he explained, was "the only identifiable element in the chain of responsibility that had sent my father from Lyons to Auschwitz." He made two trips to Bolivia, where "a little bit of the Third Reich was still alive." But when he finally found Barbie, he could not pull the trigger of his gun. "It's difficult to describe," said Goldberg. "I found him contemptible, but full of contradictions, and, well, so mediocre. All of the hate that I needed to kill him went out of me."

That was in 1975, Goldberg recalled. He had acted in desperation because France was not willing to do then what it was willing to do today: "confront its history with all its glory and shame."

"Barbie is here. He is alive. He is not like the dead who died so anonymously, without dates, times, or tombs," he continued. "It's so hard to explain to you. But the way they were killed even deprived us of mourning. Even today, my daughter sometimes asks: Why is there no grave for my grandfather?

"This trial is a chance for us to honor those who died so anonymously, so abstractly, as numbers," he said after his testimony. Painful memories, it seems, haunt not only the survivors, but their children.

Annette Kahn, a French journalist from *Le Point,* shuddered a little when Goldberg recounted his despair in court.

Annette had helped the foreign press enormously during the trial, translating difficult legal phrases, getting extra copies of depositions and motion filings. She went about her work professionally. But after Goldberg's testimony she seemed badly shaken. She took out a copy of the thick formal indictment and pointed to one name on the list of deportees.

"This is my father," she said.

Over lunch at an outdoor café near the press center, she told of her father's arrest. He was a Jewish industrialist from Paris. He had been in the Resistance near Lyons; his code name was "Renaud." He was denounced, as were so many, by a neighbor, and arrested, along with her mother, in June 1944. Annette and her brother were saved by a schoolteacher who took them in. Her mother was sent to Auschwitz.

"She didn't learn until a year later when she returned with a number on her arm that my father had been shot.

"I barely knew my father," said Annette. "I was so young when he was taken away. All I had was one of his sweaters and his handkerchief, embroidered with his initials. I kept them in a drawer for years. Somehow, I just couldn't accept the fact that he was dead. I always thought: One day he will come back; he has only lost his handkerchief.

"When I saw the police van carrying Barbie pull up to Montluc prison, where my father had been imprisoned, only then did I understand what had happened to my father. Only when I saw Barbie did I know that my father would never come back. For me, the circle was finally complete. I could finally mourn."

On a day when the trial was in recess, I visited Izieu, the tiny mountain hamlet, population 136, fifty miles east of Lyons. It was here, on the brilliant spring morning of April 6, 1944, that the Gestapo raided and arrested the occupants of the children's home. I took with me a copy in French of *The Children of Izieu: A Jewish Tragedy.*[5] The chronicle was painstakingly prepared in 1984 by Serge Klarsfeld, who hoped that the book would grant each child a posthumous identity. He believed that by painting a detailed portrait of their brief lives and their stay at Izieu in 1943 and 1944 he would remove their murders from the realm of abstraction.

At the base of the road that turns off to Izieu was a stone monument to the children, which was erected in April 1946. The obelisk is dedicated: "To the memory of 43 [sic] children of the home of Izieu, of their director, and of their five guardians, arrested by the Germans on the 6th of April, 1944, exterminated in the camps or shot in German prisons."

In addition to getting the number of deported children and their guardians wrong, the obelisk did not say that all the children here were Jews and were arrested because they were Jewish. The one non-Jewish child staying here was released immediately.

The memorial also lay total blame for the children's arrest and deportation on the Germans. It did not mention that the children were betrayed by a French neighbor, presumably a certain Lucien Bourdon, who had grown up in German-controlled Lorraine. He had lost his farm when he fled east from the German Army. But he was known to have developed good relations with the Germans in a neighboring town. One week after the arrest of the children at Izieu, Bourdon was moved back to his farm in Lorraine.[6]

The house in which the children lived was gray-painted stone, with dark green shutters and a red tile roof. It stood atop a hill with a commanding view of the Rhône River valley, a tranquil spot that the children must have loved. Mme. Taibaudier, who bought the house in 1950 and was widowed in 1986, was eager to sell the farmhouse and all its land. It was too much for her to manage alone, she said. But she had gotten used to the steady stream of visitors, especially in the last few months.

Normally she was all alone in this big empty house with its memories. It would be too much for anyone: the hand-written schedule of classes tacked to one of two old-fashioned wooden desks in the attic, the ghosts of children's voices, the commemorative plaque on the front wall of the house.

The plaque was put up at roughly the same time as the obelisk. And, like the monument at the bottom of the hill, it did not mention that the children were Jews.

The Jewish community of Lyons protested in 1987, asking the villages of Izieu and neighboring Bregnier-Cordon, which erected the obelisk, to change the inscriptions to specify that the children died because of their religion. "In the year 2000, who in Izieu will know that the children were Jews?" asked Marc Aaron, a doctor and spokesman for the Lyons Jewish community.[7]

The mayors of both villages initially denied Dr. Aaron's request, saying that the tragedy here was not only a Jewish tragedy, but a tragedy for all the people of their villages and the region. The Jews of Lyons, they complained, had only voiced protests about the memorials since Barbie's arrest. The people of Izieu and Bregnier-Cordon had lived with what had happened here ever since the war. Eventually, however, the mayors relented. In 1989, the obelisk's inscription was changed, much to the relief of Aaron and other French Jews.

But the plaque at the house has remained troubling in another respect. Its dedication is baffling: "Let the defense and the love of my fatherland be my defense before Thee, O Lord." What on earth, I thought, did that inscription have to do with the children of Izieu? Did they fight and die for France?

Eleven-year-old Liliane Gerenstein had written another kind of appeal to God during her stay at Izieu. Klarsfeld found her prayer in the house years later and included it in his touching book. "It is thanks to you," Liliane's letter said, "that I had a good life before, that I was spoiled, that I had such pretty things that others did not have. I only ask one thing," she pleaded with the Lord in printed capital letters. "BRING BACK MY PARENTS, MY POOR PARENTS, PROTECT THEM (even more than me) SO THAT I MAY SEE THEM AS SOON AS POSSIBLE. HAVE THEM COME BACK ONE MORE TIME.

"I have so much confidence in you that I'm thanking you in advance."

The Gestapo's roundup lasted only a few minutes. Sabina Zlatin, who had chosen the farm in Izieu thinking that the children of deportees would be safe there, was in Paris when the Gestapo struck. Her husband, however, was beaten and arrested and later shot. According to the villagers, the children were thrown "like packing cases" aboard the trucks. As the Gestapo vans drove back to Lyons, the children, more than half of whom were not French by origin, could be heard singing a French patriot's song, "You'll Never Have Alsace and Lorraine."[8]

On the morning of the raid, Léon Reifman, one of the children's guardians, was warned by a cry from his sister. He escaped by jumping from a second-story window of the house. It was a long way down. But he, Lea Feldblum, another guardian, and Sabina Zlatin who was in Paris, survived and returned to Lyons to testify against Barbie.

Edith Klebinder, an Austrian-born Jew, was deported to Auschwitz in the same train with the children. In a voice choked with emotion, she told the court that she remembered seeing them get off the last boxcar of the train. Because she spoke both German and French, she had been ordered to translate and was able to see which passengers were chosen for work and which for the gas chambers. Thirty-four of the children and three other adults from Izieu were gassed immediately. The remaining ten children were killed a few days later.

The main piece of evidence linking Barbie to the deportations was a telegram he sent to the central Gestapo office in Paris. "This morning the Jewish Children's Home 'Children's Colony' in East Izieu was cleaned out," the telegram stated. "Neither cash nor other valuables were found." It was signed: Barbie.

The trial dominated Lyons, particularly in its opening weeks. Marek Halter, the writer, had wanted to stage a "trial of Vichy France" to coincide with Barbie's judgment, but virtually no one wanted to reopen the old wounds of divided France.

Prosecutors and attorneys for the plaintiffs also discouraged Halter. Such a "political show," they argued, would detract from Barbie's, the best hope of prompting collective introspection about the war years in France.

Marek reluctantly acceded to the almost universal antipathy toward his plan. Instead, he joined forces with other Jews from Paris and Lyons, and a Paris-based group called S.O.S. Racisme (Stop Racism), which was fighting growing anti-Arab sentiment in France. Together, they erected a makeshift memorial to Barbie's victims in the middle of the city's main square.

"The Children of Memory," as the simple exhibit was called, was housed in a stark, cube-shaped structure that was covered by white canvas. The memorial, less than a mile from the Palais de Justice, was surrounded by the city's majestic Palais des Arts and a huge fountain depicting the Four Horsemen of the Apocalypse.

Inside were a replica of the central room of Yad Vashem, the Holocaust memorial in Jerusalem, several black-and-white photographs of concentration camps, and drawings made by children in Theresienstadt camp in Czechoslovakia. Along another wall were the names of the 24 camps in which 6,225,000 men, women, and children had perished, 5.4 million of them Jews, visitors were told. A sign, NEVER FORGET! hung over a book in which visitors were encouraged to sign. Halter said that more than 30,000 people visited the memorial during the Barbie trial, filling multiple books with inscriptions in many languages—Hebrew, Arabic, English German, and, of course, French. "After these pictures, can anyone believe that Barbie is innocent?" one inscription read. "Justice will be done!" said another. "Thank you for having made me remember," one visitor had written.

I went to the memorial one cold gray day. There was a line, as a security guard checked all purses and bags of visitors. As I left, I saw a tiny old woman with blue-white hair. She was muttering angrily to herself. "Those two young girls were giggling in the memorial," she complained, "flirting with boys at this sacred place!"

She had come to honor a friend of her family's, the Dutch consul in Lyons, who had been arrested and deported to Auschwitz for having hidden Jews. He returned after the war, she said with relief, "but from his face I knew he had seen things that were indescribable. He never talked about it. But he said just before he died: If you can ever think of a way to honor all of those who did not come back with me, do it for love of me. I know he would have wanted me to see this memorial."

Many of those who attended the trial, including students from Lyons, seemed deeply moved by the testimony. The impact on the public at large in Lyons, and throughout France, was harder to evaluate.[9] When the trial began in May, the Lyonnais seemed to revel in their city's new celebrity status, its reoccupation as it were, this time by the international press corps.

Suddenly, local characters were very much news. The restaurateurs, the town historian, the bishop were all interviewed. Reporters climbed the staircase of 12 Rue Ste. Catherine, inhaling the foul, dank air of the dimly lit old building. The former offices of the UGIF, which Barbie raided, were now the Sauna Club des Terreaux, which offered Sauna/Relaxation/Video. The nineteen-year-old who sold tickets to the club shrugged his shoulders when asked what he thought of Barbie. "What he did was terrible," he said. "But it's done. It has nothing to do with today." Would I like the "afternoon sauna special"?

Early one morning Richard Bernstein, the Paris bureau chief from *The New York Times,* and I went to the open-air marketplace to sample public opinion. The sun was rising over the old part of Lyons, and the pastel shades of the city, reflected in the ripples of the Saône River, made Lyons look slightly Florentine. The St. Antoine market, on the Quai St. Antoine, which runs along one of the two majestic rivers that converge in Lyons, was bustling by 8 A.M. The market was just across the river from the Palais de Justice, but few of the Lyonnais who were selling meat, vegetables, bread, pastries, and flowers had time or inclination to attend the proceedings.

At least one of them was old enough to have remembered Barbie's terror in Lyons. Camille Perroux was, like Barbie, seventy-four years old. He was known as the "vegetable king" of the market, where stands are awarded by seniority. Sporting a lime-green beret that covered his white hair and the tip of his bushy white eyebrows, he spoke with a certainty befitting the oldest and richest of the market's merchants, a man whose father and grandfather had sold vegetables here. Yes, he remembered Barbie.

"We should have finished him off in Bolivia," said Perroux. Prison was too good for that *salaud,* loosely translated "that son-of-a-bitch." "He has everything there in the place where he used to torture people—a television, a bed, good chow. The only thing he lacks is a woman."

Barbie, he continued, should be executed for his crimes against the Resistance and the Jews. "I'm not for capital punishment, but some crimes demand it, like Barbie's." His son, who worked in a factory on the outskirts of Lyons, had no interest in the trial, Perroux said; he was indifferent to Barbie's fate.

Yves Girerd, who sold chickens in the stand next to Perroux, was only ten when the Germans had forced him and his uncle to walk through the neighborhood at gun point. "They're like that, the Prussians," he observed. But Girerd had fought in Algeria and had seen, he said, "terrible things."

"Eight- and nine-year-old girls were raped by French Legionaires. Innocent women and children were killed. War is like that. All wars are like that. Barbie was just following orders," he asserted, as Perroux shook his head in disapproval at his thin, wiry friend in blue overalls, the proud symbol of the working class in class-ridden France. Besides, the trial was too expensive. France had better things to do with its money.

"He's old now. We should leave him in peace," Girerd pressed on. "Forty years later is too long to put someone on trial. It's supposed to be a lesson for the young, but they don't care. So it's useless. It's past. Let's forget about it."

Jacques and Lucette Seigneret disagreed about everything except the quality of the bread and cakes they sold at their stand. Lucette did not want the Barbie trial to "stir things up again" all those years after the war. She had been only a child then, she said, but she remembered the deportations from the city. "Yes, there were mainly Jews," she said. "But there were also Frenchmen and members of the Resistance." Nothing had happened to her or her family. It was better to let memories of the war die, especially those painful memories. Barbie had done terrible things. But "everyone" had helped him. The Vatican had helped him get out of France, she contended inaccurately. The United States had helped him get to South America, which was all too true.

Jacques strongly disagreed. "Barbie should be killed," he snapped at his wife. He would not say more, but Lucette told us that his father had been jailed for two months near the war's end for having hidden a Jew. Both had survived, she said, but Jacques still hated the Germans.

"Everybody knows somebody in this town who was hurt, or

something about the people who helped Barbie. That's why, you see, it's better to forget it," she said.

The divisions of opinion in the market reflected those in the city, which mirrored those in France. Most wished that the Barbie trial could quickly be put behind them, but especially denizens of this bastion of commerce, conservatism, and smugness.

Throughout its history, Lyons has been conservative. "You cannot understand the city's reaction to the trial unless you understand the fundamental conservatism of this city," said Pierre Mérindol, the author of two books about Lyons.[10]

During the 1789 revolution, Lyons was the only city in France to have a counterrevolution that killed revolutionaries. "We had no princes, only princes of industry and commerce," he said. "The only commodity that has ever counted in this city is money," Mérindol said. Lyons had always resisted two things: Paris and progress.

For years since the war, Lyons, France's third-largest city, had cultivated a myth about its role in the war. Lyonnais had long treasured their city's self-proclaimed status as the "Capital of the French Resistance."

"It wasn't true, of course," said Mérindol. "Resistance was far stronger in the mountains near Grenoble, but never mind. People here like the image."

It was true, he said, that Lyons was not occupied by the Germans until the end of 1942, and that several Resistance groups had bases here. Lyons also had one of the first clandestine newspapers—*Le Combat.* But Mérindol and historians note that Lyons had more than its share of collaborationists during the war. Thousands of Lyonnais were photographed in 1940 giving an enthusiastic welcome to Marshal Henri Philippe Pétain, the chief of the Vichy government, which collaborated with the Nazis. Joannes Ambre, a prominent lawyer of the day, wrote a pamphlet on how to resolve the Jewish problem—a document that mirrored the sentiments expressed in the anti-Jewish laws promulgated by Vichy. But whereas Vichy officials were tried for collaboration or shunned after the war, Ambre was eventually elected Deputy Mayor in Lyons after disavowing his earlier writing as a mistake of youth.

"Until the day he died in 1984, the incident never hurt his political career," said Mérindol.

Some three-quarters of French Jews were saved, but the proportion of Jews summarily executed by the Germans and their French accomplices in Lyons was the highest by far in all of France. More than 2,000 of the 11,000 Jews were deported during the war. Klarsfeld estimates that at least 400 Jewish Lyonnais were shot and burned alive in the city.

Most of the survivors who testified at the trial said that they had been denounced by neighbors and ostensible friends. Mérindol said sadly that there were so many informers in this city during the occupation that Barbie had opened a special office in the Place Bellecourt to handle all of the denunciations. "Lyons was quite anti-Semitic and extremely xenophobic. And it remains so. Only now Lyonnais hate the Arabs here more than the Jews. I'm not sure that's any reason to be encouraged about our political evolution."

André Soulier, then the Deputy Mayor of Lyons, was also saddened by his city's reaction to the trial. "Except for the first two or three days, when the trial was a media spectacle, the city of Lyons has been rather indifferent," he said.[11]

Even so, after several weeks the testimony had begun to touch some people, Soulier asserted. The trial had become "a kind of poem, a psalmody of terrible suffering." The words were beginning to register on some Lyonnais.

Perhaps, said Richard Bernstein, as we left Lyons, the effects of an event like the Barbie trial were simply slow in making themselves felt. Or perhaps Lyons was, after all, simply indifferent.

If reaction to the trial was mixed and muted in Lyons, the proceedings generated little outrage and even less interest in Paris. "Lyons is not Paris," said Bettina Baudoin, a journalist who has both French and American nationality. "Lyons is not France's capital. What happens in Lyons does not really matter. That's why the French political class was so content to have the trial in Lyons. The trial never had much effect on the political discourse of the capital."

Bettina's conclusions turned out to be something of an understatement. Some of the trial coverage, of course, startled younger French people. A lawyer friend had been taught in school about the anti-Jewish laws enacted by Vichy, he said. But because the form of proclaiming laws had not changed in France in decades, he was somewhat taken aback when he read the anti-Jewish laws in *Le Monde* when they were reprinted.

"For a moment I thought they were really new laws," said my friend Richard. "When I read them thinking they were new, the effect was stunning."

But for the most part the trial and the thousands of pages of publicity it generated seemed to skim across the surface of French society. There were a few moments of what the French called *mini* and *grand chocs.* The first occurred by accident. Soon after the trial began, *Libération,* which prides itself on being on the side of truth, published a letter to the paper that attempted to demonstrate that the annihilation of six million Jews was an impossible feat, a lie. *Libération* promptly withdrew the issue; its editor published an apology, calling the letter "unpublishable"; he dismissed the paper's letters editor and temporarily abolished the letters column.[12]

A more serious attempt by revisionists to capitalize on the interest in World War II aroused by the Barbie trial was quashed by the French government. Twenty-four hours after the trial began, the first issue of *Annals of Historical Revisionism,* a quarterly whose articles challenged the Nazi genocide against the Jews, was distributed for sale to Paris bookstores and kiosks.[13] The journal was edited by Pierre Guillaume and articles were signed by Robert Faurisson, France's premier revisionist. Its appearance at the moment when Barbie was being tried for the very crimes whose occurrence the journal denied led to angry denunciations by French civil rights and Jewish groups. On May 25, a French judge ordered a halt to the distribution of the journal, ruling that its sale during the Barbie trial was a deliberate "provocation," which might incite violence by victims of the Nazis and their families.[14]

These incidents, however, proved to be minor diversions. After it became clear in Lyons that Vergès was not going to carry out his threat to divulge the names of still-secret collaborators, the French breathed more easily, and stories about the trial in Paris slid quietly onto the back pages. This would not be a trial of France after all. Klause Barbie, of course, would be tried and convicted. But Klaus Barbie was a German.

Soon after the trial, Channel TF1, the privatized television channel, broadcast *Shoah,* Claude Lanzmann's epic documentary about the Holocaust, on four successive nights. *Le Monde* announced somewhat breathlessly that its ratings showed that 5 million Frenchmen had stayed at home to watch the broadcast. The first night had garnered 6.5 million viewers, 1.5 million more than the traditional French weekly favorite, *Mission: Impossible,* the American-produced spy series.[15]

Article upon article was written about the "return" of "memory" in France. The press was filled with self-congratulatory articles about France's willingness to confront the "ghosts of the past." "Justice and Reconciliation," proclaimed the preeminent *Le Monde,* in its lead editorial soon after Barbie was sentenced. "Justice has rendered its verdict."[16]

But then, in an odd twist, the same rambling editorial noted that it would be unjust for the German people, confronted time and again with the memories of the actions of their former government, to be subjected once more to repercussions because of the trial. Fortunately, "this aspect of things played a secondary role throughout the trial," said the mouthpiece of establishment French thinking. "French-German reconciliation is one of the reasons," the paper stated, "but not the only reason. After all, Pol Pot found henchmen to carry out massacres in every way as vile as Hitler's, and no one would think of holding the entire Cambodian people responsible.

"The guilty," the paper concluded, "could be every man: this should be the principal lesson of the Lyons trial."

Barbie as "every man"? The Nazi genocide the equivalent of the Cambodian slaughter? Evil as everywhere?

The prestigious newspaper was not alone in its relativization of the Nazi genocide. During the first week of the trial, a group called the Young Arabs of Lyons and its Suburbs, summoned reporters to a press conference to complain about the treatment of Arab immigrants in Lyons by the French government and city officials. Speaking on behalf of a coalition of Arab *"immigrés,"* as the Arabs from former French colonies are called, Djida Tazdait described their persecution by the Lyons authorities. "While he sits comfortably in his heated cell, we are being beaten by French police in the same prison corridors," Tazdait declared.

A succession of young Arab spokesmen decried the discrimination they faced in housing, education, and employment. One of them asserted that the mayor of Lyons and the chief of police were "collaborating" with commandos of the Croix-Rousse, an extremist right-wing group named after the working-class side of the major-hill of Lyons. They called for a massive demonstration to protest France's racism. "If the memory of France is short, we are the memory of the present and the future," Tazdait said. "We will not let ourselves be deported."

The recently elected conservative government intended to "deport" the Arab workers, they noted, change nationality laws to deprive them of the choice of French citizenship, and take other measures to discourage their continued stay in France. "We will not be victims like the Jews," Tazdait concluded.

After the press conference had ended, I asked Tazdait whether he was concerned that using words like "collaborating" and "deport" to describe discrimination against Arabs, however unjust, might tend to banalize the genocide against the Jews perpetrated by the Germans and their allies.

The young man stared at me blankly for a second, uncomprehending. Then he replied: "We have no choice. Those words command attention. They are covered in the press. You are here because we are using these words. We must use the Barbie trial to sound the alarm today about the growth of extreme right-wing forces in France. We can't afford to wait until it's too late."

The source of Tazdait's concern was Jean-Marie Le Pen's extreme right-wing National Front party. At the time of the Barbie trial, Le Pen was registering more than 10 percent of the national vote—and almost double that in areas in southern France with heavy immigrant populations. That made the National Front the largest extreme-right-wing movement in any major European country.

As a result, Jacques Chirac's conservative neo-Gaullist party, the Rally for the Republic, or RPR as it is called, was in a quandary over how to handle its rambunctious extreme-right-wing rival. Le Pen's xenophobic party had gained political ground.

So statements by RPR leaders reflected diverse political strains and calculations about how best to counter Le Pen. On the right was Charles Pasqua, the blunt, tough-minded Interior Minister, who favored tough measures to woo National Front supporters; on the left stood Alain Juppé, the Budget Minister, who wanted his party to distance itself from Le Pen's racist program.

These tensions in the RPR spilled out into the open during the Barbie trial. Soon after the trial was under way, Pasqua announced in Paris that he was determined to tighten up on illegal immigrants. If they would not leave France voluntarily, he was prepared to deport them—by "trainload" if necessary.

The remark stunned many on the left and within his own party. The outrage found a voice in the protest of Michel Noir, the Minister of Foreign Trade, who subsequently was elected Mayor of Lyons. Noir not only condemned his fellow party member Pasqua for a statement that gave insensitivity new meaning, he denounced his party's flirtation with the National Front. Such an alliance, he warned publicly, would not only spell disaster for the RPR but also shame for France. It would be better to lose the next presidential election than to win with Le Pen's support, he asserted.[17]

Noir's outcry was personal. His father had been deported to a concentration camp in Austria for Resistance activities. "My father told me: 'Never forget Mauthausen,' " said Noir, who was born in 1944.[18]

Privately, French political analysts dismissed Noir's statements as political opportunism. He was not considered a "heavyweight" by the *classe politique,* they explained. Whether his position had merit was clearly peripheral. The furor quickly subsided.

The RPR's political quandary was resolved four months later, paradoxically, by Le Pen himself. In an interview on a radio talk show in mid-September, Le Pen committed a gaffe of colossal proportions: he called the question of whether the Nazis had killed six million Jews in gas chambers a "detail in the history of World War II."[19]

"Are you trying to tell me [the existence of gas chambers] is a revealed truth that everyone has to believe?" Le Pen asked rhetorically. "There are historians who are debating such questions."

The outcry was overwhelming. Le Pen was denounced as a racist and anti-Semite by virtually every responsible political leader. The RPR had no choice but to adopt the course championed by the liberals: to distance itself from Le Pen and back away from some of its own harsher proposals against immigrants and its hard-line policies. Minister Pasqua even floated the idea of making it a crime to advocate historical revisionism about the Holocaust.

The National Front found itself on the defensive, pilloried and isolated. Polls conducted in the late fall of 1987 showed a significant increase in hostility toward Le Pen and his party.[20]

But once again, noted the politician Simone Veil, a new threshold of revisionism had been established. Despite the revulsion expressed by many of the French about what Le Pen later characterized as a slip of the tongue that was misinterpreted and deliberately blown up out of all proportion by the hostile French press, Veil noted that never before had a politician in France dared to make such a statement. "This is the first time that a national figure opened a debate on the reality of the Jewish genocide," she said in an interview. Because such a debate "has now been elevated to the national level," she said, "revisionist theories" challenging the existence of death camps and gas chambers had gained "national exposure."[21]

In the two-stage presidential elections in April 1988, less than a year after the Barbie trial opened, the National Front garnered 14.4 percent of the popular vote, a development that the exultant Le Pen dubbed "a political earthquake." In the parliamentary election two months later, Le Pen's party was routed (from thirty-two seats to one) and he failed to win election to the Parliament. But the drastic cut in representation resulted not from a significant lessening of support, but because of a change in the voting system.

In early 1988, the French courts ended their temporary ban on the sale of the revisionist quarterly *Annals of Historical Revisionism.* The journal went back on the newsstands. As memory of the Barbie trial faded, the publication was no longer deemed to be dangerously provocative.

Since then, the courts have rejected the prosecutor's request for a fourth trial of Barbie, which would concentrate on charges that he tortured to death French Resistance hero Jean Moulin. The resurgence of French angst over the prospect of another public exploration of the degree of collaboration in wartime France subsided once more.

Less than a year after Barbie's conviction for crimes against humanity on all 341 counts and his sentencing to life imprisonment, the trial had virtually disappeared from French political consciousness. It had neither shaken nor divided France as so many had feared. But it hadn't really registered either. Less than a year after its end, the Barbie trial had settled into the great maw of French forgetfulness.

France's historical position in the war was unique.

"Unlike Germany or Britain," France was in the camp of both the collaborators and the victors," said Claude Lanzmann, whose ten-hour film about the Holocaust, *Shoah,* has become a classic.

"That historical distinction has made France's memories of the period highly conflicting, often contradictory."[22]

The fact that France was both a winner and a loser poses painful paradoxes for the French and partly accounts for their somewhat neurotic relationship to this particular part of the past. For May 1944 is a date that signifies not only its liberation, but also "the end of a national nightmare, of Vichy and Collaboration, the memories of which remain vibrant today," wrote Robert Frank and Henry Rousso, two of France's more impressive young historians.[23] "Liberation," therefore, was a complex phenomenon that engendered simultaneously "many hopes and deep deceptions."

In addition to the winner-loser dichotomy, the war and German occupation generated enormous strife and internal tension. World War II came close to being a civil war in France. It bitterly divided families, friends, and communities.

The division was nothing new, of course, and France's relationship with its past has never been easy. France has been divided between the left and the right since its revolution in 1789. The Jacobins won, but France made its own compromise with history. It clung to the highly centralized nation-state that the revolution helped create, patriotic and deeply nationalistic. But the French never abandoned their adoration of the monarchy the revolution had deposed. Throughout its history—even today—the French have felt most comfortable when a father-king figure has headed their government. It was only a couple of years before the hundredth anniversary of the revolution that France inaugurated a permanently republican form of government, ending what had been a century of alternation between monarchy and anarchy.

France's dramatic, violent past has engendered a passionate obsession among the French with their history, but at the same time a deep-seated cynicism about it. A survey conducted in 1983 on attitudes toward World War II showed that the French have remained remarkably loyal to certain historical clichés and, in some cases, myths about themselves. "The image of a glorious France, that of General de Gaulle, dominated," wrote Frank and Rousso. "The French wanted to believe that France liberated itself, confusing their desires with historical reality." At the same time, they noted, it was difficult to conclude that France had a single "collective" or "national" memory because of its profound internal cleavages. The data indicated that even forty years after the war there was a "memory of the right," another "memory of the left," a very specific "Communist memory," and more important, "a memory of the young."

Rousso and Pascal Ory, another young French historian, argue that France's confrontation with its wartime past has undergone several stages.[24] The first was what became known as the "years of occultation," the building of the myth of a "unified, glorious France."

Its theme was articulated by General de Gaulle in a speech at the Hôtel de Ville on August 25, 1944. "Paris! Paris outraged! Paris broken! Paris martyred!" France's most revered leader said of the occupation. "But Paris liberated! Liberated by itself! Liberated by its people with the help of the armies of France, with the support and the help of all of France, of the France which fought, of the only France, of the true France, of eternal France."

As de Gaulle uttered these words, the country was in the midst of a violent purge. The Resistance was taking vengeance on the collaborationists, who had betrayed France to Germany.

The "purification" of the country between 1944 and 1955 through purges of collaborators, however, was often random and unfair, badly defined, and ultimately incomplete. Even the amnesty laws passed between 1951 and 1953 were more acts of "political revenge" than true pardons for crimes committed during the occupation. These trials and purges enhanced France's desire to repress the terrible years. So, while younger French historians have used the stage of "occultation" to refer primarily to the repression of memories of collaboration and Vichy, it also included the suppression of memories of the harsh revenge the French exacted on one another immediately after the war. Hence, the image of mass resistance and glory offered by de Gaulle became even more alluring, virtually irresistible.

This was the period in which the consensus on the basic political values and objectives that are so dominant today in France took firm root. Never again would France be conquered. Never again would she collapse morally. Never would France be part of alliances that impinged upon its ability to pursue its national interests, or which denied its freedom of political or military action. Never would France permit itself to be dictated to or become dependent on a foreign power. And most important, never again would France permit itself to be so profoundly divided.

"The lasting legacy of de Gaulle is the powerful consensus on the need for consensus," said Robert O. Paxton, the American historian of France who published in 1972 the first history of Vichy that challenged the dominant French mythology about the war.[25]

What de Gaulle did to the nation's memory was natural, very human. "De Gaulle had to give France back its honor; he had to uplift and reunify the nation by burying the profound differences between those who supported the Vichy government and those who sided from the beginning with the Resistance," said Serge Klarsfeld, the French Nazi hunter. "After all, most of the victims in France were Jews. He didn't think it was worth torturing the nation's soul just for them. I don't accept his logic," Klarsfeld added, "but I understand it."

Perhaps because of their cynicism, the French have not truly believed their semi-official history for years, many intellectuals assert. But they were pragmatic enough to see its virtues and adopt its imagery as their own.

Besides, the official Gaullist memory of France was not really a myth; it was an exaggeration. It minimized Vichy and the collaborators and the attachment of many of the French to Marshal Pétain, while it amplified the role and number of the French who resisted fascism. From the end of the war until the late 1960s, the French found it convenient to repress their more inconvenient memories, in particular, the flourishing in France of an ideological strain that closely resembled Nazism.

Instead, France's official self-image became that of de Gaulle and of Gaul fiercely resisting the invading Huns, as did the little Gaul named "Asterix," still among the most popular French cartoon characters, who was created at this time.[26]

"What you must understand is that our myths were positive," said Alain Finkielkraut, the philosopher and writer on Jewish affairs. "They enabled France to recoup and rebuild. They were not like Ernst Nolte's myths about Germany. Those are negative myths, which cannot be built upon."

While this positive image for France was being reconstructed, the war, the defeat, and the occupation were becoming "the black years" *(années noires),* those in which the quasi-civil war that raged in France was being relegated to history. "The French never really forgot," observed Paxton. "They were willfully hiding from some facts. There was a tacit agreement not to tear one another apart."

But this phase would not last. The student revolt of May 1968 that gripped French youth and other young Europeans launched a more than decade-long assault on this reassuring and simplistic model of memory. The period "between the two Mays," as it is called in France—from the May 1968 students' explosion to the election in May 1981 of François Mitterrand, France's first Socialist President—was a period of political and cultural upheaval. The death of de Gaulle and the desire of President Georges Pompidou to define his own political image deprived the French of what Rousso called the "figurehead of their retrospective heroism."

When Paxton published his book, he shocked some French intellectuals into reexamining the vision of France that permeated their own work.[27] Thoughtful articles by Harvard professor Stanley Hoffmann and other academics living outside of France were suddenly "rediscovered" with stunning effect.

Paxton's argument, which influenced the thinking of a new generation of French historians, was that the regime set up by the Germans at Vichy should not be seen simply as a product of France's defeat in war, or as a minority plot imposed by the Germans. It was, rather, a means of taking advantage of the German presence "to carry out major changes in the way Frenchmen were governed, schooled, and employed."[28]

Collaboration, he maintained and documented through meticulous research, was not a "German demand to which some Frenchmen acceded, through sympathy or guile. Collaboration was a French proposal that Hitler ultimately rejected."

France under Vichy, said Paxton, enjoyed an extraordinary range of freedom for a defeated and half-occupied state. In fact, Vichy's first hundred days took place without close, direct German political supervision. Long afterward, German influence remained essentially negative—"vetoing French proposals rather than imposing things." Vichy set up its own concentration-camp system and enacted its own racial laws against Jews without German prodding.

The government created in France may have been illegitimate, as de Gaulle maintained from exile, but it was legal. Even the United States sent an ambassador to the capital of the only legal government of any occupied country.

The Resistance, on the other hand, was the most minuscule of movements, dominated from within by the left after Germany invaded the Soviet Union, and outside the country by de Gaulle, a conservative nationalist. Its numbers were small and its status obscure. "Prominent prewar figures were virtually absent," Paxton wrote. "De Gaulle's recruits came mainly from the outcasts of the new regime and those already overseas."[29] De Gaulle's total support stood at 35,000 until well into 1942.

It was Pétain, not de Gaulle, who was a father figure for the nation, a defender of national virtues, who was going to save France. Pétain was an alluring symbol: the old *maréchal* had stopped the use of French soldiers as cannon fodder in World War I, thereby arresting widespread mutiny in the army. It was Pétain who had won the Battle of Verdun and brought honor and victory to France, albeit at a staggering cost of almost two million Frenchmen dead. The nation wanted a hero, but no more such exhausting and costly encounters. "In the summer of 1940, therefore, Pétain fitted the national mood to perfection: internally, a substitute for politics and a barrier to revolution; externally, a victorious general who would make no more war. Honor plus safety," Paxton observed.[30]

In 1972, Marcel Ophuls, the film director, brought out his four-and-a-half-hour-long film of documents and testimony about the war years. *The Sorrow and the Pity,* which emphasized the fear, the cowardice, and the anti-Semitism of the Vichy period, so shocked French audiences that the film was banned from French television until after Mitterrand came to power in 1981. In 1974, Louis Malle stunned his countrymen by producing a movie called *Lacombe, Lucien,* the story of a young rural French boy who, like thousands of others in the country, joined and fought for the pro-Nazi French militia.

A new generation of writers was also rediscovering the war years in a way that differed significantly from what was known as the *mode rétro,* the fascination during the 1970s with highly stylized caricatures of the occupation years. Young writers like Patrick Modiano reexplored the period with a fresh and candid eye.[31]

These cultural and political events combined to produce an explosive debate about the depth and breadth of the Resistance. They prompted a decade of healthy reevaluation, the beginning of a new, more balanced phase of self-perception.

"We had discovered that there was, in effect, a cadaver in the closet, and it stunk," said historian Pascal Ory, who was born in 1948. "The notion of what the Germans did to us gave way to a far more honest examination of what we had done to ourselves. Our generation, in some ways, killed de Gaulle."

"What my generation learned in schools was what the Germans did to us and made us do," said Bernard-Henri Lévy, a writer. "What we are teaching the next generation is that France had its very own fascism, a fascism in the colors of France—of blue, white and red."

The resurgence of memory was particularly strong among France's 600,000 Jews. This was attributable to some extent to the influx in the 1950s and 1960s of some 250,000 Jews from French-speaking North Africa, who had not experienced the Holocaust directly, but who were a minority determined never again to be pushed out of their homes as they had been in Arab North Africa. They were dynamic; they flourished economically in France; and they had learned as members of a minority in Arab countries how to fend for themselves in an increasingly hostile atmosphere.

Their more assertive self-consciousness conflicted with the traditional French Jewish community's penchant for blending in, for maintaining a low profile. These North African Jews were totally unlike what Marianne Sedar, a French Jewish psychoanalyst, called France's "Dreyfus Jews," a reference to Alfred Dreyfus, the nineteenth-century Jewish army captain who remained devoted to France and to the army despite his conviction and imprisonment on a trumped-up charge of espionage.[32]

Unlike their Ashkenazi counterparts, the new Jewish immigrants had not been living in France for six centuries; they were not grateful for having been the first European Jews to be granted civil rights. They were not content to be "living like a king and a Jew in Strasbourg," according to the old French Jewish adage. Their confident sense of Jewish identity in the 1980s helped prompt a more assertive self-consciousness among the French Jewish community. But many traditionalists were still intent on keeping their heads down and their identity unequivocally and solely "French."

As part of the French culture, the Jewish community partook of the spirit of the late '60s student revolt and the general reexamination of the wartime past that was under way, but de Gaulle's 1969 embargo on the sale of French arms to Israel and their government's increasingly pro-Arab stance intensified their exploration of French anti-Semitism.

In 1978, Jewish memory was jolted by a series of events. First was the public denunciation of the so-called "Holocaust lie" by

Robert Faurisson, a professor of literature at the University of Lyons. In a series of articles and a book published two years later, he denied that the Nazi gas chambers had existed. A year later, Jews, even more than non-Jewish Frenchmen, were deeply affected by the broadcast of the American-produced television miniseries *Holocaust,* which captured the imagination of hundreds of thousands of young West Europeans and garnered one of Europe's largest audiences. In October 1980, small neo-Nazi groups were held responsible for the savage attack on a synagogue on the Rue Copernic, which left four dead. Raymond Barre, who was then Prime Minister, condemned the assault by noting that, in addition to the Jews, "innocent Frenchmen" could have been killed in the attack. Such a slip-of-the-tongue embarrassed the French, for whom the sentiment was hardly shocking but who had learned that the public articulation of it was unacceptable in the post-Holocaust era.

While there is no "Jewish lobby" as such in France, the activism of a relatively few French Jews has affected the population at large. For example, the campaign waged by the Klarsfelds to locate and extradite Klaus Barbie, to document the lives of the little children of Izieu, whom he deported, to improve the quality of what French children are taught about Nazism and French collaboration, and finally to persuade French officials to confront their own complicity in the deportations, all aroused grudging interest in the war years and the Nazi genocide.

After a two-decade-long campaign, Klarsfeld succeeded in 1983 in changing the country's history books. Until then, textbooks had presented the roundups of Jews as a German operation. "And 90 percent of the French would have told you that it was the Nazis who rounded up the Jews," said Klarsfeld. "This was a major element of the real occultation," he said. Today, high school students are being taught that they were conducted by the French. "The textbooks are now impeccable," Klarsfeld said. "But it was one hell of a battle."

There was also street-by-street battle for memory. One of Klarsfeld's goals was to persuade Parisian district officials to erect plaques and monuments to French Jews on the sites of the roundups and of resistance to them. He also pressed to have existing plaques mention that those arrested and deported were mainly Jews.

Klarsfeld and others have had to do battle with the French language itself. There is not a single "Jewish survivor" in France today. In French, they are referred to only as *"déportés,"* those 70,000 anonymous people without faces or religions who were sent by equally anonymous culprits to death camps in the East. About 65,000 of them were Jews; only 6,000 non-Jewish Frenchmen shared the same fate.[33] But in French they are all *déportés*. Language has often served to obfuscate what the French would prefer not to face.

At the same time, Klarsfeld, like many of his Jewish confrères, has been intensely defensive of France's historical record. "One-fourth of the French Jews were deported; but three-quarters were saved. That couldn't have happened without massive help from non-Jews," he asserted.

Marianne Sedar agreed with Klarsfeld. But she maintained that France was, nevertheless, intensely anti-Semitic at the time and, unfortunately, that it remained culturally anti-Semitic, though the sentiment was most often latent.[34] As a young student in Paris during the occupation, she and her mother survived by moving from house to house, hiding from the French police and the Gestapo, eluding the roundups. Like many French survivors, she still kept her "Jewish bag," packed in case she might have to flee again. But now, forty years after the war, her suitcase of essentials is kept in the bedroom closet, not by the door.

"My father was so pleased to be French. He said that our neighbors and friends would protect us," she recalled. "But most did nothing. They said they would pray for us."

She probably owed her life to a school chum who took her in during the *Grande Rafle* of July 16 and 17, 1942, the largest "roundup" of Parisian Jews, in which 8,160 Jews, including 4,992 children, were arrested, held at the city's bicycle stadium for six days, and deported. "Like many of my friends, the guy who hid me was intensely anti-Semitic," Sedar said. "But his anti-Semitism was an abstraction. I was the 'exception' to the rule. Jews were bad, he and the others agreed; but the Jews they knew and liked were exceptions."

Sedar and others argue that although France's deep anti-Semitism remains strong it has simply not been fashionable to express it publicly, and certainly not politically. As in Germany, the modern face of anti-Semitism in France has often been manifested in anti-Zionism. But for the moment, right-wing resentment of Moslem Arabs in France has far surpassed the country's traditional antipathy toward Jews.

This hostility is far stronger than the home-grown traditional anti-Semitism, partly because the arrival of more than two million Arabs is linked in the French psyche with its defeat in Algeria and the loss of its colonial empire. The Jews, at least, had come to France seeking shelter and asylum from places from which France had never been ousted. They had also agreed to play by French rules. This is not the case for the Moslems, who are genuinely "foreign," who now follow France's second largest religion, and many of whom have no desire to be French.

Meanwhile, the 1980s have produced in France, as elsewhere, a spate of historical and cultural works that have continued to catalyze memory. "Our collective memory is a battlefield, a place of combat," said Bernard-Henri Lévy. There have been offenses and retreats, but we're still very much at war over this period."

Foreign historians are still making important contributions to better understanding of the wartime years, which Lévy argues is testimony to the lingering strength of the taboo. In the early 1980s, Zev Sternhell, an Israeli, touched off a furor and a lawsuit in France by asserting in his influential book *Neither Right nor Left: Fascist Ideology in France,* that the penetration of fascism in French society, particularly among intellectuals, was far deeper than historians since the war have recognized.[35]

Herbert R. Lottman, the American historian who had earlier published a biography of Pétain, wrote *The Purge,* a detailed study of the immediate postwar years, which not only documented the Resistance's often savage treatment of collaborators, but also the postwar trials and convictions of many of those who sided with Vichy.

Recently, however, the new generation of French historians, born in the intellectual vortex of the late 1960s, has come into its own. In addition to *Le Syndrome de Vichy, 1944–1948,* by Rousso, who was born in 1954, other recent works have provoked debate. Pascal Ory, for example, has argued that French collaborators were often more bloodthirsty and radical than their German counterparts.[36]

In France, as in other parts of Europe, the passage of time has prompted an outpouring of searing individual accounts of wartime experiences. In one of the most dramatic memoirs, Marguerite

Duras, a prominent French novelist, recalled the crimes and painful ambiguities of the Resistance, of which she was a member. In *The Pain,* she describes her unit's detention just after the Libération of a nondescript middle-aged Frenchman suspected of having worked for the Nazis. Duras was put in charge of interrogating him. When he refused to talk, she ordered her comrades to hit him. Little by little, the slaps turned into brutal torture. The suspect crumpled to the floor, half dead, without acknowledging his alleged crime. The war, Duras demonstrated brilliantly, could turn even brave fighters into sadistic torturers.

Her memoir is important because it challenged a part of France's mythology that was largely untouched during the 1970s assault on memory. While reassessment destroyed the myth that the Resistance was widespread, it did not attack the sacred notion of the Resistance as perfectly noble or glorious.

The resurgence in popularity of Céline, viewed by many as one of the great French writers of the century, has been cited both as evidence that France has confronted its past and as proof that it has not. Although Céline virtually created a new language composed of slang and repetition of simple words, he was also a violent anti-Semite, two of whose most vicious tracts have been banned since the war.

The issue of how Céline should be regarded has divided French intellectuals. Some, Jews in particular, have argued that he should be disregarded and his anti-Semitic polemics censored, while others maintain that France can only confront its past if it is ready to publish and debate his more odious works openly.

The French government seems content to let the intellectuals battle it out and to take action only if a consensus develops.

The Socialist President took some bold steps to prod memory in the early 1980s. President Mitterrand, for example, felt strongly that the Barbie trial would instruct the new generation of France about fascism and its evils. So one of his early actions was to negotiate Barbie's extradition with the newly elected leftist Bolivian government.

The government of "cohabitation," as the French dubbed the dual reign in 1985 and 1986 of Mitterrand as President and Jacques Chirac, of the neo-Gaullist RPR, as Prime Minister and leader of the RPR-dominated Parliament, also acted on occasion.

In 1986, Henri Roques, an obscure retired agronomist, received a doctorate from the University of Nantes after the university panel approved his thesis, which challenged a German's testimony about the existence of death camps. After vociferous protests by the French press, the government's Minister of Education overruled the jury's decision and annulled the degree—an unprecedented move in the thousand years of French academic history.

But revisionists like Faurisson and Roques, though monstrous, are marginal in France. To take action against them required neither courage nor conviction. When either was required, the French government's record has been more ambiguous. Consider the case of the Marenches files. In September 1986, Alexandre de Marenches, the former head of French intelligence, asserted in a book that there were ten tons of largely unexamined archives from the war in the possession of the French security police. Some of the documents purportedly showed that putative Resistance fighters had actually been German agents.

De Marenches argued that the documents should be sealed to prevent the age-old divisions of France from reemerging and weakening the national fabric. France could not afford the shattering of the political consensus that had enabled it to conduct an activist foreign and domestic policy.

A succession of French officials asserted that de Marenches had exaggerated the importance of the documents. The archives did not contain stunning disclosures; they would not shed new light on the unanswered questions of the war, they maintained. The French government announced later that month that the documents were being transferred to the army's historical archives, where they would be examined and processed. Since French law, however, requires that documents pertaining to national security and private individuals be sealed for sixty years, the decision effectively meant that their contents would not be revealed until all the individuals mentioned in them were dead.

The Marenches affair and the Barbie trial aroused the same kind of apprehension in France. Both held the potential for destroying not the myth of a glorious and united France, which the French had long ago discarded, but of a glorious and united Resistance. It is this component of the nation's modern image that many of the French are reluctant to abandon.

In an interview in 1986, President Mitterrand said that it was only "natural" for people to fear such disconcerting disclosures.

But, he added, he did not think that opening the archives posed a risk to the reputation of the Resistance "collectively" or to French unity and consensus. For individuals, he acknowledged, "it could cause difficulty, but it was "a responsibility we must assume."

But President Mitterrand did not do so. Though he had authority to open the archives to scholars and journalists after a preliminary national-security review, he chose not to exercise that power. And in his second term as President, the issue has not been raised again.

There are other signs of lingering political sensitivity about the period. In January 1986, more than a year before the Barbie trial got under way, a television talk show called *Droit de Réponse* broadcast the first televised debate among historians about Pétain's Vichy. For an hour, French viewers of this popular program watched historians, former Resistance members, and Pétainists debate the sources of the nation's old wounds. René Minguet, secretary-general of the Association for the Defense of the Memory of Marshal Pétain," asserted angrily that Pétain hadn't betrayed France. In the beginning, "forty million Frenchmen stood with him," said Minguet. "No one knew what was going on at Auschwitz until it was too late."

"When I was caught and tortured," recounted Serge Combret, a former Resistance member, who glared at Minguet, "the men doing the torturing weren't Hitler's men; they were Pétainists. And the portrait in the room was not that of Hitler. It was the portrait of Pétain."

The response from viewers was overwhelming. "Normally, we get about one hundred letters a day," said Georges Bonopera, one of the program's producers. "After that show, we got between seven and eight thousand. A lot of them were very intense, very violent. And they covered a wide range of subjects and were very divided. It's clear that the program touched off something of a psychodrama for France."

In May of 1986, sensitivity over the history of occupied France was reflected in an angry confrontation in the French National Assembly. The rightist legislature was considering a plan by Chirac to change the election system from proportional representation back to single-member districts. When Interior Minister Pasqua went to the podium to describe the plan, a Socialist heckled him by shouting: "You don't know your history."

Pasqua bridled and replied sarcastically that he might not know his history, but that he was "among those who helped make history while your friends were lying down before the occupiers."

Socialist and Communist legislators stormed out of the Parliament, calling Pasqua a "fascist." Pasqua said later that he had been alluding to the Communists, who found themselves in a difficult situation when the Germans invaded France in 1940 because of the Hitler-Stalin nonaggression pact that was signed the previous year.

But the Socialists insisted that Pasqua was alluding to a vote in a rump National Assembly session on July 10, 1940, when a majority of representatives, including the Socialists, gave dictatorial powers to Pétain's Vichy. Pasqua, the Socialists maintained, was challenging the notion that the left went underground to fight and the right, with the exception of de Gaulle and a few friends, tended to collaborate, or remain safely uncommitted.

President Mitterrand, who prides himself on his interest in and knowledge of French history, has firmly rejected the interpretation of the Vichy government offered by Paxton and the younger generation of French historians. In an interview, he disputed their assertion that Vichy was not simply the by-product of France's defeat in the war but was an activist French effort to use the German presence to carry out major changes in France's governance, education, and values.

Mitterrand characterized Vichy not as a fascist government that had collaborated with the Nazis, but one that was "mushy."

"It was a pathetic power, terribly weak," he said. "It was a regime of petit bourgeois, inspired by the views of the past. It was reactionary, sad, mediocre, and finally guilty, but much more because of cowardice than positive will."

He conceded that there were fascists in the Vichy government. But he added, "The country, the Vichy administration as a whole, Pétain, they were not fascist." Moreover, he maintained, "the French were not very anti-Semitic," and certainly not as anti-Semitic as central Europeans. "Not at all," he said. The anti-Jewish laws of 1940 and 1941 and concentration camps, approved without German prodding, he contended, were a product of a government that "went crazy" in its last years and "completely stuck with the Germans."

Mitterrand maintained that Pétain's fatal error was, as he put it, a lack of "lucidity." "He should never have joined Germany. He should just have been there, administering. He should never have compromised himself with Germany. He did it, and this allowed for the mistaken impression that the French were collaborationist. They had a wait-and-see policy. They were 'for Pétain—no trouble,' which is not very noble," the President asserted. "But there is still a distinction to be made."

For Mitterrand, French support for Vichy was essentially a passive phenomenon, one born of a desire to avoid conflict and a lack of vision that they were being threatened. This view conflicts with that of those who see French support for Vichy as far more activist, and the reforms that were implemented far more popular, especially its anti-Jewish laws. But it is not surprising that although France rewrote its textbooks in 1983 to include more material about French anti-Semitism and the role Frenchmen played in the arrests and deportations of Jews, the history taught in French schools is far closer to President Mitterrand's version than to Paxton's harsher rendition.

Why would Mitterrand, who fought in the Resistance himself under the code name "Morland," be so charitable to Vichy? Perhaps because Mitterrand, above all, remembers how confused and complex the situation was. Mitterrand himself worked briefly for Vichy in the office that dealt with returned prisoners of war. In 1943, he received the *francisque,* Marshal Pétain's personal decoration, although by that time he was already active in the Resistance.[37]

But from a political standpoint, Mitterrand saw de Gaulle's effort at occultation as essential for rebuilding France. It was, as he put it, "the reflex of a chief of state. I think I would have done the same," he said.

This reflex demands that the French President do whatever is necessary for France. If that means deferring painful confrontations with history by keeping the Marenches files sealed, so be it. A deep fear underlies this logic. Will a reckoning with shameful parts of France's war history undermine the country's modern consensus and resolve?

In the case of the Barbie trial, Mitterrand thought it would not. So Barbie, a German, was brought back to France, tried, and convicted. And in general, Mitterrand said, he was persuaded that despite the divisions that have always plagued this country, no matter how deep and irritating and exhausting they may be, "they have not shaken France's capacity to be a strong nation."

"In the end," he said, "the French have proven to be more patriotic than many other peoples. France has existed for a thousand years. That means it probably has a number of reasons to be proud of itself. Otherwise it would have succumbed long ago to dynastic wars, religious wars, foreign wars, and revolutions. However, France has remained France," he said.

"I don't know how the French would react if they found themselves today in a situation similar to the one we lived through," he mused. "I cannot say. But I hope they would remain fiercely partisan of their independence."

Others are not so sure. Pierre Lellouche, a strategic analyst who worked at the government-supported French Institute for International Relations and as an adviser to Jacques Chirac, said that the French do not like to expose the more sordid parts of their past precisely because they fear that the consensus about which they have become so smug could shatter. At the same time, he argued, because France had not fully examined its past, because Gaullist myths continued to prevail, the consensus was, in fact, more fragile than it appeared.

"It's true that France is the only country in Europe without a serious peace movement, that we have our nuclear *force de frappe,* our independence of action, our consensus that France must at times use force to defend its interests, as it did in Chad," Lellouche said.

"But look at what happened when the Americans sought not even our help, just our permission to overfly France, to strike a blow in Libya against terrorism. And look at how the government has negotiated and made deals with terrorists to secure the return of French citizens held in Lebanon.

"We pride ourselves on our independent commitment to freedom and the West, but are our forces in NATO?" he asked rhetorically. "Our *force de frappe* is a nuclear Maginot Line. If this country were really put to a test, would we run for cover just as we did before in Vichy? Would the same old divisions that have been covered up under the carpet reemerge? If you believe that Pétain was right because his actions helped 'save' France, and at least half of the country still believes that, what makes you think that the French would react differently if the country itself were threatened again? This is the danger of not facing one's history and absorbing its lessons."

Some French analysts find hope in current trends among the young. Survey after survey shows that French youth are less ideological, that the historical left-right dichotomy has been breaking down, that they are more willing to confront the past because it is history for them.

This trend was evident in the 1983 survey in *L'Histoire.* On one hand, the survey confirmed that the image of "glorious France, that of General de Gaulle and of the Resistance," has continued to dominate public opinion even forty years after the war.[38] Forty-seven percent, almost half of those polled, identified a picture of General de Gaulle marching down the newly liberated Champs-Élysées as the image that best captured their memory of France's liberation. Sixteen percent chose a photo of an American soldier being cheered by a crowd. And 8 percent—the smallest proportion—cited a well-known photo of a French woman collaborator having her head shaved in punishment.

On the other hand, the survey showed that young people had distinctly different images of the period. Only 28 percent of the French between the ages of eighteen and twenty-four cited the picture of de Gaulle as most evocative of the liberation, compared with the national average of 47 percent. The largest percentage, 29 percent of younger Frenchmen, cited the image of the American soldier.

Similarly, 40 percent of all those interviewed said that "the Americans" had played the determining role in France's liberation; but 34 percent—almost as many—said that the London-based French Resistance or the Maquis, Resistance fighters in France, had been the determining factor. Among those between eighteen and twenty-four years of age, however, only 23 percent attributed the liberation primarily to internal and external French resistance.

The divisions among the French by ideology and age emerge sharply when they are asked whether Pétain should have been acquitted, condemned to life imprisonment, or sentenced to death after the war. Within the general population, 31 percent said that Pétain should have been acquitted; 31 percent said they did not know; 38 percent were in favor of condemnation, 5 percent of whom favored death.

But young Frenchmen were harsher in their judgment. Their responses varied from that of the population at large: 51 percent of those less than twenty-four years old condemned Pétain; only 16 percent would have acquitted him.

"The younger the person, the more conscious he is of the important but relative role played by the Resistance, and the more determinant role played by the Americans in liberating France," concluded Frank and Rousso. "And the more aware he is of the responsibility [for what occurred during the occupation] of Pétain and Vichy."

How had they come to hold these views? Fifty-seven percent of those between the ages of eighteen and twenty-four, as compared with 40 percent of the total population surveyed, cited television as the most important factor in teaching them what they knew about the war years. For the population at large, "family stories" were the second-largest source of information, but for younger Frenchmen it was "school."

The data posed something of a paradox for Frank and Rousso. Given that the views of the young reflected history more accurately than did the memories of their parents and grandparents, the analysts wondered: "Are those who did not live through an event better able to understand it?"

At the same time, French polls have shown a sharp decline in politicization among younger French people. In January 1985, 38 percent of young people questioned were not sure whether the policies of Socialist Prime Minister Laurent Fabius were left or right.[39] An astonishing 27 percent of those surveyed declined to classify themselves on one side or another of the political spectrum. Only 28 percent thought that they had to favor the "struggle against capitalism" to vote for the French left. About half of those polled believed that "justice, generosity, and fraternity," hardly the preserve of any single party, were the all-important factors in determining how they would vote.

"Younger French people are better informed and less ideological," said a young diplomat at the French embassy in Washington. "But they also care less. They are fed up and bored with the old quarrels and divisions within their families and France."

In his own home in France, for example, he said that his grandfather, a relatively wealthy factory owner, had sided with Pétain and Vichy during the war. His father, on the other hand, had supported the Resistance.

"To this day, you cannot have a discussion of the war in my family's home in the country without a scene, without an argument or bitter words," he said. "It gets to be too much after a while. Younger people say: enough of this. For the good of France, we're putting all this behind us. We will present a united face to the world and go on with our lives."

My friend knows as a diplomat that France's effectiveness depends on not being paralyzed by these old quarrels. "We know that the public imagery of the war is false. It is not true that [the French] have not confronted their past. There has just been a tacit agreement not to dwell on the past or the false imagery of it in order to strengthen contemporary resolve," he asserted. "So the mythology, as you would call it, or exaggeration, as we would prefer it to be known, has worked," the diplomat said.

Not all find this trend reassuring. It is not moderation or a yearning for the political center that is growing among the young in France, but indifference, they say.

"The indifference of youth to political issues is widespread," said Bernard-Henri Lévy. "A sense of outrage is missing from daily life," he said in an interview. "They listen to an anti-Semitic conversation that would have been unthinkable only a decade ago without reacting. Anti-Semitism is becoming, for many of them, just another point of view. They don't get excited about it, or about anything else for that matter."

Robert Paxton once noted that while his book on Vichy caused a sensation in 1972, his second book, published in 1981 on Vichy and the Jews, did not make a ripple.[40] "It was never on *Apostrophe* or *Droit de Réponse* or any other of the talk shows," Paxton mused. There was only one printing of the book. Several explanations were possible. Perhaps the French had already absorbed and digested the history of that period between 1972 and his second work. Or perhaps they were not interested in reading another book about Jews (highly unlikely in French literary circles). Or perhaps "they simply no longer cared."

Marcel Ophuls, who recently completed a four-and-a-half-hour-long documentary about the life of Klaus Barbie, said that he feared that the indifference was being translated into "the culture of narcissism, opportunism, and materialism."

"There's a very new self-absorption growing here, a widespread emphasis now on 'making it' in young Europe," he said.

Ophuls saw this trend as a form of escape from the past, from Europe's obsession with its lost empires and great cultures. It was particularly true of France, which has never accepted its postwar status as a relatively powerful, medium-sized country, no longer the superpower of yore.

Alain Finkielkraut also considers indifference the most important new obstacle to memory. "Young people are not interested in what they consider ancient history. Films like those produced by Ophuls and Claude Lanzmann are wonderful educational tools. But how many young French people will rush out to see them?"

Perhaps it would have been better, some argue, if Barbie had been willing or able to name new names, if the trial itself had generated anguish and humiliation, if it had stunned or outraged the nation.

As Barbie lives out his life in jail, the traditional passion that the French bring to life is being slowly replaced by what many fear is the silence of indifference. Not to know is one kind of failure in a society. To know and not to care is another.

The Soviet Union

The hardest thing about being a Communist is trying to predict the past.

—Milovan Djilas, September 1988

On September 1, 1987, at 8 A.M. sharp, Svetlana Assimova started a new school year in Minsk, capital of Byelorussia. Her brown dress and white, lace-edged apron starched and pressed, sandy hair pulled neatly into the ponytail that is obligatory for all young Soviet girls, hands folded tightly in front of her, Svetlana, age thirteen, sat at her newly assigned desk at School 103.

On this morning, her eyes were riveted on a very tiny, very old lady at the front of the class. Tatyana Leonidovna Vasiliu, who admitted to being almost seventy, was wearing a chestful of medals that tinkled like tiny cymbals as she moved. Mrs. Vasiliu was talking to the class about "The War." Despite the loss of more than fourteen thousand Soviet men in Afghanistan, to most Soviet students there is still only one war: that which the West calls World War II, but which is known in the Soviet Union as the Great Patriotic War.

Much of what Mrs. Vasiliu was telling them seemed well known to Svetlana and her seventh-grade classmates. Some were restless and fidgeted as she recounted the horrors of the war in a high-pitched, squeaky voice. But their eyes grew wide when she spoke to them about the 900-day-long siege of Leningrad. She had been a nurse there. She had seen hundreds of children their age die of hunger. "We had only 125 grams of bread to eat for the whole day and much of that was mixed with sawdust to fill us up.

"You can't imagine the silence of Leningrad then," she said, "the silence of a city that is so deathly quiet because all the birds and cats and dogs, and things that make sounds have been eaten. We even ate rats, if we could find them.

"You don't even think today what's been given to you," she continued, as the children began squirming in their seats once again. "Your school is free; your books are free; you will all have jobs. The party will do its share to ensure your happiness. But you must decide what to do with your life. You must work for certain goals. And you must always remember that nothing is as dear to life as your Motherland."

Mrs. Vasiliu's recitation of her own wartime experiences is a ritual known in the Soviet Union as the "peace lesson." The lesson, of course, was about war, for when Soviets talk about peace, the thought or memory of war is never far away.

In every school throughout the vast Soviet Union—in Minsk, where I attended class that morning; in Kiev; in the Ukraine; in Moscow; in Tashkent; in Vladivostok on the Sea of Japan, a ten-hour time zone away from the Soviet Union's western border—Soviet students everywhere listen to such lessons as the first order of business of the first day of class of every school year.

In no European nation is the war as omnipresent as it is in the Soviet Union. In no other country are memories of it so vivid, or so carefully nurtured. And in no other country in Europe is it so indispensable to the state and its official ideology.

Mrs. Vasiliu's lecture in the Minsk school reflected what every Soviet adult knows and every Soviet student is taught: if you want to understand the potential of this society, look at the war. For Mrs. Vasiliu, and for millions of other Soviets, the war was the most important event in their lives. There was no mistaking her passion. But her presentation was curious in at least one respect. In her moving account of her country's suffering and ultimate triumph, she never mentioned the Holocaust.

The omission was no accident. In the West, the historical record is clear. Nazi storm troopers began mass extermination by gassing the Polish Jews living in territory that the Soviet Union and Germany had divided between them during the Hitler-Stalin Pact of 1939 and which the Germans invaded and occupied two years later. The overwhelming majority of the two million Polish Jews living in those territories had been killed by the war's end. But although the Nazis implemented the first stage of the Final Solution on this territory, and though more than 700,000 of the 3 million Soviet Jews were ultimately killed, the Soviet Union does not recognize the Holocaust as a unique, historically distinct event.[1] It does not teach its people about it in any detail. It does not officially acknowledge the disproportionate suffering or heroism of Soviet Jews during the war. And the Russian language has no accepted term for genocide against the Jews, no equivalent to the English word "Holocaust," or in Hebrew "*Shoah*."[2]

The reasons for the denial are complex. But they cannot be understood without first appreciating the centrality of World War II in Soviet history. To the Soviets the Great Patriotic War is not just another conflict in their unending struggles against internal and external enemies. The Soviet Union was forged as a nation by a thousand years of battles with neighbors and other adversaries—Tatars, Mongols, French, Poles, Germans. But the Great Patriotic War has been a fundamental touchstone of the postrevolutionary state.

While the 1917 Bolshevik Revolution sought to tear the Soviet Union out of its tsarist structure and traditions, it was the Great Patriotic War that created the modern Soviet state and cemented the more than 195 nationalities into a new Soviet empire. It was the fight against Hitler's fascism that temporarily obscured the memory of Stalin's horrific purges, the ruthless collectivizations, and state-induced famines in which millions of people died.[3]

It was the Soviet Union's struggle to survive and, ultimately, its victory in World War II, that not only unified and motivated many in this divided, strife-torn country, but more important, which vindicated and legitimized the system of government for which Lenin had laid the groundwork and which Stalin then elaborated into a dictatorship of almost unrelenting state terror. Stalin, "the great leader," had won the war. Though he singled out the "Russian people" for valor in his victory address, the Soviet peoples had fought and triumphed. Despite the vast number of real and imagined collaborators with the Nazis in the western republics closest to Germany, most Uzbeks, Ukrainians, Byelorussians, Armenians, and Jews had proven themselves loyal Soviet citizens in the struggle for their country. The Soviet Union had survived, barely, and at a harrowing price—an officially recognized cost of 20 to 25 million Soviet citizens and 10 million more wounded, 25 million made homeless, and one-third of the national wealth destroyed.[4]

"It was the moment of our greatest humiliation, but also of our greatest triumph," said Roy Medvedev, the Soviet historian whose work is finally being published inside the USSR. "The war remains more important than the 1917 revolution that created the Soviet state, than the civil war which followed its birth, than even the terror of Stalin's purges. It was truly the moment in which the Soviet Union came together as one nation, for the first time no longer divided, thrust together in a desperation that overcame the years of division and repression to save our country, everyone's country, to save our dream."[5]

The Great Patriotic War, said Medvedev, more than any other single event, helped shape the national psyche of the twentieth-century nation-state. The Soviet Union emerged from the war a destitute wreck, but amid the debris of war were the beginnings of the awesome modern Soviet empire, more than twice as large as the United States, with 40 percent more people.

The war is still spoken about in hushed, almost religious terms; the cult of the war is virtually a secular religion that has replaced Russian Orthodoxy as the country's moral framework for many Soviets.[6] And the victory is portrayed as an ordeal in which goodness and justice—embodied in the Soviet state—triumphed over almost unimaginable adversity and evil—the implacable fascist enemy. And given America's late entry into the war, the Soviets did so virtually single-handedly.[7]

The cost was almost unimaginable in Western terms. One need only compare the official casualty statistics: Germany lost 3.8 milion with 780,000 seriously wounded; Italy, 77,500; the United Kingdom, 311,100 with 86,000 seriously wounded; the United States, which entered only in 1942, lost 292,000 with 670,000 wounded.[8] In sum, Soviet losses were 40 times those of Britain, 70 times those of the United States. And these are only the official figures, which most Western and some Soviet historians believe underestimate the Soviet Union's actual losses.[9]

As a result, war memorials are everywhere. In every Soviet city, village, and hamlet, in virtually every large office, there is at least one memorial to the Great Patriotic War.

Virtually all Soviets, whatever their race, religion, nationality, or political coloration, even dissidents and refuseniks, agree that it is difficult to overestimate the importance of the war to the national psyche. "You are born, your parents bundle you up and take you to a war memorial," said Jewish dissident Nathan, né Anatoly, Sharansky, in an interview shortly after he immigrated to Israel.[10] "When you're in school, you are taken to the eternal flame honoring the tomb of the unknown soldier in Moscow. In spring, there are trips to war memorials in other parts of the Soviet Union. Immediately after you get married, you go lay a wreath near the eternal flame at your local war memorial or cemetery. It is impossible to separate memories of the war from modern Soviet life. The war is too essential."

More than forty years after its end, the war has remained a major intellectual theme of Soviet society. The United States Library of Congress contains roughly 7,800 books in the English language about World War II. The Soviet Union has published roughly 20,000.[11]

Just as there is a "correct" line in Soviet politics, there is a "correct" view of history, and hence of war history in particular. Deviations from the political line of the moment are bad enough, but because the war is a cornerstone of Soviet national consciousness, deviations from the country's official line on the war are tantamount to historical heresy, political sacrilege.

But since Mikhail S. Gorbachev has come to power, the Soviet Union has been embroiled in a dramatic, turbulent debate over precisely this pivotal event and other critical moments in its official past. The Soviet press and academic journals have been filled with articles reassessing key events and individuals connected with the war. Newspapers and literary journals have carried articles containing information that would never have been published before and which are still derided by many conservatives.

Stalin's image as the victorious military "genius," as he called himself, has been decimated by a barrage of savage attacks in plays, films, and the increasingly assertive, but still state-controlled, press. Critics have accused him of grievous mistakes born of paranoia—such as murdering most of the senior Soviet officer corps in purges before the war, an action that Soviet officials now blame for having doubled the country's losses.

Gorbachev has personally ordered the construction of a memorial to the victims of Stalin's purges. Nikolai Bukharin, the celebrated Communist leader executed by Stalin in the 1930s, has been rehabilitated, and even Trotsky is no longer the traitor and spy that Stalin made him out to be.[12] The years in which Leonid I. Brezhnev ruled have become known as the "era of stagnation"; his son-in-law was put on trial and convicted of corruption in the fall of 1988.

In August 1988, Viktor R. Yashchenko, the country's chief map-maker, acknowledged to the government newspaper *Izvestia* that even the country's official geography was fiction. For the past fifty years, Soviet cartographers had routinely falsified Soviet maps on orders from the secret police, relocating cities, rivers, and streets to confuse a putative enemy.

By the end of 1988, an unprecedented debate had erupted in the Soviet press and professional historical forums over the justification for the 1939 Hitler-Stalin Pact, the agreement in which the Soviet Union and Nazi Germany divided Eastern Europe between them, a source of shame for modern Soviets.

And in the spring of 1988, Soviet authorities withdrew all history textbooks and canceled history examinations in secondary schools, unsure of which questions about the war could be asked and what constituted correct answers.

Even more startling, the Soviet Union has begun taking tentative steps toward including the Holocaust in the realm of historical reassessment. In July 1988, archivists from the United States and the Soviet Union signed a historic agreement granting Western scholars access for the first time to Soviet archives relating to Nazi occupation and the Holocaust. Raul Hilberg, the prominent Holocaust historian, and other members of the delegation representing the U.S. Archives and the U.S. Holocaust Council, were shown a sampling of documents from the archives in Moscow, two republics, and one region. They were given not only German documents, but also some local Ukrainian, Lithuanian, and Latvian police records describing in detail the degree and nature of cooperation with the Nazi occupiers. Such documents had never been seen before by American scholars, said Sybil Milton, a member of the delegation and a research curator at the United States Holocaust Memorial Museum in Washington.[13]

Gorbachev's reassessment is not the first. A fictitious historian in a 1960s play by Edward Radzinsky, quoted in Geoffrey Hosking's *A History of the Soviet Union,* reflects the confusion and timidity of many Soviet intellectuals prompted by previous bouts of historical reassessment. "My first work was about Shamil," Radzinsky's character said. "Shamil was the leader of a national liberation movement. But views changed . . . and at the end of the 1930s, he began to be considered an agent of imperialism. So I confessed my mistake. Then, during the war, he became the head of a liberation movement again. So I confessed that I had made a mistake in confessing my mistake. Later, in 1949, he once again became an agent, so I confessed that I had . . . well, you see how it was. I had been mistaken so often that I began to think I was just one great big mistake."[14]

Mikhail Geller and Alexander Nekrich, in their pioneering work on Soviet society, concluded long before *glasnost* and *perestroika* that the rewriting of Soviet history has been such a persistent feature of Soviet intellectual life as to constitute a virtual "nationalization of memory."[15]

Gorbachev's critics do not believe that his campaign has been aimed at "denationalizing" memory. The best that can be hoped for in the current round of revisionism, they say, is that the gap between what is widely known and what is officially said may be substantially narrowed.

Moreover, this latest round of historical reassessment, like previous episodes, was not the result of grassroots pressure, nor was it even favored by the public at large. In this sense, it differs fundamentally from the debates in the democracies of Western and even Eastern Europe, where events, such as the Klaus Barbie trial in France, Kurt Waldheim's election in Austria, and the upheavals in Warsaw and other cities, have prompted bitter eruptions of long-suppressed memories of the war and, to some extent, a voluntary reexamination of those years.

The battle for memory in the Soviet Union, by contrast, has been mostly official. It has been dictated from above. And that is its ultimate paradox and, some maintain, its key weakness. Because the latest reexamination of history has been promoted by Gorbachev for political purposes, its continuation depends largely on the political survival of this man and his cadre.

While many in the West remain cautious, many Soviet intellectuals have rallied around the reassessment. They maintain that it reflects long-standing Russian tradition. Since tsarist times, all change has come from the top. Therefore, the reopening of pages of history and the opening of the society in general should not be denigrated simply because Soviet leaders initiated it. In an authoritarian, traditionalist system, how else could the process have begun?[16]

For supporters, the only critical issue is whether it will continue. How many "white spots," as Soviets call the black holes in Russian history, will wind up being confronted? How much historical truth will be acknowledged and revealed?

Many historians and intellectuals have argued that while Khrushchev's attack on Stalin in 1956 was more pointed, nothing on the scale of the current changes and reassessment has occurred before in the modern Soviet state. They have portrayed the historical debate not only as a reflection of an even deeper Soviet struggle to overcome the deadening legacy of the country's authoritarian past, but also as an indispensable precursor to the Soviet Union's effort to change its political and economic policies.

"For forty years the war has legitimized the government of a state that can't even feed itself," said one Western diplomat. "The war, the suffering, the horrors they endured have been drilled into them to get them to accept the sacrifices they have been making ever since: the lines, the shortages, the repression. The economic and political sacrifices are always justified by leaders who say—if there is another war, next time we will be ready."

Therefore, by confronting and debunking some of the most-cherished myths about the war, the current leadership risks undermining its own legitimacy. In this sense, the effort by Gorbachev, the first Soviet leader who was too young to fight in the war, to de-Stalinize the country intellectually and economically has been truly bold, or as skeptics say, foolhardy.

Glasnost intellectuals maintained, often in disturbingly identical language, that Gorbachev's campaign to reexamine history, Russia's war experience under Stalin in particular, was crucial to his ambitious goal of restructuring the Communist Party and his country. "A succession of Russian leaders have tried to rewrite history, but this is different," asserted Medvedev, once among the staunchest critics of a succession of Soviet regimes, but now officially in favor. "Now we're determined not just to lay down a new correct line of history. We're trying to seek the truth."

Russian intellectuals and reformers are captivated by the momentous struggle. They have been euphoric about the battle against their country's authoritarian tradition, the groping toward alien concepts like free speech and a free press, elected officials and true civil rights and liberties, and the search for what Soviet analysts call a "normal" society. They might fail; they know that. But at least in its initial stages, the officially blessed reexamination of history in the USSR has generated more excitement, drama, and vibrancy than have any of the freewheeling, but desultory, sometimes bitter debates taking place in the democracies of Western Europe.

Such enthusiasm is especially curious because it continues to be shadowed by the subliminal cynicism and wariness bred of decades of quashed hopes and repression, and because it is not shared by the masses, the *narod* in whose name the reassessment is being conducted. The people have greeted the new campaign with intense skepticism and a slightly hostile indifference. However repressive and inefficient, the Soviet Union's eighteen-million-strong bureaucracy managed to meet their basic needs in previous regimes with little or no initiative on their part. Yes, there have been endless lines; but for forty years there has also been a free lunch.

In my visits to Moscow, I quickly sensed the exhilaration, the fervor of *perestroika,* but only more slowly the disquiet resulting from the officially sponsored debate. Underlying the euphoria was a grim reality, which, like the KGB itself, never quite left me. It was the realization that this period, this excitement, was a luxury due to an accident, or in Marxian terms, a product of history called Gorbachev. The discussions could stop or, more precisely, be stopped at any moment. *Glasnost* existed by the grace of Gorbachev. It was not widely seen as something necessarily desirable and essential for a vibrant society.[17]

While the United States takes pride in its ability to integrate peoples from more than one hundred nations in one vast melting pot, that concept has been anathema to many in the Soviet Union. And this has served to complicate the already complex status of Soviet Jews.

From the revolution on, Soviet governments have grappled with the problem of how to subdue, co-opt, and control the more than one hundred distinct nationalities that now comprise the Soviet empire—only twenty-two of which have more than a million people, but each of which boasts a separate language, culture, and historical memory.[18]

Gorbachev has removed the nationalities question from the list of banned political subjects. The reform program encouraged demands for greater autonomy and independence from Moscow by the Baltic states, Armenia, and even Georgia, Stalin's native republic.

Until the 1988 conflict over the territory of Nagorno-Karabakh between Armenia and Azerbaijan and the mass protests in the Baltics, no nationality had proven as problematic for the Soviet government as the country's nearly two million Jews. Russian anti-Semitism has run so deep, for so long, and antipathy to Jews has been so widespread that Jews have been the country's traditional scapegoats, the brunt of jokes in good times and vicious pogroms in the bad. Resented by officials in Moscow, they have been discriminated against in most of the country's republics.

But, above all, Jews have been robbed of a major component of their identity by the Soviet Union's unwillingness to acknowledge that, apart from the Nazi war against the USSR, the Germans and their collaborators waged a genocidal campaign against the Jews that nearly resulted in their extermination in Europe. With rare exceptions, Jews have been all but written out of Soviet versions of the Great Patriotic War.

The official Soviet version of the war barely mentions the Nazi genocide inflicted on Europe's Jews. Six million were relatively few, they say, when compared with the twenty million Soviet war dead. Since the war, Soviet officials and citizens have been deeply resentful of what they have described as an effort by Jews to monopolize wartime suffering. As a result, the Soviet government has conducted what many Western analysts regard as a calculated campaign to erase a Jewish past.

Not a single book devoted to anti-Semitism has been published officially in the USSR in more than fifty years, William Korey, an expert on Soviet Jewish history, wrote recently.[19] The famous *Black Book,* in which Soviet writers Vasily Grossman and Ilya Ehrenburg meticulously documented the struggles of Soviet Jews against the Nazis, and their fate, has been suppressed in the Soviet Union for more than forty years. The silence surrounding the destruction of Europe's Jews was broken before Gorbachev on rare occasions in the '50s and '60s, first when *The Diary of Anne Frank* was published in Russian translation, and later when a similar story appeared about the life of a young girl in the Vilna ghetto.

Because knowledge of the Holocaust is absent from Soviet life,

Soviet citizens have by and large been unable to appreciate the significance of the creation of the state of Israel, or the special relationship that Soviet Jews and other Jews have with the Jewish state. While knowledge of the Holocaust might not make Soviets more sympathetic to Israel or to the country's Jews, the lack of information has heightened non-Jewish resentment of the Jewish emigration movement. "What they know about Soviet Jews is that here are a group of people who do fairly well by Soviet standards, who tend to be highly educated and have good jobs, who want to desert their country," said Celestine Bohlen, former Moscow correspondent for *The Washington Post.*[20]

Without an awareness of the Holocaust, Soviet Jewish demands for immigration to Israel have served to fuel Russian anti-Semitism and the xenophobia that is the hallmark of Pamyat and other right-wing, nationalist groups. The resentment many Soviets feel toward the country's Jews has been exacerbated by the campaigns of American Jewish groups to "free Soviet Jewry," which for many years concentrated almost exclusively on emigration, rather than on securing greater religious and national rights for Soviet Jews.

The plight of Soviet Jews is particularly bitter because so many Jews played pivotal roles in the Bolshevik Revolution and its early leadership. Although a succession of Soviet leaders ultimately adopted Lenin's vision that the only answer to the Jewish problem was assimilation, Jews had long flocked to the revolutionary movement. Badly treated by most of the tsarist governments, they were disproportionately represented in the revolution's senior ranks: Trotsky, Zinoviev, Kamenev, Sverdlov, Radek, to name but a few.

From the early stages of the revolution, the Soviet government regarded the Jews not as a religious group, but as a nationality, one ostensibly equal to all others. But even in the beginning there were restrictions. Hebrew, the Jews' religious language, was banned, and Yiddish, spoken by many Jews in Russia, was designated their national tongue. And unlike most other nationalities, Jews had no territorial homeland of their own inside the USSR.

In May 1934, the government declared the area of Birobidzhan, a swampy, mosquito-infested area in southeastern Siberia on the Manchurian border, a "national Jewish unit, administratively and territorially." It was designated an "autonomous region," rather than the more important designation of an "autonomous republic." Few Jews lived in Birobidzhan, an agricultural area, and fewer still wanted to go to this wretched region to build a homeland. The designation of Birobidzhan as a Jewish national unit ultimately became yet another way of trying to push this activist minority, geographically and symbolically, out of the mainstream of Soviet life. Stalinist purges in 1936–37 and in 1948–49 twice put an end to what had been short periods of immigration of Jews and the development of an autonomous Jewish life and culture there.[21]

The resistance to giving Jews greater national rights has been not only unreasonable but often counterproductive. Unlike Ukrainians and Byelorussians, Soviet Jews are relatively few in number; they pose no threat to the Soviet empire. But unlike most other nationalities, they can claim a potential homeland outside the USSR —Israel. And although the Soviet Union voted in favor of the creation of the Israeli state in the United Nations, anti-Jewish measures increased markedly as concerns about a relationship between Soviet Jews and the fledgling Jewish state blossomed.

While the enormity of Soviet losses might explain the government's resistance to acknowledging a higher status as "victims" for any single ethnic group, its resistance to honoring the disproportionate Jewish heroism in the war is inexplicable, except through anti-Semitism. Though Soviet Jews constituted the eleventh-largest nationality, they were the third most highly decorated minority in the Great Patriotic War. But there is not yet a single official memorial in the country dedicated exclusively to that heroism, or to their suffering.

There have been signs, however, that even this is changing. Eager to remove the issue of treatment of Jews from the East-West bargaining table and to enhance the Soviet role in the Mideast by improving relations with Israel, Gorbachev seems to have adopted a three-pronged policy toward his nation's Jews. First, he has substantially increased emigration for Jews who wish to leave. Second, he has facilitated assimilation for those who wish to stay by permitting children of mixed marriages to identify themselves officially as non-Jews. Third and most internally problematic, he has taken steps to make life easier for Jews who wish to remain and to identify themselves as Jews by nationality and by practicing their religion.

In January 1988, American opera star Regina Resnik and her husband told *The New York Times* that the Lithuanian authorities had granted them permission to finance the construction of a Holocaust memorial in the capital in honor of Lithuania's murdered Jews. Moscow did not object, they said. It would be the first such official memorial in the country.

In late 1988, Edgar M. Bronfman, chairman of the World Jewish Congress, announced that Moscow had agreed to permit Hebrew to be taught in synagogues. In January 1989, Adolf Shayevitch, the officially appointed rabbi of the Moscow synagogue, stated in a letter to the WJC that he had resigned from the Anti-Zionist Committee, which had operated since 1983 as a vehicle for criticizing Israel and spreading anti-Semitic propaganda. The group, he disclosed, would be dismantled by the year's end, but that did not occur.[22]

That same month, Moscow Radio announced the formal rehabilitation of several members of the Anti-Fascist Committee who were arrested in 1948 and killed after mock trials four years later. The Anti-Fascist Committee had been founded by some of the Soviet Union's most prominent Jewish intellectuals and cultural figures during the Great Patriotic War to rally support in the West for their country. The broadcast called the allegations of "state crimes and spying" for which they were imprisoned or killed in the late '40s and early '50s "groundless" and "fabricated," and concluded that the charges had been used "as the pretext for repressive measures."[23]

In February 1989, the country's first officially sanctioned Jewish cultural center opened its doors. The new center was named for Solomon Mikhoels, the chairman of the Anti-Fascist Committee, the country's most prominent Yiddish actor, and a leading cultural figure, who was killed in the Stalinist purges of 1948. The center represented a "historic softening of Soviet policy towards its Jewish minority," said Bronfman. Even more extraordinary, its inauguration featured a poster exhibit on the Holocaust. The exhibition of posters and pictures of Holocaust artifacts and history, donated by the Simon Wiesenthal Center of Los Angeles, was the first officially sanctioned exhibition devoted exclusively to that topic.

Despite these steps, many Jews in the Soviet Union and Western analysts have remained skeptical about whether the Jews and Judaism will thrive here. Will the center be permitted to operate without official resistance? Will Jews no longer be harassed? Has Soviet unwillingness to make any form of "honorable mention" for Jewish suffering and heroism come to an end? Will the Holocaust become part of Soviet orthodoxy?

The concern is well grounded. Resistance to the more relaxed official attitude toward Jews and other Gorbachev policies remains strong, and not merely among rightists.

"Gypsies and Slavs were also singled out for extinction," asserted Georgi Arbatov, director of the United States and Canada Institute, a Soviet official whose father was a highly assimilated Russian Jew.[24] "We lost twenty million people during the war, some of whom were Jews. So why divide the dead? Why make people think that the Jews, they really are different, entitled to special or different treatment? To do so would be counterproductive. It would prompt even greater anti-Semitism here."[25]

During my visits, I met Jews who have struggled tenaciously to overcome anti-Semitism and other barriers. Official discrimination led some Jews to emigrate, others to stay and use Gorbachev's historical reassessment of the war years to press harder for individual human rights, for recognition of Jewish identity and a Jewish past—of their suffering and heroism.

There were also courageous non-Jewish writers, artists, academics, and intellectuals who saw the fate of the Jews and of other national minorities as part of their own struggle for *glasnost* and *perestroika*, a key to building a more pluralistic, more humane, more democratic society.

These unsung warriors—Jew and gentile alike—live in Moscow, in Minsk, in Leningrad, in Kiev, in the Baltics, and in other far-flung cities of the Soviet Union. The success or failure of their efforts can be seen as an important barometer of what Gorbachev's reassessment and the reform program have been able to accomplish and what remains undone. Here are some of the stories of these people, and these places.

Perhaps no other region of the Soviet Union suffered under German occupation as much as Byelorussia, the country's fourth most populous republic, situated in northwestern Russia, the European part of the country. According to official statistics, one out of every four inhabitants—2.2 million non-Jews and virtually the entire Minsk ghetto of 80,000—died during the war. The massacres and destruction were such that the region did not regain its prewar population of 10 million until 1979. Officials said there are more than 6,500 war memorials in Byelorussia alone.[26]

Drawn by the enormity of this devastation, I traveled to Minsk with Bill Keller, of the Moscow bureau of *The New York Times.* The capital of the region, Minsk is one of the thirteen officially designated "hero" cities because of its suffering and valor during the war.

My spirits sank as Nonna Tovmasyan, our enthusiastic thirty-eight-year-old Intourist guide, drove with us from the airport past endless rows of monotonous housing blocks, the same blocks that ring the outskirts of Moscow and which form the vast majority of the housing here. The Russians have dubbed these structures "Khrushchevyiya," officially a reference to their mass construction under Khrushchev, but also a pun in Russian meaning "slums."

Indeed, the designation "hero city" meant that almost nothing was left of prewar Minsk except a few carefully preserved houses and cottages that were occupied mostly by artists and older Soviets, who do not miss the amenities of apartment life.

Minsk dates its origins to 1067, old even by Russian standards. But the oldest remaining structure was a Russian Orthodox church, built in 1609. The city, it turned out, was not entirely flattened during the war: only 82 percent of it—the opera and ballet house, 47 schools, 24 kindergartens, 3 hospitals, and the Palace of Young Pioneers. In Minsk alone, some 200,000 were killed.

The old city along the river was gone. The city itself sprawls in determined drabness eastward. Boasting 1.6 million inhabitants, postwar Minsk was planned to accommodate a maximum of 2 million residents. But the region has been growing more rapidly than envisaged and attracting not only Byelorussians from small villages and towns but also Russians and minorities from other regions.

The Byelorussian capital, it turned out, was filled with young men and women burning with *glasnost* and *perestroika.* Life was good in Minsk, young party officials said. All things were possible under *perestroika* and *glasnost.* The city was blossoming economically and the region presented young Byelorussians with a wide range of cultural, intellectual, and entrepreneurial opportunities. Their enthusiasm did much to obliterate the dreariness of our physical surroundings.

But as soon as we turned to the reason for my visit—the Great Patriotic War—the spirit of optimism dissipated. Once again we were reminded of this society's rigidities—of what could and could not as yet be changed. In Minsk, as elsewhere, rigidity, or ideological bedrock, was usually connected to some aspect of the war; it mirrored the Soviet Union's reluctance to confront a past that did not suit its official self-image. What we found in Minsk also reflected much about the depth of lingering anti-Semitism in this region and about the Soviet Union's insistence on having its history its own way.

Our lesson began at the Minsk Museum of the Great Patriotic War, one of the city's most cherished institutions, the oldest war museum in Russia, said Genady Barkun, its deputy director. The museum's first home was inaugurated in November 1945, six months after the war ended. Its new, more spacious three-story quarters opened in January 1965. Since then, it had received more than 11 million visitors. The Minsk war museum is by far the region's largest, but more than 57 million people had toured its five branches, scattered throughout Byelorussia.

"If you live in this area, you feel very close to the war," said Dr. Barkun, who was born and raised in a village near Minsk. "Remembering the war is not an effort here. It's natural, indeed unavoidable, given what happened here."

The museum consists of thirty rooms full of war memorabilia, truly chambers of horror. There were pieces of the jackets worn by the first Byelorussian soldiers who had faced the 5.5 million Germans who crossed the border at 4 A.M. on June 4, 1941, when Germany declared war against Russia. There were posters, photos, canteens, parts of the engine of a plane commanded by a pilot who was killed flying his aircraft into a German tank division after he ran out of ammunition. There were mockups of what the Russians called "concentration camps" in which thousands of Byelorussians had died.

Bill and I were deeply impressed by the place, by the devotion of people who worked there. But all of these testaments could not equal the emotional power of a sequence of photographs on display over the entrance to one of the main galleries of the museum.

The girl in the first photo was young, barely a woman. She had light wavy hair and a firm expression that showed no trace of fear. She and two male companions were being led through the streets of Minsk by S.S. soldiers. Around her neck was a large sign in German and Russian: "WE ARE PARTISANS AND HAVE SHOT AT GERMAN SOLDIERS." The date is October 26, 1941.

In the second photograph, a German soldier, without expression, was fastening a rope around her neck.

In the next, the rope was taut and her face contorted in the agony of someone who in a moment would be dead.

Of all the exhibits in the museum, there was no more dramatic reflection of the efficient savagery of the German occupation, and the heroism of those who died fighting it, than this sequence of enlarged black-and-white photographs.

"These are pictures of the first partisans ever to have been publicly executed on Soviet territory by the Fascist German occupation," said Nonna, who guided us through the museum. She had seen the photos dozens of times, she said; they never failed to move her. "The first partisan killed was a woman," she noted proudly.

The two men were identified soon after the war as Kirill Trus and Volodya Sherbatseyvich, partisans of Byelorussian origin. But the girl has remained officially *nyeizvestnaya*—"unknown."

Since they were found more than twenty years ago, the pictures have been widely reproduced in Soviet textbooks, in the state encyclopedia, in film documentaries, and in museums like this one in Minsk. Literally millions of visitors to the Minsk Museum have gazed in stunned silence at the images.

But one citizen of Minsk could not bring himself to look at those photographs. Zahir I. Azgur, prominent sculptor, a "Distinguished Artist" of the Soviet Union, delegate to the Supreme Soviet of Byelorussia (the Byelorussian legislature), chairman of the regional "Peace Fund," and member of several official committees, had not visited the war museum for years. Because to him the heroine was not unknown.

Her name was Masha Bruskina, he told Bill and me. She was his niece.

"I cannot bear to go there. I'm afraid to meet with Mashinka," he said, shifting away eyes that have seen much in his eighty years. "In the museum she is anonymous, a person without a name, without relatives—including me."

Azgur was not alone in asserting that the unknown heroine was not unkown. In investigations conducted by journalists in Moscow and in Minsk, more than two decades ago, more than twenty people—including Masha's father, her school principal, and classmates at Middle School No. 28, most of whom have since died or, like Azgur, were very old—identified the unknown heroine as Masha Bruskina.

So why was this heroine still officially unidentified?

"Stupidity and meanness of the local Byelorussian bureaucrats, who don't like people from Moscow telling them what to do," said Ada Dikhtyar, a Moscow journalist who helped uncover the heroine's identity in 1968.

Officials in Minsk, by contrast, insisted that the evidence was not conclusive. "The experts have said that there is no absolute certainty that the girl was Masha Bruskina," asserted Barkun of the Minsk war museum. "Many people claimed at the time that the girl was their relative. They produced pictures of their daughters and cousins and friends, which also resembled the partisan. To make a mistake would not only be unscientific and unjust to history, but it would offend others who believe that she is their kin."

Lev Ovsishcher, a Jewish war hero who immigrated to Israel in 1988, had an alternative explanation. Masha Bruskina has not been officially recognized because she, like her uncle Azgur, was a Jew.

"The men who hanged with her were Byelorussians. They were identified almost immediately," Ovsishcher said.

"The KGB in Minsk know who betrayed her, who led the operation to capture her. They know the names of those who arrested them and who put the rope around her neck. The three of them fought together; they died together. How could they not know who she is?"

Ada Dikhtyar also admitted to being disheartened. An attractive woman in her fifties who bears an uncanny resemblance to the young heroine she investigated, Dikhtyar greeted us in her apartment in Moscow, overlooking the Moskva River.

Under Gorbachev, she said, she could talk about the evidence openly, without any apparent hint of fear. But Mrs. Dikhtyar's dogged pursuit of the truth spoke volumes not only about the determination of Soviet intellectuals like her, but also about the Soviet Union's disdain for unofficial truth.

After a fellow journalist who worked on the case with her published their findings in 1968 in *Trud*, the official trade-union newspaper, he lost his job. The author of a similar article published in the local paper in Minsk, also in 1968, was chastised for his journalistic shortcomings and also dismissed. After her broadcast about Masha Bruskina was aired in 1970, officials accused Ada Dikhtyar of having failed to clear her broadcast with local party officials; she was told she would not broadcast on the radio again. But she refused to stop.

Her involvement with the story began in 1968 when Lev Arkadyev, a friend and screenwriter working on a film about the war, told her about the photographs he had seen in the Minsk Museum. He was puzzled by the dead girl's anonymity and resolved to identify her.

At the time Mrs. Dikhtyar was a reporter for the Soviet Youth radio station, Yunost. Captivated by the memory of the photos, she readily agreed to help.

"I, too, had seen a photo of the girl in a school textbook," she said. "I didn't dwell on it, but somehow that picture stuck with me.

"Besides," she said, "we considered our project very patriotic. We raise our children here from kindergarten through college on the Second World War. Schoolchildren visit and send postcards to war veterans as class projects. They buy food for disabled veterans and perform other services to help them. The Young Pioneers, our scouts, frequently 'adopt' heroes and heroines of the war as their mascots. They collect information about their lives and study their heroic deeds.

"Sometimes they try to track down people missing in the war, or try to discover how certain individuals or groups of partisans died. It's almost a national pastime: filling in the blank spots in our war history.

"Having them do these things is much better than simply telling children about the war," she asserted. "It's a way of exposing them to the consequences of war, of enabling them to share in the suffering. It humanizes children."

So she and Lev began their work expecting that they would be supported wholeheartedly by Moscow and Byelorussian authorities.

"When we began," she said, "neither of us considered the heroine's nationality important. To us, it was all the same if she was a Byelorussian, a Ukrainian, or a Jew. Why would that matter, we thought? There were many Jewish heroes of the war. Even the secretary of the Byelorussian underground party during the war was a Jew."

So they contacted local officials in Minsk. "We couldn't understand it at the time," she said, "but from the outset they refused to cooperate."

Why were reporters from Moscow prying into Byelorussian affairs? they were asked. What did they hope to prove? Did they believe that Communist party officials in Byelorussia were hiding something? Who had authorized this investigation anyway?

Virtually all their requests for information or access to official archives were denied or ignored. The KGB in Minsk, for example, even refused to give them access to the records of a traitor, a Soviet soldier who had cracked under torture and had been among those who betrayed the three partisans.

Frustrated and bewildered by the official response, they enlisted the help of a reporter on the local paper, the *Evening Minsk*. The paper, apparently unaware of the official stonewall of their inquiry, published a picture of the unknown heroine and a plea for information about her identity.

Responses trickled in, until more than twenty of the respondents had identified the heroine as Masha Bruskina. Some said she had a father who was living outside of Moscow, and Mrs. Dikhtyar managed to locate him.

Shortly after the war, he, too, had written a letter to the *Evening Minsk*, pleading for information about his daughter, from whom he was separated during the war. The war had been traumatic for him; he had been mentally unstable ever since, Mrs. Dikhtyar said. He had spent lengthy periods in mental hospitals.

He was in a psychiatric hospital when Mrs. Dikhtyar found him in the late 1960s. But his second wife gave to Ada and Lev the letters she had received in response to his appeal for information about Masha. She had not shown them to her husband, she told them, fearful that they would only further upset his precarious mental state.

The letters we held in our hands were torn and fragile and yellow with age. But time had not diminished their passion. And through them a portrait of young Masha Bruskina emerged.

"Greetings, Comrade Bruskin," began one note to Masha's father, written in 1944. "Your letter reached me by chance. I work as a secretary in local government and open the mail.

"I knew Masha Bruskina very well before the war. I lived together in the ghetto with Masha and your wife. I can assure you that your daughter died during the war like a heroine. Masha was not just executed like so many others, including my family, in the ghetto in Minsk. She was a very special case.

"She worked in a local hospital; she was secretly helping the partisans.

"I, too, was a partisan. And I know about the death of Masha in great detail. But to this day I cannot bear to write about it."

As soon as she saw the letter, Mrs. Dikhtyar decided that she had to find its author. Pursuing a truly Western-style investigative journalism in a country not known for its commitment to the art form, Mrs. Dikhtyar tracked down its author in Leningrad and went to see her.

The woman let out a shout when she looked at the photo. She turned her head away, unable to look at it more closely, Mrs. Dikhtyar recalled.

But the woman in Leningrad confirmed that the girl in the photo was Masha Bruskina. Yes, she had lived in the same apartment with Masha in the ghetto, she said. The Germans had come to arrest Masha in September. They had put her in prison. Masha had been severely tortured.

She said her own father had seen the Germans hang Masha in October 1941. Masha's lifeless body had been left hanging outside the factory alongside her two dead comrades for several days as a warning to other partisans.

Masha's mother, disregarding the danger, went to the factory to try to have her daughter's body taken down. She was so distraught by the sight that she went mad, the woman recounted. Masha's mother returned to the ghetto. She was killed by the Nazis in the pogrom that leveled the ghetto and destroyed virtually all of its inhabitants.

Additional information about Masha's brief life and death came to Mrs. Dikhtyar through what she considered an unlikely source: members of a Lithuanian battalion that had collaborated with the Nazis in their occupation of Minsk.

For Soviet officials, the extent of the collaboration with the Nazis in Byelorussia, in the Ukraine, in Lithuania and Latvia, has remained one of the "white spots" of history. The Soviet authorities have acknowledged, of course, that there were "instances" of collaboration with the Germans. In some cases—like the Crimean Tatars—such instances of collaboration, or merely the threat of it, were used by Soviet authorities to justify the mass relocation of whole peoples.

But apart from these cases, collaborators have almost always been portrayed as exceptions—individual traitors to their country. The notion that whole groups of Slavs and non-Russians were initially sympathetic to the Nazi invaders as "liberators" from the Bolshevik Russian state is still anathema to Soviets. As a result, officials in Minsk never mentioned to us the presence of the Lithuanian battalion in their region during the war when they spoke of the German occupation.

"So they didn't tell you that it was a Lithuanian photographer in the battalion who took those photos? That it was he who gave them to the authorities and later to us?" said Mrs. Dikhtyar, allowing herself a bitter smile.

In the 1960s, she explained, Soviet officials were still actively pursuing war criminals in Lithuania. Many of the officials of the Lithuanian battalion that had helped occupy Minsk had fled the country after the war. But some had stayed in Lithuania. They had changed their names, hidden their identities, and a few even continued meeting to continue their "fascist Lithuanian independence movement," as Mrs. Dikhtyar put it.

In the '60s, party officials in Lithuania were compiling evidence against the battalion in Minsk and those who served in it. Some of this evidence was given to Mrs. Dikhtyar and Arkadyev. "It's sickening, really," she said, shaking her head. "When we went to the place of heroes, the Ministry of Internal Affairs in Minsk, we got no help. But when we turned to the Lithuanians in Kaunas, we received a lot of cooperation."

At the time of her inquiry, much was being written about the battalion, because the Soviets had identified several of its members who had fled to the West and were pressing for their return to the Soviet Union to stand trial for war crimes.[27] Among the more famous was Z. Ignatavicius, who had served as the battalion's priest. He had fled to the Vatican after the war, and despite repeated appeals by Moscow, Pope Pius XII had refused the Soviet Union's plea to extradite him.

She showed us a September 1971 issue of a Lithuanian magazine that had documented some of the priest's activities during the war. There in black-and-white was a photograph of a smiling Father Ignatavicius, seated alongside the Pope.

"There are still a lot of war criminals in the West," she said. "This good priest, for example, died peacefully at the Vatican."

The battalion's photographer had taken the photos of the executions of Minsk partisans, the first three of whom were Masha and her two comrades. Before the war, his photographs had been much celebrated in Lithuania. After the Germans invaded and conquered the country, the photographer, an ardent Lithuanian nationalist, had a much-acclaimed exhibit of his pictures portraying German success at winning the hearts and minds of Lithuanians. Then after the Soviets regained control of the country, the chameleon photographer had another officially blessed exhibit. This time, his photographs paid tribute to the courageous Russian soldiers who had liberated Soviet territory from the fascist invaders.

He had spent some time in a prisoner-of-war camp after the war, of course. But he was not a soldier, and thus was not considered a traitor and was soon released.

Through the accounts of the photographer and other members of the battalion, Mrs. Dikhtyar was able to learn the final pieces of the mystery surrounding Masha Bruskina's betrayal.

Masha was a dedicated young Communist who was better assimilated than many Jews in Minsk. She had lightened her hair and used her mother's name, which was not distinctively Jewish. After the Germans had invaded Minsk, she had gone to work in a Minsk hospital that was converted by the Nazis into a prison camp for wounded Soviet soldiers. There she cared for patients, but also stole medicine, medical instruments, and identification papers for the partisans who were operating in the forests surrounding the city. Masha was a small part of an essential chain of supplies that enabled Soviet officers to escape and an officially estimated 400,000 Byelorussian partisans to continue fighting and disrupting the German occupation.

She was betrayed by one of those she had nursed in the hospital, a wounded Soviet officer, whose name has not been released. After her arrest, she was severely tortured. But she did not talk, according to officials in Lithuania. She went to her death with her head erect and her pride intact. She was seventeen.

Mrs. Dikhtyar also received information about Masha from Azgur, Masha's uncle. We found the famous sculptor in September 1987 at his Minsk studio, a spacious loft, bathed in sunlight.

Strands of silver hair protruding from under his navy blue beret, a faded silk scarf draped dramatically around his neck, with the rimless eyeglasses favored by Trotsky and by Western radicals of the 1960s, Azgur seemed a made-to-order sculptor from Moscow central casting. For years he had labored here in the studio, whose very size, location, and equipment bespoke his status as an officially favored artist. During the war, he had fled to Moscow, but after the Soviet victory he had returned to the city and region he loved.

"Two hundred and thirteen of my works were destroyed during the war," he said. "Since then, I've worked here to honor those people who built their own lives in an internationalist manner, and those who helped others rebuild their lives." His busts and statues represent an eclectic group of heroes—the Russian lions of history and culture, of course, but also Franklin D. Roosevelt, Winston Churchill, and even Stalin—all fighters of fascism, he said.

"I'm not a sculptor of historical figures," he challenged us in an ebullient, animated style. "I'm a sculptural historian. I study faces and find truth."

And what was the truth, we asked, about Masha Bruskina?

Azgur, usually a study in perpetual motion, suddenly grew still, his body collapsing slightly like an accordion. "Masha . . . was my niece," the words blurted out.

"I recognized her instantly when I saw her photo in the *Evening Minsk*. I wrote a letter identifying her to the paper. They published an article agreeing with me in 1968. But she has still not been officially recognized. Someone is preventing her from being recognized," he said. "I still can't understand why."

Could he be mistaken about the girl's identity?

"I'm a professional sculptor," said the connoisseur of faces, pointing to his eyes. "She lived at my house before the war. No. I could not be mistaken about my own flesh and blood."

He had taken a small photo of Masha dressed in her Young Pioneer uniform to an "expert," but the expert, whom he did not identify, said that it was impossible to determine whether the unknown heroine was the same girl, based on so small and old a photograph.

But a man of his standing in the Party, a distinguished artist with connections to the authorities, a member of the legislature, surely he must have been well positioned to challenge the expert's determination? Why had he not?

"I wasn't seeking any personal privileges out of my action," he said defensively. "I was afraid people might think that I was trying to glorify myself by making her a heroine. To me she was not a heroine. She was a victim of the war. Like my own mother."

Was it possible, I asked, that Masha had not been recognized because she was a Jew?

"I deny that," he declared. "It is not possible in this country. I'm not saying that we don't have anti-Semites. There are some. Like everywhere. But they do not command our lives here.

"An expert can be a fool, and by chance an expert can be an anti-Semite. But I don't blame him or the system for it. I simply say that his vision is different from mine."

But why did he not raise the question now, with new experts and in a new political climate in Moscow, if not in Minsk?

Azgur said he no longer had the photo. He had lost it, he said. Besides, no one from the museum had ever come to see him to ask him about Masha. "I consider that a lack of respect for me."

And it was too late. "I'm eighty. It was such a long time ago," he added, seeking to continue the studio tour and change the subject.

Some Jews contended that Azgur had not pressed the matter because he, like so many of the privileged Jews and non-Russian minorities in the Soviet Union, were loath to speak out and risk their privileges by being branded troublemakers. In an authoritarian system like this one, the cost of candor or conscience could be high.

But remembering the pain on Azgur's face when we mentioned Masha's name, fear of losing status did not seem to be a satisfactory explanation for his silence, and in a country that demands compassion for individuals, it was surely the least-charitable explanation. There was, after all, far more to fear than the loss of a studio and commissions.

Azgur might have been willing to raise the issue with the authorities had he not harbored a deeper anxiety: he might have feared that they would say no. Refusing his appeal would inevitably raise the question of why. And this, in turn, might lead him to question whether it was really one "expert" who was an anti-Semite, really "someone," as he put it, who was preventing her from being recognized, or whether, rather, it was a system that even forty years later, for whatever reasons, still found it in its interest not to identify the unknown heroine officially as Masha Bruskina.

Such a denial would have forced him to question the very underpinnings of his art and his life—his belief in this system, in his country and its inherent virtues. That might have been too great a risk for any true believer in the Communist faith.

So Azgur had chosen instead to go on sculpting the heroes and heroines of his imagination, to portray the figures of a world that he would like to see rather than that which existed. His lifelike reproductions of heroes, metal replicas of real men and women, were without warts and weaknesses, the epitome of Soviet realism. There were no lines and wrinkles on their faces, no flaws, no tears.

"I'm in an interesting position," he observed quietly. "I have a certain peace, an inner pride when I think of the niece who lived in my house and grew before my eyes. On the other hand, there is a deep inner sadness because she is not officially recognized. This will be my everlasting sadness, for the rest of my life."

For her part, Mrs. Dikhtyar admitted that she was often saddened, more often frustrated, by her pursuit of official recognition for Masha. But she was younger than Azgur, she said, and unlike him had never abandoned hope that one day Masha Bruskina's name would appear in the Minsk war museum and throughout the Soviet Union. Eventually, the Soviet Union would grant Masha Bruskina her rightful place in history because, quite simply, there was no longer any logical reason not to do so.

Mrs. Dikhtyar noted that when she and Arkadyev began investigating the Bruskina affair anti-Semitism in the Soviet Union was particularly acute. Israel had just demolished its Arab foes in the Six-Day War of 1967. Moscow, under pressure from its Arab allies, had severed diplomatic ties with Israel.

Within the USSR, there was heavy official propaganda against Israel and Zionists abroad and particularly at home. The state-encouraged anti-Zionist committees, thinly veiled forums for virulent anti-Semitic attacks, were being formed throughout the country. Soviet Jews and their supporters were under scrutiny everywhere.

That period of history had ended, she said. Moscow was busy taking steps to reestablish ties with Israel, attempting to play a larger role in the search for stability, if not peace, in the Middle East, and the anti-Zionist committees were being disbanded, or at least officially discouraged.

Moreover, Mrs. Dikhtyar, like so many Russian intellectuals, was convinced that the new spirit of *glasnost* and *perestroika* championed by Gorbachev would eventually help end Masha's official anonymity.

She knew she faced obstacles. Jews had been resented in Byelorussia ever since the Russian Empire annexed the territory in the eighteenth century. In addition to the deeply ingrained anti-Semitism, she had to confront the resistance of a stubborn local bureaucracy that did not like outsiders telling them what to do, and far more important, the chauvinism and ethnic jealousies that were particularly acute about the Great Patriotic War.

In addition to losing 2.2 million Byelorussians—one out of four—in the war, this was a region in which there had been substantial collaboration with the Nazis. Much of the killing inside the ghetto was done by Soviet collaborators who were Byelorussians and other minorities who hated Jews, and who hoped that their betrayal would make Nazi Germany more sympathetic to their nationalist aspirations.

The case of Masha Bruskina has been ensnared in what Bill Keller called a "treacherous web of official truth and historical reality," and as these words are being written, this has been sufficient to ensure her official anonymity.

In 1988 after Keller publicized the case in *The New York Times,* the Byelorussian authorities established a commission to examine the issue. Much to the Jewish community's delight, Ada Dikhtyar was named one of its members.[28] But shortly before it was scheduled to meet, another of its members wrote an open letter to the *Evening Minsk* denouncing the inquiry and stating his view that there was no proof that the unknown heroine was Masha Bruskina. Mrs. Dikhtyar, enraged by the letter, demanded that its author be thrown off the commission. Her request was refused. So she has boycotted the few meetings the commission has held.

There has been no mention of Masha Bruskina in the *Soviet War Encyclopedia*, no tribute to her quiet poise and dignity in death, no general recognition of her name.

But there is a memorial of sorts in her honor, thanks, once again, to Mrs. Dikhtyar and Mr. Arkadyev.

When Masha's father died in the early 1970s, they decided to help give him a decent burial. A nurse at the psychiatric hospital in Moscow where he died told them that he had never stopped talking about his daughter Masha, who had been killed by the Germans during the war.

Mrs. Dikhtyar and Mr. Arkadyev arranged for Masha's father's ashes to be interred in the Central Crematorium in Moscow. Accompanied by Azgur, they held a small memorial service for the father and for Masha one wintry morning.

On the front of the small rectangular box that encloses his ashes are his name, carved in stone, and a picture of his beloved daughter. A small plaque hangs alongside the photo. It reads: TO MY DAUGHTER MASHA, EXECUTED BY THE FASCISTS. 1924–1941.

Unlike Minsk, which was virtually flattened during the war, less than half of the magnificent city of Kiev, the "Mother of Russia, the heart of the Ukraine," was destroyed. The most impressive sites—the Cathedral of St. Sophia; the Mariinsky Palace, an eighteenth-century jewel; the eleventh-century Monastery of the Caves, a honeycomb of caverns hidden inside the hilly right bank of the broad Dnieper River; one of the ancient "gates of Kiev" of Moussorgsky's *Pictures at an Exhibition;* the sprawling gardens and palaces of a succession of princes; the golden onion domes of the splendid eighteenth-century churches, heavily influenced by Byzantium—all remain gloriously intact.

The Ukraine has traditionally been the gateway between Scandinavia and the Black Sea, and its capital, Kiev, is the Soviet Union's third-largest and, at fifteen hundred years of age, its oldest city. It was here that Russian Orthodoxy was established in the tenth century, that Prince Vladimir decided to conduct a mass baptism of ten thousand Russians in the Dnieper so that the soul of Russia would become Christian.

If the ornate churches and golden domes have come to symbolize the ancient traditions of this city and the region, the Ukraine's modern monument is a stone's throw from the medieval Monastery of the Caves. It is the sixty-five-acre Great Patriotic War "Memorial Complex," a tribute to the 5 million people of the Ukraine who died during the war, one-sixth of the population; to the more than 250 villages razed by the Germans; and to the 4 million Soviets who were sent off to Germany for hard labor, more than 100,000 of whom were from Kiev. In this city, 195,000 were killed. In 1941, 900,000 people had lived here. By 1943, only 183,000 were left.[29]

Each day, more than 6,500 visitors, 10,500 on weekends, tour the complex. They walk in mass guided tours through the "Tunnel of Suffering," which portrays in rock carvings the soldiers, civilians, partisans, and workers who fought to save Mother Russia from the fascist invaders. They wander onto the Plaza of Victory, a gigantic gray stone plaza used for ceremonial occasions; and they visit the vast war museum. With 16 halls that contain 10,000 exhibits, it is the largest of its kind in the Soviet Union and the third most popular museum in the entire country. Only the Hermitage of Leningrad and the Pushkin of Moscow attract more visitors.

The Cathedral of St. Sophia is the city's most ancient landmark but Kiev's modern signature is the "motherland" statue that crowns the war museum. Constructed in 1981, this almost grotesque statue of stainless steel is more than 185 feet high, the entire monument being more than three hundred feet tall, a small skyscraper of suffering and triumph. Mother Russia, clad in a flowing Greek toga, her arms stretched over her head, towers above the complex and the city itself, dwarfing even the most elaborate of the church domes. In her left hand, the steel mother holds the shield of Russia; in her right, she brandishes a gargantuan sword pointed at the sky.

This Mother Russia and the Memorial Complex are de rigueur for official visitors and Soviet schoolchildren. But there is another monument to the war that is less frequently visited. It is a far less impressive memorial that was built in the summer of 1976 in honor of more than 100,000 Soviet citizens who were killed by the Nazis at Babi Yar.[30]

The monument is odd by Soviet standards. Though wildly emotional, like most artistic portrayals of Soviet heroism or pain, it is relatively understated when compared to others. Also it is situated near the city's perimeter. The eleven bronze figures—a woman clutching a young child, a soldier, a sailor, a farmer, a well-dressed man, and so on—are huddled together atop a concrete slab in a triangular form about twenty feet above the ground. The slab symbolizes the ridge of the vast ravine into which the bodies fell after being machine-gunned by the Germans.

Beyond the statue lies a well-manicured semicircle of lawn, about fifty yards long. At the edge of the lawn are rows of red poppies symbolizing blood, and beyond that, a ring of trees.

The day I visited the monument with my Intourist guide, Tanya Petrakova, no one else was there. The silence was a sharp contrast to the noisy throngs that congregated at the Kiev Memorial Complex in the heart of town, which we had visited only an hour earlier.

"Babi Yar," said Tanya, means "women's ravine." It was here, on the outskirts of town, that women had come to do their washing. Tanya, who was half Ukrainian and half Russian, said she did not know how many Jews had died here. No one had ever asked her the question, she added, her tone suspicious and defensive.

Soon after the Germans occupied Kiev, she recounted, all the Jews were ordered to assemble in the town center. They were instructed to bring food for four to five days' travel, and all of their valuables. These were confiscated, and the Jews forced to march in procession to the ravine. The date was September 29, 1941. They were lined up at the ravine's edge and machine-gunned. Their bodies fell over into the ravine. To ensure that all were dead, the Germans wandered among the corpses, shooting any bodies that showed tremors of life.

"They began with the Jews, but continued with the rest of the population," Tanya said.

As the Soviet Army advanced, the killings increased. The Germans, who burned the bodies as the ravine filled, sifted the ashes for jewels or anything else of value that the victims might have swallowed or hidden. In April 1943, just before the city was liberated, the Germans tried to hide the evidence of the massacres, and the ravine was constantly ablaze. Heavy smoke from the burning bodies hung over the city for two days.

When Kiev was freed, there were still bodies burning in the ravine, said Tanya. "The horror was discovered and revealed to all."

But only part of the horror was revealed. The official government report on the massacre, released six months after Kiev's liberation, described the Nazi crimes against Soviet citizens. Jews were never specifically mentioned.[31] Today there is an inscription in Ukrainian on the plaque at the foot of the frieze: "Here in 1941–1943, the German Fascist invaders executed more than 100,000 citizens of Kiev and prisoners of war."

When I returned to the hotel, I leafed through the official guidebooks and the reference material I had brought to find a description of the monument. In the latest edition of the *Kiev Encyclopedia,* which was published in 1986 by the Chief Editorial Board of the Ukrainian-Soviet Encyclopedia, I found a small notation about Babi Yar. "A place of mass destruction by Hitlerites of the general population of the city of Kiev," the book states. "Overall, more than 100,000 citizens died. Here was erected the memorial to the Soviet citizens, soldiers, and officers of the Soviet Army shot by the German Fascists at Babi Yar."

The description was accurate, as far as it went. Babi Yar was, indeed, an infamous place of mass destruction, the first Nazi conveyor belt of death. But the reference omits the fact that at least

50,000 of those killed at Babi Yar were Jews, 33,771 in the first two days alone. This had been one of the first places of Jewish mass destruction, before the installation of gas chambers. Ukrainians and other Soviet citizens also were shot here, but Jews were selected for extermination first, and they died here in disproportionate numbers.

Because Babi Yar was first and foremost a place of Jewish suffering, the Soviet Union has been reluctant, almost from the end of the war, even to acknowledge what had happened. William Korey, the expert on Soviet Jewry, notes that early plans for a monument by A. V. Vlasov, a well-known architect of his day, and B. Ovchinnikov, an artist, were quietly shelved in the late '40s. In March 1949, Savva Golovanivsky, a Ukrainian-Jewish poet who had written sympathetically about the victims of Babi Yar, was denounced in the Soviet press for "defamation of the Soviet nation."[32]

But the past would not remain silent. The issue was finally brought to center stage by Yevgeny Yevtushenko, the poet, who in September 1961 wrote a poem bemoaning the fact that decades after the slaughter, no monument stood over Babi Yar, a key link in the chain of European Jewish genocide.

Even the poem which caused a furor, however, was not the verse that Yevtushenko had written. That original version was recited by Yevtushenko to twelve hundred students in Moscow three days before its official publication in *Literaturnaia Gazeta.* The "International," the Communist anthem, he recited that day, could "thunder forth" only when anti-Semitism was "buried for good." But bigoted sentiments, he continued, still arose "on the vapors of alcohol and in conversations after drinking."

The poem that appeared in the journal made no reference to the "International" or to the intoxicated revelations of unsocialist instincts. But the poem was attacked nonetheless by two leading Soviet literary ideologists as ideologically incorrect.

Two years later, no less a literary critic than Party Secretary Khrushchev attacked the poem at a conference of writers and artists in Moscow. Yevtushenko, Khrushchev said in his address, had shown "ignorance of historical facts" by asserting that Babi Yar was a historical example of anti-Semitism. "Comrade Yevtushenko," Khrushchev stated at the time, "the poem has no place here."

When Yevtushenko protested that anti-Semitism in the Soviet

Union still had resonance, Khrushchev insisted that it was "not a problem."

"It is a problem, Nikita Sergeievich," Yevtushenko replied. "It cannot be denied and it cannot be suppressed. It is necessary to come to grips with it time and again. . . . We cannot go forward to Communism with such a heavy load of Judophobia."[33]

The exchange had sprung to mind as I stood at the base of the monument, trying to imagine the place of mass extermination as it must have looked then. But I could not. The area I saw was rather flat. There was no deep ditch, no ravine into which thousands of bodies could have fallen. The metal figures seemed to be falling over onto a neatly manicured lawn a mere twenty feet below. How could this tree-rimmed semicircle have been the place where thousands of people had fallen into a mass grave each day?

Tanya, my guide, offered an explanation. After the war, the city had grown rapidly. The ravine had been filled in with earth and a park was established here. Housing had sprung up around Babi Yar. The building was continuing. Down the slight incline to the right of the monument soared a giant new television tower. "That's the latest, along with the new sports complex, which is being built over there," she said, pointing to the giant steel tower that dwarfed the monument.

Her answer, it turned out, was only partly correct. I learned the other part later in my visit from Lev Elbert, a Jew from Kiev who had applied for permission to immigrate from Kiev to Israel in 1978. Since then, he and his family had endured the typical life of a refusenik—the loss of his job, KGB searches of their home, the seizure of books and manuscripts and letters from friends, the exclusion of their son from privileged schools and clubs, and finally periods in prison.

Lev had fought back. He and his wife, Hannah, had gone on well-publicized hunger strikes to protest his treatment in jail and the government's refusal to let his family emigrate. Their case had become well known. They had invited me to a seder dinner on Friday night at their apartment in Kiev.

A medium-sized man with piercing blue eyes and a tough gaze, Lev lived not far from Babi Yar. He had grown up in Kiev. His wife's grandparents had been shot there. He spoke about what the Jewish people had endured in the Soviet Union and what he feared would be their fate here.

He was a Zionist, he said. He had decided to sacrifice any hope of a productive life in the Soviet Union by applying to emigrate, because by denying the Holocaust and Soviet Jewish suffering during the war, "those bastards are trying to exterminate our souls."[34]

But "the bastards" had built a monument, even if belatedly, I replied. They took any tourist who wished to visit Babi Yar to see it.

"No," he declared. "They take you to *their* monument. They do not take you to Babi Yar, the actual place where the slaughter took place."

He offered to take me there the next morning at 7 A.M. We would meet at "their" monument, he instructed. "And this time don't bring Tanya," he said. "I'll give you an unorthodox tour of the real Babi Yar."

It was cold on Saturday morning. I could see my breath. I took the trolley and arrived early, so I was standing at the foot of the monument, shivering, when Lev arrived on foot.

He stared at the official monument in disgust. "This is a false monument," he said. "There is a Ukrainian woman, a Ukrainian soldier, a sailor, a bureaucrat, a Ukrainian partisan. But none of these figures are Jews. These are not Jewish faces. And, of course, the inscription is in Ukrainian, not in Yiddish or Hebrew or even Russian, not in a single language that the descendants of the majority of those who died here consider their mother tongue," he continued.

But the greatest sacrilege, he said, was that this was not even the spot where the Jews and others had been killed. This was not Babi Yar.

We walked together across the semicircle of lawn, past the poppies and the trees, across the road, into a large park. "This," said Lev, "is Kiev's new recreation park, part of the new sports complex."

The destruction of the Ukraine's Jews had begun before the Germans had ordered the Jews of Kiev to assemble for what was to become their death march to the ravine. Kiev, the heartland of the Orthodox Church, was since the time of the tsars the most vitriolically anti-Semitic bastion in Russia. And during the time of the tsars, thousands of Jews had been killed in a succession of pogroms.

After the October Revolution, more were killed in the vicious civil war between the Reds and the Whites. Though Jews were finally offered a degree of protection by the young Soviet government, the respite was short-lived.

During the first weeks of the German occupation, Kiev and the Ukraine were racked by spontaneous pogroms. Press reports of the time and hundreds of eyewitness accounts indicated that the Ukrainian population had received the German invaders with enthusiasm, viewing them as "liberators" from the horrors of Stalin's collectivizations and purges. For every German battalion in occupied Ukraine, there were roughly five local battalions of comparable size supporting them.[35]

Hundreds of thousands of collaborators in the western or Polish Ukraine, gleeful at the prospect of eventual liberation from Soviet rule by the more civilized Germans, began rounding up Jews throughout the region, murdering men, women, and children and pillaging their homes. They even established their own concentration camps. The most infamous was at Shubkov, near Rovno, where western Ukrainians imprisoned and tortured Jewish inmates.

Although collaboration was so widespread, virtually all Soviet descriptions of the situation here, to this day, portray collaborators as a tiny, hated minority of misfits and traitors.

Enthusiasm for the new occupiers cooled quickly and disenchantment set in, but only as Ukrainians began to understand that the Slavs were also viewed as subhuman by the perfect German race. Some turned and began fighting the Germans, the part of history highlighted by modern Soviet history books and articles. What goes unsaid is that as late as 1944, when the Germans were in retreat, Western historians estimate the number of Ukrainians still fighting alongside the Nazis at 220,000.[36]

The Ukrainian zeal for killing Jews was not initially well viewed by the German fascists. They would deal with the Jews in their own way: a methodical, well-organized slaughter was far preferable to the outbursts of violence taking place throughout the countryside. And the proliferation of Ukrainian nationalist groups, armed and fighting, posed a deeper threat to Germany's plans for the breadbasket of the Soviet Union and its inhabitants, who were needed for forced labor in the factories and fields of Germany. So when the Germans learned of the camps for Jews, they ordered the Ukrainians to dismantle them.

"A tiny minority of Ukrainians tried to help the Jews during that dreadful time," said Lev, as we walked through the sports park. "But most were content to see us stoned and dragged from our houses, or murdered on the spot."

It was still early when Lev and I entered the park. Young women with babies in strollers walked along the concrete pathways. Old men strolled along the grass. Old women sat on benches, reading newspapers and gossiping. A group of young boys kicked a soccer ball across a field. There were even a few Soviet joggers in shorts, minus the omnipresent American Walkmans.

Lev guided me past this scene of pastoral simplicity into a heavily wooded area. Suddenly, the ground began to rise. The terrain was covered with densely packed shrubs and trees. The pathways disappeared and the soil became rocky and difficult to navigate. Thorns from wild bushes scratched my arms and face. I felt that I had entered a jungle and clung to Lev's arm for support. We were no more than half a mile from the monument, but this wild, untended place seemed a million miles away from the neatly cut lawns and rows of flowers, the official tribute to Ukrainian suffering.

Lev stopped when we got to the top of what seemed to be a hill, though visibility was minimal because of the foliage. "Look down," he instructed, separating the leaves and branches of the densely packed trees and foliage with his powerful hands. "See the real Babi Yar."

The ravine suddenly appeared below me. There was a vast, deep ditch, a staggering fifty-foot drop that made me slightly dizzy as I stared down into it.

"It used to be even deeper, about 150 feet," said Lev. "But in 1961, the government tried to build a sports stadium on this land. Workers began filling the ravine with silt. Less than a year later, the dam here gave way and the silt poured down the slope, killing some Kievites, and ruining the project.

"People here said it was the Jews' revenge for having been disturbed," he said. So the stadium idea was abandoned and plans for the "recreation park" took its place.

The land we had walked through to get to the ridge, said Lev, was Kiev's old Jewish cemetery. To build the park and the sports complex, bulldozers had ripped through the tombstones, crushing the marble and the skeletons with their iron teeth. "They wanted to blot out not only the memory of Babi Yar, of this infamous ravine, but also any trace of the traditional resting place of the city's Jewish population," Lev said bitterly.

"They destroyed the cemetery to build a recreation park. They preserved the Russian civilian cemetery and the military cemetery next door. Those graves are very well maintained. But here people now walk and jog and play ball and make love on the ashes of the Jewish people."

There were still remnants of the tombstones. As we walked back to the main road, I stumbled and fell across a protruding stone. It was engraved, and Lev translated it for me: "TO THE UNFORGETTABLE MEMORY OF MARIA FREINDLICH (PERTCHUK). DIED—MARCH 17, 1937."

I wanted to take the stone remnant with me, to rescue it from oblivion, from being ground up under the foundations of the cable television center planned for this site. But Lev said no. The authorities would disapprove. I could get into trouble.

We walked back to the road in silence. The morning's frosty mist had cleared and I realized that my face was covered with sweat.

Along the road stood a very old house. It was the old synagogue, Lev told me. It had been restored after the war and was now used as the administrative office for the park.

"In 1978, two years after the monument at Babi Yar was built at its new and improved location, we Jews applied for permission to say Kaddish at the memorial to honor our dead with our traditional prayer for them. We never received the courtesy of a written reply, of course. The authorities in Kiev have never sanctioned a Jewish religious service here. When we assembled years later without official permission, the KGB used the Institute of Immunology across the street from the monument to hold and interrogate those of us who had participated.

"From the Jewish point of view, the destruction of the body is not as important as the destruction of the soul," he said. "And that's what they have been intent on destroying. We don't claim any exclusivity in the massacre at Babi Yar. We know that many Ukrainians and prisoners of war and Russians were shot here too. But the Jewish deaths should be acknowledged. We were singled out to die here first. And more of us died as a people than they did.

"But they will not acknowledge it: not Khrushchev, not Brezhnev, not even Gorbachev. They are still trying to blot out the memory of what happened here—by hiding the actual place of slaughter, by destroying the city's major Jewish cemetery, by making no mention in any textbook of the fact that a disproportionate number of those who died here were Jews, that the Jews of Kiev were assembled for mass destruction first. Our identity has been denied, obliterated in the mass of 'Soviet citizens' who suffered during the war.

"They have been trying to destroy memory so that history can be changed to conform with their ideology. They will never accept us here as Jews. Now perhaps you see why my family and I must leave this place, must leave this country. I am not willing to be destroyed. I am not willing to lose my soul."

In late 1987, three months after my visit, Lev and Hannah Elbert received permission to emigrate. Soon after, Soviet authorities also permitted for the first time a solemn commemorative event in honor of the martyrs of Babi Yar, not in Kiev, but in Moscow.

Several hundred Jews attended the ceremony in the Jewish section of a local cemetery on the outskirts of Moscow. Yosef Begun, who also had received permission to emigrate after more than fifteen years of waiting, complained about the absence of any reference to the slaughter of Jews at the Babi Yar memorial. A Jewish nonrefusenik, Yuri Sokol, urged the Soviet Union to confront and quash anti-Semitism. Samuil Zivs, a Jew who heads the official Anti-Zionist Committee, reflected the official Soviet view by asserting that the Jews who were executed at Babi Yar had died defending their homeland.

Lev, who was still in Kiev and unable to attend the ceremony, made one last pilgrimage to the tree-covered ravine Babi Yar. He took his son with him, to the actual site, so that he, at least, would never forget what had happened here.

Alexander Schlayon, fifty-six, known to his friends as Sasha, has been obsessed for many years with Babi Yar. A thin, balding man with sad hazel eyes, Schlayon is a Jew, but a secular member of his faith with no desire to leave his birthplace of Kiev or the Soviet Union.

When we met in Kiev in the fall of 1987, he described himself as a filmmaker, though he hadn't made a film in eight years. In fact, he made only one film. It was called *Babi Yar*.

The film has been shown in the Soviet Union and abroad since 1981, but Schlayon insisted that none of the three versions that have been screened is the film he made. It was the work of editors, of "assassins" who "murdered" his cinematic tribute to the Jews who died at Babi Yar.

"I lost part of my family there," said Sasha. "I lost the friends of my childhood."

Schlayon is alive today because he and his mother were evacuated to a safer city when his father went to fight at the front. After the war, he moved to Moscow and worked as an editor at the central television station. In 1980, he returned to Kiev and decided to try to make a documentary film about Babi Yar. "In forty years since the war, there wasn't a single book or film about the slaughter here," he said.

He anticipated resistance, but thanks to the interest of a rising young associate in the film industry, Vitaly Korotich, now the editor of the *glasnost* magazine *Ogonyok,* the project was approved and work begun under Ukratelye Film of Kiev.

Schlayon filmed interviews with dozens of witnesses and survivors, traveled to Germany to examine records and the Nuremberg archives, and assembled what he asserted was the most complete description of the slaughter ever compiled in the Soviet Union.

Working feverishly against a production deadline, he suffered a heart attack in December 1980 when the film was almost finished. "I was exhausted, sleeping two or three hours a day, working day and night in the studio trying to finish on time, editing photographs and interviews so horribly depressing that I could barely watch them."

Korotich, he said, took over the final editing of the film. Schlayon was appalled when he saw the final product. "They had changed the entire film. There was almost nothing about the Jews who had been killed at Babi Yar. In fact, there were only one or two brief references to Jews in the entire film. All the witnesses who had described what had happened to the Jews had been edited out. It was no longer my film."

The day before the film was to be screened in Kiev in 1981, Schlayon sent a telegram to the judicial authorities trying to stop its distribution. He received no response. He sued in the People's Court in Radiansky to protect his author's rights, but the court refused to hear the case. A succession of appeals to Korotich, to the courts, to the influential filmmakers' union were rejected.

Schlayon was discharged from the project. He began to be harassed by the authorities and hounded by critical articles in the press. The film union accused him of having forged his diploma in filmmaking, a charge that barred him from working on other films. The KGB broke into his apartment and seized the material he had assembled to complete a book on Babi Yar. Months later, it was returned, without explanation. His wife was asked to produce their marriage license to prove that they were truly married. Newspaper articles attacked him for spreading "Zionist propaganda."

"Because my film focused on the Jewish tragedy at Babi Yar, they accused me of having made an exclusively Jewish film, one that served the interests of the Zionists. They speculated that I was on the Zionists' payroll. I couldn't fight them," he said.

"I finished my book on Babi Yar six years ago—five hundred pages of it, including some of the interviews with witnesses that were eliminated from the film," he said. "But no one here wants to publish it."

In September 1983, *Birobidzhaner Shtern,* the daily newspaper in the Jewish autonomous region, published excerpts of his book in Yiddish, but no Russian-language journal has done so.

He tried to appeal for help to Korotich, Schlayon recounted, but Korotich refused to help him restore parts of the film. "When we argued once, he told me that he didn't want to be accused of having made a 'Jewish' film," Schlayon asserted.

He has not worked since the dispute; he has lived off the salary of his wife, an art historian, and meager earnings from the few freelance articles he has managed to publish. He has been offered other jobs, but has continued to insist that he is a filmmaker who wants work in his field. Penury, he said with a shrug, was "the price one must sometimes pay here to maintain one's dignity."

Throughout his ordeal, however, he has not lost hope that one day his film will be seen in its original version. *Glasnost* has dramatically improved the situation for writers and creators, he said. "But unfortunately these changes have not yet reached Kiev."

In January 1987, Schlayon received a telephone call that raised his hope. He was asked to meet with the head of ideology of the Ukrainian Communist Party. But the official did not want to discuss the film. He offered instead to try to find him work as a translator in his department.

"I told him I did not want charity," Schlayon explained. "I told him I wanted work in my field, that I wanted my film restored, and that I wanted to work on another film. But first my film must be restored. People without a past have no future, I told him. That is true for the Jews here, and it is true for me."

Back in Moscow, Korotich's usually cheerful face suddenly clouded when I mentioned Alexander Schlayon and the film they had made together. "Ah, poor Schlayon," he said, fidgeting in the chair behind his desk at the headquarters of *Ogonyok.* "It is sad. Alexander has become a jealous and bitter man."

Korotich confirmed that Schlayon had come to him in the late 1970s, seeking his help in making a film about Babi Yar. "He had no experience as a director," Korotich said. "He had been a technician at the Moscow television center. But I felt that we needed such a film, and I felt equally strongly that the film needed a Jewish director. So I agreed to help him and work with him on the project. I helped get him access to archives. I helped get him travel money."

The film that Schlayon made was "very powerful, very emotional, but it was not a particularly good film, and definitely not a truthful film," Korotich asserted. "He portrayed the war as one essentially between Germans and Jews. He also included all kinds of material that was not relevant to what had happened at Babi Yar," he continued. "For example, he included footage of the Warsaw Ghetto uprising. It was interesting, of course, but not relevant to his film.

"Of course the Jews suffered," he said. "We all know they suffered more than others. But the Germans killed Byelorussians and Ukrainians with the same enthusiasm as they did Jews. This country isn't France or Germany, where mostly Jews died. Here, everyone suffered, so why divide the dead?"

Korotich denied having edited the references to the Jewish genocide at Babi Yar out of the film. "I did not edit the film. I could not have. I was only the commentator in the film. I am not a film editor."

The editing, he said, was done by "officials," whose names he could no longer recall.

"But I encouraged Schlayon to write his book, and I have been very active in promoting Jewish art and literature in this country. And I believe that there should be a monument to the Jews who died in our country during the war. Perhaps in one of the ghettos. We will almost surely have such a monument one day."

The episode was apparently difficult for Korotich. As a Ukrainian he seemed to resent personally what he saw as the effort by Jews to monopolize suffering during the war. He was a child during the war, he said, and his memory of Babi Yar was different from Schlayon's.

"It is true that many Jews were killed here. Due in part to our own propaganda, many Jews had looked to the German invaders as liberators. Hardly anyone thought that Germans would kill the Jews. Germans were civilized, organized people, free traders, unlike the Communists. So when the Jews were ordered to show up with two days of food and clothing in the central square, rumors spread throughout the Ukrainian community.

"The main rumor was that the Rothschilds had paid to transport the Jews of Kiev to Palestine, or some other good place. The Jews are smart, we Ukrainians thought. If they are going someplace, we wanted to go too. So many Ukrainians showed up in the square that day."

The Ukrainians were eventually weeded out by the Germans, of course. But ultimately their fate was the same as the Jews'. "First they killed Jews, then everybody else," he said.

The statistics spoke for themselves, he maintained. One-third of the 900,000 people of Kiev were Jewish. At the end of the war, the city's population stood at 100,000. The rest escaped, were deported or killed. The 800,000 were not only Jews.

"I remember it all too well," he insisted. "We all suffered. My aunt and my father-in-law were killed. They were Ukrainians, not Jews. Jews must not be singled out for a special role in our national suffering. It can only backfire on them and further strain the fabric of our society."

"There is no Soviet history, as such. It's an oxymoron," said Roy Medvedev, the tall, calm, distinguished historian who after years of political isolation has become intellectually chic under Gorbachev.

"History in my country changes with each change in Soviet leadership. So instead of history there is Soviet mythology, alleged history, which serves as the main instrument of ideology, of state legitimation. My work," he said, "has been devoted to challenging the rigid subordination of history to politics."

Because of repeated purges of government archives, history

could not be found in official books and archives. "It is locked away in people's memories," Medvedev said.

As a result, there is not a "collective memory" as such about the Great Patriotic War, even though it is the pivotal event of modern Soviet history. Attitudes toward it, Medvedev said, depended on one's age, experience, even one's gender.

Those born no later than the early 1920s, many of whom fought from the very beginning, remembered the war as "the most terrible, most important event" of their lives. "They knew only retreats, humiliation, and devastation," he said.

Only about 20 percent of them made it home; the rest were killed or captured, and most who were taken prisoner died in captivity. Those who did return were changed men. They were determined that their country would never again give away the smallest piece of land to anyone, for any reason.

The second generation of the war—his own—also saw death and destruction, but "on the attack, on offensives. Of course we were shocked by the losses," he said. Between 40 and 50 percent survived. "But we saw a more heroic war. Somehow our factories and military turned out the weapons and the officers we needed. We felt ourselves a part of a powerful organism, struggling to survive and to vanquish our enemies. Yes, many of my friends died; my brother, Zhores, was badly wounded. But it is less humiliating to die during an offensive. When you're retreating, there is no time even to bury the dead."

The third generation was Gorbachev's own. They remembered the war as children—the dislocations, the loss of parents and grandparents, the hunger. "The overriding memory of people in their forties and fifties is the hardship," he said.

Finally, there was his son's generation—the fourth generation —those for whom the Great Patriotic War was history. Soviet citizens born ten years after the war or more have had it drummed into them, but "many have rebelled against the propaganda," said Medvedev.

"My son, who is thirty, has no interest in politics. He grew up during the years of stagnation. It was a time of great lies through culture and art. Maybe that's why he and so many in his generation rejected it. He's a chemist, a 'specialist.' He doesn't even read the newspapers. Lacking any spiritual or moral nourishment, this generation has grown up very cynical, very apolitical," said Medvedev.

"When I try to talk to him about the tragedy, about the suffering, he says, So, is that how you justify life here today? Is that what you want for me? There the conversation ends. He's quite typical of his generation, I fear. They are not Gorbachev supporters. They don't believe in anything."

There was also a gender gap of sorts in attitudes toward the war. The men died, but it was older women who were most bitter. "They carry the heaviest burden of the war, for they lost fathers, brothers, lovers, sons. When a soldier died, his life ended. But his wife lived on, often childless, alone, for the rest of her life. There were no more grooms; they would never again become brides. Older women today still hate the Germans for this deprivation. They have never forgiven."[37]

Despite these differences, Medvedev argued, the war had bred in the Soviet people as a whole what he termed, borrowing from the Jews, a "never again" consciousness. "My generation feels that we won the war. It helped ease the pain of the terror of the '30s. In my own case, I had watched my father being taken away by Stalin's men when I was thirteen. But all the war generations believe that our country must never again be humiliated, that we must be strong, that everyone must be afraid of us, that this is our only protection."

Not for nothing, others agreed, does the Russian word *kremlin* mean "fortress."

Under Gorbachev's reassessment, the old taboos about Stalin and the war have been falling, one by one. While many pages of Soviet history are still blank, important chapters and crucial footnotes have been filled in. The reassessment has struck a responsive chord. The newspaper *Literary Gazette* has published hundreds of letters decrying the injustices of the Stalin years and appealing for rehabilitation and the restoration of pension rights and other benefits to those deprived of them during Stalin's purges. In 1987 alone, the newspaper reported, it received more than ten thousand letters on this theme.

Having arrived at the official consensus that Stalin was a tyrant who made dreadful mistakes, the Soviet Union has begun grappling publicly with deeper, even more painful questions: Was Stalin necessary? What was it in the Soviet system that made him possible? And did part of the blame not rest with Lenin, the still largely untouched god of the Communist faith?

Some Western scholars and students of the Soviet Union do not regard the intellectual furor over the ghosts of the past as either fundamentally significant or essential to the economic and political reforms Gorbachev has been trying to impose.

Patrick Cockburn, Moscow bureau chief for the London *Financial Times* from 1984 to 1988, argued in an interview that Soviet intellectuals like Gorbachev's have focused on historical reassessment because, first of all, they were Marxists and Marxists think history is important. In addition, he said, concentrating on the past was a form of escapism from problems for which they have no solutions. "It's less risky to discuss Stalin's crimes than to confront the enormous problems facing this society," Cockburn said. How can the USSR rationalize the incredibly inefficient system of production? How can the need for greater decentralization be balanced against the Soviet government's goal of developing the poorest regions of the country? How can the Communist party be reanimated? What can be done about deep-seated anti-Semitism here?

"Intellectuals address none of these real issues. Their answer is always: Let's build a Pasternak Museum, or a monument to Stalin's victims," Cockburn concluded.

Though the shortcomings of the productive sector have become all too obvious, the progress achieved so far under Stalin, Khrushchev, Brezhnev, and the succession of Soviet leaders has not been forgotten by many Soviet citizens. And they have resented the attacks by intellectuals on the men who won the war and enabled their society to develop. The feeling is shared by many in the Soviet bureaucracy—some eighteen million strong. These people were, in effect, the winners of the Soviet system, the men and their families whom Stalin put in place. While Western journalists tended to see the battles over history and the future in terms of "good" and "bad" guys, they were really between the winners and the losers of the system. And here the "bad guys" won.

It is one thing for a democracy to engage in a historical reassessment of the war years as in France, where de Gaulle's Resistance movement triumphed, or in Germany, where the constitution, laws, and leadership were totally changed after the war. It is quite another to do so in an authoritarian system that is still ruled by the bureaucracy that was shaped by, that condoned and conducted the purges, the collectivizations, and the colossal war mistakes the society is trying to reexamine.

Yuri N. Afanasyev, a burly man in his early fifties who trains

Soviet archivists and is a key intellectual champion of the historical reassessment and *perestroika*, argued that the Soviet Union would never be a "normal" country—less authoritarian, less fearful, more pluralistic, more democratic, and economically productive—unless it confronted the lies of its past.[38]

True or not, most Soviet academics and intellectuals who support Gorbachev's *glasnost* and *perestroika* ardently believe this, which in a country like the Soviet Union tends to make it so.

Afanasyev, a historian who has specialized in both Communist Party and French history, said that rewriting the nation's history is a prerequisite to broader social and political change in the USSR for several reasons.

First, history is simply more important to the Soviets than to most Americans, or even to most Europeans. For Europeans, obsession with their history usually focuses on the antiquity of their civilization. This is not true in the Soviet Union, which developed far later as a nation-state, whose current form of government is only seventy years old.

For Soviets, history is a key frame of reference in ways that are difficult for most Americans even to comprehend. Ordinary workers tend to know key dates in their city's and region's life. And it is not unusual for people to have spent several generations in a city or region, and therefore to be even more profoundly attached to it.

A second, more pragmatic reason for the reassessment is that Soviet intellectuals demand it as the price of their support for Gorbachev's sweeping reforms. The intelligentsia would probably not have signed on so early or as ardently unless Gorbachev had been willing to challenge the mythology that the Soviet regime called history. Many of them had found this humiliating as social scientists. Long before Gorbachev, Soviet historians knew that their profession was riddled with lies and politically useful self-delusions and that Western historians dismissed them as serious scholars. They were chafing at the historical bit, sneaking historical truths between the lines of what they wrote, watching them be disclosed covertly by playwrights and other less "serious" observers in Soviet eyes. The truth was hidden between the lines of Mikhail F. Shatrov's "historical" plays, hinted at by writers in a few published novels and in manuscripts that would never be printed, and alluded to in a few films that managed to emerge relatively unscathed from the censor's office.

Thanks to the reassessment, many historians and other writers and intellectuals have been able to reclaim some intellectual dignity. As a result, they are numbered among Gorbachev's staunchest supporters.

Finally, Afanasyev argued, history and political ideology in the Soviet Union are inexorably linked. To change the latter, one must alter the former. That is how it had always been, even under the tsars. Under Communism, the tendency had grown stronger.

"We are Marxists, so for us there is a historical dialectic, a clear link between thoughts about the past and the direction of our future," Afanasyev said.

Under Khrushchev, many Communists concluded that Stalinism was a politically undesirable legacy. They decided to get rid of it. They tried to do so by the same authoritarian means he would have applied.

"What did Khrushchev do? He threw Stalin's corpse out of the mausoleum in Red Square. Very scientific. It solved nothing," Afanasyev asserted.

To overcome the legacy of Stalinism, he added, the roots and political structures that made it possible must be examined and rejected. In other words, to de-Stalinize the country, Gorbachev must destroy Stalin.

Specifically, that means permitting historians to fill in the white spots of history, those that the censors had "whited out" of the country's past. "It's a very human form of work," he continued. "It has meant restoring facts, figures, and faces. It has meant rehumanizing a dehumanized society; it means confronting and reforming what we have today: 'deformed' socialism."

The memory of the war years constitutes the heart of this reformation, because despite the awesome destruction and suffering, it was one of the few times in which Soviet men and women felt free. "The war conjures up not only pain, but pride and nostalgia for a period in which citizens stood together, voluntarily, to defend the motherland," asserted Medvedev.

There are few inspiring memories of the Stalin era, so remembrance of that wartime freedom and personal sacrifice, of almost miraculous economic production and intense patriotism, are among the happy ones. Hence, they are cherished; they die hard. Efforts to face Stalin's record and mistakes squarely have been increasingly resented by many ordinary Soviet citizens and denounced by conservative leaders in a thinly veiled attack on Gorbachev's policies.

In a loudly applauded speech at the party conference in June 1988, Yuri V. Bondarev, a well-known writer, accused the press of "immorality" in its criticism of Stalin and his legacy. "Our press, which destroys, denigrates and casts into the cesspool our past life and experience, is erecting an ugly monument to thoughtlessness," he said.[39] "We do not need to destroy our past in order to build our future."

Among the most critical vehicles of memory, one that has advanced Afanasyev's goal of "rehumanizing" Soviet society, or "filling in the faces of our history," is a strong oral tradition. A case in point is Nikolai Bukharin, the Communist leader whom Stalin killed in the 1930s for having opposed collectivization of the nation's farms. Sensing his fate, Bukharin composed a short letter of defense days before his arrest. His wife, Anna Mikhailovna Larina, learned Bukharin's last testament and preserved it in her memory for fifty years—through imprisonment, exile, and obloquy—until a generation of Communists emerged who were willing to grant his final request.

"He read it to me over and over aloud until he was convinced I had it by heart," said Larina, a small, dignified old woman, who was twenty-four at the time. He then made her swear to fight until he was exonerated of charges that he had betrayed the revolution that he had helped create. Knowing that Stalin would burn such a testament, were his envoys to find it, "he destroyed the letter himself," she said.[40]

In February 1988, the verdict of treason against her husband—whose ideas are reflected in some of Gorbachev's proposals—was overturned. Bukharin's words, safeguarded in the memory of Anna Larina, finally found their way onto the front pages of *Pravda, Izvestia,* and *Moscow News.* "I have never been a traitor. You should know, comrades, that there is a drop of my blood on the banner which you will carry on your triumphant march to Communism."

Another fruit of this tradition is the memoir of a young man who in 1948 witnessed the arrest of his father, a leader of the Jewish Anti-Fascist Committee. The committee, founded in the early 1940s and composed of some of the nation's most prominent Jews, had rallied support in the West for the USSR during the war.

What is known is that in October 1948 committee leaders were summoned to the Kremlin for an emergency meeting with senior Soviet officials. A lengthy discussion was held. The meeting adjourned. Later that night, virtually all the committee leaders who had attended were arrested and imprisoned. Four years later, these heroes of the Great Patriotic War were executed. A few of the luckier members were given lengthy prison sentences.

What occurred at the meeting has long been a source of debate. In his memoirs, Khrushchev, who did not attend the session, said that the Jews had tried to persuade Soviet leaders that Birobidzhan, the officially designated Jewish region where only 5 percent of Soviet Jews lived, should be declared the Jewish national homeland and that all Jews in Russia should be sent there. Other historians say that the Jews proposed the creation of an autonomous Jewish republic in the Crimea. Still others say that the meeting broke up over arguments about the treatment of Soviet Jews and anti-Semitism that was condoned by the government.

But the memoir given to me by a friend during one of my visits to the Soviet Union offers another version of what happened that night, a fateful event in Soviet Jewish history and one that has never been discussed officially. The memoir was written years after that fateful meeting by the son of one of the participants.[41] It is based largely on a reconstruction of what his father told him and what other members told their families between their return from the meeting and 3 A.M., when the Soviet secret police roused them from their beds and arrested them. The author of this memoir never saw his father again.

According to the memoir, the JAC members were welcomed by Mikhail Suslov, Secretary of the Central Committee. Suslov told them that the government, prompted by concern about the future of the Jewish people, had decided to create a real Jewish homeland inside the Soviet Union for all Soviet Jews. The Jewish autonomous region of Birobidzhan would be elevated to an autonomous republic, and Jews from inside and outside the Soviet Union would be "encouraged" to go there. The republic would be a model of social and economic progress, the memoir quotes Suslov as saying. It would show Israel, which was fast becoming a "marionette of imperialism," that the Soviet Union offered a "progressive" alternative to the road chosen by Israel, which "was leading its people to an inevitable catastrophe."

Jews did not need another catastrophe, Suslov told them. "Six million is a minimum of those who were killed" during the Great Patriotic War, he said.

The Jewish leaders, appalled at Suslov's proposal, attempted diplomatically to explain their objections. Solomon Lozovsky, president of the international of revolutionary trade unions (PROFINTERN) a Central Committee member, and one of the most prominent members of the JAC, protested that Jews had no natural territorial homeland, that their only land was that of all the lands of the USSR where they resided. Their destinies, he argued, were linked to those of the Russian, Ukrainian, Byelorussian, and other peoples with whom they were "struggling and creating a common motherland."

What would happen to those who refused to relocate? He could never advocate such a course to fellow Jews, Lozovsky said. A similar argument was voiced by Peretz Markish, a member of the Presidium and the most prominent Jewish writer of his day. Jews, he said, could not be cut off from their culture and transplanted to a region as foreign to them as Birobidzhan. Hadn't Jews suffered enough?

The memoir states that Suslov was "fidgeting in his chair" by the time the meeting was adjourned; it would continue the next day, he told them. "Before dawn," the memoir recounts, "all were arrested." There is no mention of such a meeting with the JAC in Suslov's own memoirs. And given the meticulous destruction of potentially embarrassing records by Stalin and his successors, exactly what transpired that night in Soviet Jewish history may never be corroborated in documents.

But thanks to the country's oral tradition, this story and others like it have been told and retold around kitchen tables from one generation to the next. In a country as repressive as the Soviet Union, such accounts, despite their obvious flaws, are indispensable in filling in what is missing in Soviet history.

The tradition has been reinforced by the physical and emotional closeness of Soviet families. Since so many were directly touched by the war, memories of those experiences are keenly felt to this day by the grandparents and even the parents of young Soviets, many of whom share apartments because of the housing shortage in most Soviet cities. The war years have remained a topic of discussion in many families.

"Official focus on the war is almost unnecessary," said André Baranov, a writer at *Komsomolskaya Pravda,* the youth organization's newspaper.[42] For Baranov, the war is not ancient history. He has seen it daily, not only in yellowing photographs of fallen comrades his father still keeps at home, but in the shrapnel in his father's arm, and the other severe injuries he incurred.

A second vehicle of memory in the Soviet Union is the spirit of many of Russia's best artists. While it is obvious that honest debate always seems more precious in societies in which it is forbidden, the traditional devotion of Russians to their artists and creators has served the cause of *glasnost* and historical reassessment. It is the playwrights, filmmakers, poets, writers, and artists who have challenged shibboleths and helped mold the debate more than the historians and other scholars.

Yevgeny Yevtushenko's poem expressing admiration and compassion for Bukharin was published in January 1988, months before the Soviet government formally rehabilitated him. More than twenty-five years earlier, his poem about Babi Yar helped embarrass the authorities into building a monument to the massacred.

Heavy Sand, by Anatoli Rybakov, which was published inside the Soviet Union in 1978 more than ten years after it was written, recounts the travails and heroism of a Jewish family in the Ukraine, one of the few published novels in Soviet literature to focus on Jews.

Today, Shatrov's plays have inspired debate and set the stage for the official resurrection of some of the Bolshevik Revolution's once-purged figures. Shatrov, who is fifty-six—one year younger than Gorbachev—has attacked Stalin with a fervor that transcends politics. "My father participated in the revolution," he recalled one day at his apartment overlooking the Moskva River. "He was executed in 1937, at the height of Stalin's purges. For what? For nothing."[43]

His mother was arrested in 1949 and released from a labor camp only in 1958. "For what? For being the wife of her husband twelve years earlier."

Aleksei Rykov, who was executed with Bukharin after a political show trial in 1938, was Shatrov's uncle by marriage. All killed—for nothing.

Shatrov has relished the unusual role—that of surrogate historian—which he and his fellow artists have been playing in the unfolding of the Soviet Union's new history. And he praised Afanasyev and other "bold" Soviet historians.

"The question is always what aches in a person. With me it is my soul that aches. I cannot say why Afanasyev's soul aches and the souls of others do not. What can you expect from them? They have withstood so much for sixty years; they have put up with so much. To write the truth is difficult, not only for historians, but for everybody in this society. But you have to decide once and for all what you are doing, what you are living for."

Alexander Askoldov, a film director, has also benefited from the liberalized atmosphere for artists and writers in Moscow. For more than twenty years, his film, *Commissar,* sat on the censor's shelf. It had been his first, his only film. But now *Commissar*, which portrays a Jewish family's struggle for survival and dignity during the years of the civil war and its selfless assistance to a female Russian commissar, has been shown inside the Soviet Union and touted at film festivals abroad.

Being an honest filmmaker in the Soviet Union, Askoldov said, is somewhat akin to "being a tightrope walker without a net." After his fall from the high wire back in 1976, he lived on his "wife's salary, an obsessive conviction to fight so that one day [the] film would be shown, and occasional glimmers of hope."[44]

Like Shatrov's father, Askoldov's father fought in the revolution and throughout the civil war; he was shot in 1937. His mother was imprisoned when he was five. Though he is not Jewish, he was helped as a child by a Jewish family, a memory that gave him the idea for *Commissar.*

"You cannot imagine the life led by us 'sons of the enemies of the people,'" said Askoldov, whose quiet indignation smolders within him to this day. "There was a hatred of all of us. It was a shadow that you always knew was there. It's like anti-Semitism."

Expressions of the Great Patriotic War or the Holocaust in modern Soviet paintings are less common. But in Minsk, concentration-camp scenes painted by Mikhail Savitsky, the head of the Young Artists Studio, have been on display at the Great Patriotic War Museum since 1980. His large, painfully detailed tableaux fill a side room of the museum. One depicts a concentration-camp inmate hurling himself against barbed wire in a suicide attempt. Another shows camp inmates hauling away wagonloads of skeletal corpses.

Savitsky, a gaunt, white-haired painter, whose vast, sun-filled studio belied his self-deprecating characterization of himself as a painter on the "margins" of Soviet art, is, rather, a "Distinguished Artist" of the Soviet Union. During the war, he was a non-Jewish prisoner at several concentration camps: Buchenwald, Dora, and

Dachau, where he was finally liberated by American troops. "I can never forget what I saw there, and what you see is what I remember," he said, one cold, bright afternoon in the late fall of 1987.[45] "A human mind cannot comprehend the life inside a concentration camp." Over the years, he said, several of his exhibits were canceled by the authorities. "I guess I wasn't engaged in 'right' thinking."

Among the most controversial were his concentration-camp paintings and others depicting the horrors of the war. "I depicted real people, afraid, but still fighting, not shouting hurrah in the streets. I painted partisans burying children—their own children.

"Human memory is subject to alteration. A person who was fighting then would screen out today the pain of the loss of fellow fighters, the horrible conditions every soldier faced. The glorious battles were not so glorious. They were bloody and savage. I don't like war. And that's why I painted these pictures."

Memories of the war were being erased. They were becoming "rose-colored," and that, he warned, would alter the entire modern generation's attitude toward the war.

"Over time, the memory of a nation—that war was a catastrophe—does not change. And people here know the truth. Whatever is finally written in books will never affect the memory of the nation. People will only say when they read it, 'Truth, at last.' In this country, only the 'history' keeps changing."

But Savitsky's concentration-camp paintings are not without paradox. One of those that hangs in the museum—a painting that portrays a Nazi guard and a ghoulish *kapo* (an inmate recruited as a Nazi helper) standing in front of a pile of white cadavers—was repainted by him at the instructions of Minsk Communist Party officials. Members of Minsk's Jewish community had found the painting blatantly anti-Semitic, because the uniform of the *kapo*, who seemed to be smiling at the slaughter, bore a Star of David.

The incident highlights another potential aid to memory in the Soviet Union: the enormous power of the Soviet government to fill in the more gaping holes, to right historical wrongs, and to authorize the replacement of official mythology with a truer version of the past. Under Gorbachev, this has been done to a far greater extent than ever before.

But the opposite may also take place. A later generation of powerful Soviet leaders might decide one day to "revise" Gorbachev's truths. What would remain of this period of enlightenment is heatedly debated by Moscow intellectuals.

Judicial proceedings in the Soviet Union, as in the West, have also enhanced memory. The continuing trials of war criminals and collaborators, for example, serve to jog Soviet memories about the war. The Soviet Union has engaged in a protracted effort to identify and extradite those who killed Soviet civilians during the war.

For many years, the Soviet office responsible for tracking down and prosecuting war criminals had no official counterpart in the United States. The U.S. Office of Special Investigations was created within the Justice Department at Congress's insistence only in 1976, and even then in the face of administration opposition.[46] American officials in the OSI say that the Soviets have been scrupulous in their presentation of records and documents justifying their requests for extradition of alleged war criminals. Cooperation, they say, is excellent.

As recently as August 1988, the Soviets tried and sentenced to death someone whom Tass identified only as "a Soviet citizen who took part in Nazi massacres of the local population in the Ukraine during World War Two."[47] However, because war crimes trials, like most Soviet trials, are not open to the public, they have had only a limited role in educating young Soviets about the crimes of the past.

Finally, monuments, memorials, and official and unofficial commemorations serve to keep the memory of the war alive. Visits to Great Patriotic War museums are an essential part of their education system. No official foreign delegation or group tour visits Leningrad without being taken to the Piskareskaya Cemetery, where more than 550,000 Soviet victims of the siege of Leningrad are buried in mass graves.

Progress has been made by Jews and other minorities in their efforts to stage officially blessed commemorations. In September 1988, the government gave a permit to Jews in Moscow who wished to commemorate Babi Yar and the slaughter of Jews in the Minsk ghetto. That same month, the government agreed to permit the construction in Lithuania of the nation's first monument to the "Holocaust," a word that has not been used in the Soviet Union to refer to the Nazi destruction of Soviet and European Jews. Officials in the Ukraine have also begun debating whether a word about the Jews should be added to the plaque describing the massacre at Babi

Yar. Some have suggested that a separate memorial to the Jews be built closer to the ravine. Similar campaigns for memory, even when unsuccessful, have taught not only young Jews and other minorities, but young people in general about the unofficially acknowledged parts of their compatriots' past.

Finally, another boon to memory has been the rise of the so-called Twentieth Party Congress generation. These men and women—now in their fifties, like Gorbachev—were young when Khrushchev made his dramatic attack on Stalin at the congress and launched his liberalization program. They were awed and inspired by the attempt. They never forgot the heady spirit of those years.

Their passion today reflects a widespread craving among Soviet intellectuals to "repersonalize" and repoliticize a society that has become highly depersonalized, ever more passive and indifferent. This very emotional yearning plays into the hands of memory. Soviets, too, have learned that abstraction prompts amnesia.

Hence, historians like Medvedev and Afanasyev repeatedly endorse the need, for example, to publish the names of as many of Stalin's victims as possible, as well as those of their executioners.

"What we need to do is to restore facts, figures, faces," Afanasyev said. "We used to speak in hushed tones of the 'cult of personality' here. We dared not even say whose.

"We have a feeling now that this is our last chance. After the war, after Stalin died, there was so much hope that things would improve. But that hope was killed off. We became slaves, serfs without passports, without food or money. We lived under constant scrutiny. Those were horrible years in which modern public consciousness was formed.

"Those years fostered social passivity and alcoholism. People were reduced to the level of cattle," he said quietly. "Then the Twentieth Party Congress in 1956 opened our eyes. It was a very emotional thing for us. We have never forgotten it. We define our generation in terms of it. And it is what makes us want so very much to involve young people in that spirit today.

"I want to cry out to them: Don't be afraid. Open up your minds! Open your souls! Learn your history!

"They must learn about not only the calamity of war that came to our house. They must know about the evil that has lived inside it for so long."

. . .

Alongside Russian traditions that prompt remembrance, there are equally powerful forces and traditions that work against memory and Gorbachev's ambitious efforts.

A stratagem for burying memory often employed by Soviet officials is the deliberate distortion of historical truth through terminology. For the rest of the Western world, the war that devastated the continent of Europe and resulted in fifty million deaths is known as the Second World War. Most historians date the war from September 1, 1939, when Germany invaded Poland, to 1945, when Germany and Japan surrendered. This is not the case in the Soviet Union.

The Great Patriotic War that has been talked and written about until recently in the USSR began on June 22, 1941, when Nazi Germany stunned Stalin by invading the Ukraine. The designation has been useful. It has enabled the Soviets to teach their children about a war that is crucial to the national psyche without dwelling on such unpleasant events as the 1939 Hitler-Stalin Pact, when Stalin allied his country with fascism.

It has also enabled the Soviet Union to avoid detailed mention of the Red Army's quiet move into eastern Poland under the Pact's protocol, and the Soviets' subsequent seizure and occupation of that territory, the Polish Ukrainian and Byelorussian provinces. Under Sovietization of the territory, more than 200,000 Polish men and women were taken to prisons and labor camps inside the Soviet Union, where many died. The puppet "progressive groups" then dutifully requested that the occupied territory be incorporated into the Soviet Union, where it remains to this day. All this occurred more than one year before a single German fired upon a Soviet soldier.

Concentration on the Great Patriotic War also enables Soviet historians to ignore Stepan Bandera, a priest and fervent Ukrainian nationalist, who mobilized a ragtag army of thousands of his compatriots to fight the Soviet Union. Although he is regarded by many historians as a homicidal maniac, a despicable and unsavory killer, quelling the revolt required a large-scale Soviet military operation—including tanks, aircraft, heavy artillery, and an elaborate police intelligence operation. Bandera so plagued the Soviet Union even years after the end of the war that the NKVD, the Soviet secret police and KGB predecessor, finally managed to assassinate him in West Germany years later. But Bandera's activities and the strength of and support for his rebellion have never been widely publicized in the Soviet Union.[48]

Collaboration, in general, is yet another key phenomenon that has largely defied reassessment or public debate. Soviet resistance to acknowledging it has been particularly unfortunate for the country's Jews, since so many of them died at the hands of collaborationists.

The Great Patriotic War permits the Soviet Union to separate its seizure and annexation of Lithuania, Latvia, and Estonia in 1940 from the war and the Hitler-Stalin Pact. Western historians estimate that more than 170,000 people in these republics were arrested, put into cattle trucks, and deported to Siberia. Most never returned. Only under Gorbachev has the pact been criticized.

Finally, recounting the Great Patriotic War permits Soviet historians to gloss over their country's "Winter War" of 1939–40 against Finland. Only after thousands of Finns had died defending their country against Soviet aggression, and only after the full weight of the Red Army was brought to bear against them, did the Finnish government sue for peace. The cost of the war was devastating for the Soviets while they should have been preparing for their impending confrontation with Germany. More than fifty thousand Soviet soldiers died; countless more were wounded.

An even more telling example of a war-related distortion of fact through terminology is the Soviet Union's memorial at Khatyn, about an hour from Minsk, which commemorates the destruction of Byelorussian villages by the Germans. The memorial's simplicity sets it apart from most other Soviet war monuments. It reminded me of the Vietnam war memorial in Washington, whose abstract, austere design also invites contemplation.

Khatyn was once a village on the road to Vitebsk and the home of 149 peasants. The Germans burned it to the ground as a warning to partisans. Today, a white marble walkway connects the spots where each of the village's twenty-six huts once stood. In their places stand twenty-six plain concrete obelisks, each with a small black bell at the top. The bells peal every thirty seconds. There is also a "cemetery of villages," 186 tombstones bearing the names of lost villages, those destroyed by the Nazis and never rebuilt. A "Wall of Memory" stands at the end of the cemetery. Inscribed on this replica of a prison wall are the names of 260 camps—"concentration camps" my guide called them—where 205,000 Byelorussians were killed between 1941 and 1944, victims of shootings, starvation, immolation, disease, and gassings in mobile trucks whose exhaust pipes were turned inside.

My guide, Nonna Tovmasyan, could reel off by heart the names of the camps and their casualty rates: Polotsk, 150,000; Gomel, 100,000; Volkovysk, 20,000; Orsha, 19,000. Two of the camps were reserved for children, whom the Germans kept as blood donors for their soldiers, she said. One million of the more than 2 million Byelorussians who died in the war were civilians.

But something beyond aesthetics makes the Khatyn memorial noteworthy. Nonna had never heard of another place of mass slaughter only 175 miles from Khatyn. She had never heard of the Katyn Forest, 10 miles west of Smolensk, a few hours from this memorial village. She was not alone. Few Soviets have been told about the place where, during their occupation of Poland in 1940, Soviet soldiers systematically murdered more than 4,000 Polish officers, the élite of the country, and dumped their bodies into mass graves.

The name of Khatyn village and the name of Katyn Forest are different in Russian, spelled and pronounced somewhat differently. But they are not all that different. Why choose this spot to commemorate the destruction of more than a hundred Byelorussian villages? Why pick the name of this particular village for the memorial?

Vitaly Korotich, of the *glasnost* journal *Ogonyok,* called the similarity in names "useful" and not truly misleading. "Both sites were places of slaughter," he said.

The Soviet government might one day be forced to acknowledge its predecessor's responsibility for the country's horrendous massacre at a spot with a similar name, as Poland has now officially demanded. In August 1988, the foundations of a new Soviet memorial were laid at the edge of Katyn Forest. Polish and Soviet officials laid wreaths at the base of a commemorative plaque, which reads: "A memorial complex to Polish officers who perished at Katyn and a monument to the Soviet prisoners-of-war will be erected in this place." No mention is made of how the Polish soldiers died or who killed them.[49]

And the Khatyn monument outside of Minsk, built in 1969 and visited by more than 25 million people, will almost surely not be renamed. Whether intentionally or not, the name of the monument serves to blur the memory of the Soviet massacre of Polish officers.

In spite of greater freedom, the subordination of historians to politicians remains an impediment to memory. A military commission has been working on a new ten-volume history of the Great Patriotic War, but it was Gorbachev and his supporters who selected its members, and it was Gorbachev who named himself titular head of another commission to review party records and archives, and to present what Tass has described as a "definitive" version of the Communist party's history.[50] Historians cannot work without access to archives. And in the Soviet Union, access continues to be limited to those designated by the state.[51]

The 1988 U.S.-Soviet archival exchange agreement, providing access to Soviet state and republic archives, was unprecedented and represents a breakthrough. But Afanasyev, for one, has remained discouraged by the lack of a comparable opening of party archives. In a state in which the party is the only organ that has really mattered, the continued inaccessibility of this material to scholars and journalists immeasurably complicates independent historical analysis.

Even Gorbachev's speeches have been read by many party officials as new sets of official guidance. Afanasyev said that he viewed Gorbachev's pronouncements as an invitation to debate.

"But many of my colleagues still see it as gospel. People at the archives came to me after his speech with words underlined. They said, Gorbachev says this, but you are writing that. When you see his speeches in that way, you will always remain in the dark," he concluded.

Just as elements of Marxist ideology have reinforced the mechanisms of memory, other elements of it have had the opposite effect. Belief in a "scientific" unfolding of history, or a "historical dialectic," for example, has prompted interest in events of the past that have shaped the present. But it also implies that there is only one "correct" interpretation of the unfolding, as opposed to several different analyses that might be partially valid.

Thus, most Soviet commentators, when asked whether Gorbachev could achieve the changes he desires without reexamining the past, responded in the negative. But most, when pressed, added that they believe that Gorbachev is the product of what Korotich has called "historical necessity." They stress that his effort to reassess history will not result in several competing interpretations of primordial events of the past, but in a single, "logical" rendition of the "truth."

"We must show history as logical," said Korotich. "We must show Gorbachev as a logical part of our historical development. Just as Stalin was a logical part of our history, our fight against Stalin is now also logical. We need one history, one line. I'm not a proponent of letting one hundred historical flowers bloom."[52]

The fact that such words were uttered by Korotich, whom many Western analysts regard as a leading reformer, an articulate exponent of Gorbachev's "new thinking," illustrates the depth of the problem.

Even Afanasyev, without doubt one of the most passionate and enlightened of the proponents of historical *glasnost,* espouses an unshakable belief in what he terms "scientific" history. For example, he said, he was uncomfortable with compatriots, such as the playwright Shatrov, who attacked Stalin simply because of his "deviations" from Leninism. Lenin was not a god, he said.

A fair enough viewpoint. But Afanasyev went on to add: "It's not scientific. It won't allow our society to move forward."

This notion of history as a conveyor belt of Progress, moving inexorably toward a more enlightened future state, is similar to, but quite distinct from, the Western notion of examining history in order to avoid repeating mistakes. The Soviet view makes history almost an adjunct of official dogma, despite Afanasyev's desire not to do so. It is a deeply entrenched attitude among Communists that is part and parcel of the Soviet Union's quandary.

Another vehicle of historical distortion is rationalization, which, of course, is not confined to the Soviet Union. But it is especially pronounced in Soviet officials' justification of their country's unwillingness to acknowledge the Holocaust and Soviet Jewry's disproportionate suffering during the war.

Dr. Arbatov has clearly articulated the reasoning. "As in the United States, the extermination of the Jews is well known here," he asserted during one of several interviews at his spacious office at the U.S.A.-Canada Institute one icy day in January 1988. "But our perspective is different from yours and from that of the Europeans. Here, it wasn't only Jews the Nazis wanted to kill as many of as possible. They wanted to level and destroy Leningrad. They wanted to kill all POWs. They wanted to preserve only as many Slavs as necessary for work and agriculture.

"OK. Six million Jews died. But one million Soviets died in Leningrad alone. What's six million when you've lost twenty million?

"Yes," he continued, "we should write about the Jewish genocide. We should acknowledge it. It should be depicted—and to some extent it is, though maybe not enough—in our literature and films and history. But we will not enhance *glasnost* by dividing the dead. There is not a single monument in this country to the war dead of a single nationality, not even to the Russians. And I don't want to begin separating the dead by nationality now. It is improper."

Korotich said that the Jewish situation was particularly delicate in some of the republics outside of the Russian republic. Consider, he said, his own republic of the Ukraine. "Because so many Jews were active from the beginning in the Communist Party, Jews played the role of Russians in the national republics. You can still hear it today. The Jews took our land; the Jews ate our sausage; the Jews took our money. It's a lot easier to blame the Jews than the Russians. So in our country one must be doubly careful about singling them out for special tribute. It could backfire," he warned.

Portraying Jews as the major victims of the war in his country, Arbatov agreed, might well create "a counterreaction on the part of people who suffered here. It could wind up being very dangerous for Jews."

The nature of the threat was rarely articulated. But it emanates from another product of *glasnost*—the resurgence of Russian nationalism, among the strongest of the nationalist movements. Its most prominent organ of expression in the mid-1980s was Pamyat, which, paradoxically, means "memory," in Russian. Thanks to *glasnost,* Pamyat's anti-Semitism and xenophobia, too, have been able to surface.

Gorbachev's toleration of a greater degree of nationalism within the USSR has granted the anti-Semitic, anti-Communist, traditionalist nationalist movements greater expression. Since Pamyat has been permitted to organize and stage protests, Jews in Moscow and other republics have grown fearful about what could be a resurgence of overt anti-Semitism, a new round of intensified persecution of Jews. Many activists have received warnings from supporters of Pamyat. Anti-Semitic incidents have been increasing.

There is no doubt that Russian nationalism is a potent force in the Soviet Union, and the authorities have done little to discourage it.

While feelings of the leadership toward Pamyat and similar groups are mixed, officials have often cited Pamyat as a justification for not reexamining and fighting the deeply entrenched cultural anti-Semitism in the Soviet Union. Crudely put: we are denying the disproportionate Jewish suffering and heroism during the war in order to protect the Jews.

A more compelling explanation can be found, however, in Russian anti-Semitism itself, a centuries-old tradition perpetuated by a succession of Soviet goverments. It was Stalin who initially refused to admit that Jews had suffered more than non-Jews on Soviet territory. Khrushchev then adopted the "Do not divide the dead" policy and made it his own. Since his era, this position has been the official policy of most Soviet leaders, including Gorbachev.

Jews are more hopeful now that their situation will change. The Soviet people have not been told why, but Jews have been permitted under Gorbachev to emigrate in greater numbers. The definition of those eligible to emigrate as Jews has been narrowed, but emigration—up to fifteen thousand in 1988—has increased. For the rest of the country's 1.8 million Jews, who have chosen to stay in the Soviet Union, or at least not to apply to leave, a greater degree of cultural self-expression has been slowly tolerated. Though Hebrew has not been officially recognized as a legitimate language and Jewish cultural associations have still not been granted the privilege of official registration in most of the republics, the authorities have given informal approval to Jewish gatherings—such as the rally at the main cemetery in Moscow and in 1989 in Kiev to commemorate the slaughter of Jews and other Soviet citizens at Babi Yar. In November, Soviet officials agreed to let Hebrew be taught within official synagogues, the first step, many Soviet Jews hope, toward replacing Yiddish as the official Jewish language. A Jewish Cultural Center opened in Moscow in February 1989. That same year, some thirty Jewish children began attending some afternoon courses at the Moscow synagogue.

Soviet experts say that Soviet Jewish emigration and a more tolerant official attitude toward Jews who remain in the country are inexorably tied to Gorbachev's *glasnost* and *perestroika.* But will the sweeping reform program continue? Optimists say that the process will continue because it must. There is no going back to a system that has failed so miserably.

But some remain pessimistic. One Soviet scholar put it this way: Gorbachev's reforms could be likened to a country's decision to switch driving from the left- to the right-hand side of the road.

"The problem," he said, "is how to accomplish this. What you don't do is say: O.K. We'll do it sequentially. Tomorrow we will start with the trucks."

Soviet society is so riddled with passivity, fear and inefficiency it has thus far proven impossible to correct problems in one sector without profoundly destabilizing others. But despite the obstacles the Soviet Union has been doing what many European nations have been reluctant to do: it has been confronting its wartime experiences squarely and facing unpleasant truths about itself.

Ultimately, however, transforming the Soviet Union into what Korotich has called a "normal" country might be beyond the ability of any single leader. For it is one thing, the skeptics say, to encourage the Soviet Union to face the mirror of its past; it is quite another to escape its legacy.

The United States

The desperation among Holocaust survivors in America has become almost palpable. It was articulated in 1989 by Elie Wiesel, who more than any other individual has built an international reputation on bearing witness to the Holocaust. "I have an occasional nightmare now," he said. "I wake up shivering, thinking that when we die, no one will be able to persuade people that the Holocaust occurred."

He is not alone. Most of the survivors have died or are dying. Soon, all will be gone. Consequently, many have become obsessed of late with speaking out. They feel compelled to tell their stories now, before it is too late. They want the world to know what they experienced only forty-five years ago. They want other Americans to take notice and remember.

This was not always the case. Immediately after the war, the survivors who came to America wanted to forget their experiences and build new lives. The communities in which they lived encouraged little else.

"We came from a deportation camp in Germany to the Lower East Side of New York in 1950; I was ten years old," said Abraham H. Foxman, national director of the Anti-Defamation League of

B'nai B'rith, the nation's largest Jewish organization. "When I look back, I think that the survivors felt guilty that they had survived. They were embarrassed about things they had to do to live through those years. But their isolation, or whatever else they felt, was reinforced by our neighbors. They expected us to look like we had come right out of a camp—emaciated, wounded. They hinted that they wanted to know what we had gone through, only they didn't really. My parents tried to explain at first. But they stopped. It simply wasn't worth it."

The 1950s were years of public assimilation and private pain. People like Foxman's father wrote, but mostly for themselves, in diaries and in memoirs, few of which were published. Foxman found his father's moving manuscript about life in the death camps, written in the early 1950s, only after his father died.

What happened inside survivor homes depended on what individual survivors had endured in the camps and on their personalities. Some could talk of little else with their children. Others could not discuss it at all.

Outside their homes, there was little support for these victims. Their pain was not recognized by organized American Jewry. Survivors were not exactly excluded as a group; but they were not included either. Neither the Jewish community—nor gentiles—were interested in their harrowing tales. Only one group of Americans had any detailed knowledge of or interest in the catastrophe—soldiers who had seen the concentration camps. But the stories of what they had witnessed in Europe made little dent in the nation's consciousness.

So most survivors buried their memories by keeping busy. They learned English, built businesses, created new identities, raised families. They were preoccupied not just with survival but with succeeding in this new land.

This concern was shared by most Jews. As late as 1957, Nathan Glazer, the sociologist, pondered why American Jews seemed so relatively uninterested in the two most cataclysmic events of Judaism in the twentieth century—the Holocaust and the creation of the state of Israel.[1]

The suppression of memory began to end with the trial of Adolf Eichmann in Israel in 1961. "I remember it vividly," said Leon Wieseltier, literary editor of *The New Republic* and a Jewish scholar, whose mother survived the Russian and German occupation of

Schodnica, a village in Poland.[2] "Everything stopped in our house during the trial," he said. "There was a total, eerie silence."

"The trial was the first event to awaken survivor consciousness, to touch even some nonsurvivor Jews deeply," said Michael Nutkiewicz, the son of survivors and the director of the Martyrs Memorial and Museum of the Holocaust in Los Angeles. "It was really the first time that survivors were telling their stories in public, expressing their pain on television, before the world."

In Los Angeles, survivors hesitantly approached the Jewish Federation and other institutions, seeking their support for a public monument to those who had perished. The initial response from Jewish groups there and in other cities was cool. Few had any interest in promoting projects that might reopen unhealed wounds. Even in American universities and among intellectuals curiosity was slight. Hannah Arendt had generated controversy through her coverage of the Eichmann trial and her provocative analysis of what came to be known as the "banality of evil." But Raul Hilberg, the author of what is widely regarded as the bible of Holocaust studies, did not publish his work until 1961. "And Elie Wiesel was just barely eking out a living," said Rabbi Irving Greenberg, president of the National Jewish Center for Learning and Leadership. "Nobody was interested then in what he had to say."

This period of hesitation ended decisively and abruptly with Israel's Six-Day War in 1967. The impact of the war on the American public, and on American Jews in particular, is difficult to overestimate.

"All of a sudden the Jewish community had understood that the Israelis might be defeated by the Arabs, that there might be a second Holocaust for the Jews. The fears for Jewish collective safety pushed all the Holocaust buttons," said Nutkiewicz.

Michael Berenbaum, the project director of the United States Holocaust Memorial Museum, arrived in Israel the day before the war began. "I remember thinking: if my people are going to die, I want to die with them," he recalled. "I had vowed that if Israel lost the war, I would return to the United States and marry a non-Jewish woman so that my children would be free of the trauma of being Jews. We were either going to turn around our history or the lineage would end with me."

While the prospect of defeat triggered despair among Jews everywhere, Israel's stunning victory helped empower the Jewish community in America. Jewish men began sporting yarmulkes and gold Stars of David. Six-Day War jokes spread through the country. Synagogue membership soared. Jews suddenly began seeing themselves as the descendants of biblical cowboys—Jewish Clint Eastwoods.

Because Jews no longer felt so absolutely vulnerable, they could finally confront the period of their most intense vulnerability. "After the '67 war, the Jews were finally safe. It became 'safe' to talk about the Holocaust, 'safe' to talk about growing Jewish power here at home," Nutkiewicz recalled.

The Six-Day War destroyed vestiges of anti-Zionism within the American Jewish community. For gentiles, it legitimized Israel as an ally capable of victory, and hence worthy of support on pragmatic as well as moral grounds.

It also transformed the Holocaust into a quasi-religious event, a sign not only of suffering, but also of resurrection, somewhat akin to Christ's crucifixion and the resurrection for Christians. Though the Jewish victims of the Nazi genocide did not choose to die for their faith, the Holocaust became for some Jews after the Arab-Israeli war a militant symbol, a reason for the redemption of the Jewish people through a triumphant state. Fascination grew with the instruments of the near destruction of the Jews. Auschwitz, once a metaphor for death and barbarism, became a sacred site.

The catastrophe that had speeded the creation of a Jewish state in Israel after the Second World War had two decades later activated and enhanced a sense of identity among Jews in America.

Jews, of course, had long been active in America in human-rights causes—most important, the civil rights movement. But the growing awareness of the Holocaust in the wake of the 1967 war led children of Holocaust survivors and other young Jews to feel that they had a special obligation to try to right perceived wrongs in America. Activism was the key, indifference the Jewish equivalent of one of Catholicism's mortal sins. And that activism affected issues that had seemingly little to do with Jewish interests.

"You can't grow up in a family whose members have numbers on their arms and remain indifferent to your country's involvement in a war like Vietnam," said Mark Rudd, the former student radical who spearheaded the 1968 rebellion at Columbia University in protest against the Vietnam War. Addressing the audience at a twenty-year commemoration of the strike, Rudd said that he had equated the American involvement in Vietnam with the German occupation of Europe.

"But we were not going to be good Nazis," said Rudd, recounting motivations he had not shared with most of us at the time. "I was not going to stand by and watch American planes drop napalm on innocent women and children. I was not going to let my country burn innocents alive and do nothing."

Yes, he conceded, his group had erred in embracing violence. "But we did not just go along."[3]

Rudd said that neither he nor any of the other Jewish leaders of the student revolt (and the majority were Jews) had identified themselves strongly as Jews during their rebellion. Almost none was religious at the time. "But we acted as Jews," he said, "because we were afraid that our country was perpetrating a second Holocaust."

The Arab-Israeli war coincided with the emerging financial success of the survivors in America, another key factor in the growing awareness of the Holocaust. By the mid-1960s, many survivors had accumulated significant wealth; they were eager to use it for causes close to their hearts. By the mid-1970s, their children were organizing, which in turn encouraged many of the parents to become more active.

The dynamism of the survivors, once again, mirrored growing Jewish activism in general. The political and economic success of Jews in America and the decline in anti-Semitism had gradually enabled Jews to "emerge from the closet," said Stuart Eizenstat, an attorney and the Domestic Policy Adviser to President Carter. "Jews were no longer the frightened minority of the pre-war period," said Eizenstat. "This was a country in which Jews were permitted to have interests and to push for them. Clout had become respectable." By the mid-1980s, more than seventy Jewish groups were registered as lobbyists in Washington.

In the decade after the Arab-Israeli war, the Holocaust became one of those issues around which Jews organized and lobbied. There was nothing inherently exploitative in the Jewish push for monuments, memorials, and public tributes to the period of their most intense suffering. But the linkage of the Holocaust with campaigns to raise money and enhance support for the state of Israel marked the beginning of serious abuse and misuse of the Holocaust.

American Jews discovered that the Holocaust could be used as a weapon not only for garnering sympathy at home, but also for insisting on unquestioning support for Israel abroad. Some Jews who had been active in the civil rights movement and "dovish" toward the war in Vietnam, could, by calling upon the memory of the Holocaust, become increasingly intolerant and "hawkish" on Israel's behalf.

The power of Holocaust imagery was not lost on Israel's enemies. At the United Nations, the Arabs and Soviets started describing the Israelis as aggressors. Crude comparisons were made between Israelis and Nazis. American Jews, in turn, responded by portraying themselves and all Jews as potential Holocaust victims.

Menachem Begin was elected Israel's Prime Minister in 1977. Begin, who had fled Central Europe and the Nazis, raised the specter of the Holocaust whenever an issue surfaced that involved an actual or perceived threat to Israel's security. In the United States, the slogan "Never Again!" came not only from the lips of Meir Kahane and other extremists, but also from secular, assimilated Jews who had only a nodding acquaintance with the precepts of their faith and who, before the war, had manifested little sense of Jewish identity.

Menachem Z. Rosensaft, a lawyer and the founding chairman of the International Network of Children of Jewish Holocaust Survivors, deplored what he viewed as the growing politicization and popularization of the Holocaust in the late 1970s. "By that time, the Holocaust had definitely caught on. It had been widely popularized in films and television docudramas," said Rosensaft, who was born in 1948 in Bergen-Belsen after it had become a camp for displaced persons. "There was a lot of amateur pop psychology floating around. There were a lot of people talking about 'transmission trauma' and the like. Neither I nor the other Holocaust survivor children in our group recognized the portrait being painted of us," he said.

In 1981, after the first world gathering of survivors in Israel, Rosensaft and survivor offspring from several different countries decided to form an umbrella organization to redirect their efforts. "We felt the best way to honor those who had died was to look at the experience in a broad moral context."

While his parents worked on building monuments and museums and other projects in honor of those who had perished, Rosensaft's small group, in addition to staging commemorations, worked to win congressional approval of ratification of the international genocide convention, to free Soviet and Ethiopian Jews to emigrate, to end apartheid in South Africa, to rescue Vietnamese boat people, and to preserve Yiddish culture in America. While his mother was helping to plan a new museum in Washington to honor the Holocaust's victims, Rosensaft met in Sweden with Yasir Arafat and other representatives of the Palestine Liberation Organization.[4]

The meeting with Arafat anguished and enraged many Jewish supporters of Israel. How could a child of survivors have betrayed the memory of those who had perished by meeting with an avowed enemy of Israel and the Jewish people?

"We [the offspring] are not survivors," Rosensaft explained. "Only the survivors have the right to use the terminology of survivors. All Jews are not survivors, as some Jews have been saying recently. That is nonsense." Children of survivors had no special privileges or rights, he continued. "What we do have is a unique relationship to the Holocaust because of our relationship with our parents. We have a particular sensitivity to the events of the war and the Holocaust which others in our generation do not have. And that gives us a special responsibility, not just to talk to ourselves about ourselves. We have a specific duty to share our awareness with others, to ensure that others, Jews and gentiles alike, understand why remembrance of these events is important."

While many American Jews have strongly opposed Rosensaft's views on how the Holocaust should be translated into modern political life, they have shared his desire to see the event made a part of American memory. It is American Jews who, quite naturally, have taken the lead in the wide range of commemoration projects.[5]

Since October 1980, when the Congress unanimously embraced in law and in the name of the American people the duty of "Holocaust Remembrance," projects have proliferated throughout the country. From North Dakota, with its five hundred Jews, to New York, home of nearly half the nation's six million Jewish Americans, commemoration projects are under way.

A fifty-six-page directory of Holocaust institutions in the United States published in 1987 by the United States Holocaust Memorial Council listed ninety-eight American institutions—nineteen museums, forty-eight resource centers, thirty-four archival facilities, twelve memorials, twenty-six research institutes, and five libraries. Though some of these facilities overlap and fit into several categories, the directory did not include many of the hundreds of small private study groups, like the one in Palm Springs, California, the Holocaust Survivors of the Desert. These tiny clusters of survivors and their children and grandchildren have been meeting with little publicity throughout the nation.

Representative Stephen J. Solarz, Democrat of Brooklyn, whose district is home to more Jews than Jerusalem, said he had never believed that Jews would be so successful in transforming the Holocaust into part of the nation's officially recognized civic culture. The critical moment, in his view, came on November 1, 1978, when President Carter created the President's Commission on the Holocaust and charged its thirty-four members, the majority of them Jews, with exploring how the nation should commemorate the Holocaust.

The commission, chaired by Elie Wiesel, produced a report ten months later that contained several recommendations.[6] First, the panel concluded that any memorial to the Holocaust should be, as Wiesel put it, a "living" monument. Hence, the group recommended that a museum be built rather than an abstract statue or monument similar to the Vietnam War Memorial. Second, it was agreed that the national Holocaust museum should be built with private donations on federal land in the nation's capital. Third, the report recommended that the President implement a resolution approved earlier by Congress designating national Days of Remembrance of Victims of the Holocaust.[7] Fourth, the group urged that a Committee on Conscience of prominent private citizens be established to sound an alarm whenever and wherever human rights were violated.

Only one of the commission's recommendations was not implemented, the most forward-looking of its proposals—the Committee on Conscience. The State Department and the White House vigorously opposed it. Neither favored the establishment of an officially sanctioned, private group of human-rights busybodies who might offer competing assessments of various international human-rights crises and the efficacy of the U.S. government's efforts to resolve them.

"Our proposals were fine as long as they did not ask the government to extend the lessons of the Holocaust to our current foreign and national security policies," said Hyman Bookbinder, a long-time lobbyist for the American Jewish Committee and an original member of the Holocaust Commission and the Holocaust Council that succeeded it. The Committee on Conscience had been his idea, and he was bitterly disappointed when the proposal was shelved.

The government's rejection of the Committee on Conscience proved just the first of several setbacks for Jews lobbying for national commemoration of the Holocaust. In Washington in the spring of 1985, Jews suffered a bitter political defeat.

Much has been written about Bitburg as a German-American crisis. But Bitburg was a domestic crisis as well. It was the first instance of serious political strain between organized American Jewry and the Reagan Administration, whose relations until then had been impeccable. It was also one of the first highly publicized political struggles in the United States over which form of Holocaust commemoration was appropriate.

The Jewish community's anguish about President Reagan's Bitburg visit was compounded by remarks he made while defending his planned trip against protests from Jews, veterans groups, the American Legion, and the press. On April 18, 1985, less than a month before the visit, Reagan told broadcasters and editors: "There is nothing wrong with visiting that cemetery where those young men are victims of Nazism also. . . . They were victims, just as surely as the victims in the concentration camps."

His statements stunned American Jews. The President of the United States, known for his staunch support for Israel and his empathy for Jews, had equated the women and children who had died in concentration camp gas chambers with the men who had helped put them there. Bergen-Belsen equaled Bitburg.

The U.S. Holocaust Memorial Council, which succeeded the commission and was also chaired by Elie Wiesel, held two emergency sessions to discuss whether its members should resign in protest. Wiesel argued that the entire council should resign. But there was resistance, particularly from the survivors. Some felt that the museum project had to take precedence. Others were unwilling to risk alienating an American President, who, but for Bitburg, had an extraordinary record of support for Israel and for Jewish interests at home. "They felt strongly that it would be a mistake for history's sake to resign, so we were outvoted, by considerable margins," recalled Wiesel. In the end, not a single member of the council resigned.[8]

"The Bitburg affair made American Jews feel vulnerable," wrote Geoffrey Hartman, the scholar, soon after the affair. "Not because they doubted the soundness of the American system or the good will of the president." Rather, Jews felt exposed because "they understood, again, their dependence on that good will."[9]

Hartman found Bitburg particularly troubling because "despite the attention the Holocaust had received . . . one could not count on the facts being known or their significance being understood. Publicity, media exposure and Days of Remembrance have been less than successful in conveying the enormity of the Shoah. 'Bitburg' disclosed that what understanding there was at the highest level of government led not to sensitivity, but only to sentimentality."[10]

According to a 1988 survey commissioned by the American Jewish Committee, Jews have grown increasingly anxious about American anti-Semitism and anti-Israeli sentiments. More than 75 percent of the Jews surveyed said that anti-Semitism in America was "a serious problem for American Jews," the highest level recorded since AJC surveys first posed the question in 1983. Similarly, when asked whether "virtually all positions of influence in America are open to Jews," only 25 percent agreed, the lowest figure in any previous poll.[11]

Steven M. Cohen, a professor of sociology at Queens College, City University of New York, who conducted the survey, attributed the anxiety about anti-Semitism to fears about the Reverend Jesse Jackson, who was at the time a contender for the Democratic presidential nomination, and to the rift between Jews and blacks in general.

But others argue that the roots of Jewish anxiety in America are deeper, that the invisible umbilical cord between Jews in America and Israel has played a role. Just as Israel's victory over the Arabs in 1967 served to empower and embolden Jews in America, Israel's mounting problems in quelling the Intifada and the growing chorus of protests about its actions in the occupied territories have fueled Jewish insecurity in America. Although a majority of American Jews have never set foot in Israel, the perception that Israel is locked into a hopeless, unwinnable struggle with the Palestinians, that another Holocaust might be possible, has prompted widespread anxiety about their own well-being in the United States. This, in turn, has made some Jews feel vulnerable, as they did before the '67 Arab-Israeli war, and uncomfortable once again with efforts to commemorate the Holocaust.

This growing sense of vulnerability has ignited an intense debate over how the Holocaust should be commemorated in the United States. In a nation as heterogeneous as America, where so many ethnic and religious groups compete for a place in the nation's historical consciousness, what form of national remembrance is appropriate?

For the most part, the arguments have attracted little public notice. They have taken place mainly within Jewish homes and Jewish organizations. But increasingly, of late, Jews and non-Jews alike have begun to ask, quietly, whether the proliferation of Holocaust museums throughout the land, and especially the construction of the $147 million U.S. Holocaust Memorial Museum on the National Mall in the heart of the nation's capital, is the best way to preserve the memory of this terrible event. Yes, the genocide in Europe has relevance for all Americans,[12] but aren't too many Jews, young ones in particular, already obsessed with the Holocaust? Hasn't the construction of so many monuments in such prominent places risked turning the Holocaust in the eyes of non-Jewish Americans into little more than a Jewish obsession, the "Shoah *Shtik,*" as one academic called it?[12]

In the possession of the most politically oriented Jews, has the Holocaust not become a blunt, aggressive weapon wielded to secure unquestioned support for Israel or special sympathy at home? The repeated use of the Holocaust to shame non-Jews into feeling guilt had become so much a part of popular Jewish culture by the end of the 1980s that it led one exasperated commentator to complain that "a Jew gets a parking ticket and he starts screaming about the Holocaust."[13]

In an article written almost a decade ago that remains controversial to this day, Robert Alter warned that "serious distortions of the Holocaust itself and, what is worse, of Jewish life occur when the Holocaust is commercialized, politicized, theologized, and academicized."[14] Making the Holocaust a fundamental touchstone of Jewish values, he argued, was bound to lead to distortions of emphasis and priority.

Deborah Lipstadt, a prominent Jewish writer, identified another risk inherent in Jewish preoccupation with the Holocaust and the resulting museum projects, especially the Washington museum. The placement and subject matter of the Washington memorial risk giving many non-Jews who have little direct knowledge of or contact with Jews an image of them as "perpetual victims," she has argued. "Is that really the impression that American Jews want to project?"

"For many years, survivors were virtually ignored by the Jewish community," said Leon Wieseltier of *The New Republic.*[15] "Only about ten years ago did the term 'survivor' become an honorific title. But once American Jews decided to make the Holocaust a part of their civic religion, survivors became the American Jewish equivalent of saints and relics."

Some survivors, too, deprived for so many years of respectful listeners to their stories, have come to see themselves as the conscience of American Jewry. Among the chosen people, they have become the chosen chosen.

"We still speak with an accent; we are green . . . but the green of emeralds," said Ben Meed, a survivor and member of the Holocaust Council, in recent remarks at a remembrance dinner. "We are the emeralds of American Jewry."[16]

The Holocaust industry has created a new vocabulary and way to measure time. Jewish writers have said that since World War II time can be charted as "before" and "after" Auschwitz. The American Jewish Committee survey in 1988 reflected the pivotal place in Jewish consciousness that the Holocaust has come to occupy. When asked whether they agreed with the statement that the "Exodus from Egypt and the giving of the Torah [the basic laws and commandments] to the Jewish people means more to me as a Jew than do the Holocaust and the founding of the State of Israel," only 14 percent said they agreed. Sixty-nine percent said they disagreed; 18 percent were uncertain.[17]

"The centrality of the Holocaust for American Jews amounts virtually to a cult of death," said Wieseltier. "How many American Jews know anything about the Jewish medieval poets, the wealth of culture, the Jewish philosophers? To American Jews, the six million who died were born a few minutes, at best a few years before they were killed."

Wieseltier has argued that this concentration on the Holocaust is dangerous for the soul and sanity of American Jewry. "Paying respects to those who perished in the Holocaust has become a political litmus test of respect for Jewish interests," he observed. "But the Holocaust is not a Jewish interest. It is a Jewish memory, a Jewish trauma, a Jewish experience."

"I think there has been too much emphasis among Jews on the Holocaust," Lipstadt agreed. "If you only look at the Holocaust, you develop what Salo Baron called the 'lachrymose theory of Jewish history.' The tearful becomes the prototype. Jews come to see themselves and gentiles come to see them as perennial sufferers. In other words, it risks letting the enemy define us. Yes, we should try to understand and remember the Holocaust," she said, "but within the context of what we are trying to preserve—a special heritage and tradition. If our image is only of suffering, we will have robbed ourselves of the joy and replenishment that Jewish tradition has always fostered."

What many Jews and non-Jews have come to fear is that this most terrible of events is becoming just another cause, just another fund-raising vehicle for a wide variety of interests. The memory of those who perished in the gas chambers of Auschwitz is being demeaned by the crass use of these deaths in bad made-for-television movies and trashy novels. Vulgarization takes many forms in pluralistic America. But it always results in a denial of dignity, in a gross distortion of the Holocaust for contemporary goals and ends. Saul Friedlander, among the first to detect the trend, warned of the sometimes unwitting effort to remove the component of horror and mystery from the event. Europe's most searing genocide was being transformed into an American version of kitsch.[30]

Wieseltier dubbed the phenomenon the "gentrification" of the Holocaust. "This is inevitable when the Holocaust is torn from its context and served up in culturally palatable portions," said Wieseltier.

This vulgarization is a new form of historical titillation. And in a society like America's, where the public attention span is measured in seconds and minutes rather than years or decades, where fad is often confused with trend, where sentimentality replaces insight and empathy, it represents a considerable threat to dignified remembrance.

The possibility that the Holocaust museums may lack dignity is a major concern of Friedlander, Wieseltier, and other critics.

Henry Kissinger, who fled Nazi Germany with his family in

1938, has objected to the national museum on more pragmatic grounds. He asserted in an interview that a museum on the Mall, next to monuments honoring America's founding fathers, constitutes, as he put it, "too high a profile" for American Jews. Kissinger has raised money for the Holocaust museum being built in New York City, which, given its large Jewish population, is an appropriate site for such an institution, he maintained. "But building a memorial on national ground is likely only to reignite anti-Semitism."[18]

Who will want to visit these chambers of horror, the skeptics ask? Will parents want to take their children there? Will the museums' constituency be broader than Jews, who need little reminding of the genocide? Will the Washington museum have meaning for non-Jews who come to the nation's capital to see the Air and Space Museum and the National Gallery of Art?

Irene Kirkland, an Auschwitz survivor who has lived much of her life in Israel and America, expressed yet another concern. Israel, she said, has already built a Holocaust museum, the emotionally wrenching memorial in Jerusalem known as Yad Vashem. Since the Holocaust was a Jewish catastrophe, she argued, a national memorial is appropriate only in Israel.[19]

Many agree, though given the sacred status of the projects within Jewish circles, they are reluctant to say so publicly. While it is now evident that the United States did not do enough to prevent the genocide in Europe or to stop it once it had started, the Holocaust is not an American experience. Americans did not do it, nor were they its targets or victims.

World War II, by contrast, is part of the American experience, one very different from the terror of the camps. While more than 292,000 Americans died and 670,000 were wounded, the war for most Americans was a fundamentally positive experience. It regenerated the depressed economy, completed the wreckage of European economic and military supremacy, and enabled America to emerge as the world's undisputed superpower. But even the war was not fought at home. So the world's bloodiest conflict has proven less difficult for Americans to confront than the Civil War, or more recently the war in Vietnam, where the lack of a national consensus about its necessity triggered bitterness and recriminations that have endured to this day.

If national remembrance has proven problematic in countries

that have a direct connection to the Holocaust, commemorations in the United States have raised different and in some ways broader questions about preserving the memory of painful events. What is the best way of fostering memory of such an event in a country in which what is being commemorated is so truly foreign?

Such questions have not daunted those Jews intent on building monuments. Supporters of the Holocaust museums and other projects have been bewildered, and in some cases outraged, by such concerns. They point out that after Israel, the largest number of survivors live in the United States. Second, Americans helped free those in the camps. Third, America's defeat of fascism ultimately saved not only countless Jews, Gypsies, and others who would have been slated for destruction, it rescued freedom, democracy, and decency.

Another reason for building a memorial in Washington, supporters have argued, is that such a museum is a useful antidote to America's infatuation with technology, so predominant in other museums and memorials on the Mall. "While the Air and Space Museum glorified the wondrous capabilities of technological know-how, the Holocaust museum will reveal the dark side of technology," Michael Berenbaum said of his museum. "When applied to Treblinka, it permitted 150 people to kill 900,000 in 18 months at a cost of .05 cents per person. There should be at least one reminder of that grisly statistic among the nation's monuments."

Max Kampelman, President Reagan's chief arms control negotiator and a Holocaust Council member, acknowledged that the Holocaust did not have roots in the American experience or tradition. "But we have statues all over the country of foreign heroes, and we accept them as part of our national landscape," he said. "The Europeans probably should have built such museums in their capitals, but they haven't and most probably won't. Only Israel did, because it is a state run by Jews. But our building will demonstrate the tolerance of our culture, its ability to empathize with the suffering of all its people. Our decision to build such a museum says something about our commitment to human rights and to the kind of nation we want to be."

It also says something about the status and confidence of American Jews. "A generation ago, American Jews would never have sought national recognition for a fundamentally Jewish issue," said Berenbaum. "Only a generation that feels at home as Jews, at home as Americans, and secure as American Jews can confront the issue and demand such recognition. Jews who resist the notion of a Holocaust museum on federal land," he said, "tend to be those who are not comfortable as Jews or as Americans.

Finally, proponents argue, there is another reason for embracing this Jewish passion as America's own in the form of brick and mortar on the National Mall. Given the nature of America's fast-moving society and the disappearance through death or the passage of time of other vehicles of memory, this country, more than its European allies, needs to enshrine the memory of this unique event in a physical place. When there are no more war-crimes trials, no more Kurt Waldheims to shun, no more survivors to tell their stories, there will be a museum devoted to an event that an American government considered important enough for all its citizens, not just Jews, to remember.

There is no doubt that those charged with finding ways to commemorate the Holocaust passionately believe that America owes the Jews recognition of their past suffering and survival. They note that the Vietnam War Memorial, too, was initially controversial, that veterans groups and other critics deplored the abstract monument because it was not heroic, and that some had argued it had no place on the Mall.

But the Vietnam War Memorial, whose planning began about the same time as the Holocaust Museum's, is a very different project. Vietnam is part of the nation's past. And the design selected seems intended not to teach visitors about the war but rather to prompt questions about it.

Some Jewish activists, by contrast, seem to be trying to graft foreign experience onto the nation's civil culture by building centers designed to educate Americans about the Holocaust and to encourage them to derive moral lessons from it. That is a far more ambitious goal than simply paying tribute to those who died.

The core challenge of all the Holocaust museum projects, but the Washington memorial in particular, was identified early on by Berenbaum. The genocide was aimed at Jews. Its victims were disproportionately Jews. But how could this Jewish tragedy be made relevant to the overwhemingly non-Jewish American people? Would the fact that the Holocaust was an extermination system aimed at Jews be de-emphasized to give the museum a more "American" character, a universal appeal and relevance?

"The Americanization of the Holocaust, the clash of myths, comes to the fore when we consider the inclusion in a commemorative ceremony of the Armenians, of other nationalities who suffered under Nazism and who perceive themselves, correctly or incorrectly, as victims of Nazism," Berenbaum wrote in the early 1980s. "How does one do justice to the Jewish experience in an American context that inevitably presses toward universalization?"[20]

The proponents of Holocaust museums have tried to preserve both goals: to maintain the specificity of the Holocaust as a distinctly Jewish catastrophe, and to attract a broad American audience that will find the commemoration meaningful and relevant to them. They have also struggled with the difficult issue of how honest—that is, how horrific—should these museums be. How can the savagery of the Holocaust be conveyed without alienating visitors, without forcing them to flee? Each of the museums has attempted to resolve the inherent tension in different ways; in almost every case, these efforts have bred controversy and compromises that have made some of the survivors and other participants deeply uncomfortable.

The two largest Holocaust projects under way in America are the construction of museums in Los Angeles and Washington. They have adopted very different approaches to commemoration. And the controversy surrounding each of them suggests that in remembrance of the Holocaust good intentions may often not be enough.

There is no more holy night in Hollywood's secular culture than the annual festival of camera and lights—the Academy Awards. Anyone who is anyone in this company town attends the Oscars to watch the American film industry do what it does best, honor itself.

In 1982, the bestowal of the Academy's prize for "Best Documentary Feature" came about midway in the nationally televised, heavily viewed broadcast. A blonde Hollywood starlet, in dangling rhinestone earrings and décolleté, asked for the envelope, please, in which the name of the winner was concealed.

The music softened; the drums rolled; the envelope was opened.

"And the winner is . . ." she said breathlessly, "the winner is . . . *Genocide!*"

The audience leapt to their feet as Rabbi Marvin Hier bounded down the aisle. As founder and director of the Simon Wiesenthal Center, which had co-produced the film, Hier had elected to accept the Oscar for the eighty-eight-minute documentary on the Holocaust. In black-tie and black yarmulke, clutching the golden tribute with both hands, he waited for the applause to subside. In lieu of the traditional expressions of thanks to one's mother and colleagues, he said solemnly: "This film is dedicated to the victims of the Holocaust. They have no graves, but their memories will live on until the end of time."

The music swelled and the audience cheered the film and its ebullient producer, Rabbi Hier, surely the only Orthodox rabbi ever to win an Academy Award.[21]

To his critics and even some of his supporters, Hier's Academy Award has come to symbolize what his institution represents—the intersection of Hollywood and the Holocaust. Perhaps it was inevitable, given the nature of American society, that the Holocaust and Hollywood would find each other, for as more cynical Jewish activists have said of the burgeoning interest in the Holocaust: "There is no business like *Shoah* Business." The enormous success of the Simon Wiesenthal Center, however, has given new meaning to what was once a macabre in-house joke.

While many other Jewish activists and groups are jealous of what he has achieved since his arrival in Los Angeles in 1977, some have argued that Rabbi Hier has exploited the Holocaust for well-intentioned but nonetheless political ends. His approach, they have warned, will not only distort Jewish identity and activism, it will ultimately undermine commemoration efforts.

Without doubt, the center's prosperity is attributable almost entirely to Rabbi Hier. Friend and foe alike consider Hier a genius of sorts, an energetic promoter who has almost single-handedly built the center into a political force to be reckoned with in Jewish and lay circles far beyond Los Angeles. He is a study in perpetual motion. Even when he is sitting down, he is not sitting still. A hand reaches for the phone between words. His arms wave; his legs cross. There is so much to do.

"We've moved far beyond the Holocaust," Hier said. "We've become a full-fledged Jewish defense agency. We're a social-action agency, a human rights organization. We respond quickly, whenever and wherever anti-Semitism appears. In fact, we've become one of the largest Jewish membership organizations in the country

—some 380,000 families make regular contributions to it. This support gives us independence. That's why our critics don't like us. We're Orthodox, we're quick, we're aggressive, and we're successful. B'nai B'rith has been around for ninety years. We're the new boys on the block."[22]

The block that Marvin Hier occupies is on West Pico Boulevard, not in Hollywood at all, but in West Los Angeles, the vibrant, expanding part of the city. This was the land and vacant building that Hier purchased when he arrived in L.A. with a check for $500,000 from Samuel Belzberg, a wealthy businessman from Vancouver, British Columbia. Within two weeks of his arrival, Hier had put $200,000 down on the $900,000 property that would eventually become the site for the $38 million complex under construction since the summer of 1988. The eight-story, 165,000-square-foot building will have as its centerpiece a Holocaust museum, Beit Hashoah, which means "House of Destruction," although in English the museum is being called the Museum of Tolerance, a rather deliberately nebulous name. Also being built are a 7,000-square-foot library, 4,000-square-foot archives, a 350-seat auditorium, a film studio and media center, three-level underground parking for nearly 300 cars, and ample room for the seminars and offices.

The center has established offices in New York, Chicago, Miami, Toronto, Jerusalem, Paris, and Washington. Its staff numbers forty-eight, more than seventy when its branches are included. "On the spot researchers throughout Europe and the Middle East monitor trends and developments involving right-wing extremism and Arab anti-Semitism," states Hier's glossy twenty-eight-page fund-raising brochure.

The slickly written booklet invites the reader to help create "the first major Holocaust Center in the English-speaking world." This formulation carefully distinguishes Hier's center from its counterpart in Israel, Yad Vashem, which is not English-speaking, and many of whose members have been highly critical in private of Hier's activities and approach. It also separates his center from the U.S. Holocaust Memorial Museum in Washington, which is far larger, but scheduled to be completed after Hier's. It appears to discount the Martyrs Memorial and Museum of the Holocaust, which opened about the same time as the Wiesenthal Center and is located just a few minutes' ride away. The Martyrs Museum, housed in and affiliated with the Jewish Federation of Los Angeles, has a budget of only $125,000 a year compared with Hier's annual $9 million operating fund. So it probably does not qualify as a "major" center.

From his temporary offices in the center's original building, Hier oversees the center's multifaceted activities. These, too, have gone far beyond commemorating the Holocaust. They have included the boycott against CBS-TV for casting Vanessa Redgrave, a PLO sympathizer, in the role of a Holocaust heroine in its television movie *Playing for Time;* a successful campaign to have West Germany extend its statute of limitations on prosecuting Nazi war criminals; and an unsuccessful petition drive to encourage the Vatican to recognize Israel. Since 1978, the center has published a wide variety of reports on instances of anti-Semitism and racism throughout the world, in addition to its annual compendium of articles by leading Holocaust scholars. It has launched a weekly radio news program that is aired by the Congressionally funded National Public Radio. It has been compiling a videotape archive of Holocaust survivor testimony.

Through its Nazi-hunting unit, it provided a list to British Prime Minister Margaret Thatcher of seventeen suspected Nazi war criminals believed to be living in the United Kingdom in 1986. A year later, it gave a similar document to the Justice Department's Office of Special Investigations. Hier acknowledged that on the American list, which included seventy-four Americans of Lithuanian and Latvian origin allegedly involved in war crimes before immigrating to the U.S., were individuals already known to OSI and some who had even died, but the center's charges received wide attention in the press.[23]

That kind of publicity has meant much to Rabbi Hier. "It means everything to him," said Gary Rosenblatt, editor of the Baltimore *Jewish Times* and author of the first detailed article about the center.[24] "One of his admirers put it well," Rosenblatt recalled in an interview. "He's half yeshiva, half Disneyland."

How did Rabbi Marvin Hier become the hub of this Holocaust remembrance universe in Hollywood?

Fate, Rabbi Hier asserted, played a role in the center's creation. He had always been interested in the Holocaust and in young people, he said. Born in New York City in 1939, he was not the son of Holocaust survivors. His parents had come from Poland some twenty years before the Shoah. "But everyone on my father's side of the family was wiped out. And beyond my own immediate loss, I was always obsessed with the event, this extraordinary event in which one-third of the Jewish people were exterminated!"

As assistant rabbi at age twenty-five and eventually chief rabbi of a small congregation in Vancouver, the home of some twenty thousand Jews, Hier had taken his students to visit concentration camps throughout Europe. He loved working in Canada, where he had lived since 1962, he said. "But I also knew that Vancouver was not the place to focus on the Holocaust. The international place of memory for the Shoah was in Israel, but the strongest nation on earth was the United States." A visit to Los Angeles persuaded him that this was the perfect city for the next stage of his life's work.

"There were so many people here already, and so many more moving to the Sun Belt. But in terms of Jewish culture and education, it was one hundred years behind New York. It really was the new frontier, ripe for development," he said.

But Hier knew no one in Los Angeles and had no money. That, he said, is when fate intervened. During a sabbatical in Jerusalem in 1976, he went to see the "dean" of Hasidic rabbis, the Rabbi of Ger, to whom thousands of Orthodox Jews flocked on holy days for a blessing. He told the rabbi of his dream of founding a Holocaust educational center in Los Angeles. But how could he do it without friends and financing?

"This is the mystical part of the story," Hier recounted with growing excitement. "The Rebbe Gerer said to me: 'Go immediately. You will have great success.' "

That was on a Sunday. On Tuesday, he was back in Vancouver attending a wedding when he happened to chat with another guest, Samuel Belzberg, who had accumulated a substantial fortune. Hier had worked closely with Belzberg's children and had helped bring them closer to their religion. Hier outlined his vision for a Holocaust center in Los Angeles that would both remember the Holocaust and help renew Jewish culture. The two men met again the next day, and by the end of the meeting, Hier walked away with a $500,000 check from Belzberg and a pledge of further support for his project.

"The picture of the Rebbe Gerer hangs in my house to this day!" Hier exclaimed.

Another picture hangs in Marvin Hier's office, that of Simon

Wiesenthal, the famed Austrian Nazi hunter after whom the center is named. The saga of how Wiesenthal came to be associated with Hier is the source of a bitter controversy within the Jewish community of Los Angeles over whether Hier "stole" Wiesenthal from the older Martyrs Museum project. The episode provides clues about Hier's operating style and the bitterness felt toward him by some of the survivors.

Holocaust survivor groups in Los Angeles had been attempting to build some kind of memorial since 1962, according to Michael Nutkiewicz, the Martyrs Museum's former director. In the late 1960s, the Jewish Federation agreed without much enthusiasm to provide the survivors with some space and staff, provided they were able to raise funds for the project themselves. In 1973, the survivors held their first major fund-raising dinner. The guest of honor was Simon Wiesenthal.

Planning for the new museum proceeded, but sluggishly. Another fund-raising dinner was planned in 1977, and once again Wiesenthal agreed to attend as the guest of honor. But shortly before the dinner he canceled abruptly; the dinner was called off.

The survivors learned only later that Rabbi Hier had flown to Vienna to make Wiesenthal what amounted to a better offer. Hier's project was not merely talk. He already had the money to build a center, which he was prepared to establish in Wiesenthal's name. In addition, Wiesenthal's financially strapped Nazi-hunting center in Vienna would receive $5,000 a month from Marvin Hier's center.

"He never asked for it. It was something our board voluntarily and unanimously agreed to do. There was absolutely no quid pro quo," Hier insisted. He had sought out Wiesenthal because he had admired Wiesenthal's work, and because both he and Belzberg wanted the Los Angeles center to help him track down Nazi war criminals. "What Elie Wiesel is in eloquence and writing, Simon Wiesenthal is in terms of action," Hier explained.

But many of those associated with the Martyrs Museum were furious. They charged that Hier had essentially talked Wiesenthal into "franchising" his name and reputation to a Holocaust entrepreneur. Moreover, he had undercut the Martyrs Museum project by denying it the key attraction for its fund-raising dinner. To ease tensions, Rabbi Hier donated $25,000 to the Martyrs Museum to compensate the project for its losses. But bitterness between the two institutions has lingered.

"The Martyrs Museum is a survivors' museum," said Nutkiewicz. "It is a memorial which addresses the past and the people who suffered and who are still in pain. It is also a tiny jewel dedicated to dignified remembrance of the Jewish Holocaust and, most importantly, to educating young people about that traumatic event."

Fred Diament, an Auschwitz survivor who is associated both with the Martyrs Museum and the U.S. Holocaust Memorial Museum in Washington, stressed that the Martyrs project was responsible to the Jewish Federation, the elected representatives of the Los Angeles Jewish community. "We, the survivors, are part and parcel of that broader community. Unlike Hier, who stages his own ceremonies on the Days of Remembrance, we commemorate those days with the rest of the Jewish community. Because we are part of the Federation, we must be historically accurate and conduct our commemorations with dignity. We are not like Hier, who is out there on his own, doing his own thing," Diament said.

Leon Wieseltier said that the paucity of survivors involved in the creation of the Simon Wiesenthal Center partly accounted for its difficulties in presenting the Holocaust with authenticity. "Nonsurvivors did not smell the camps; we did not live it. When we think of the Holocaust, we see it in black and white; our images come from the photos and newsreels. The difference between survivors and every other Jew is that the survivors remember it in color."

Hier's supporters point to numerous accomplishments, most of which result from the center's ability to act quickly, without being constrained by Jewish Federation bureaucracy or any other organization. When Russian Jewish activists were given permission to open a Jewish cultural center in early 1989, it was Rabbi Hier who quickly assembled his poster exhibit on the Holocaust and installed it in the Moscow center to coincide with its opening.[25] The night before the opening of the center, Hier secured permission to screen *Genocide* for an audience of close to one thousand Russians. Both the exhibition and the screening were remarkable given traditional Soviet reluctance to discuss the massacre of Soviet Jews as distinct from the suffering of all Soviet citizens.

During the Bush-Dukakis 1988 presidential contest, it was the Simon Wiesenthal Center that helped identify and publicize the presence of four former Nazi collaborators on Bush's panel of supporters of Baltic origin. The Bush campaign promptly dismissed the four.

While he has stressed that the Jewish people need "allies" in their fight against anti-Semitism and intolerance, Rabbi Hier parts company with other Jewish leaders who believe that good relations between Jews and gentiles must take precedence over other goals. In 1989, for example, he urged Jews not to visit Poland until the church agreed to honor its 1987 agreement and move a controversial Carmelite convent from the grounds of Auschwitz. In 1987, he refused to meet with Pope John Paul II as part of a Jewish delegation after the Catholic leader invited Kurt Waldheim to the Vatican and publicly praised him there without mentioning his wartime service for the Nazis.

Some accuse Hier of histrionics, of using his stance simply to attract more publicity. But he has maintained a consistently hardline position, one to which he adhered despite the tensions it caused between him and Simon Wiesenthal, who was at the time still defending the Austrian President.

Paradoxically, one of the center's finest products has received the least publicity. Its annual, containing essays by leading Holocaust scholars, which is edited by Sybil Milton and Henry Friedlander, has been widely praised by academics. But few outside the field even know of its existence. "I suppose it is not what interests Rabbi Hier and the center," said David Altshuler, director of the Museum of Jewish Heritage in New York.

Grabbing the public's attention through mass media does interest Hier. And this has led to charges that he has "trivialized" the Holocaust through slick productions, films such as *Genocide.* While some film critics attacked the film for a slickness akin to that of the center itself, others agreed that *Genocide,* nevertheless, was emotionally powerful and thought-provoking.[26]

"Look," said Hier, defending his emphasis on film, television, and radio, "young people today don't read. We can pretend that they do and that they'll learn about the Holocaust in their classrooms. But they won't. So you have to give them information about this period and its moral lessons in a form that they are used to receiving it—the tube."

He also defends his use of actors and actresses to generate interest in the Holocaust. When Simon Wiesenthal turned seventy-five in 1983, Hier organized what the center itself described as a "star-studded" birthday dinner for him. Some fifteen hundred people turned out for the gala, which was chaired by Elizabeth Taylor.

"We're in Hollywood; this is the home of the film industry," Hier exclaimed. "So sure we use stars. But they are like most people. They're actors; we're all actors. They memorize scripts. But when they come in contact with this event, that is the part of the script that they never forget."

In 1988, Hier celebrated Wiesenthal's eightieth birthday with two gala dinners, one in Los Angeles on October 30, where President Reagan and Nancy Reagan were honored just before the presidential election, and another in December in New York City.

The New York dinner, which netted $700,000, was chaired by a Republican, Ronald S. Lauder, former U.S. Ambassador to Austria; the Mistress of Ceremonies was Lesley Stahl of CBS. But the main tribute to Wiesenthal was given by West German Chancellor Helmut Kohl, the architect of Bitburg.

The selection of Chancellor Kohl to honor Wiesenthal appalled many in New York's survivor community, but so did the speech that Rabbi Hier delivered on the occasion. With the West German Chancellor and his wife seated on the dais, Hier launched into a detailed and gory description of atrocities committed by German camp guards and soldiers during the war.

"It was a ghastly evening," said another of the honored guests in attendance that night. "Perhaps Kohl should not have been invited. But having been invited, subjecting him and his country to this sort of humiliation in front of a thousand people was inappropriate to say the least. Only a Chancellor of West Germany would have sat there and taken it."

Such stunts have succeeded, as Hier put it, in "grabbing" the attention of young people in particular. But others are offended. "Yes," said Menachem Rosensaft, "he has grabbed young people emotionally; he has mobilized their energy. But where is he taking them? Toward what end?"

One serious criticism of the center is that Rabbi Hier is instilling mainly fear and guilt in young Jews, not the sensitivity and understanding they need to combat anti-Semitism, intolerance, hatred, and oppression.

In 1983, Rosenblatt noted in his article on the center, a mailing prepared by an advertising agency was sent to hundreds of thousands of Jews. Its goal was to raise funds for the center's new

"Nazi-Watch Program." It claimed that a "new wave of anti-Semitism is sweeping Europe," and that it was being "fueled by Americans who are supplying both leadership and material to rebuild Nazism in Europe." Anti-Semitic networks were on the rise in Europe and the United States, "INDEED, ALL OVER THE WORLD!" the letter proclaimed. Hatred and anti-Semitism were on the rise in the United States, "threatening all we hold dear."[27]

The letter was long on shock value but short on fact. Justice Department officials maintained that networks of neo-Nazis were neither strong nor well financed and that incidents of anti-Semitism in the United States were on the decline. The letter was a deliberate exaggeration of the threat of a resurgence of anti-Semitism for fund-raising purposes, critics charged.

Privately, officials of the Anti-Defamation League, which has been monitoring anti-Semitism in the United States and abroad for decades, have complained that Hier's work is duplicative of theirs, and that Hier's exaggerations frighten people, which is politically irresponsible and dangerous.

"Marvin Hier battens upon the same view of the world as anti-Semites," said Wieseltier. "Both live in a world that wants the Jews dead, in which there is no distinction drawn between identity and morbidity, in which what happened in Germany can happen here, so you have to be constantly on guard. But history in context tells us that it cannot happen here. Not now. Not in the near future."

Rosensaft argued that Hier's concentration on the Holocaust, on the alleged rise of anti-Semitism throughout the world, risks creating a false and negative sense of Jewish identity. Using the Holocaust to ignite social activism removes this watershed event from its historical context. "You don't promote understanding by taking the Holocaust out of world and Jewish history," he warned. The effort to build social activism on the Holocaust rather than seeing it as a critical episode in history would produce perverse results.

"I have an eleven-year-old daughter," Rosensaft said. "I want her to have a positive attitude towards Judaism, a spiritual and moral understanding of its values, which, in turn, will make her want to embrace the faith and become part of it. That won't happen if you tell your kids: the point of being Jewish is to make sure that we don't get killed again."

What history teaches, as opposed to Marvin Hier, he said, was to make distinctions. "My daughter knows that there is world history, and Jewish history, and that there was a watershed event in that history in which evil reached its climax," said Rosensaft. "She knows that there has been a long history of anti-Semitism, that as a result, her grandparents went through the most horrendous ordeal. She knows that there is anti-Semitism in the Soviet Union and that it has led to the persecution of Jews there. But she also knows that the Soviet Union is not Nazi Germany. She knows that not all anti-Semites want to kill people, that some just say or write bad things, that not all anti-Semites want to send her to a gas chamber."

Removing the Holocaust from the context of history, in sum, would create a sense neither of true identity nor of history. It would create Jews who do not like Hitler.

There is a second, more subtle consideration. Learning about the Holocaust may inspire outrage and social activism in younger Jews, but that is no substitute for knowledge of the faith and for living according to Jewish values. "To suggest that awareness of the Holocaust is why we fight apartheid in South Africa risks implying that we wouldn't be fighting apartheid were it not for the Holocaust," Rosensaft asserted. "The fight against hatred and oppression should not be something we Jews do because there was a Holocaust."

Some critics have accused Hier and other activists in the new remembrance industry of "politicizing" the Holocaust. Hier has insisted that the center is politically nonpartisan, studiously neutral. (And friends say that Hier is a Democrat.) But the bestowal of awards to the Reagans days before a presidential election raise questions about that contention. It was no accident that George Bush visited the center during the 1988 campaign, critics charge.

Hier, his detractors say, has used the Holocaust to promote support for hard-line men and principles, in Israel and in the United States. Moreover, they accuse him of exploiting the Holocaust to build a political power base for himself and his center. "Rabbi Marvin Hier has become a self-appointed spokesman for American Jewish interests," said Wieseltier. "There is something morbid, morally and historically wrong, and a little obscene, about the notion that one's professional relationship to the Holocaust qualifies one to speak on behalf of a living community. Why don't the manufacturers of the Yortzeit candles that we burn for the dead speak to the President about Jewish interests? Hier is one big Yortzeit candle manufacturer."

Also, Wieseltier argued, Hier's linkage of the Holocaust and American politics has vulgarized both. "He and his operation have no right to desecrate the memory of millions of dead Jews by glibly associating their memory with the center's politics."

The Holocaust is politically neutral, he maintained. All it should teach is activism: that Jews must do whatever they can to prevent other Jews from being killed. There has been a legitimate disagreement within the Jewish community about what prevents the killing of Jews. With respect to Israel, for example, some say that giving back the West Bank will prevent it; others say clinging to the territories will do that.

"But Rabbi Hier preaches that if you really understand what happened at Treblinka, you won't ever give up the West Bank and you'll always vote Republican," Wieseltier asserted.

Another implicit message of the Wiesenthal Center is that the Holocaust helped validate the state of Israel. Remembering the Holocaust leads to staunch support of Israel. Those who criticize Israeli policy, therefore, do Israel no favor. This attitude was reflected in the center's recent coverage of the Intifada, the Palestinian uprising in the occupied territories. "The 'War of Stones' still underway on the West Bank and the Gaza Strip represents the most serious domestic threat Israel has faced since becoming an independent state," stated the newsletter of May 1988. "It has brought a hail of criticism from the international community and a mixed chorus of advice and criticism even from some American Jews. The international media—with 700 correspondents in Israel taking advantage of press freedom unheard of in any recent theater of conflict—has succeeded in bringing the stark images of the violent confrontations—if not perspective—into American living rooms."[28]

"American Jewish intellectuals and some leaders in the community have no business trying to dictate a sister democracy's future election results, or final borders," Rabbi Hier wrote in a Memphis newspaper in February 1988. "It is not their sons and daughters whose lives are on the line; it is not their homes which are in range of Katusha rockets; it is not their cars which have to run the gauntlet of stones. Israel's future cannot be held hostage to their social 'embarrassment.' "[29]

Rosensaft and others have said that such comments reflect the use of the Holocaust to discipline American Jews. An American Jew who was horrified by an Israeli government that authorized its soldiers to break Palestinian bones should shut up. A Jew who criticized Israel was risking another Holocaust. Since when, Hier's critics ask, has criticism been equated with abandonment?

Rosensaft and others dispute Hier's implicit assertion that an uncriticizable Israel is the best way to remember the victims and prevent a recurrence of persecution. "That formulation does both Israel and the Holocaust a disservice," he said. Israel, he asserted, should be supported by Jews "not because they feel guilty about not having done enough to prevent the Holocaust, but because the Jewish people are entitled to a land of their own."

Critics of the Simon Wiesenthal Center have also complained about the use of the Holocaust to justify lobbying for Jewish interests. They have been enraged by its use by Jewish lobbyists—"You must do this for the Jews because there was a Holocaust." If the Holocaust had never happened, Jewish Americans would still have interests. And lobbying on behalf of those interests is not a response to Auschwitz. "It is normal behavior in an open society," said Wieseltier. "In this society, Jews are permitted to have interests and lobby for them, for the first time ever."

Questions of style are among the objections to what Marvin Hier is doing in Los Angeles. Some familiar with plans for the Museum of Tolerance accuse Hier of attempting to make a "sound and light" show out of the Holocaust. Some of the most grotesque proposals for the museum were rejected. Hier turned down, for example, an exhibit in which visitors would walk into an actual railroad cattle car; he also rejected a proposal to pipe in simulated screams of dying people. But questions of taste remain.

The museum, explains the center's fund-raising brochure, is divided into two main sections: "the story of human behavior and prejudice—focusing on human rights in America—and the story of the most extreme example of man's inhumanity to man—the Holocaust."

The brochure continues: "Through historical artifacts, documents, newsreel film, photos, and state-of-the-art multimedia technology—interactive computerized displays, audio-visuals and multimedia presentations, three-dimensional models—you experience a living social document."

In the museum's "Interactive Tower," visitors can explore specific examples of prejudice and minority oppression in America by selecting subjects on a touch-screen computer. "You witness the Civil Rights struggle in America and the inspirational story of Dr.

Martin Luther King, Jr." In a special-exhibit theater, visitors will "experience a panorama of two thousand years of anti-Semitism—and learn about the contributions made by Jews throughout history."

"Entering the Museum's second exhibit area, you are introduced to another innovation in museumology," the document states, "a series of exhibits that tell their story without written text. You are led by computer-synchronized light, color, and sound through a succession of tableaus that take you back in time. You are in Europe before and during the Holocaust. You hear the actual words of the victims, the victimizers, the heroes, and the apathetic bystanders.

"As a searchlight comes on—you are at a replica of the gates of Auschwitz. You imagine Jews being stripped, clothed in prison garb, numbered, having their heads shaved. You see historical film footage of Jews being 'selected' for work—or the gas chamber. . . . A searchlight sweeps the boundary fence. You are introduced to the hell that was Auschwitz. You imagine that you are following the final steps of the victims along the rough ground . . . you view actual film records of the discoveries made by the Allies when they liberated the camps . . . and you hear echoes of the victims—those who survived and those who did not.

"As you are about to leave the Holocaust section of the museum, how do you feel? Perplexed. Sad. Angry. Disgusted. Stunned. Ashamed. How could human beings sink to such depths of depravity? How could civilized people commit such crimes against humanity?"

The museum will bring visitors back to the present "quickly" by having them enter a "Situation Room," where the Center's own communications network will monitor, on banks of video display terminals, "injustice and inhumanity taking place NOW in the United States and around the world."

This high-tech approach to an almost unimaginable horror has appalled many Holocaust scholars, Jews, and non-Jews alike. "People like Hier," said Wieseltier, "do not understand the distinction between commemoration and entertainment."

Saul Friedlander, the Israeli historian whose parents were killed at Auschwitz, warned in the early 1980s about an impending explosion of Holocaust-related kitsch in response to the growing modern fascination with the event. To Friedlander, Hier's Center epitomizes what he has long feared—the degradation of the Holocaust in the name of commemorating it.[30]

The Simon Wiesenthal Center may well be the most egregious example of its genre. But it is not alone. Taking note of Hier's success, several Jewish organizations and causes have taken up the Holocaust as a fund-raising theme. Since 1985, remembrance dinners have been hosted by Israel Bonds as part of its fund-raising campaign. The first recipient of its award was Elie Wiesel, who had always refused to speak at fund raisers for Holocaust-related projects, but who subsequently permitted his name to be given to the award.

"Israel Bonds should be bought on their own merits; they should be bought to promote a strong Israel," said Rosensaft. "Having the memory of the Holocaust exploited to sell a coupon-bearing bond is, to say the very least, inappropriate."

In America, the lowest common denominator often sets the agenda. The Holocaust is not immune from this tendency. For several years, the Simon Wiesenthal Center warned of an alleged alarming rise in anti-Semitism in America. The measurements used by the ADL did not properly assess the danger, Rabbi Hier maintained. But in 1988, ADL itself, impressed by the success of the Wiesenthal Center's politics of shame and fear, also struck a more alarmist tone in its report on anti-Semitic incidents. The 1988 report, published in February, found that it described as a "significant increase" in vandalism and other anti-Semitic actions. But the number of incidents cited in the report was small by European standards and especially in the context of soaring American crime statistics.

The lowering of vulgarity thresholds has also been reflected in publishing. In the late '70s, Stein & Day, the relatively small but highly respected house which effectively closed in 1987, published the Warsaw Ghetto diaries of Adam Czerniakow, the head of the Judenraut. Czerniakow killed himself in 1942 after learning that the children from the ghetto were being sent to Treblinka. The appearance of the volume in English was an important event in publishing circles. Literary critics were shocked when an advertisement for the book contained a note of endorsement from Albert Speer, Hitler's friend and chief Nazi architect.

Call it vulgarization of the Holocaust, or simply bad taste. There will be many imitators ready to rush through the door that Rabbi Marvin Hier has opened. Hier makes no apologies for his center or his style. One man's "scare tactics" are another's "early warning system."

"We Jews have a very bad record at prediction," said Hier. "We're like the baseball hitter who is up to bat with two strikes against him. That's the proper attitude for Jews. We shouldn't be going around saying: it cannot happen again. It cannot happen here. We Americans have never been tested."

It is impossible to overemphasize the Holocaust, he replied to his critics. "I would rather be accused of overemphasizing the Holocaust than of being wrong again and facing the consequences of having been wrong." The consequences of overemphasis, he said, are not negative: Jews would feel more Jewish. "That is not a major crime in a generation that faces a major threat of assimilation, the true threat to Jewish culture," he continued. "There are many Jews who have been hanging on to their Judaism by a single thread. When these people focus on an experience like the Holocaust, there are suddenly more threads."

Marvin Hier points to what he considers the major vindication of his center and its Holocaust activities—its impressive success. "I do not believe that people are sheep or fools," he said. "We have an enormous following. When the stock market crashed, the Simon Wiesenthal's fund raising was actually up. Our detractors are jealous."

"Rabbis and others tell us we should be motivated by joy rather than fear, by commitment rather than paranoia," Rosenblatt wrote more than four years ago. "They say such preoccupation with the anti-Semitism of the present and the past creates a climate of depression, isolation and mistrust—and renders virtually all other issues inconsequential by comparison. But the success of the Simon Wiesenthal Center tells us otherwise. For while scholars, statistics and sermons may point towards a more positive Judaism, the phenomenal growth of the Wiesenthal Center suggests that the haunting memory of the Holocaust is, for better or worse, what makes millions of Jews feel like Jews."[31]

On a crisp and sunny winter day in October 1988, some fifteen hundred people assembled on a barren plot of land near the National Mall for the unveiling of the cornerstone of an extraordinary museum, tucked in among the Washington, Lincoln, and Jefferson memorials.

Nothing quite like it had ever been constructed in the nation's capital, as the men and women gathered here were well aware. Among the legislators and diplomats and religious and lay civic leaders were some of the nation's most prominent Jews—writers, artists, government officials, men of commerce and industry. Virtually the entire leadership of the national Jewish organizations was represented.

They stood side by side, some arm in arm, on the artificial tarmac, under the billowing tent that had been erected for the occasion. A few held handkerchiefs to dab away their tears as President Reagan pulled a golden cord and exposed the single giant block of granite that was to be the museum's foundation stone.

In the front rows were leading figures of the museum campaign. There were the tough-minded real-estate developers: Harvey ("Bud") Meyerhoff, the project's chairman, and Albert ("Sonny") Abramson, whose fund-raising skills and pragmatism had become indispensable. There was William J. Lowenberg, a businessman from San Francisco. "Forty-five years ago, I stood before Josef Mengele in Auschwitz without hope and without a country," Lowenberg, a survivor of eight camps, told those assembled. "Before the day was over, I had a number tattooed on my arm and was condemned to be without a name. I could not possibly have imagined that today I would stand in your presence as a free and secure citizen of this great nation.

"In the shadows of the gas chambers," he said, he and other survivors were given a sacred obligation, a duty they would share for the rest of their lives: to remind the world not to forget. "For me, a survivor of Auschwitz and Dachau, and for all of my fellow survivors, this is a moment of immense consolation." He spoke haltingly. "We are grateful beyond words that the American people will know our tragic story and will transmit it from generation to generation."

Hadassah Rosensaft, the energetic head of the museum's archives committee, had been liberated from Bergen-Belsen. Her brother had been killed fighting in the Zionist underground. Her mother and father and sister, her first husband, and her five-year-old child had all been killed at Auschwitz. "As I looked at the cornerstone that day," she said, "I understood for the first time that our museum had become a reality."[32]

"It was a very special moment for me," recalled Mark E. Talisman, director of the Washington office of the Council of Jewish

Federations and former vice chairman of the United States Holocaust Memorial Council, which was charged with building the museum. "For years I had sleepless nights and had a secret fear," he told me. "I had always felt a desolation, an incomprehension that one-third of my people had been permitted to die, that 75 percent of European Jewry, the most cultivated, had been exterminated. Images of the one million children who were killed would flash through my mind. They looked so much like my own children! So I had always wanted to do something in my lifetime to help others remember them."

"I wish my father could have lived to see this," said Abraham Foxman, the national director of the Anti-Defamation League, the son of a Pole who survived the Vilna Ghetto and died in the United States in the late 1970s. "Time, they say, brings justice," his father had written in his memoir. "But often it is an unmerciful wrongdoer, and one of its great wrongs is that it makes us forget. Let us oppose the 'law of time' and the verdict of being forgotten."

The ceremony was a moving triumph for survivors and those who had shared the dream of building a memorial. It seemed an exquisite occasion of harmony and solidarity.

But this was not the case. Some of those in attendance had set aside their differences to savor the presidential tribute to their labor. The lofty rhetoric about remembrance masked bitterness that the nine-year effort to build a museum had engendered. The acrimony was so deep-seated that Elie Wiesel, the founding spirit and first chairman of the commission and the council that succeeded it, and others who had played key roles in the project's early days chose not to attend the ceremony.

The tensions were not primarily the result of the clash of egos, though personality differences had surely exacerbated them. At the heart of the bitterness were conflicting answers to profound questions about how best to honor the memory of those killed. What kind of Holocaust would be remembered? Most critically, whose suffering would be included in a Holocaust museum? That of the Jews alone? Or of the four, or six, or eleven, or twenty million "others," depending on which historian is doing the counting?

"Given the incredible intellectual challenges inherent in such a project, tensions were inevitable," said Michael Berenbaum, the theology professor who since 1988 has been the museum's project director.

Other projects have resolved tensions inherent in Holocaust commemoration in different ways. There is no question that the Holocaust museum under construction in New York, home to three million of America's Jews, will focus primarily on the fate of Europe's Jews during World War II. "Ours will be a Jewish museum," said David Altshuler, an academic once associated with the Washington museum, and currently the director of the New York museum. But its name, the Museum of Jewish Heritage—A Living Memorial to the Holocaust, also reflects Altshuler's desire to emphasize the Holocaust as part of a continuum of Jewish life that includes history before and life after that cataclysm.

The Simon Wiesenthal Center in Los Angeles has adopted a diametrically different approach. Although the center itself has raised most of its funds from Jews and defines the Holocaust inside its museum's walls as a Jewish tragedy relevant to all people who wish to prevent similar occurrences, its name, the Museum of Tolerance, reflects both "its pedagogical aim (tolerance) and the plural audience it hopes to attract," said James Young, the scholar.[33]

The U.S. Holocaust Memorial Museum is somewhere between these conceptual opposites. "The museum's definition was a political compromise which preserved the essence of Elie Wiesel's insistence on the Holocaust as a Jewish event, while at the same time, enabled the project to reach out to others who had suffered," said Stuart Eizenstat. The definition, in other words, would maintain the historical integrity of the event itself, while being responsive to the politics and pluralistic demands of American life.

The compromise emerged in the early stages of planning; it was first formally and publicly articulated by Wiesel in his "Report to the President" on the Holocaust Commission's deliberations.[34] "The Holocaust," he wrote, "was the systematic, bureaucratic extermination of six million Jews by the Nazis and their collaborators as a central act of state during the Second World War; as night descended, millions of other peoples were swept into this net of death." Or, as he also put it, "The Event is essentially Jewish, yet its interpretation is universal. The universality of the Holocaust lies in its uniqueness."

Robert Greenberger, a journalist who first examined the project in detail, described the compromise succinctly. "All Jews were victims, but not all the victims were Jews. Hence, all would be represented in the museum."[35] Through this artful formulation, the museum would be able to focus on the Jewish aspect of the tragedy, without denying a place on the rostrum of suffering to non-Jews. For without the participation of gentiles, participants in the project agreed, the museum would never be sanctioned as a "national" monument.

Nevertheless, some of the survivors remained uneasy with the compromise. "It was a persistent split," said Mrs. Rosensaft. "Survivors would have preferred that the museum be 150 percent Jewish, that it concentrate exclusively on the Jewish genocide. But we couldn't do that because this was, after all, an American national monument; it had to include the suffering of others."

Survivors, in particular, were troubled by what they called the potential "dilution" of the Jewish nature of the Holocaust. They knew that this had occurred at other American memorials. Finding itself short of funds, the Babi Yar Memorial Committee in Denver, for example, was able to complete its memorial—an afterthought to a condominium project—only after the local Ukrainian community agreed to contribute money, according to Young. "The Babi Yar Memorial there now commemorates 'The Two Hundred Thousand Victims who died at Babi Yar, Kiev, Ukraine, USSR, September 19, 1941–November 6, 1943. The Majority Jews with Ukrainians and Others.' " Had the time of slaughter been limited to the first three days after September 29, however, the plaque, if it were historically accurate, would have been able to mention only the slaughter of Jews, and perhaps the Ukrainians who helped kill them, Young observed.[36] Survivors on the Holocaust Council were determined that the Washington museum would not make such a compromise. Yet the memorial itself was the product partly of typically American political pressures and compromises.

The idea was initially promoted in 1977 by three Jewish officials in the Carter Administration—Eizenstat; Mark Siegel, a liaison with the Jewish community who worked on the White House staff; and Ellen Goldstein, a staff member of the Domestic Policy Council. Eizenstat said he had been concerned not only about the erosion of memory of the war among people of his generation and younger, but also about the incidents of Holocaust revisionism that seemed to be fueling this amnesia.[37]

Siegel was initially more concerned with securing ratification of the Genocide Treaty, which had languished for years without Senate approval. He thought that as part of the campaign the White

House might propose capping ratification of the treaty with the construction of a memorial to the Holocaust, which was, after all, the twentieth century's most egregious genocide.[38]

Siegel asked Goldstein to prepare a memorandum on how other nations had commemorated the Holocaust. Goldstein quickly sensed the potential political benefit of the remembrance gap to the Carter Administration. In her memorandum, she encouraged Siegel to persuade Carter to stop by the small Center for Holocaust Studies in New York on his next trip. "Perhaps President Carter can begin to heal the rift between himself and the Jewish population by visiting the Center on his visit to New York" she wrote.[39]

Siegel sent President Carter a memorandum suggesting that the United States consider establishing a national memorial. The proposal went nowhere, Siegel said, until almost a year later, when relations between Carter and the typically pro-Democratic Jewish community had plummeted. American Jewish leaders were furious that Carter had endorsed a "homeland" for Palestinians, that United Nations envoy Andrew Young had met with a representative of the Palestine Liberation Organization in New York, and that National Security Adviser Zbigniew Brzezinski had been quoted as vowing to "break the back" of the Jewish lobby on Capitol Hill. Carter had also beaten the usually invincible Jewish lobby by ramming through Congress a major sale of F-15 fighter aircraft to Saudi Arabia. Siegel resigned over the sale.

In March 1978, Goldstein sent a second memorandum concerning the creation of a national Holocaust memorial, this time to Eizenstat. "An item in William Safire's March 27 column [in *The New York Times*] reminded me of this memorial question," the memo states. Safire, in discussing the Nazis' right to march in Skokie, Illinois, had written that "America has no vivid reminder of the horror of the Final Solution. But we have a reminder not even Israelis can boast: our own homegrown handful of Nazis."

Building such a memorial might be "an appropriate gesture in honor of Israel's thirtieth anniversary and a symbol of the United States's support of Israel's birth and continued life," she wrote.[40] While Goldstein never mentioned the strained Israeli-American ties, she did worry that "such a move might appear to some people to be glib public relations."

The following June, President Carter surprised a large group of rabbis at a meeting in the Rose Garden by saying that he had decided to appoint a commission to consider the construction of a Holocaust memorial.

Eizenstat insisted that the memorial was not conceived as a way of placating Carter's angry Jewish constituency. The timing of the decision, he said, was "coincidental." The memorandum he sent to the President made no mention of any potential political benefit to the administration.[41]

Siegel, who had left the White House by then, disagreed. "Politics obviously played a role," he maintained. The memorial had gone nowhere until the Jews became a potentially serious political problem for the Democrats because of the F-15 sale. "Only then was it resurrected." But this did not trouble him, he added, because "frankly, I wanted a memorial built. I liked the outcome." Similar pragmatism was expressed at the time by Berenbaum. "Jewish tradition has always recognized mixed motives and sought to utilize them in positive ways," he wrote in 1982.[42]

The key divisive issue of how universal the memorial would be emerged almost immediately. Anne Wexler, a presidential aide who was the liaison with various ethnic groups and Democratic constituencies, argued strenuously that neither the commission that was to decide what kind of memorial to build nor the council that succeeded it to supervise its construction should be composed solely of Jews. The panels had to be representative of all people who had suffered at Hitler's hands during the war, she argued. If the representation was not broad-based, the recommendations would not win congressional backing.

But Elie Wiesel, whom Carter had appointed as the commission's chairman at Eizenstat's strong urging, insisted that the groups be composed mainly of Jewish survivors. Slowly he accepted the membership of a few "righteous gentiles," those Christian immigrants who had helped save Jews. "Then Anne pressed for the inclusion of Lithuanian immigrants involved in resistance against the Nazis, and Elie became very upset," Eizenstat recalled. "The Lithuanians, Elie argued, had been part of the problem, not the solution." But Wexler prevailed.

At one early meeting of the Holocaust Commission, Rabbi Irving Greenberg, the panel's former director, argued for the broadest possible representation of Holocaust victims. One survivor became almost hysterical. He had seen his brother stomped to death by a Polish guard at Auschwitz. Was Greenberg suggesting that the

Poles be put in the same memorial as his brother? "There was a lot of pain all around," Rabbi Greenberg recalled.[43]

Wiesel ultimately accepted a rather diverse group of Americans on the commission and then the council. And the decision to make the project more universal, more inclusive, affected almost all other basic decisions.

Many of the conflicts over universality sprang from the commission's initial determination that the most fitting memorial for the Holocaust dead was a "living" museum. According to commission members, all but one member of the panel favored the construction of a museum rather than a monument or other type of memorial. Wiesel and the others felt strongly that whatever was built had to help educate people, young Americans in particular. A simple, eloquent statement like that ultimately made by the Vietnam War Memorial would not suffice. Worse, it might not even be noticed.

"Elie said that there were a thousand monuments in Washington, but who even knew they were there? He wanted to build something more distinctive, something that would be different from the statues and memorial plaques that littered the nation's capital."

Only Lucy S. Dawidowicz, the Holocaust historian, disagreed. She favored building a memorial, one of "compelling austerity," preferably located in New York, "the center of the Jewish population in the United States and the cultural crossroads of the modern world." At a commission meeting, she expressed her fear that a museum on a grand scale might give the appearance of "celebrating rather than commemorating the Holocaust." She said in an interview she was so concerned about the form a grandiose museum would take that she, alone, refused to sign the commission's recommendations when the panel's final report was issued.

Once the concept of a museum was endorsed, disputes over its contents and enormous cost were inevitable. From the beginning, Carter insisted that no money for construction of such a memorial be appropriated from federal funds.[44] The deficit was spiraling out of control; moreover, Eizenstat said, "Carter believed that because the project was not a war memorial, but of particular interest to the Jewish community, Jews should be able to raise money for it."

Jews on the commission agreed. "We thought it would look grubby for the Jewish community to seek federal funds," said Hyman Bookbinder, a Democrat and longtime lobbyist for the

American Jewish Committee. "After $3 billion a year for Israel, it would have been unseemly to beg for $100 million for a museum."[45]

Moreover, the commission members thought that a nationwide fund-raising campaign for such a museum would educate Jews and non-Jewish Americans about the Holocaust. But, despite talk of the project's universal audience, pragmatists recognized from the beginning that the museum would be "specific" when it came to fund raising. If Jews cared about this project, they would have to finance it.

The politically explosive potential of the memorial was heightened by a second crisis in the project's early days, a conflict over whether the Turkish deportation of the Armenians between 1915 and 1923 would be included in the museum as an example of a previous genocide. Set Momjian, an Armenian-born businessman, was appointed to the council and insisted that it should be. And he immediately pledged $1 million to the fledgling project on behalf of the Armenian community to ensure that it would be. "There was an implicit, if not explicit, understanding that the gift would result in the inclusion of the Armenian massacres in the museum's permanent exhibit," said Eizenstat.

But when the Turkish Ambassador to the United States learned of this, he visited Eizenstat at the White House. "I had many blunt and difficult meetings during those years, but this was the most difficult," Eizenstat recalled.

The Ambassador reminded him that Turkey had been hospitable to Jews over the centuries. Though neutral during the war, Turkey had given refuge to many Jews fleeing Hitler. In modern times, it was the home of a large and thriving Jewish population, and it was one of the few states with a Moslem majority that had established and maintained diplomatic relations with Israel. Including the Armenians in the museum, the Ambassador warned, would not only affect relations between Turkey and Israel, it would also mean that "Turkey could no longer guarantee the safety of Jews in Turkey," Eizenstat quoted the Ambassador as saying.[46]

Turkey received support from an unlikely third party. Several council members said that Israeli officials had urged them to heed Turkey's concerns. Israel's flag flew over the consulate in Ankara.

Discord also erupted over the council's relationship with the Federal Republic of Germany. From the beginning, the project troubled Helmut Kohl, who was then the leader of the conservative Christian Democratic Union. Kohl expressed his concerns in 1980 to his key advisers, including Peter Petersen, a Christian Democrat and member of the Bundestag.[47] "What would a young German visiting the United States think when he passed the Holocaust Museum on the Mall?" Peterson said. "What would he feel when he saw his country's entire history reduced to these twelve terrible years? Was this the way in which the United States was going to treat its most valued European ally?"

A friend in Congress arranged a meeting in New York between Petersen and Wiesel in the winter of 1983. By that time, Kohl had become Chancellor.

"It was an extraordinary conversation," Petersen recounted. "I told him about my background—that I had not only been a member of the Hitler Youth, that I had been an enthusiastic one!" Petersen admitted that he had been bitterly disappointed when Hitler lost the war, and that he had initially considered the stories about the camps lies, Allied propaganda. For him, Hitler was God; National Socialism was his religion. The Allies hadn't won because they were right or morally superior to Germans, he said. "They won because you had more guns and bombs."

But in 1945 his father, who had not been political, brought a Jewish survivor home to talk to "his crazy son who still believed in Hitler," Petersen said. The man's stories about Bergen-Belsen shook young Petersen's Nazi faith to its core. "My first instinct was one of shame, to flee Germany. I wanted to go somewhere else, anywhere that we could escape it," Petersen said. "But my father got very angry. He told me: you ran after the Nazi flag like everybody else. That was understandable. But having done that, you do not have the right to leave now that your country needs you. You will stay here and work to make sure that what happened never occurs again.

"So I did. And I refused to engage in the self-pity that was so common at the time. Hitler had stolen our youth and betrayed our innocence, people would say! I knew instinctively that we could not base a new nation on self-pity. Instead, I worked then, and have continued all my life since then, to fight the moral indifference that made the Holocaust possible."

Wiesel listened carefully, Petersen said. "The man who had refused even to meet with the German Ambassador in Washington was willing to listen to me."

Finally, Petersen made his appeal. More than half of the Germans alive today were not even born when the war ended. The Federal Republic had worked long and hard to establish a more moral record in the world, to become an ardent democracy at home and a staunch supporter of Israel and America abroad. In view of all this, could the new museum not take account of Germany's extraordinary evolution? Yes, he said, he knew that the museum would be built. But did it have to stop with Auschwitz? Could it not include Germany's help in building a strong Israel, in giving more than 100 billion Deutschmarks in reparations? Could it not include some kind words about the new Germany?

Petersen said that Wiesel had replied: "I am not a judge; I am a witness." But, Petersen added, Wiesel agreed that one could not condemn a whole people today for what their fathers and grandfathers had done. "He said it would be unfair to blame my son."

At the end of the long meeting, they agreed to form a group of six Germans and six Americans to discuss what had been learned since the war and other issues raised that afternoon. Chancellor Kohl appointed the six personally. The group met first in early 1984.

Through these visits, he and Wiesel became friends, Petersen said. Wiesel invited him and other German members of their committee to attend some of the Holocaust Council meetings in Washington so that they could better appreciate the type of memorial being planned. He appeared at the meeting at which Wiesel resigned in late 1986.

"I came to respect Wiesel enormously," Petersen said. "So when he was nominated for the Nobel Peace Prize, I helped get eighty members of the Bundestag to write the Nobel committee in support of his nomination. When he finally won the prize, he invited me to attend the ceremony in Stockholm—the only German there!"

These contacts between the Germans and the Holocaust Council ended abruptly after Wiesel resigned. "After Meyerhoff took over, he reorganized our little group out of existence. I tried to meet with him several times," Petersen said. "He and the others have always refused to do so." The Germans felt wounded by their exclusion from the project.

In fact, most council members had not known of Wiesel's invitation to Petersen to attend council meetings. Some were appalled when they were told, particularly the survivors. Council members confirmed that after Wiesel's departure, it became unofficial policy not to meet with German officials to discuss the museum's thrust or contents. "I don't make deals with Germans," Lowenberg told a friend.

The relationship with Germany, however, was not the issue that drove Wiesel from the council. What made him resign, he has said, was his growing concern that the project was becoming too politicized, too "homogenized," and that this would ultimately degrade the quality of the tribute he had hoped to pay to Holocaust victims. "Either this place will be a sanctuary, or it will be an abomination," Wiesel told a friend before he resigned in December.

Even Wiesel's admirers acknowledge, however, that his strengths were spiritual, not practical. He came to be seen by many on the council as a poor choice for translating the themes of remembrance and commemoration into concrete and mortar. He trusted only a handful of survivors and was reluctant to delegate authority, they said. Since the council met infrequently, key decisions piled up without resolution. Wiesel also declined, as he had always done as a matter of principle, to give fund-raising speeches or to host other commercial events to raise money for the project. "The project," he told friends, "is too sacred to be cheapened or demeaned by commercialization or politicization."

But in addition to his concerns about the project's tone and direction, Wiesel told one friend privately, that he felt he lacked the pragmatism and management skills needed to transform his vision into reality. "My monument is one of words," he said. In his letter of resignation, Wiesel alluded to his managerial shortcomings. "At this stage of its development," he wrote, "the council needs a Chairman with expertise in management, administration, finance, and construction. As you know, all these fields are alien to me, hence my decision to step down and allow you to appoint a successor who will fill the needs of the hour."

Congress had set a deadline by which the council had to show substantial progress. Most believed that included a site for the museum and significant financial pledges. The deadline was approaching, but the council had neither.

Fund raising, in particular, was faring poorly. Wiesel told friends that the council had $30 million in pledges by the time he left his post.[48] But the total cost of the building, content, and endowment was projected in 1986 at about $100 million.

Wiesel turned for help to the council's developers, Sonny

Abramson and later Bud Meyerhoff. Within weeks of joining the museum development committee, Abramson got the project moving quickly and on a much grander scale. Wiesel had favored opening a relatively small museum in a single red-brick structure near the Mall, a structure known as the "Auditor's Complex."

But the developers favored tearing it down and building a giant structure.

Abramson demanded that his development committee be given authority to act without approval of Wiesel or the council. Abramson threatened to resign unless he was given more autonomy.[49] He got it. But relations between Wiesel and the developers had deteriorated beyond repair. A few weeks later, Wiesel left the council.

After he resigned, Wiesel told friends that growing politicization of the project was jeopardizing its soul. Consider, he said, the tasteless decision to name parts of the museum after the largest donors. Minutes from the meeting of June 17, 1987, indicate that the executive committee discussed two proposals. First, it voted unanimously not to accept funds from either Germany or the Soviet Union and to consider gifts from other governments and foreigners on a case-by-case basis. Second, "Chairman Meyerhoff noted that in addition to the $1 million commitment from him and his wife, Lyn, the Meyerhoff family had pledged $5 million. The 500-seat Main Auditorium will be named for his father, Joseph Meyerhoff," the minutes state, without further explanation.[50] Since then, the council has approved the naming of the museum's cinema-lecture hall for another larger donor, the Helena Rubinstein Foundation.[51]

Berenbaum, the project director, stressed that the council eventually banned named plaques in the heart of the museum—the Hall of Remembrance and the Hall of Witness. But some council members have said privately that they are uncomfortable with such personal tributes as a quid pro quo for large contributions in any part of the building.

Another unseemly aspect of the project has been the growing competition within the Jewish community for membership on the Holocaust Council. "For a while, they were almost killing one another to be appointed," said Deborah Lipstadt, the Holocaust scholar. "By the time that museum opens, blood will have been shed over who will speak at the ribbon-cutting ceremony."

The competition reflects an even more disconcerting rivalry

among Jewish groups to seize the Holocaust as their special preserve. Membership has not been growing in most of the alphabet soup of established Jewish groups—the AJC's (American Jewish Committee and American Jewish Congress), the ADL (Anti-Defamation League of B'nai B'rith), and the like. The Simon Wiesenthal Center, which grabbed the issue early, is the exception. "These groups are fighting for survival and for prominence," said Lipstadt, with only a trace of irony. "And the Holocaust is a very prominent issue."

By the time Wiesel resigned, the bitterness within the council ran so deep that each side was spreading calumnies about the other. Some council members—including Meyerhoff and Abramson, who declined to be interviewed for this book—refused to discuss the museum with journalists. Almost no one wanted to be identified in this book by name. Wiesel supporters charged that Abramson and Meyerhoff were intent on contributing so much money to the Holocaust Museum that it would eventually be renamed the Abramson-Meyerhoff Memorial Holocaust Museum. Defenders of the builders were asserting, again not for quotation, that Wiesel had only stayed on the council to lobby for his Nobel Prize, and that he had, in fact, resigned less than three months after he had won it. Internal Jewish politics are notoriously fierce. But the rancor generated by the issue of how best to commemorate the Holocaust stunned even the most seasoned observers.

"At one point, the tensions were so great that I feared that pettiness, along with philosophical divisions, might actually sink or stain the project," said Talisman. "That things ever got to that point was somehow truly incomprehensible to me."

For several months, a critical debate raged within the council's key "content" committee over how much and what kind of technology is appropriate in a museum intended to highlight the danger of technology harnessed to death. The issue has been particularly sensitive because the Simon Wiesenthal Center's Museum of Tolerance plans extensive use of technology, which has prompted charges that it is turning Holocaust commemoration into Disneyland.

As a result, many of the survivors have favored emphasis on the museum's collection of more than four thousand Holocaust artifacts—striped camp uniforms, a Torah smuggled into Auschwitz, the ticket and passport of an ill-fated passenger on the ship the *St. Louis,* the ship loaded with Jewish passengers which the United

States turned away, and the patches of cloth in the form of a yellow star that Jews had to wear in different European countries.

Fred Diament, a California businessman, Raul Hilberg, the Holocaust scholar, and others warned repeatedly that commemoration could slip into a "sound and light show" if technology were to take priority over artifacts. "I think we can do it with dignity," said Diament. "We have all been aware of the problem."

In late 1989, the content committee approved a $3–6 million "Interactive Learning Center," to be called the "Hall of Knowledge," in which those interested in finding out more about a particular exhibit could do so. The center's goal, said Berenbaum, is to turn the passive viewer into an active participant. "Let's say you saw something about the Einsatzgruppen [the security police units that played a key role in exterminating Jews] and you wanted to know more," he said. "You could sit in front of a terminal or computer screen and ask questions about them. Who were they? Where did they operate? Were they only Germans? The point is to activate the visitor."

The computer system, which will accommodate sixty tourists at a time, was designed by Yechiam Halevy, an Israeli who has provided similar software to the Israeli Defence Forces. Earlier versions of some of the technology contemplated for the center has been used in the Museum of the Diaspora, at Tel Aviv University in Israel. But critics note that technology employed by other museums might not be appropriate for a Holocaust museum in America.

One idea that the committee rejected was using computers to simulate what is known in Holocaustology as "choiceless choices." For example, a family is hiding in the attic; the Gestapo are searching the house; the baby starts to cry. What do you do?

"We will not use computer technology to play Holocaust simulation games," vowed Berenbaum, the project director, "at least as long as I am here."

But senior officials have led a precarious existence at the Washington project. In eight years, four people have held the post of executive director. And because a museum's collection and technology must constantly evolve, there are no guarantees that today's dignified museum may not become tomorrow's trendier, jazzier experiment. Even the continued assembly of Holocaust "artifacts" has had ghoulish overtones. The museum staff has taken pride in the "authenticity" of the objects it will display to future visitors. But what will tourists think of walking through the "authentic" railroad car that took Jews from the Warsaw Ghetto to their deaths at Treblinka, or a "genuine" barracks from Birkenau that will be placed in a permanent exhibition hall? How will they feel about walking down a corridor at the museum on the "original" cobblestones from the Warsaw ghetto, a gift from the Polish government? And how will young visitors to the museum react to the display of a room full of camp victims' clothes, another of shoes, and a third filled with womens' hair?

A final unresolved issue is whether the museum will have what its detractors have called a "happy ending." Will it emphasize the continuation of life through the survivors, the creation of the state of Israel, the flourishing of the Jewish community in America, fascism's defeat? Will it instill in the visitor a sense that individual commitment to fighting racial intolerance and hatred can make a difference?

Or will it leave the visitor with a sense of horror and shame about the all too recent past? Will it make the visitor feel shame about the fact that America did virtually nothing to stop the slaughter once it had begun? Will it stress the story of the "liberators," or the reasons why Congress refused to approve a resolution that would have permitted twenty thousand children under fourteen—hardly a threat to the American unemployed—to find shelter in America?[52] Will it emphasize that because of the State Department's administrative policies, only twenty-one thousand refugees were allowed to enter the United States during the three and one half years that this nation was at war with Germany, 10 percent of those who could have been admitted under immigration quotas during that period?

"You're asking me: will the moral message of our museum be that good triumphed in the end?" said Berenbaum. "No. That will not be our message. There are at least six million reasons to dispute that. But we must transmit a belief that good can triumph over evil if people do not become passive or indifferent bystanders. I think that there is a world of difference between the two messages."

Alex H. was telling his story of survival. Seated stiffly on a couch in a small, sparsely furnished room, he was alone but for a woman asking him questions and a young man with a video camera. "In that camp of Lauenstein [a Nazi labor camp] I was so hungry that I don't know what I would have ate," Alex H. said softly. "We were sleeping on the floor and next to me was another camp inmate. I don't know how old he was—he looked old. And we just got our ration of bread, and he was already so sick that he wouldn't eat that bread. And I was laying next to him, waiting that he should die, so that I can . . ." Alex H. stopped. His eyes filled with tears; he swallowed his breath. Several seconds passed as he struggled to regain his composure and finish his sentence. "So that I can . . . grab his bread."[53]

In the stories that survivors have been telling for posterity here at Yale, the silences are as eloquent as words.

"In the pause between the 'can' and the scrupulously chosen 'grab' lies an internalized history of remorse and humiliation that is given birth only through an audience's collaboration with that prolonged moment of painful, searching silence," wrote Lawrence L. Langer, who has been watching hours of the videotapes for a book he is writing.[54]

In testimony after testimony, those who have come to Yale since 1981 to tell their tales of pain, loss, of sorrow and despair, and ultimately of their survival, reached a point at which they could no longer find the words to describe what they had endured. It was then that the camera took over. It captured the hesitation, the averted glance, the ironic smile, the flash of pain at a memory, the fidgeting, the sighs, the errant tear, the silent search for the right phrase to translate the inexplicable. Those images transcended the space of silence.

Thanks to the camera, the stories were no longer simply words on a page absent their teller; they were no longer disembodied tales. These were suddenly very real people, recounting their pasts in ways as different as the experiences themselves. It was their silences that spoke most clearly.

For more than a decade, projects have been under way to record the experiences of Holocaust survivors on videotape. These testimonies have been taped, catalogued, indexed, edited, sometimes transcribed, and circulated to schools and educational institutions by videotape projects at Yale, UCLA, and other research centers.

The projects are an alternative to the museums being built around the country, but they, too, have stirred controversy.[55] Some historians have argued that these individual accounts, out of their broader context, produce poor, unfactual history. Other critics have voiced concern that these stories might arouse a ghoulish fascination with the survivors' suffering, a voyeurism in horror, an identification with the evil portrayed, or with its perpetrators. Finally, there is the risk of sensationalism, that the videotaped interviews might degenerate into what Geoffrey Hartman, the Yale project's faculty adviser, called the "talk-show format, with the host gushing over the survivor, how strong, heroic, wonderful such a person must be." Television, Hartman warned, often produces a sense of unreality.[56]

But after visiting the Video Archive for Holocaust Testimonies at Yale, I believe that the videotaped oral histories of Holocaust survivors being compiled at Yale and elsewhere are among the most powerful ways of transmitting the memory of the Holocaust to those who did not experience it.

Explaining his goal of assembling an "Archive of Conscience" on which future educators and filmmakers might rely, Hartman, who teaches English and comparative literature at Yale, asserted that "these living portraits are the nearest our descendants can come to a generation already passing from the scene."[57]

Long after the last survivor with a number on his or her arm has died, young people will be able to hear the individual's story in his own words, in his own voice. He will be able to search a human face and look for a human response. When so much imagination is required even to understand that the Holocaust could have occurred, the presence of a living person who suffered and endured it eliminates the need for one vast intellectual and emotional leap.

Hartman has argued that there is no substitute for the survivors' testimony. No one can speak for them. And no one else can tell us what they have to say.

So videotapes are probably the most effective weapon against revisionists and revisionism. It is impossible to watch and listen to Renée G. describe the sound of wailing in her Polish village after a Gestapo roundup as "a whole town crying," or to Helen K. recount how her brother died in her arms when they were crammed into a cattle car en route to Majdanek, and question whether these events look place.

While revisionists might cite inconsistencies and discrepancies in the survivors' accounts, they cannot diminish the authenticity of their voices and the power of their experiences. The survivors' accounts are particularly convincing because they, too, often express disbelief about what they endured. "I cannot believe what my eyes have seen," said Helen K.

The Yale tapes are also effective because the project's directors have carefully defined its goals and limitations, what they can and cannot do. Hartman, for one, has stressed that these oral histories are not histories as such and cannot be substituted for studying the past. Just as there are public myths about the Holocaust, there are also survivor myths. Many of those who told of their arrival at concentration camps, for example, recalled having seen Mengele, the angel of death, standing on the train platform to greet them. Mengele, of course, could not possibly have been in so many camps at the same time. But they believe that he was there. Similarly, many of the women who talked about life in the camps were persuaded that the Nazis had given them something to stop them from menstruating. Science tells us that starvation has this effect, but the myth has remained widespread among female survivors, and hence is often repeated in their testimonies.

So these accounts are no substitute for history, but they are invaluable. First, they help shatter public myths about the Holocaust. It is widely believed in America, for instance, that the liberation of the camps was a joyous event for those being set free. But many of the witnesses said they experienced incredible pain and loneliness almost immediately after their liberation. For many, the liberation was not joyous. It was then that they realized for the first time the scope of their loss.

"Oral history does not try to turn the survivor into a historian," Hartman wrote, "but to value him as a human witness to a dehumanizing situation. We cannot allow only images made by the perpetrators to inhabit our memory."[58]

James Young, a Jewish-studies scholar, argued that the power of the tapes was in their portrayal of Holocaust victims not as piles of corpses stacked like cordwood, or as skeletal figures in oversized striped uniforms, but as whole, healthy human beings, well-groomed, self-possessed, pillars of their communities, outwardly well-mended and thriving. "By showing us whole human beings, however inwardly scarred they are, the videotapes rehumanize the survivors, and in so doing, rehumanize the murdered victims as well," Young said. By relocating both victims and survivors in the human community, "the tapes might return just a fraction of the dignity and humanity the Nazis attempted to destroy."[59]

At Yale, the archive has been strengthened immeasurably by the inclusion of testimonies from non-Jewish survivors and observers. One of the most moving accounts was the testimony of a Jesuit priest, identified as Father John S., who described watching a deportation of Jews from Poland. The scene had made "a terrifying impression."

As a young seminary student, he had sneaked up to a train station where he had heard moaning and crying during the night. He found a hole in the wooden fence that had been erected around the station. "It was a cattle train," he said, "right in front of me, just about two tracks from the fence . . . it was opened by an SS soldier. . . . And the impression was terrible because it was terribly packed. I literally saw what you see in pictures, mothers with children, and old people . . . and one man immediately jumped off, and I always remembered his face because he looked a little bit like my father. . . . I did not hear what he said to the German soldier . . . but his behavior was polite . . . what I made out was that he was asking for water. And immediately the SS soldier . . . clubbed him down . . . [into] insensitivity. And whether he died or was later put on the train [I don't know]. And then I ran away. I was so scared and I was so upset; I never saw anything like this in my life. I simply ran away."

The interviewer, who was not photographed, asked whether he had told anyone what he had seen. The question seemed to stun Father John, who was suddenly forced to grapple with his own moral responsibility. Gentle but persistent questioning eventually resulted in self-realization. "Jewish people were deported all around me and I did nothing," he said. "I panicked; no, I did not know what to do."

The incident, he said, was the tragedy of his life. He wished he could live his life again. "Today I might be ready to run in front of the train and lie down," he said. "Today, maybe, I would cry out —protest. At the time, I was immobilized. I ran away. I was utterly unprepared."

It is, indeed, the nakedness of these accounts that permits us to relate to them so strongly. The viewer can find a little of himself in the accounts. Dr. Menachem S., now a gynecologist, survived the war in Krakow, Poland, as a street child. His parents were persuaded that he would be safer depending on the kindness of strangers than staying with them. Several Poles had taken him in—a woman who permitted him to pray to the picture of his mother instead of the crucifix on the wall. "I used to pray: 'Dear God let this war end and let my mother come back and get me,'" he said. Prostitutes who worked in a brothel some three miles from a camp originally gave him food and a place to live. "People on the marginal side of society helped one another," Dr. S. recalled.

After the war had ended and his first child was born, he went out and purchased nearly $400 worth of toys for his newborn infant. When his wife returned to their small apartment, she was stunned. What had possessed him? A baby could not use an electric train and a rocking horse and the other expensive items they could ill afford.

"It took me some time to realize that I was buying the toys for me," Menachem S. said, adding with a wry smile, "And it was then I began wondering: what are we doing to the next generation?"

Helen K., of Warsaw, described her marriage to a man she had known before the war. "My husband was the only person who knew who I was," she said, in a starkly simple explanation of how life in a concentration camp had transformed her.

Rabbi Baruch G., of Poland, told of his suffering after liberation from the concentration camp. "I suffered more from loneliness and isolation than I did during the Holocaust period." He described the joy he first felt at his son's bar mitzvah, years later, safe in the United States. All his wife's relatives were assembled for the party, a grand occasion. "But then I looked around," he said, his voice breaking. "There was no one on my side.

"You are alone," he said. "Life around you seems to be normal, but you are abnormal."

The Yale project directors have encouraged the witnesses to talk about life before the Nazis came to power. Helping to re-create the world that was destroyed is part of the educational value of the taped archives, they maintain. Discussion of life before the Holocaust has also served to make these witnesses seem more like real people rather than "survivors." So does their talk about present injustices. One striking aspect of the testimonies is how many of the survivors discuss the pain they feel about the boat people, blacks in South Africa, their fear that the world might once again turn its back on instances of genocide.

The witnesses at the Barbie trial in Lyons and in New Haven had much in common. Both described their vivid and harrowing experiences at the hands of the Nazis. Both sets of testimonies have provided indelible personal records of atrocity and suffering almost unimaginable to most of their countrymen. But survivors who testified in Lyons did not testify about the camps. They spoke of what Barbie had done to them in Lyons, before he had sent them to the camps. Those who testified about Barbie were describing events that were one step removed from camps, the core of the Holocaust.

Those who recorded their testimony for the Yale archive have not limited their experiences to a time and place. They have been encouraged to testify about their lives before they were shattered by National Socialism, about their confinement and transportation to the camps, about life and death inside them, about their experiences during liberation and their emotions after it. Their words are as close as those who have never experienced what they did can come to understanding their world.

The tapes are invaluable in that they combat memory's most virulent enemy—abstraction. "When I listen to some of the women witnesses," said Joanne Rudof, a former Hebrew teacher who is the project's manager, "I realize that these videotapes help restore my sense of their humanity. I'm listening to a person who could be my grandmother. The more I listen and watch, the more I understand that there is no survivor experience, as such. There are survivor experiences, as varied and multifaceted as the people who had them," she said. "It has become impossible for me to generalize about them."

The Yale testimonies, said Hartman, "focus on the individual rather than the mass, on each person's embodied and ongoing story, on the mind as it struggles with its memories, making sense of or simply facing them, on transmitting in oral form each version of survival."

These very individual accounts are the opposite of the survivor footage taken by the British immediately after the liberation of Bergen-Belsen. There are no numbing images of bulldozers crashing into soil containing thousands of skeletons, of masses of ghostly faces with hollow cheeks and black empty eyes. "No matter how hard I try," said Joanne Rudof at Yale, "I cannot imagine six million exterminated. But I can understand each of these stories."

Rudof and Hartman, with the aid of volunteer interviewers and two graduate-student assistants, are the custodians of what by 1989 totaled some thirteen hundred videotaped testimonies.

The archives did not begin at Yale, but as a grassroots project within New Haven. Dori Laub, a child survivor who had become a psychiatrist, the head of the local survivors' organization, and a television interviewer with her own program, started trying to raise money for filming survivor testimony in 1979. The spark was the television series *Holocaust.* Though the program scored record ratings and was widely credited with having prompted interest in the Holocaust among young Americans and Europeans, survivors in Connecticut and elsewhere were angered by what they saw as the program's trivialization of the searing experiences.

"Everything had been taken from them. Now television was trying to take away their stories too," said Rudof.

Armed with one video camera and enough film for four one-hour-long interviews, Laub and an associate filmed the first four witnesses in May 1979. Geoffrey Hartman's wife, a survivor, was one of them.

The New Haven Farband, a Jewish organization with a large number of survivors as members, donated $5,000 to the project, encouraged by the initial interviews. Public attention and press stories generated more interest, more funding, and more survivors who wished to tell their stories.

The video archivists had conducted two hundred interviews by the time the project moved to Yale. A $300,000 grant from the Charles E. Revson Foundation enabled the university to open a small but professional videotape archive and to continue filming interviews. More than $500,000 of the project's $750,000 endowment goal has been raised. But the project is poorly funded, considering that it has operated on less than what is required for one made-for-television movie.

The Yale Video Archive now provides assistance to some twenty affiliated projects throughout the country. Affiliated projects accept the Yale project's insistence on trained, noninterventionist interviewers, on providing support for the witness before and after he gives his testimony, on safeguarding a witnesses' privacy, and on the use of the testimonies solely for educational purposes. The Yale videotapes are expected to be displayed by the United States Holocaust Memorial Museum. And the project has been preparing a major video unit on the Holocaust for high schools. Facing History and Ourselves, a Boston-based educational foundation, has been using the Yale histories as the heart of a program dealing with testimony excerpts, with a teachers' manual and teacher-training workshops. In 1987, the project circulated more than 115 edited tapes to schools throughout the country, many more Catholic than Jewish schools.

While the project would like to encourage more of the estimated fifty thousand survivors still alive in this country to come forward and testify, Yale has strict rules on solicitations. "People who come to bear witness are volunteers," she stressed. "We do not send more than one letter of invitation. We feel that this is something that survivors must want to do. Otherwise, it would simply be too painful."

She accepts the fact, therefore, that those who choose to bear witness are a self-selected group, who may have different perceptions and attitudes from those who still cannot or will not discuss their experiences.

Exploitation, of course, is a risk inherent in such a project. Hartman and others have taken precautions to ensure that people who were so desperately exploited once in their lives do not suffer the same humiliation again. Hence, no full names appear on the television screen. And access to the Yale archive, housed in Sterling Library, is restricted to families of the witnesses, students of the Holocaust, and scholars.

Yale can be expected to face something of a dilemma when the distribution of the tapes becomes broader. Will they be able to guarantee the tapes' use for "educational" purposes? Will they be on display for all of America to see in the national Holocaust Museum or the Simon Wiesenthal Center of Tolerance? Will schoolchildren find themselves watching and listening to the emotionally wrenching accounts of these people as they breeze through the museum in a half-hour tour? Will they be shown them in class outside of their historical context? Will the American penchant for education on the cheap reduce them to a quick and easy alternative to sustained, sensitive instruction about the Holocaust?

Hartman was quick to identify the risk. "Video-testimonies should not be used to substitute emotion for thought, or tears for the scholar's resolute and continuous inquiry into the character of the perpetrators, their methods, the nature of the system, or other issues of conscience."[60]

In America, that is no easy commandment. There may, in fact, turn out to be a trade-off between the number of people who can see the taped testimonies and the dignity of the setting in which they are seen.

If the testimonies are not available to many Americans, the films and documentaries now pouring out of Hollywood will be.

In democracies, it is difficult to impose quality controls on such projects, or on the use of them. As time passes, greater exploitation seems inevitable. Americans will get the Holocaust that Yale or that Hollywood gives them, the Holocaust of fact, or of imagination.

Conclusions

My grandmother was a tiny, deceptively frail-looking woman with white hair, a fierce temperament, and an infuriating habit of speaking to my father in Russian or Yiddish, neither of which I understood. Despite decades in this country, she never mastered more than a smattering of English.

Given our language gap, she and I did not speak much. But as a child, I spent hours in silent wonderment watching her furiously chop beets and onions for what my father proclaimed "the world's greatest borscht." She had been poor beyond description in Russia. As a child, she had witnessed a series of vicious pogroms. She was a shrewd woman, with intelligent eyes, who had never gone to school. She had lost two of her seven children to disease and misfortune.

My father said that when he was a boy his mother loved to sing and dance. But there seemed to be little joy left in her by the time I was born. The only pleasure she relished was cooking for us, and making sure that we ate every bite.

On one such occasion at our home in Miami Beach, the whole family was assembled in the kitchen, watching television, as my grandmother pulverized an onion for that evening's soup. The broadcaster interrupted his newcast to announce that there had just been a terrible airplane crash moments before the program had begun. It was feared that all on board—more than one hundred people—had perished.

My normally loquacious father fell silent. My Irish Catholic mother, who was terrified of flying even in the calmest of skies, gasped.

Grandmother Lena stopped chopping for a moment. Turning to my father, all but ignoring my mother and me, she asked in broken English: "How many Jews were on board?"

My grandmother had suffered in Europe. And she had responded to her suffering in a very European way. The conclusion she drew from her own experience, even after she got to freedom and safety in America, was that concern about her fellow human beings had to be rationed. No human tragedy could be measured as such. It was the fate of her people that mattered. If an airliner went down, she would dole out her sympathy based on the number of Jews on board.

Born an American, I drew the opposite conclusions. My experience with Judaism and Jewish activists taught me—as Hyman Bookbinder never tired of reminding me—that there could be no Jewish welfare without general well-being. I concluded that the Holocaust suggests that Jews and all threatened minorities need allies in their societies, that no minority can survive in political and cultural isolation.

So at times while writing this book, I found myself losing patience with the debate over whether the Holocaust was, or was not, a uniquely Jewish experience. Of course the Holocaust was unique and, yes, it happened to the Jews. The Jews were singled out for total eradication, and for senseless, even counterproductive slaughter, since the genocide required resources that the Germans diverted from their war effort. But the Holocaust was a tragedy for Western civilization as well.

Could anyone not believe that it called into question the underpinnings of "civilized" society? Could anyone doubt that it undermined for a long time to come the spiritual authority of the Catholic Church and other churches that put their institutional interests above the tenets of their faith? Was it possible to have older European friends and not know that the war had destroyed their families and their world?

No, most of the "others," as they are often callously called, did not die in gas chambers. Their suffering is not comparable to that of the Jews as a people. Except for Gypsies, no other group was singled out for total extermination by the Nazis. But that does not mean that the memory of their tragedy matters less or is any less compelling. The war that produced the Holocaust was a universal tragedy not only because six million Jews were deliberately killed. It was a universal catastrophe because the allegedly civilized world let it happen.

Western Europe today seems prosperous, self-assured, and tranquil enough. But beneath the crust, the lava of memory smolders. Only when a society is forced to confront these memories—by a Jenninger speech in Germany, a Waldheim election in Austria, or a Barbie trial in France—does the bitterness, the hatred, and the anti-Semitism, along with the guilt and defensiveness, burst forth with what seems astonishing power and vehemence.

In every country, every culture I explored, irrespective of national character or political ideology, a particularly national form of self-deception has usually triumphed over self-revelation. The need to evade has most often transcended illumination.

It does not help to quote Santayana—that those who refuse to learn from history are bound to repeat it. For history, as Geoffrey Hartman astutely observed, sends decidedly mixed messages. Was it inevitable that Jews in Germany, the most successful and among the most assimilated in Europe, would be singled out as vermin fit only for extermination?

The so-called "lessons" of the war and the Holocaust are now being written and rewritten. But the Holocaust does not "teach." It is not a religion or an ideology. It cannot provide a moral or political framework for living one's life. The Holocaust exhausts. It defies. It negates. And it raises frightening questions, such as what did the Jews of Europe do to incur such wrath? How could Europe's most cultured people have devised the West's most efficient, neatly implemented genocide? Why did so many people follow Hitler? Why did relatively few resist?

While the vehicles of remembrance differ from society to society, the mechanisms of suppression tend to be similar. Cultures suppress what they would like to forget in remarkably similar ways, even when the events themselves are strikingly different. Events such as Stalin's brutal collectivization and purges in the USSR, the Dreyfus affair and Klaus Barbie's crimes and collaboration in

France, Kurt Waldheim's war service in Austria, Wounded Knee or My Lai for Americans, or the Holocaust almost everywhere, are not comparable. But that does not imply that they cannot and will not be compared. One thing they have in common is the desire of the people and societies responsible for them to forget them or evade responsibility for them. They become alike in the way in which we come to think of them, or to suppress them.

Cultures tend to employ the same vehicles to suppress pain and unpleasant memories as individuals: denial, the shifting of blame, rationalization, and relativization.

In almost every country, denial, the least sophisticated form of suppression, is the easiest to combat. The unabashed revisionists who deny that the Holocaust took place have no intellectual credibility in Europe or the United States; their audience has been extremely limited and is likely to remain so. Even the Soviet Union does not deny that there was a Final Solution for Jews; it has simply chosen not to emphasize their disproportionate slaughter and suffering.

Shifting blame is also a common form of amnesia; the Austrians have most finely perfected it as a technique for blaming others and exonerating themselves for their political and moral failings. But shifting blame, which enables the perpetrator to see himself as a victim, is a common defense mechanism throughout Western Europe and the Soviet Union. The Soviets blame the Nazis in part for the mass suffering Stalin inflicted on them. In its own national mythology, France failed to resist not because it was a nation that had not wanted to fight another war, but because it had been so quickly "overwhelmed" by Germany.

Rationalization and relativization are the most common, insidious, and hence problematic forms of the suppression of memory. Examples in Europe and the United States abound. The United States did not do more to rescue Jews because priority had to be placed on winning the war. True as far as it goes, but that is not the sole explanation. Or there was no "proof" of what the Germans were doing to the Jews until it was too late. Completely untrue, as historians Walter Laqueur and David Wyman have devastatingly demonstrated.[1] As for the American officials who read the reports and heard the intelligence and saw the aerial reconnaissance pictures of Auschwitz, what they read and heard and saw was, as Deborah Lipstadt concluded, "Beyond Belief."

Relativization, what Lipstadt has called the "yes, but" syndrome, is one of the trickier forms of rationalization. "Yes, six million Jews were killed by the Germans, but the United States also committed mass murder. Did they not drop a second (implicitly unnecessary) nuclear weapon on Nagasaki? Yes, the Germans slaughtered Jews, but was Hitler not a response to Stalin? Yes, the Germans massacred Jews, but did the Soviet Union not kill more than a million Germans on the eastern front? Yes, the Jewish genocide in Europe was horrific, but was not Pol Pot's slaughter of his own people—between one and three million, no one will ever know for sure—equally reprehensible?"

Tragedies will always be compared. Saying that the Holocaust was unique will not prevent that. For it is natural, as Israeli scholar Yehuda Bauer has argued, for the Holocaust to be placed in historical context, to be compared with events before and after. "If what happened to the Jews was unique, then [the Holocaust] took place outside of history, and it becomes a mysterious event, an upside-down miracle, so to speak, an event of religious significance in the sense that it is not man-made," he wrote of the problematic nature of the Holocaust. If, on the other hand, "it is not unique, then where are the precedents or parallels?"[2]

It is also understandable, as the scholar James Young noted, that Holocaust imagery would be applied to other genocides and slaughters, even if they predated the Final Solution. The Armenians, for example, describe their suffering at the hands of the Turks as the "Armenian Holocaust," though their tragedy occurred twenty-five years before Germany's extermination of the Jews. To the extent that Nazism and the Holocaust have come to symbolize evil, Armenians and other victims of racial or religious hatred will inevitably seek to appropriate that symbol as a metaphor for their own despair. That the Palestinians should seek to portray themselves as the modern-day historical equivalent of Jews and the Israelis as Nazis is understandable. That the West should fail to note the differences or to challenge the analogy is not. On the other hand, it is equally unacceptable for American Jews and Israelis to discount Palestinian suffering simply because the plight of Palestinians is not comparable to that of the slaughtered Jews.

The expression of one's tragedy in the metaphor of another people's sorrow does not imply that the tragedies are equal in intent or scale. But the sloppy use of Holocaust language to evoke the imagery of Nazi terror for noncomparable situations has contributed, often inadvertently, to the relativization of the Jewish genocide. Even Elie Wiesel, who has argued most eloquently for the uniqueness of the Holocaust, has warned in writing and speeches of the dangers of a "nuclear holocaust."

Imprecise language is a culprit in many cultures. In France, where love of the nuance of language borders on obsession, the use of the term *déporté,* "deported," masks a historically painful distinction. The Jew who was deported as part of the Final Solution becomes the linguistic equal of the Resistance hero who made a conscious decision to fight fascism. Both were deported. And the fate of neither is revealed in this word.

The American penchant for calling victims "martyrs" also blurs. John F. Kennedy, for example, was called a martyr because he was killed when he went to Texas in 1963 to campaign. Martyrs are those who choose to die for their beliefs—like Masha Bruskina. The children of Izieu did not choose Auschwitz. Most of the six million Jews who died in Europe had no choice. The use of the term "martyr" may be well intentioned, since it attempts to add some posthumous grandeur to the slaughter. But it distorts as it tries to give a meaning to the inexplicable.

In some countries, the memory of trauma remains more tenacious than in others. The durability of a memory depends in part on the nature of what is being remembered. Wounded Knee and My Lai were unpardonable massacres, but what is more often recalled is the broader context in which they occurred—the dispossession of the Indians and the war in Vietnam.

The quality and veracity of memory also depend on who is doing the remembering. Some nations and cultures are simply better than others at remembering. Jews, for example, are geniuses at transmitting memory. They have done so not only by making memory a fundamental touchstone of the faith. They have also devised powerful family-based rituals for sharing the memory of suffering and victory. The Passover seder occurs once a year—not often enough to become routinized and boring and not so infrequently as to be unfamiliar. Through recitation of a well-known story—accompanied by food and wine that help evoke the period—Jews are reminded not only of their bondage and humiliation as slaves in Egypt but of their glorious liberation and Exodus, their long and arduous journey into independence and the promised land. And unlike the Christian churches, where Christ's sacrifice is commemorated in public services, the Passover seder is held not in a public place, but in the home, where most of our most powerful memories reside.

Armenians, too, are skilled at remembrance. A people like the Jews whose history is laced with suffering, Armenians have traditionally placed a premium on transmitting the memory of their trauma as a means of perpetuating a sense of cultural identity, a bond shared by all their scattered flock.

Some societies remember better because they value history—the French, for example, who study themselves and perpetually take their national pulse. For some countries, such as the Soviet Union, history is a form of political legitimation. So emphasis is placed on remembrance, even if what is being remembered is partly mythology.

As I was writing, I occasionally asked myself: Since remembering the past, particularly painful episodes is so arduous, why bother? Does it really matter that Europeans do not dwell on the war? Will the world be any worse off if the United States does not commemorate the Holocaust?

Knowing and remembering the evil in history and in each of us might not prevent a recurrence of genocide. But ignorance of history or suppression of memory removes the surest defense we have, however inadequate, against such gigantic cruelty and indifference to it. There is always a danger of overreaction—the fear that every form of cruelty will inexorably lead to a new Holocaust. But that Europeans and Americans failed to react quickly and decisively to Pol Pot's genocide in Cambodia is alarming evidence that the memory of the Holocaust has not sufficiently sensitized Western democracies to the consequences of violations of human rights elsewhere in the world. On a much smaller scale, the delayed and initially weak response by Western intellectuals to Iran's death warrant against writer Salman Rushdie suggests that even those who should be most aware of the dangers of intolerance are not yet equipped to act as moral and intellectual guardians of the precious freedoms and liberties we enjoy.

The memory of evil has not transformed human nature. A new generation of flawed men and women now control the awesomely destructive weapons of the new age. One need not talk of "nuclear holocaust" to be concerned about the consequences of the proliferation and potential use of such weapons anywhere on the planet. The two superpowers that are the custodians of atomic arsenals should pay the closest attention to World War II and the Holocaust.

How best can this be done? How can the memory of the Holocaust be transmitted most effectively?

No single vehicle of memory is perfect; there is no perfect solution waiting for well-intentioned societies to discover and implement. Each has impressive limitations.

Consider, for example, the writing and teaching of history. In France, Robert Paxton's pioneering book on Vichy helped shape young French historians who have, in turn, helped the French confront the past more boldly. In the Soviet Union, historians are being given access, often for the first time, to a wealth of archival material that may enable them to learn much about their wartime past, if the present political trends continue, that is, if Gorbachev prevails and does not shift direction. But while the work of historians affects a society's intellectuals, it is far harder to translate their work and its significance to the society at large.

Historical films and docudramas such as Marcel Ophuls's *The Sorrow and the Pity* and Claude Lanzmann's *Shoah* are effective. But these works, too, are seen mostly by highly educated people. Television's mega-mini-series *Holocaust* and other efforts to translate the Holocaust for mass audiences have proven far more effective at imparting knowledge about and interest in the event. But they risk romanticizing and trivializing history's most complex phenomenon. And in the end, even celluloid is fleeting. The raw power of *Holocaust* has faded dramatically over time as film techniques have advanced and the sophistication of audiences has grown.

Then there are commemorations. They are most common in Germany and the Soviet Union. In the United States, commemorations tend to focus on joyous occasions: the Fourth of July celebration, the Bicentennial, Thanksgiving. But while Americans commemorate Memorial Day, the country has no special national commemoration for the Civil War.

In Germany, where commemorations have become part of a veritable industry of *Angst,* the results are mixed. If poorly conceived or insensitively conducted, like the harebrained gathering at Bitburg, commemorations can be counterproductive, prompting defensiveness and amnesia rather than collective introspection. My experience in Fulda indicated that commemorations can be effective catalysts of memory for those who have experienced an event. But they often seem to be less effective for those too young to remember what is being commemorated.

Another prompter of memory is war-crimes trials and judicial proceedings against those who committed atrocities. But given the age of the perpetrators, such trials will soon end. And even when they are held, the distance from the event, coupled with the failing memory of the victims, sometimes results in doubts about the process itself. In the case of Klaus Barbie, legitimate concerns were raised by respected French officials and intellectuals about whether this trial of a German Gestapo officer in Lyons was a truly useful vehicle for exploring France's role in the war. On the other hand, the transcripts of such trials provide an enduring, permanent record of atrocities, a document that can be used as ammunition against those who may one day seek to challenge the existence or scale of the Nazi Holocaust.

Not only the perpetrators of war crimes are dying, the victims are too. And when they are gone, we will lose the single most valuable and emotionally compelling source of information about that horrific event. Menachem Rosensaft once noted that he could never feel the pain his parents felt. No matter how many times he had heard about the camps, he would never really know what it had been like to wake up to the black sun of Auschwitz.

Similarly, we can never know what he has felt. For watching and listening to his parents has given him and other children of survivors a special relationship to the Holocaust. They do not draw from the traumas the same conclusions as their parents, of course, but the so-called "second generation" has a proximity to the suffering that most of us cannot share.

Perhaps the closest we can come is to watch a survivor speak to us on film. I have never met "Helen K." or "Leon S.," who shared their painful memories with the video archivists at Yale. But I shall never forget their words either. And I continue to believe that their own stories, told to us in their own hauntingly painful, sometimes contradictory words, can do more to make future generations begin to understand the incomprehensible than any other single vehicle of memory. These portraits would not be possible without video technology, the same technology that Rabbi Hier and the other Holocaust entrepreneurs are using to stage the Holocaust shows they hope will broaden their audience. But unlike the sound-and-light shows, the video archives are highly personal documents. They "repersonalize" those who suffered. The victims become people, not numbers.

These personal accounts of the Holocaust are not history; they cannot be substituted for factual accounts of the events and analyses of how they could have occurred. But they accomplish something that few history texts can: they stir our emotions; they make us feel the survivor's pain, the bystander's confusion. In attempting to understand the Holocaust, empathy counts for much.

The quantity of instruction about the Holocaust has been increasing and its quality improving. But the lessons of history being imparted vary widely and are difficult to regulate or monitor in Germany, the United States, and other countries where national education is the responsibility of states and even smaller political entities. Such decentralization prompts healthy differences and divergent approaches to remembrance. But it also means that the national government is limited in terms of how it can promote memory and what kind of memory it can promote through the schools. Education, moreover, is a protracted, undramatic process that often holds too little attraction for societies like the United States, where quick fixes and prompt results are more highly valued.

Many thoughtful Jews have argued that political tests of strength —such as the Waldheim election in Austria and the Bitburg affair in America—are educational and help spark debate, and hence enliven memory. The Waldheim election surely had that effect in the United States and in Western Europe. But Austrians argue, and public opinion surveys support their view, that the Waldheim election had the opposite effect on the Austrians. The Waldheim affair made Austrians more defensive about the past, not less so. It made them feel more, not less, like victims. It made them close their minds to the unpleasant truths they were hearing. It did not illuminate. The confrontational nature of this vehicle of memory made people shun the past, rather than explore it.

Moreover, the Germans, the French, and even the Dutch savored the Waldheim scandal in Austria to some extent. It enabled them to compare themselves and their postwar remembrance records favorably. There is no indication that the Waldheim affair made those countries more reflective about their own moral failings during the war. Ultimately, the Waldheim controversy may prompt a future generation of Austrians to debate the past more candidly, to become more politically sensitive and less anti-Semitic, especially once their national embarrassment subsides. But there is little proof that it has had this effect to date.

The Soviet Union is the master of another vehicle of memory—official rewriting of history. Though such rewriting is much denigrated in the West, all governments, even nonauthoritarian ones, make judgments about how much they want their citizens to know about the past. The opening of the archives in the Soviet Union is in some ways the Soviet version of American government's Freedom of Information Act and sunshine laws. But while the Soviets have taken steps to open the vaults of an exceedingly painful, often disgraceful past, the inherent weakness of this official mechanism of memory is that the process can and may be stopped as abruptly as it began. If a society takes the view that memory should be the purview of the state, the search for facts and explanations will remain subservient to political objectives and regimes.

There are more creative efforts at prompting memory being tried in the United States than in any other country. America's diversity and its pluralism have given birth to a thousand different remembrance projects, even a moving Holocaust "comic" book, which is intelligent and brutally poignant, not funny at all.[3] What such efforts may lack in taste, they compensate for in sincerity, originality, and enthusiasm.

What fosters memory of the Holocaust? Essentially, any intellectual tool, any mechanism, any tradition that reduces its abstraction will do so, any way of making individuals and peoples and nations remember that before the Holocaust was a national and international catastrophe, it was a family tragedy, an individual loss. History books and education are important. But my memory of a single infant's leather shoe encased in glass at Yad Vashem in Jerusalem is as powerful.

Abstraction is memory's most ardent enemy. It kills because it encourages distance, and often indifference. We must remind ourselves that the Holocaust was not six million. It was one, plus one, plus one. . . . Only in understanding that civilized people must defend the one, by one, by one . . . can the Holocaust, the incomprehensible, be given meaning.

Notes

GERMANY

1. Fulda, "Der Jüdische Friedhof in Fulda," Reihe *Dokumentationen zur Stadtgeschichte,* No. 2, February 1980.
2. The German Information Center in New York City reports that in 1988 there were too many commemoration ceremonies throughout the Federal Republic for them to maintain a complete list. According to Moritz Neumann, director of the Regional Association of Jewish Communities in Hesse, the first German city to stage such a commemoration was Frankfurt. Once a great center of German Jewish culture, Frankfurt boasted a Jewish population of 30,000, one of the largest in all Germany, roughly comparable to the country's Jewish population today. Interview, May 31, Frankfurt.
3. Interview, May 25, 1987.
4. Michael Berenbaum, manuscript for book of essays on memory and the Holocaust.
5. Interview, Fulda, May 30, 1987.
6. Interview, Paul Gwosdz, Fulda town councillor, May 28, 1987.
7. Saul Friedlander, interview about his work on Pope Pius.
8. The observations about the commemoration were made to me May 24–29, 1987, in conversations with survivors and other participants.
9. Wolfgang Hamberger, speech marking commemoration of Jewish Cultural Center, May 27, 1987, p. 4.
10. The schedule was so taxing that it led one survivor to quip: "At this pace, they are finally going to kill me."
11. In addition to more than two dozen interviews with Jews from 7 countries, a questionnaire containing 23 questions about the Fulda commemoration was sent one month after the meeting to the 168 heads of households the Mayor's office recorded as having attended the conference. Seventy-eight participants replied,

the majority from the United States, but also from Israel, France, Britain, Germany, and even Zimbabwe. In some cases, the questionnaires were followed up by telephone interviews. In addition to answering the questions, some of the participants sent articles they had written for their local newspapers, pictures and mementos of the visit or their childhood in Fulda, and in two cases, diaries they had kept during the conference. This effort, of course, was not a scientific survey. I did not attempt to reach those who refused to attend the commemoration, or those who failed to respond to the questionnaire. But the responses provided some general guidance on how participants felt about their visit afterward, about whether their feelings about Germany had changed as a result of their visit, and about the most enjoyable and difficult aspects of the trip.

12. Nancy Campus, "The Holocaust: the Need to Know," Scarsdale *Inquirer,* July 17, 1987.
13. Ibid.
14. I use the word *Kristallnacht* with reservations. It was the word chosen by the Nazis to describe the state-ordered destruction of synagogues and Jewish homes and businesses. But the English translation, "Night of Broken Glass," does not begin to convey the terror and destruction of that episode, or the fact that for many historians it marked a critical turning point in Hitler's war against the Jews. I have chosen to use this word because it has become well known in English and in other languages. Other formulations that would avoid this Nazi terminology are, alas, too clumsy for repetition.
15. Elisabeth Noelle-Neumann, "The Possibilities and Limits of Opinion Polls as a Scientific Means of Determining the True State of Public Opinion," paper presented to the NATO Conference in Brussels, November 19, 1987. See also "Die NATO-Experten und das Publikum; Das Problem der Akzeptanz von Verteidigungspolitik," Dokumentation des Beitrags in der Frankfurter *Allgemeinen Zeitung,* No. 168, July, 22, 1988.
16. Interview, Bochum, August 1986.
17. The expression in German is "vergangenheitsbewaltigung," which translates literally "to conquer the past," or "to overcome . . . ," "to surmount . . . ," or "to master. . . ." Several German commentators have noted the awkwardness of this concept. Josef Joffe, foreign editor and columnist of the *Süddeutsche Zeitung* in Munich, noted in a 1985 essay in *The New Republic* that the expression in German would lead an observer to conclude that "history is not remembrance, but a duel, not the 'seamless web' of past and present, but an ancient foe who must at last be bested." It has been rejected by many historians and social commentators as superficial and misleading in that it seems to imply "overcoming" the past. President Richard von Weizsäcker rejected the term in his extraordinary speech to the Bundestag on May 8, 1985, following the Bitburg debate and offered in its place the formulation for contemplating the past that has more or less become ritual in the Federal Republic, the most widely accepted way of expressing the need to confront Nazi history. See Charles S. Maier, *The Unmasterable Past,* Cambridge, Harvard University Press, 1988. See also Frederick Weil, "The Imperfectly Mastered Past: Anti-Semitism in West Germany Since the Holocaust," in *New German Critique,* No. 20, spring, summer, 1980.
18. Fritz Stern, *Dreams and Delusions,* New York, Alfred A. Knopf, 1987, p. 18.
19. Ibid.
20. Interview, Frankfurt, September 1986.
21. "Some German Struggles with Memory," in *Bitburg in Moral and Political Perspective,* edited by Geoffrey H. Hartman, Bloomington, Indiana University Press, 1986, p. 29.

22. K. D. Bracher, *The End of the Weimar Republic,* Ring-Verlag, 1955; 16th edition, 1978.
23. Interview, Geneva, July 1986. Cited in Friedlander's essay in Hartman, ed., op. cit.
24. For an excellent discussion of the origins of the historians' debate, see Gordon Craig, *New York Review of Books,* October 8, 1987, and Charles Maier, op. cit.
25. Andreas Hillgruber, *Hitler's Strategie: Politik und Kriegsführung, 1940–41* (2d edition, 1965; Munich, Bernard & Graefe, 1987).
26. Charles S. Maier, "Immoral Equivalence," *The New Republic,* December 1, 1986, p. 36.
27. "Between Myth and Revisionism? The Third Reich in the Perspective of the 1980's," in *Aspects of the Third Reich,* edited by H. W. Koch, London, Macmillan, 1985, pp. 17–38.
28. Interview, Munich, August 1986.
29. Jürgen Habermas, "Compensating for Loss: The Apologetic Tendencies in the Chronicling of Modern German History," in *Die Zeit,* July 11, 1986.
30. Eberhard Jackel, "Die elende Praxis der Untersteller," in *Die Zeit,* September 13, 1986.
31. James E. Young, "The Texture of Memory: Holocaust Memorials and Meaning," New York University, paper delivered at conference "Memory for the Future," Oxford, England, July 1988.
32. Interviews with Josef Joffe, Washington and Munich, 1986 and 1988.
33. Serge Schmemann, "Bonn Journal: Facing the Mirror of German History," *The New York Times,* October 21, 1988, p. 4.
34. Vera Laska, *Nazism, Resistance and Holocaust in World War II: A Bibliography,* Metuchen, N.J., 1985, p. xvii; citation from Michael R. Marrus, *The Holocaust in History* published for Brandeis University Press by University Press of New England, Hanover, and London, 1987, p. 6.
35. Friedlander, op. cit., p. 30.
36. Raul Hilberg, "Bitburg as Symbol," in Hartman, ed., op. cit.
37. Paxton's assertion in an interview (September 1986) is supported by German polling data. Elisabeth Noelle-Neumann, head of the Allensbach Research Institute, concluded in *Die Verletzte Nation, Deutsche Verlags-Anstalt,* published in 1987, that the gulf between parents and children in West Germany was broader and deeper than in nine other European countries and the United States. Based on 16,000 interviews, she found that only 49 percent of West Germans believe they have the same views as their parents on morality, compared with 84 percent in the U.S. and 76 percent in Britain. This gulf, she concluded, was partly responsible for the general feeling of dissatisfaction and restlessness that was so striking in her survey of Germans.
38. Peter Schneider, "Hitler's Shadow, On Being a Self-Conscious German," *Harper's,* September 1986, p. 52.
39. See Hartman, ed., op. cit.
40. Schneider op. cit., pp. 49–54.
41. James M. Markham, "West German TV Specials Spark Debate on Reconciliation with Nazi Era," *The New York Times,* April 24, 1985, p. C17.
42. Interview, Bochum, August 1986.
43. Markham, op. cit.
44. Saul Friedlander, *Reflections of Nazism: An Essay on Kitsch and Death,* New York, Harper & Row, 1984.
45. Interview, Washington, February 1989.
46. Interview, Richard R. Burt, former U.S. Ambassador to Germany, Washington, March 5, 1989.

47. Interview, Paris, November 1986. See also "Soviet and American Policies in the Opinion of Germans in the Federal Republic of Germany," study commissioned by Friedrich-Ebert-Stiftung, the foundation sponsored by the Social Democrats and *Stern* Magazine, September 1988.
48. Interview with Michael Stürmer, Washington, D.C., October 1987.
49. For this account of the origins of the Bitburg controversy, I am indebted to Raul Hilberg, "Bitburg as Symbol," in Hartman, ed., op. cit., and interviews with Pierre Hassner, Saul Friedlander, William Griffith, Josef Joffe, Peter Petersen, Richard Burt, and Helmut Sonnenfeldt.
50. "Beyond the Zero Hour: The Creation of a Civil Culture in Postwar Germany," speech by Richard R. Burt, Ambassador of the U.S.A. to the Federal Republic of Germany, German-American Institute, Amerikahaus, Nuremberg, May 23, 1986.
51. Telephone interview, February 8, 1989. See also Serge Schmemann, "A Very German Storm: Dust Settles and Unsettles," *The New York Times,* December 14, 1988, p. A4.
52. Interview, Washington D.C., December 15, 1988.
53. Feldman notes that approximately 40 percent of all federal compensation payments awarded—some 25 billion marks by 1985—have gone to individual Israelis. Between 1959 and 1978, Israel was among the top four recipients of German development aid; it ranked first in terms of per capita contributions. West Germany, population 50 million, still sends more tourists to Israel than any other country except the United States. And the largest number of "twin" cities and towns in Israel have come from the Federal Republic.
54. Lily Gardner Feldman, "German Morality and Israel," in *The Federal Republic of Germany at Forty,* edited by Peter Merkl.
55. *The Week in Germany,* German Information Center newsletter, September 16, 1988.
56. "The Treatment of the Holocaust in Textbooks," edited by Randolph L. Braham, Social Science Monographs, Boulder, Colorado, and Institute for Holocaust Studies of the City University of New York, 1987.
57. Ibid.
58. Timothy Garton Ash, *New York Review of Books,* December 1989.
59. Ibid.

AUSTRIA

1. Gordon A. Craig, "The Waldheim File," *New York Review of Books,* October 9, 1986, p. 3.
2. Ibid.
3. Paul Hofmann, *The Viennese,* New York, Anchor Press, Doubleday, 1988.
4. Interview, September 1986.
5. The *New Columbia Encyclopedia,* edited by William H. Harris and Judith S. Levey, New York and London, Columbia University Press, 1975.
6. Hofmann, op. cit., p. 305.
7. Interview, September 1986.
8. Hofmann, op. cit., pp. 37–39.
9. Stefan Zweig, *The World of Yesterday,* University of Nebraska, 1964; Frankfurt, 1970, p. 28.
10. Hilde Spiel, *Vienna's Golden Autumn, 1866–1938,* Weidenfeld & Nicolson.
11. Jean-Marc Gonin, "Autriche: l'antisemitisme raconté aux enfants," *Libération,* Saturday and Sunday, July 12–13 edition, p. 22.
12. Robert Knight, "The Waldheim Context: Austria and Nazism," *Times Literary Supplement,* London, October 3, 1986.

13. Radomir Luza, *The Resistance in Austria, 1938–1945,* University of Minnesota Press, 1984.
14. Evan Burr Bukey, *Hitler's Hometown: Linz, Austria, 1908–1945,* Indiana University Press, 1986.
15. Interview, 1988.
16. Robert Knight, op. cit.
17. Ibid.
18. John Bunzl, "Austrian Identity and Anti-Semitism," published in *Patterns of Prejudice,* Institute of Jewish Affairs, vol. 21, no. 1 (Spring 1987). The article quotes a fascinating poll based on interviews conducted by the British between September 1946 and February 1948 (during the Allied occupation). The interviews showed that only 42.6 percent of respondents thought that National Socialism was a "bad idea." As many as 38.1 percent thought it was a "good idea, but badly executed." And 20.8 percent had no opinion at all. The survey is quoted in an article, "Entnazifizierung," by Oliver Rathkolb.
19. Ibid., p. 4.
20. Gruber's statement cited in Robert Knight, op. cit.
21. Geoffrey Wheatcroft, "Absurd Reich," *The New Republic,* March 28, 1988, p. 14.
22. Oliver Rathkolb, *Gesellschaft und Politik am Beginn der Zweiten Republik,* Hermann Boehlaus Nachf, Wien, 1985.
23. Ibid., p. 59.
24. Ibid., p. 69.
25. Ibid., p. 70.
26. Ibid.
27. Ibid., p. 72.
28. Ibid., p. 73.
29. John Tagliabue, "Files Show Kurt Waldheim Served Under War Criminal," *The New York Times,* March 4, 1986.
30. Interview. February 1, 1989. Eli Rosenbaum, now of the Justice Department's Nazi-prosecuting OSI, was the investigator for the World Jewish Congress who unearthed documents and photos that established Waldheim's service with General Loehr. He said that both he and Elan Steinberg, executive director of the WJC, believed at the time that the revelations would force Waldheim to withdraw his nomination. "Austria is the only country in Europe in which a man with his record could run and could be elected," Steinberg said in an interview on February 1, 1989, in New York City.
31. The following summary of Kurt Waldheim's military career is based on reports in *The New York Times* and on an impressive account of Waldheim's wartime record published by the World Jewish Congress. The document is entitled "Kurt Waldheim's Hidden Past: An Interim Report to the President, World Jewish Congress," published on June 2, 1986, six days before Waldheim was elected President. Written by Eli M. Rosenbaum, General Counsel, New York.
32. Ibid., pp. 26–29.
33. Hofmann, op. cit., p. 326.
34. According to a voting-analysis study commissioned by Waldheim's People's Party, 55 percent of voters between the ages of 19 and 29 cast ballots for Waldheim, compared with 47 percent of those 30–44, 52 percent of those 45–59, 49 percent of those 60–69, and 43 percent of those 70 years of age or older. The survey is based on an exit poll conducted during the first election on May 4, 1986. The results are contained in a report by Fritz Plasser, "The Austrian Presidential Elections 1986 from the Viewpoint of Opinion Research," presented at the EDU–Campaign Manager Seminar, Vienna, September 9–11, 1986.

35. Ernst Gehmacher, France Birk, and Guenther Ogris, "Die Waldheim-Wahl, Eine erste Analyse," *Journal für Sozialforschung,* 26.Jg. 1986, p. 327.
36. In the poll published by the *Journal,* 57 percent cited his role as a "statesman" as the key reason for their vote for Waldheim; only 25 percent, the lowest percentage, said they had supported him because they found him "sympathetic." The reverse is true for Steyrer: 57 percent said they had voted for him because they liked him; only 30 percent considered him a statesman.
37. Jane Kramer, "Letter from Europe," *The New Yorker,* June 30, 1986, pp. 65–77.
38. John Tagliabue, "A Tense Time Now for Jews of Vienna," *The New York Times,* April 10, 1986.
39. Interview, Vienna, September 1986.
40. Interview, Vienna, September 1986.
41. Interview, New York, February 1989.
42. Interview, Neal Sher, director, OSI, New York, February 1, 1989.
43. Interview, New York, February 9, 1989.
44. Henry Kamm, "Vienna Journal: A New Yorker's Anguish in the Land of Waldheim," *The New York Times,* October 9, 1987.
45. Robert J. McCartney, "Waldheim Statement on Jews Cited," *The Washington Post,* February 14, 1988.
46. Serge Schmemann, "Waldheim Assails 'Slanders,' Vows Not to Step Down," *The New York Times,* February 16, 1988, p. 1.
47. Bunzl, op. cit., p. 6.
48. Ibid.
49. "The Truth About Austria," III S/87, Special Edition, edited by Eberhard Strohal, Auslandsosterreicherwerk, Vienna, p. 21.
50. Reuters North European Service report, February 2, 1987.
51. "Waldheim and the Watch List Decision: Anti-American and Anti-Semitic Reporting in Austrian Print Media," by Maximilian Gottschlich and Karl Obermair, Department of Journalism and Communication Research, University of Vienna, June 1987. Prepared for the Anti-Defamation League of B'nai B'rith, European Office.
52. *The New York Times,* November 29, 1988.
53. The poll was conducted on behalf of the League of Jewish Friendship, a group of mostly non-Jewish Austrians committed to religious and political harmony between Jews and gentiles. Haerfer said that the results of the survey astonished the group and researchers at the center alike. "I was simply unprepared to find a resurgence of such vitriol," he said in a telephone interview.
54. Telephone interview, Vienna, February 1989.
55. The survey results might also be interpreted as an indication that the roots of the political education and acculturation of Austrians after the war are not deep.
56. Telephone interview, February 1, 1989.
57. Interviews, Israeli officials, Washington and New York, December 1987.
58. "Austrian Parliament Votes to Pay Victims of Nazis," by Peter Hoffer, *The Washington Post,* March 24, 1988.

THE NETHERLANDS

1. Associated Press report from Arnhem, October 16, 1985.
2. Interview, Velp, January 6, 1987.
3. Telephone interview, Anne Frank Foundation, July 1989. The documentation department of the Anne Frank Foundation in Amsterdam reports that there has

been a steady increase in numbers of visitors to the Anne Frank house since it was opened in May 1960. Some 9,000 visitors came that first year; a decade later the number had risen to 182,000. By 1980 the house received 330,000; 502,000 people visited in 1985. In 1990 museum officials expect 600,000 tourists.

4. Interview, Amsterdam, January 6, 1987.
5. A. Harry Paape, Rijksinstitut voor Oorlogsdocumentatie, War Documents Institute, interview, January 7, 1987. "NSB" stands for Nationaal-Socialistische Beweging in Nederland.
6. Ibid., p. 232.
7. Dr. L. de Jong, interview, January 7, 1986.
8. Jacob Presser, *The Destruction of the Dutch Jews.* Translated by Arnold Pomerans, New York, E. P. Dutton, 1969.
9. Death estimates differ from source to source because an estimated 20,000 Jews of German or Austrian origin had fled to Holland and were included by the Nazis in death tolls. Dr. Presser estimates that Dutch Jewish victims of the war totaled about 90,000 (p. 539).
10. Presser, op. cit., p. 540.
11. Interview, January 7, 1989.
12. Interview, Washington, D.C., October 1988.
13. Presser, op. cit., pp. 538–39.
14. Miep Gies, *Anne Frank Remembered,* New York, Simon and Schuster, 1987. Prologue.
15. Luigi Barzini, *The Europeans,* New York, Penguin Books, 1984, p. 204.
16. Presser, op. cit., p. 4.
17. Interview, Amsterdam, January 9, 1987.
18. Interview, Amsterdam, January 8, 1987.
19. Presser, op. cit., p. 12.
20. Interview, Amsterdam, January 5, 1987.
21. Presser, op. cit., p. 35.
22. Ibid., p. 38. Presser and de Jong also note that about 20,000 of those who registered were not even Dutch, but Germans, Poles, and Jews from other countries who had fled to Holland for safety.
23. Ibid., p. 37.
24. Ibid.
25. Ibid., p. 48.
26. Ibid., p. 277.
27. Ibid., p. 270.
28. "Enquiry Commission, part VIIc, p. 783. Cited by Presser, ibid., p. 264.
29. Interview, Amsterdam, January 5, 1987.
30. Presser, op. cit., p. 543.
31. Interview, Amsterdam, January 6, 1987.

FRANCE

1. Interview, Simone Veil, August 1986.
2. Interview, Alain Finkielkraut, May 15, 1987, by Judith Miller and Richard Bernstein, *The New York Times* Paris bureau chief, Lyons.
3. Interview, Paris, May 18, 1986.
4. Erna Paris, *Unhealed Wounds, France and the Klaus Barbie Affair,* New York, Grove Press, 1985, p. 94.
5. In English, the word "Jewish" is not used. The title reads: *The Children of Izieu: A*

Human Tragedy, by Serge Klarsfeld. In English, it is published by Harry N. Abrams, New York, 1985. The original French version was published in 1984, in Paris.

6. Interview with Serge Klarsfeld, May 16, 1986. For other accounts of Lucien Bourdon's involvement in the arrest of the Izieu children, see Hugh Nissenson, *The Elephant and My Jewish Problem,* New York, Harper & Row, 1988, pp. 191–202. Ted Morgan, "Voices from the Barbie Trial," *The New York Times Magazine,* August 2, 1987, pp. 36 and 44. Efforts to reach Bourdon for comment were not successful.
7. Richard Bernstein, "Remembering 44 Children: Sorrow, Pity, and More," *The New York Times,* April 8, 1987.
8. Ibid., p. 34.
9. Just before the Barbie trial began, an opinion poll carried out by the French polling firm IPSOS for the Paris daily *Le Monde* showed considerable interest in the trial. According to the survey, the results of which were published in *Le Monde* (May 2, 1987) and later in "Patterns of Prejudice," London, Institute of Jewish Affairs, vol. 21, no. 2 (Summer 1987), 51 percent of the 900 people aged fifteen and over polled in April said they intended to follow the trial very closely. Sixty-eight percent said that French officials were right in obtaining Barbie's extradition from Bolivia; 13 percent said they were wrong; 19 percent had no opinion. Sixty-four percent said that the trial should take place even though the events themselves occurred more than 40 years ago; 25 percent were against the trial. An even larger percent, 72 percent, said that "justice" was the word that best characterized their attitude toward the events of 1942–1944; 19 percent chose the word *oubli,* or forgetting. Sixty-six percent said the trial would allow young people to gain more knowledge of the history of the occupation. While 68 percent of those who held this view were under twenty-five, only 43 percent of them said they planned to follow the trial very or fairly closely; 53 percent said they would follow it from afar. Interest in the trial or belief that it should be held did not seem related to ideology.

   When asked, "Why is Barbie going to be tried in Lyons?" 40 percent replied, for crimes committed during World War II; 22 percent said for the genocide of the Jews; and only 6 percent replied for crimes against humanity.

   Sixty-three percent said they were "very" or "rather" interested in World War II. Thirty-six percent said they had "little" or "no" interest in the war at all.

   A similar poll was not conducted after the trial, so there is little way of knowing whether or not the trial significantly shifted public opinion in France. But the survey shows clearly that the concerns about the trial shared by many members of the French *class politique,* the small élite who constitute the French political establishment, were not shared by the general public.
10. Pierre Mérindol, *Lyon, le Sang et l'Argent,* Éditions Alain Moreau, Paris, 1978. *Lyon, le Sang et l'Encre,* Éditions Alain Moreau, Paris, 1987.
11. Richard Bernstein, "Lyons Reacts Quietly, with Some Indifference to the Trial," *The New York Times.* Interview with Soulier, May 25, 1987.
12. "Courrier Piège," *Libération,* July, May 29, 1987, p. 45.
13. See *Annales d'Histoire Révisionniste,* no. 1, spring 1987, Nouvelles Messageries de la Presse Parisienne, Paris.
14. *Le Matin,* "L'éditeur de Faurisson demande réparation," Ariane Bouissou, November 18, 1987, p. 12.
15. "Cinq million de Français ont regardé 'Shoah,' " *Le Monde,* August 2, 1987.
16. "Justice et Réconciliation," *Le Monde,* July 6, 1987, p. 1.
17. See *Le Monde,* May 15, 1987.

18. "Michel Noir: N'oublie jamais Mauthausen me disait mon père," *Le Monde,* Friday, May 22, 1987, p. 8.
19. For a written account of the RTL broadcast, see Le Matin, "Le Pen considere les chambres à gaz comme 'un point de detail,' " September 15, 1987, p. 1.
20. "L'audience du Front National a subi un net recul dans l'opinion," poll by Sofres for *Le Monde* and RTL, *Le Monde,* November 4, 1987, p. 1.
21. "Le Pen's Holocaust Remarks Part of an Alarming Trend: French Ex-minister," Agence France Presse, September 1987.
22. Interview, Paris, October 1986.
23. "Quarante ans après: les Français et la Libération," *L'Histoire. Sommaire No. 67,* May 1984. Robert Frank and Henri Rousso analyze the results of a poll conducted by Louis-Harris France for the monthly journal. The survey, conducted December 21–26, 1983, included 1,000 people, randomly selected.
24. Interview, Pascal Ory, Paris, September 1, 1986.
25. Interview, Paris, August 11, 1986.
26. Henry Rousso, "The Reactions in France: The Sounds of Silence," essay in *Bitburg in Moral and Political Perspective,* p. 53.
27. Robert Paxton, *Vichy France, Old Guard and New Order, 1940–1944,* New York, W. W. Norton, 1972.
28. Ibid., p. 33
29. Ibid., p. 42
30. Ibid., p. 35
31. The author of more than ten novels, Modiano is among France's most prolific younger writers; he is of Egyptian Jewish origin. Many of his books, such as *La Place de l'Étoile* (Gallimard, 1968), explore themes from the war years and the occupation. In *Place de d'Étoile,* a pun on the name of France's celebrated square, Place of the Star, and the yellow star that Jews were forced to wear in occupied France, Modiano begins with the following story: "In June, 1942, a German officer approached a young man and asked him: 'Excuse me, sir, where is the Place de l'Étoile?'
32. "The young man pointed to the left side of his chest." For what is widely regarded as the definitive account of the celebrated scandal that tore France asunder, see Jean-Denis Bredin, *The Affair: The Case of Alfred Dreyfus,* translated by Jeffrey Mehlman, George Braziller, New York, 1986.
33. Robert Paxton, *Vichy France,* p. 183. Specifically, Paxton notes that 60,000–65,000 of those deported were Jews, mostly foreigners who had relied upon traditional French hospitality. Only 2,800 of all the deportees returned.
34. Interview, December 21, 1986.
35. Sternhell, Zev. *Neither Right nor Left: Fascist Ideology in France,* translated by David Maisel, University of California Press, 1986. The lawsuit referred to was brought in 1983 by Bertrand de Jouvenel, an elderly political scientist and writer. He claimed that Sternhell had libeled him by accusing him of having harbored fascist sympathies. In February 1984, the court sentenced Sternhell and his publisher to pay Jouvenel the sum of one franc, a symbolic extraction of damages. For a discussion of the trial and France's ambivalence about the book and its conclusions, see "The Road to Vichy," a review of Sternhell's book by Saul Friedlander, *The New Republic,* December 15, 1986, pp. 26–33.
36. For an excellent analysis of the confrontation with the past in Western Europe, see the European edition of *Newsweek,* April 20, 1987, "Ghosts of the Nazis," by Scott Sullivan, European regional editor, pp. 20–28.
37. Catherine Nay, *Le Noir et le Rouge,* Éditions Grasset et Sasquelle, Paris, 1984.
38. *L'Histoire,* op cit., pp. 61–71.

39. Poll conducted by SOFRES for the newspaper *Libération,* January 9–12, 1986.
40. Robert Paxton, and Michael R. Marrus, *Vichy France and the Jews,* Calmann-Lévy, Paris, 1981. English edition: New York, Schocken Books, 1983.

THE SOVIET UNION

1. Raul Hilberg, *The Destruction of the European Jews,* New York, Holmes & Meier, 1985, p. 339. Hilberg notes that the estimate of 700,000 Soviet Jewish deaths includes the country as its borders were defined in 1937. After the Hitler-Stalin Pact of 1939 and the subsequent division of some Polish territory by Germany and the USSR, the Jewish population under Soviet control increased by 2 million Jews to a total of 5 million, according to H. H. Ben-Sasson, *A History of the Jewish People,* Cambridge, Harvard University Press, 1976, p. 978. The overwhelming majority of the 2 million Polish Jews living in Soviet-controlled territory were killed or transported to concentration camps. So the number of Jews killed in Soviet-controlled territory was actually much larger than 700,000.
2. William Korey, "Soviet Treatment of the Holocaust, History's Memory Hole," essay to be published in forthcoming volume *Remembering for the Future,* Pergamon Press.
3. Historians offer wildly varying casualty figures for the collectivizations, state-induced famines, and terror. Robert Conquest, in *Harvest of Sorrow,* estimates the death toll for ridding the country of kulaks and through famine at about 14.5 million. New York, Oxford University Press, 1986, p. 301. He is quoted by Geoffrey Hosking in *A History of the Soviet Union* as estimating deaths from the terror between 1936 and 1950 at 12 million. London, Fontana Press/Collins, 1985, p. 203. Hosking puts the casualties of the Stalin terror at between 15 and 20 million (p. 203). Moshe Lewin, the émigré historian, has estimated that as many as 10 million were affected by "de-kulakization." Vladimir Tikhonov, a member of the Soviet Academy of Agricultural Sciences, wrote in the April 1988 issue of the weekly tabloid *Argument and Fact* that 10 million farmers had been "repressed" during the collectivization program in the '30s. Although he did not state that millions had died, his figure for "repressions" was the highest ever published. Official histories published earlier insisted that only wealthy farmers had been punished by Stalin. (See David Remnick, "Academician Details Stalin's 1930s Terror," *The Washington Post,* April 5, 1988.) The same tabloid quoted historian Roy Medvedev as estimating the number of Stalin's victims—those who were killed, deported, or imprisoned—at 40 million, the largest figure printed to date. See "Stalin's Victims," Associated Press, Moscow, February 4, 1989.
4. Geoffrey Hosking, op. cit., p. 297. Some recent reports in the Soviet press have estimated the death toll to be as high as 36 million.
5. Interview, Moscow, January 1988.
6. Nina Tumarkin, a historian at Harvard's Russian Research Center, explores this topic at greater length in an upcoming book, whose working title is *Russia Remembers the War.*
7. American and Allied fears of Soviet capabilities and aspirations undoubtedly contributed to the delay in launching the Allied invasion that would relieve pressure on the Red Army and enable it to both defeat the Nazis and move toward the West. For an excellent account of Allied motives and the decision to delay an American invasion for 23 months, see David Eisenhower, *Eisenhower: At War,* New York, Random House, 1986, particularly pp. 72–100.
8. *Encyclopedia Americana,* World War II, vol. 17, pp. 529–30. *Encyclopedia Britannica,* see "Japan occupied by the Allies."

9. Interviews: Medvedev, January 1988; Uri Afanasyev, January 1988.
10. Interview, Washington, D.C., December, 1987.
11. "The Summit: Exhuming the Corpse," *Newsweek,* December 14, 1987, p. 44. Chart on "Reading" in the Soviet Union compared with the United States.
12. Craig R. Whitney, "The New Trotsky: No Longer a Devil," *The New York Times,* January 16, 1989, p. A3.
13. Interview, Washington, D.C., January 1989.
14. Hosking, op. cit., p. 248.
15. Mikhail Geller, and Alexander Nekrich, *Utopiya u vlasti,* 2 vols., London, Overseas Publications Interchange, 1982. Cited by Hosking, p. 183. (U.S. edition: Mikhail Heller and Aleksandr Nekrich, *Utopia in Power,* New York, Summit Books, 1986.)
16. Interviews, Medvedev, Afanasyev, Vitaly Korotich, 1987 and 1988.
17. Bill Keller, "Another Soviet Taboo Is Broken: Paper Attacks Communist Party," *The New York Times,* February 9, 1989, p. 1. Gorbachev himself has mostly been exempt from glasnost. An important exception was an article published in February 1989 in *Neva*, the Leningrad literary and political monthly, which attacked both the Communist party and its leader. The article written by Sergei Y. Andreyev, whom the magazine identified as a 35-year-old geologist from western Siberia, asserted that the party had ignored the interests of the public to become the instrument of a "new class" of managerial bureaucrats. It also accused Gorbachev of contradicting himself by advocating greater diversity of opinion while simultaneously banning opposition parties that might compete with the Communist party. The article created a sensation that winter, but since then there have been few imitators.
18. Paul A. Goble, "Gorbachev and the Soviet Nationality Problem," in *Soviet Society Under Gorbachev*, Maurice Friedberg and Heyward Isham, editors, New York, M. E. Sharpe, 1987.
19. Korey, op. cit.
20. Interview, New York, March 15, 1989.
21. *Encyclopedia Judaica*, pp. 1044–50.
22. Ari Goldman, *The New York Times,* Jan. 4, 1989, p. 9.
23. Foreign Broadcast Information Service, Daily Report, SOV-89-016, January 26, 1989. Moscow Domestic Service in Russian, January 26, 1989.
24. Arbatov is not correct. Most historians agree that Gypsies were designated like the Jews for extermination; but plans for their eradication were never as fully developed or implemented as for Jews. Slavs were to be used as slave labor. Those not needed for work were to be destroyed. But they were not, as a race of people, slated for total annihilation.
25. Interview, Moscow, September 1987. A follow-up interview was held, also in Moscow, in January 1988.
26. Interview, Genady Barkun, deputy director, Minsk Museum of the Great Patriotic War, September 1987.
27. The battalion commander who ordered Masha Bruskina's execution is said by the Simon Wiesenthal Center in Los Angeles, California, to be Antanas Gecas, a Lithuanian who immigrated to Scotland after the war, and who, as of December 1988, was still alive. Britain has refused requests by the Soviet Union and the Simon Wiesenthal Center for his extradition to stand trial for war crimes.
28. Bill Keller, telephone interview, March 1989.
29. This estimate was provided by officials at the war museum. But Vladimir Petrov, who lived in Kiev in 1943, and other Soviet experts say that the population was double that at the war's end. The devastation to the inhabitants and the city's infrastructure, in any case, was immense.

30. The estimate of the slaughter at Babi Yar remains controversial. Estimates range from 80,000 to 200,000. The total is important in that it enables historians to make a judgment about what proportion of those who died at Babi Yar were Jews.
31. Korey, op. cit.
32. William Korey, "The Soviet Cage: Anti-Semitism in Russia," New York, Viking, 1973.
33. Ibid.
34. Interview, Kiev, September 1987.
35. Hilberg, op. cit., p. 139. Hilberg, quoting German statistics, reports that as of October 1942 there were 3,849 Schutzpolizei (German city police) and 5,614 Gendarmerie (rural police) in the occupied Soviet Ukraine. There were 14,163 "indigenous" Schutzpolizei and 54,794 Gendarmerie. These units played an important role in the second sweep of Jews in the occupied Soviet Union.
36. Hosking, op. cit.
37. The argument is supported by Jean Bethlce Ehlstein's *Women and War,* New York, Basic Books, 1987. It is also borne out by a recent, highly unusual Soviet-American poll. The poll of 939 Moscow residents, results of which were published in May 1988, was conducted by the Institute for Sociological Research, a branch of the Soviet Academy of Sciences, for *The New York Times* and CBS News. It clearly showed that Moscow women were generally more conservative and more orthodox than men, in sharp contrast to opinion in America. They were far more inclined than their male counterparts to say that the Soviet Union needed greater military strength than the United States; they were more skeptical of arms-control treaties, and far more chauvinistic about the superiority of life in the Soviet Union.
38. Interview, Moscow, January, 1988.
39. Philip Taubman, *The New York Times,* September 27, 1988.
40. Felicity Barringer, *The New York Times,* Feb. 8, 1988.
41. The memoir is based on the son's memories, plus discussions with several of the wives and children of other participants in the meeting that night. Several had written down accounts of the meeting. But given the meticulous destruction of potentially embarrassing records by Stalin and his successors, our knowledge of the dispute that night comes mainly from these oral accounts, transmitted and retransmitted around dozens of kitchen tables from one generation to the next. Such accounts, despite their flaws, are indispensable in filling in the "white spots" of Soviet history.

    The entire memoir is printed as an appendix. Soviet and American Russian experts who have seen it believe it to be an authentic account.
42. Interview, Moscow, January 1988.
43. Unpublished notes from interview by Bill Keller, *The New York Times,* January 1988.
44. Interview, Moscow, September 1987.
45. Interview, Minsk, September 1987.
46. Interviews. Elizabeth Holtzman, Washington, D.C., 1987, 1988.
47. "World News Briefs," *Financial Times,* August 6–7, 1988.
48. "Khrushchev Remembers," op. cit., p. 141. Boston, Little Brown, 1970.
49. Tass, "Soviet Spokesman on Memorial under Construction at Katyn," August 30, 1988. Moscow.
50. Tass, General Sergei Radzievsky, interview, August 14, 1987.
51. Afanasyev has called for the opening of all party and state archives to scholars after a twenty- to forty-year hiatus. He was hopeful at the beginning of 1988 that such a rule would be adopted, even though he feared that many vital documents

no longer existed owing to the succession of purges by secret police chiefs and general secretaries. A revised rule regarding access to historical archives was drafted in the summer of 1988, but many historians, including Afanasyev, found it too limited.

52. Interview, Moscow, January 1988.

THE UNITED STATES

1. Nathan Glazer. *American Judaism,* University of Chicago Press, Chicago, 1957. Reprinted 1989. See Introduction.
2. The story of Stella Wieseltier, née Backenroth, one of seventeen children of a wealthy Jewish oil magnate, is recounted in the stunningly evocative collection of short stories *Hasidic Tales of the Holocaust,* by Yaffa Eliach, Random House, New York, 1982.
3. Speech by Mark Rudd, April 22, 1988, Columbia Strike Reunion, Wood Auditorium, Avery Hall, Columbia University, New York.
4. Interview, New York, January 8, 1989. Rosensaft concedes that his participation, as part of a five-member group of Jews, at the meeting on December 6 and 7 in Stockholm with Arafat has stirred controversy within Jewish circles. But he has ardently defended the meeting, calling it "politically naïve" to think that the Israeli-Palestinian conflict can be settled without participation of the Palestinians themselves. For the moment, they are represented by the PLO. One participant at the meeting, not Rosensaft, said that he began his presentation by telling Arafat and the other PLO officials: "I was born in Bergen-Belsen. My mother and father are Holocaust survivors. My grandparents were killed in the camps. So were many members of each of their families. Nothing is dearer to me, save my own country, than the survival of the state of Israel. And that, Mr. Arafat, is why I have come to talk to you about peace." Arafat stared silently at the forty-year-old lawyer for some time. He never commented on the Holocaust.
5. It was also the Jewish community, once again, that led efforts to hunt down Nazi war criminals in America. Thanks to the persistence of former Representative Elizabeth Holtzman, the New York Democrat, representing her constituency, Congress created a special office in the Justice Department in 1979 to hunt down Nazi war criminals in the United States, strip them of their citizenship, and deport them. Since then, the Office of Special Investigations, which in 1988 had 12 lawyers, 8 historians, and 2 investigators, has lost only 2 completed cases. With an annual budget of roughly $3 million, OSI had deported or removed from the United States some 25 accused war criminals by the end of 1988. It had stripped 30 naturalized Americans of their citizenship, and had another 25 cases pending in the courts. In 1988, OSI officials said some 600 investigations were under way.
6. Report to the President, President's Commission on the Holocaust, Chairman, Elie Wiesel, September 27, 1979.
7. It was Senator John Danforth, an ordained Episcopal minister, who proposed independently of and prior to President Carter's formation of the Holocaust Commission that April 28–29, 1979, the thirty-fourth anniversary of the liberation of Dachau by American troops, be designated as national days of remembrance for victims of the Holocaust. He said in an interview that he was motivated in part by having watched the television mini-series *Holocaust,* which was broadcast in the U.S. in April 1978. The first national Holocaust commemoration ceremony was held in the Rotunda of the U.S. Capitol on April 24, 1979. The simple candle-lighting ceremony was presided over by President Carter, giving the affair the chief executive's personal imprimatur. Since then, commemoration

ceremonies have been held in state capitals and major cities throughout the country.

8. In an interview in January 1989, Wiesel said that he had wanted to resign, "but not as an individual. I felt then, and I still do, that my own resignation, or that of one or two council members, would have had little impact. So I stayed on for a while longer. But a resignation, 'en masse,' would have been politically significant." Wiesel, nevertheless, succeeded in publicizing and dramatizing the issue at a White House ceremony awarding him the Congressional Gold Medal of Achievement. In a brief, emotional speech, Wiesel implored Reagan to cancel the cemetery visit. "That place, Mr. President, is not your place," Wiesel said. "Your place is with the victims of the S.S."
9. *Bitburg in Moral and Political Perspective,* edited by Geoffrey H. Hartman, Indiana University Press, Bloomington, 1986. Introduction, p. 9.
10. Ibid., p. 8.
11. Steven M. Cohen, Queens College, City University of New York, Market Facts, Inc., national survey commissioned by the American Jewish Committee, October 13, 1988.
12. Saul Friedlander, interview, New York, November 1989.
13. "Nervous Times, Big Check, and a Bit of Noise," Michael M. Thomas, *The New York Observer,* September 4, 1989, p. 1.
14. Robert Alter, "Deformations of the Holocaust," *Commentary,* February 1981, pp. 48–54.
15. Interview, Washington, D.C., December 21, 1988.
16. Remarks by Ben Meed, Fourth Annual International Elie Wiesel Holocaust Remembrance Award Dinner, December 4, 1988, New York, reported in the *Forward,* January 13, 1989, p. 17.
17. Survey conducted by Market Fact, Inc., in April and May 1988 for the American Jewish Committee.
18. Interview, New York, April 1989.
19. Interview, Washington D.C., February 1989.
20. Michael Berenbaum, "On the Politics of Public Commemoration of the Holocaust," *Shoah,* Fall/Winter, 1981–82, pp. 6, 7, 8, 9, and 37.
21. For this observation, and many others in this chapter on the Simon Wiesenthal Center, I am indebted to Gary Rosenblatt, who wrote the first major critical article on Rabbi Hier, and who shared with me his insights into the center, the Holocaust, the Los Angeles Jewish community, and its politics. His article, still a classic, appeared in the Baltimore *Jewish Times,* September 14, 1984, pp. 62–74. "The Simon Wiesenthal Center: State-of-the-art Activism or Hollywood Hype?"
22. Interview with Rabbi Marvin Hier, founder and dean of the Simon Wiesenthal Center, Los Angeles, November 28, 1988.
23. Pete Yost, Associated Press, Washington, D.C., February 13, 1987.
24. Rosenblatt, op. cit.
25. The exhibition, which accompanied the opening of the Jewish Cultural Center in Moscow, was the first exhibition on the extermination of the Jews shown inside the USSR. The Soviet Union does not recognize the Holocaust as such, arguing traditionally that all Soviet citizens suffered equally during the war.
26. Rosenblatt quotes Stephen Hunter, the Baltimore *Morning Sun* film critic, as saying that he was "powerfully put off by the slickness" of the film, which, he wrote, seemed at times to be a "guided tour of the Holocaust courtesy of a very preppy advertising agency." While the effect was "unsettling, even offensive," the film was nonetheless "so scorching that it transcends technique in the end. It becomes almost unbearably moving." Quoted in op. cit., p. 69.
27. Ibid., p. 64.

28. "Commitment," vol. 3, no. 1 (October 1988), Simon Wiesenthal Center, Los Angeles, Calif.
29. Marvin Hier and Abraham Cooper, "Realities, Fantasies of the 'Shepherds' War," *The Commercial Appeal,* Memphis, February 26, 1988. Reprinted in "Response," Simon Wiesenthal Center, May 1988.
30. Friedlander does not mention the center but refers to the vulgarization of Holocaust imagery in "Reflections of Nazism: Death and Kitsch."
31. Gary Rosenblatt, op. cit., p. 74.
32. Telephone interview, January 1989.
33. James E. Young, *Writing and Rewriting the Holocaust,* Bloomington, Indiana University Press, 1988, p. 188.
34. "Report to the President," President's Commission on the Holocaust, September 27, 1979, pp. iii and 3.
35. I am indebted to two fine articles by Robert Greenberger. The first, "Painful Witness," published by *Regardies Magazine* in November 1988, was one of the first in-depth examinations of the Holocaust Memorial project to appear in the non-Jewish press. The second, entitled simply "Museum," was circulated in February 1989 to Jewish newspapers by the Fund for Jewish Journalism. Mr. Greenberger provided an advance copy of the manuscript.
36. Young, "Whose Holocaust?" *The Jerusalem Post,* International Edition, week ending June 24, 1989.
37. Interview, Washington, D.C., January 4, 1989.
38. Interview, February 23, 1989.
39. White House memorandum, June 21, 1977.
40. White House memorandum, March 28, 1978.
41. White House memorandum, April 28, 1978.
42. Berenbaum, op. cit., p. 37.
43. Greenberger, op. cit., p. 7, and interview.
44. Conversation with former President Carter, New York, March 1989.
45. Interview, Washington, D.C., January 1989.
46. The Turkish Embassy said that the ambassador had no recollection of having made such an explicit threat to Eizenstat. But he did confirm that Turkey was adamantly opposed to the inclusion of the Armenian tragedy in the museum, as currently planned.
47. Peter Petersen, interview, Washington, D.C., December 10, 1988.
48. Financial Reports, Fiscal Year 1988 through December 31, 1987, United States Holocaust Memorial Council. The "Campaign Pledge/Receipt Report" as of December 31, 1987, showed that more than $44 million had been pledged by the end of 1987. Council figures showed that as of September 30, 1987, the council had more than $29 million in pledges, thus supporting Wiesel's assertion. But his critics note that it had taken the council six years to raise that sum, that most of this had not actually been paid, and that serious fund raising (meaning securing very large pledges from a few wealthy donors) only began after Meyerhoff and Lowenberg took control. As of December 1988, more than $55 million had been pledged to the project, whose cost was then estimated at well over $100 million.
49. In a letter to Elie Wiesel, dated November 11, 1986, Meyerhoff warned that unless fundamental changes were made, "the Museum will not be built—certainly not within the requirements of time, budget or expression of its mission." The changes he proposed, which ceded power to the Development Committee, would eliminate what he described as the "waste, acrimony, and in the vernacular much 'spinning of wheels' " that "charitably" characterized the council's operations.
50. Minutes from the meeting of the Executive Committee, United States Holocaust

Memorial Council, Wednesday, June 17, 1987, p. 4. Copies of the minutes were provided by other council members. Eventually, the council provided a copy as a courtesy to the author only after the American Civil Liberties Union protested that the council was covered by the Sunshine and Freedom of Information acts. But the council has continued to maintain that the public has neither the right to attend meetings nor the right to see minutes or documents it produces.

51. Greenberger, op. cit., p. 10.
52. For a definitive account of U.S. inaction, see David S. Wyman, *The Abandonment of the Jews,* New York, Pantheon, 1984.
53. Alex H., T–210 Fortunoff Video Archives, Yale University, Sterling Library. Also cited are testimonies of Menachem S., T–152; Helen K., T–58; John S., T–216; Renée G., T–5; Rabbi Baruch G., T–295.
54. Lawrence L. Langer, "Holocaust Testimonies and Their Audience," *Orim: A Jewish Journal at Yale,* pp. 96–111.
55. For an excellent discussion of the role and value of such videotape archives, see Young's *Writing and Rewriting the Holocaust.*
56. Geoffrey H. Hartman, "Preserving the Personal Story: The Role of Video Documentation," *Dimensions, A Journal of Holocaust Studies,* vol. 1, no. 1 (Spring 1985).
57. Geoffrey H. Hartman, "Learning from Survivors: Notes on the Video Archive at Yale," in *Remembering for the Future,* Oxford, Pergamon Press, 1988, pp. 1713–16.
58. Ibid., p. 1714.
59. Young, op. cit. p. 163.
60. Hartman, "Preserving the Personal Story . . . ," p. 17.

CONCLUSIONS

1. Walter Laqueur, *The Terrible Secret,* New York, Penguin Books, 1982. David S. Wyman, *The Abandonment of the Jews,* New York, Pantheon Books, 1984.
2. James E. Young, *Writing and Rewriting the Holocaust,* p. 88, quoting Yehuda Bauer in *The Holocaust in Historical Perspective,* Seattle, University of Washington Press, 1978, p. 31.
3. Art Spiegelman, *Maus: A Survivor's Tale,* New York, Pantheon, 1986.

Acknowledgments

Writing a book, unlike working for a newspaper, is a lonely endeavor. But there have been several people who have made it less so by providing information, insights, and encouragement. Many are already cited in this book. But several are not.

First, the book owes its existence in part to A. M. Rosenthal, the former executive editor of *The New York Times* and now its distinguished columnist, who had a habit of pushing reporters and editors to their intellectual limits (and sometimes beyond them.) In the summer of 1986, I sketched out a rather vague proposal about comparing memories of the Holocaust in France, where I was then based, and in three other European countries. He gave me eight weeks to explore the topic, enormous time for a daily newspaper, which not unreasonably, expects its correspondents to file daily. Les Gelb, the deputy editorial page editor, listened to my theories and read sections of the book. Craig Whitney, the former Washington Bureau Chief, enabled me to continue working on the book while serving in Washington as his deputy. Martin Arnold, the media editor, forgave me for spending part of many a morning with Simon and Schuster instead of with him; he, too, gave much appreciated advice and support. Lynn Nesbit, my agent, encouraged me to turn my magazine piece into a book; she also found the perfect publisher.

In France, Larry Maisel and Susan Grant believed in this project even more than I did at times, helped find French and Dutch survivors willing to discuss the war with me, and shared their thoughts and reservations about mine over so many moments of precious friendship. Richard Vilanova, Jean-Baptiste Toulouse, and Andre Soussens helped translate the often frustrating French and provided friendship and insight. Anne Aghion, then the office manager of *The New York Times* Paris bureau, organized trips, helped edit the magazine piece that provided the core of the book, and kept me going. So did my friend, the filmmaker Gudie Lawaetz.

My researchers in France, Marie Lascombes and Alice Sedar, and in Germany, Beata Thewald, kept me abreast of relevant development long after I left Europe.

The Soviet Union was a less frustrating place to work than it can normally be thanks to Bill Keller, with whom I traveled and from whom I learned much about the country. Phil Taubman and Felicity Barringer, also *Times* colleagues, were warm hosts and loyal friends. Special thanks to Victor Klimenko for the graph and Mark Belenky, who translated several key interviews for me.

Most of the book was written in Washington, where I am indebted to Jerrold and Leona Schecter for lending me books, encouraging the project, and making sure that I ate dinner. Hal Sonnenfeldt, Nelson Ledsky, Bill Griffith, Charles Maier, and Ron Asmus advised on the German chapter. Igor Belousovitch helped with the Soviet Union. Vladimir Petrov corrected mistakes in my rendition of Russian history, refined ideas, and read the manuscript. Naomi Rosenblatt's stimulating Bible classes contributed more than she will ever know. Jo Tate, my assistant in the Washington bureau, helped organized my files and my life. Nancy Walker was the most inquiring, spirited researcher/translator/editor/friend a writer could have. In addition to Michael Berenbaum, Martin Smith, a gifted filmmaker, and Sam Eskanezi of the Holocaust Museum in Washington explained the thrust and goals of the project. Though we often disagreed, I retain enormous respect for their intentions and integrity.

In New York, Eva Fogleman and Jerome Chanes provided material, as did Hyman Haves, in Los Angeles. Zvi Gitelman's advice on the Soviet Union was enormously valuable.

I owe special thanks to Bernard Lewis, whose work has shaped so much of my thinking about the Mideast, who took the time to read and comment on the manuscript. So did Martin Mayer and Karin Lissakers, my friends and fellow writers. There are a few more people without whom this book would not have been written —Saul Friedlander, whose work and guidance led me to believe much of what I do about how best to remember the Holocaust; Bob Blackwill, whose friendship, editing and support were indispensable; Bill Safire, whose own work, discipline, and loyalty to friendship have set such a fine example; Joan Buck, a gifted writer and friend who urged napping when the words would not flow; and Jason Epstein, who challenged several of my more misguided notions in the book and heard more about the Holocaust than any editor or friend needed or wanted to know.

I want to thank Carl Schorske, my teacher at Princeton, for his powerful insights on Austria. Annette Insdorf and Anton Kaes, for their work on the role of film in molding impressions of the Holocaust. Nechama Tec, who survived and explored who helped and why. Mark Belenky, for translating the Russian memoir. And Ed Klein, for putting these issues on the cover of *The New York Times Magazine.*

Finally, I want to thank George Hodgman, for his patient and thoughtful editing. Above all, I am indebted to Alice Mayhew, not only for the title, but for understanding what this book was really about, and for making it so much better than it was when I gave it to her.

Judith Miller
New York, January, 1990

Index

Aaron, Marc, 127
Abramson, Albert ("Sonny"), 252, 262–263, 264
Academy Awards, 236–37
Adenauer, Konrad, 38
Adler, Alfred, 63
Adler, Isfried, 24–25
Adler, Jeffrey S., 28
Adler, Yoram, 24–25, 28
Afanasyev, Yuri N., 201–3, 204, 207–8, 211, 215, 216, 299*n*–300*n*
Algerian War, 116, 120, 131, 147
Alter, Robert, 230
Altshuler, David, 243, 254
Ambre, Joannes, 132
American Jewish Committee (AJC), 229, 231, 264
American Jewish Congress (AJC), 264
Amersfoort Camp, 97
Anderl von Rinn, 66
Andreyev, Sergei Y., 298*n*
Annals of Historical Revisionism, 134, 138
Anschluss, 61–62, 65, 66, 67, 85, 86
Anti-Defamation League of B'nai B'rith (ADL), 88, 245, 250, 264
Anti-Fascist Committee, 170, 204–6
anti-Semitism, 45, 56, 237, 238, 239, 243, 244, 245, 246, 251, 279
  in Austria, 62, 63, 65–66, 69, 76–82, 87–90, 92, 287
  in France, 114, 117, 133, 143, 144, 146–47, 148, 151, 152, 156
  hypersensitivity to, 29
  in Netherlands, 99, 101, 109
  in Soviet Union, 167–71, 173, 182, 183–84, 188–92, 194, 205, 217–18, 246
  in United States, 224, 229, 233, 245, 250
anti-Zionism, 146, 183, 223
Anti-Zionist Committee, 170
Apostrophe, 156
Arab-Israeli War (1967), 183, 222–23, 224, 229, 230
Arabs, 144, 225
  sentiments against, in France, 129, 133, 135–36, 146–47
  see also Palestinians
Arafat, Yasir, 226, 300*n*
Arbatov, Georgi, 171, 216–17, 298*n*
Archives, U.S., 163
Arendt, Hannah, 222

Arkadyev, Lev, 176–77, 179, 183, 184–185
Armenians, 236, 259, 281, 283, 302*n*
Ascher, A., 104
Ash, Timothy Garton, 59
Askoldov, Alexander, 208
Auschwitz, 25, 37, 75, 97, 100, 150, 223, 232, 248, 249, 252, 257, 261, 264, 280, 285, 303*n*
  Lyonnais sent to, 123, 124, 125, 128, 129–30
  Polish Carmelite nuns at, 11, 243
Austria, 10, 15, 61–92, 97, 279, 280, 286–87
  anti-Semitism in, 62, 63, 65–66, 69, 76–82, 87–90, 92, 287
  campaign against Jews in, 67
  de-Nazification in, 69–72
  educational programs in, 69, 79, 86–87
  "first victim" myth in, 62, 68–69, 72–73, 76, 88
  former Nazis in government of, 71–72
  history of, 63–66
  ignorance of war years in, 67–68
  lack of resistance in, 66
  National Socialism accepted in, 65–66, 68, 76, 292*n*
  opinion polls in, 87–88, 89–90, 92
  pinpricks to memory in, 73
  postwar settlement on, 68–69
  reparations paid by, 69, 91
  support for Nazis in, 61–62, 67
  Waldheim affair in, 10, 11, 62–64, 67, 72, 73–92, 95, 164, 243, 279, 280, 286–87, 292*n*
  xenophobia in, 63, 76, 77, 79, 87
  year of commemorations and remembrance in, 83, 85–86, 89, 91
Austria Today, 72
Azgur, Zahir I., 174, 175, 180–83, 184

Babi Yar, 186–98, 207, 210–11, 218
  actual site of killings at, 190, 192–94
  description of executions at, 187
  disproportionate toll among Jews at, 187–88, 193–94
  estimate of slaughter at, 299*n*
  film on, 194–97
  monument at, 186, 187, 189, 190, 210–11
  solemn commemoration of, 194, 210
  Yevtushenko and, 188–89, 207
Babi Yar, 194–197
Babi Yar Memorial (Denver), 255
Badinter, Robert, 115
Bandera, Stephan, 212–13
Baranov, André, 206–7
Barbie, Klaus, 112–38, 145, 148, 149, 152, 156, 157, 164, 279, 285
  absent from courtroom, 119–20, 122
  apprehension about trial of, 112–18, 295*n*
  charges against, 113, 116
  defense strategy for, 116, 120–21
  first trial of, 115
  Izieu raid and, 123, 126–28
  Lyonnais' views on, 130–33
  media coverage of, 122–23
  memorial in Lyons to victims of, 129–130
  opinion poll before trial of, 295*n*
  Parisians' views on, 133–34
  testimony against, 123–25, 128, 271–272
  tracking down of, 115, 120
Barkun, Genady, 173, 175
Baron, Salo, 232
Barre, Raymond, 145
Barzini, Luigi, 99
Baudoin, Bettina, 133–34
Bauer, Yehuda, 281
Becker, Boris, 43
Beckerman, Ruth, 65, 67, 80–81, 82
Begin, Menachem, 225
Begun, Yosef, 194
Belgium, 15, 99, 100
Belzberg, Samuel, 238, 239, 240
Berenbaum, Michael, 15–16, 222, 234–35, 236, 253, 257, 263, 265, 266
Bergen-Belsen, 97, 260, 272
Berlin Wall, 46, 57–58
Bernstein, Richard, 130, 133
Birkenau, 266
Birobidzhan, 168–69, 205–6
Birobidzhaner Shtern, 196
Bitburg affair, 11, 45, 47–50, 51, 54, 55, 228–29, 244, 284, 286, 301*n*
Black Book (Grossman and Ehrenburg), 167
Blaisse, Mark, 110–11
Bloom, Alan, 27

B'nai B'rith, 238
  Anti-Defamation League of (ADL), 88, 245, 250, 264
Bohlen, Celestine, 168
Bondarev, Yuri V., 204
Bonopera, Georges, 150
Bookbinder, Hyman, 228, 258–59, 278
Boot, Das, 43–44
Bourdon, Lucien, 126
Bourguburgu, Danielle, 113–14
Bourguburgu, Jean-Marie, 113
Bracher, K. D., 33
Brandt, Willy, 59
Brezhnev, Leonid I., 163, 193, 201
Bronfman, Edgar M., 83, 85, 170
Bruck, Wolfram, 57
Bruskina, Masha, 174–85, 282, 298*n*
Brzezinski, Zbigniew, 256
Bucheim, Lothar-Gunthar, 44
Bukharin, Nikolai, 162–63, 204, 207
Bunzl, John, 68, 87
Burt, Ambassador Richard R., 50
Bush, George, 242–43, 246
Byelorussia, 171–85, 212
  anti-Semitism in, 183–84
  Bruskina affair in, 174–85, 282, 298*n*
  collaboration in, 178–80, 184
  devastation in, 171–72
  Khatyn memorial in, 213–14

Cambodia, 41, 116, 135, 281, 283
Campus, Nancy, 20–21
Carter, Jimmy, 227, 255, 256–57, 258, 300*n*
Catholic Church, 278
CBS-TV, 239
Céline, Louis-Ferdinand (Louis Destouches), 113, 148
Census Bureau (Netherlands), 102, 103
Center for Holocaust Studies (New York), 256
Children of Izieu: A Jewish Tragedy, The (Klarsfeld), 126, 127
"Children of Memory, The," 129
Chirac, Jacques, 136, 148, 150, 153
Christ, 223, 283
Christian, Gerold, 64
Chronicle of the Persecution of the Jews (Hertzberg), 103
Cockburn, Patrick, 201
Cohen, Steven M., 229
Cojot-Goldberg, Michel, 124–25
Cold War, 38–39, 69
  end of, 57–60
Combat, Le, 132
Combret, Serge, 150
commemorations, 284–85
  Bitburg affair and, 11, 45, 47–50, 51, 54, 55, 228–29, 244, 284, 286, 301*n*
  at Fulda, 13–16, 18–32, 55, 285, 288*n*–89*n*
  of Kristallnacht, 52–54, 57
  in Soviet Union, 170, 194, 210–11, 242, 284, 301*n*
  in United States, 222, 226–44, 248–249, 251–66, 284, 300*n*–301*n*
  year of, in Austria, 83, 85–86, 89, 91
  younger generation not engaged by, 29–31, 55
Commissar, 208
Committee on Conscience, 227–28
Communist Party of Soviet Union, 165, 215, 217, 298*n*
  Twentieth Congress of, 211
Communist Party of Ukraine, 196
Congress, U.S., 210, 226, 227, 230, 256, 262, 266, 300*n*
Craig, Gordon A., 62, 67
Crimean Tatars, 178
Croix-Rousse, 135–36
Czechoslovakia, 17
Czerniakow, Adam, 250
Czernin, Hubertus, 74

Dachau, 10, 124, 300*n*
Danforth, John, 300*n*
Dawidowicz, Lucy S., 258
Days of Remembrance of the Victims of Holocaust, 47, 227, 229, 242, 300*n*
de Gaulle, Charles, 144, 151
  mythology crafted by, 114, 139, 140, 141, 152, 154
  in Resistance, 115, 142–43, 201
de Grout, Cyp, 102
DeHoyos, Stanislas, 120–21
de Jong, Louis, 98, 99, 102, 107–8, 109
Dekking, A. F., 105–7
Dekking, Maryanne van Raamstonk, 105–6, 107, 108, 111
Dekking, Yara, 105–6, 109–10, 111
de la Bella, Simon, 101
de Marenches, Alexandre, 149

de-Nazification:
in Austria, 69–72
in Germany, 38
"déportés," 146, 282
de Vlugt, W., 101
Diament, Fred, 242, 265
Diary of Anne Frank, The, 167
Dikhtyar, Ada, 175–80, 183–85
Djilas, Milovan, 158
Dollfuss, Engelbert, 74
Dreyfus, Alfred, 144, 279
Droit de Réponse, 150, 156
Duras, Marguerite, 147–48
Dutch Jewish Council, 97, 103–4

education, 287
in Austria, 69, 79, 86–87
in France, 145, 152
in Germany, 30, 55–56, 286
in Soviet Union, 158–59, 163
in United States, 286
Ehlers, Peter, 53
Ehrenburg, Ilya, 167
Eichmann, Adolf, 39, 67, 118, 221–22
Eizenstat, Stuart, 224, 254, 255, 257, 258, 259, 302*n*
Elbert, Lev, 189–94
Estonia, 213
European Community, 58, 85
Evening Minsk, 177, 181, 184
Express, L', 83

Fabius, Laurent, 155
Facing History and Ourselves, 273–74
fascism:
abuse of term, 40–41
describing periphery vs. core of, 41–42
Fassbinder, Rainer Werner, 44–45
Faurisson, Robert, 134, 145, 149
Feldblum, Lea, 128
Feldman, Lily Gardner, 54, 57, 291*n*
films about Holocaust, 43, 134–35, 138, 143, 145, 156, 194–97, 236–37, 242, 243, 273, 284, 300*n,* 301*n,* 303*n*
Fingerhood, Doris, 20, 24
Fingerhood, Steven, 22, 24, 28–29
Finkielkraut, Alain, 117, 121–22, 141, 157
Finland, 213
Fleischer, Hagen, 84
Foxman, Abraham H., 220–21, 253
France, 10–11, 15, 60, 112–57, 201, 279–80, 282
anti-Arab sentiments in, 129, 133, 135–36, 146–47
anti-Jewish laws in, 132, 133–34, 151, 152
anti-Semitism in, 114, 117, 133, 143, 144, 146–47, 148, 151, 152, 156
attitudes of young people in, 154–57
Barbie trial in, 112–38, 145, 148, 149, 152, 156, 157, 164, 279, 285, 295*n*
chauvinism and nationalism in, 114–115
collaborationists purged in, 140, 147
deportation of Jews from, 114, 120, 121, 123, 124–25, 131, 133, 145, 146, 152, 296*n*
elections of 1988 in, 136–38
growing indifference in, 156–57
history as interest in, 115, 139, 283, 284
internal divisions in, 139–40, 141, 149, 152, 153, 154, 155–56
Jews saved in, 146
language of obfuscation in, 145–46, 282
liberation of, 139, 140, 154
Marenches files in, 149–50, 152
myths and historical clichés in, 139–142, 148, 149, 154, 156
North African Jews in, 144
"occultation" stage in, 140–41, 145, 152
patriotism in, 153
period "between two Mays" in, 142
Resistance in, *see* Resistance, French
resurgence of memory in, 142–45, 147–48, 150
student revolt in, 39, 142, 144
textbook reform in, 145, 152
Vichy government in, 114, 128–29, 132, 133–34, 139–43, 147, 150–53, 155, 156, 284
Waldheim scandal and, 286–87
winner-loser dichotomy in, 138–39
Frank, Anne, 10, 95–96, 98, 108, 111
Frank, Otto, 108
Frank, Robert, 139–40, 155
Frankfurter Allgemeine Zeitung, 35–37
Frankfurt ghetto, 56–57

Anne Frank Museum (Amsterdam), 96, 293*n*–94*n*
Freedom party (Austria), 71–72, 73
French Revolution, 114, 132, 139
Friedlander, Henry, 55, 243
Friedlander, Saul, 11, 33, 38, 41, 44, 232, 249
Frischenschleger, Friedhelm, 73
Fulda, 13–32, 56
  history of, 16–17, 25
  Jewish school in, 19, 27
  reunion of Holocaust survivors from, 13–16, 18–32, 55, 285, 288*n*–89*n*
  war memories of gentiles in, 26–27
Fulda House (Jerusalem), 27
Fürst, Michael, 53
Furth, Eva, 100–101, 103, 108

Gecas, Antanas, 298*n*
Geller, Mikhail, 164
General Union of French Jews (UGIF), 120, 123, 130
Genocide, 236–37, 242, 243, 301*n*
Genocide Treaty, 226, 255–56
Gerbrandy, P. S., 104
Gerenstein, Liliane, 127–28
Gerer, Rebbe, 240
German Culture Week, 56
Germany:
  division of, 31–32, 46, 58
  reunification of, 46, 58–60
Germany, Democratic Republic of (East Germany), 10, 46, 57–60
Germany, Federal Republic of (West Germany), 10, 13–60, 69, 91, 117, 135, 161, 201, 239, 279
  attitudes of young people in, 29–31, 55, 290*n*
  attitudes toward past within popular and political culture in, 38–39
  Bitburg affair and, 45, 47–50, 51, 54, 55, 284
  commemorations in, 13–16, 18–32, 55, 284–85, 288*n*–89*n*
  compensation awarded by, 54–55, 291*n*
  democratic tradition in, 50
  de-Nazification in, 38
  education about Holocaust in, 30, 55–56, 286
  end of Cold War and, 57–60
  guilt vs. historical responsibility of, 27–28, 51
  historical revisionism in, 32–37, 41–51
  Jenninger affair in, 52–54, 56–57
  lack of internal reconciliation in, 54–55, 56–57
  longing for heroes in, 43–44
  "mastering past" in, 32, 51, 289*n*
  proliferation of historical works in, 37–38
  Schlusstrich concept in, 11, 44–45, 47–50
  student riots in, 39–41, 45
  U.S. Holocaust Memorial Museum and, 259–62, 263
  Waldheim scandal and, 286–87
Gestapo, 97, 112, 115, 120, 123, 126, 128
Girerd, Yves, 131
glasnost, 165, 166, 171, 172, 183, 195, 196, 202, 207, 217, 218–19, 298*n*
Glazer, Nathan, 221
Hermann Goering Works (Linz), 70–71
Goldstein, Ellen, 255, 256
Golovanivsky, Savva, 188
Gorbachev, Mikhail, 57, 183, 193, 198, 199, 204, 211, 284, 298*n*
  economic and political reforms of, 202, 210, 218–19; *see also glasnost, perestroika*
  historical reassessment and, 162–66, 171, 175, 200–203, 209–10, 212, 213, 215-16
  nationalities and, 167, 217
  and policy toward Jews, 169, 171
Graff, Michael, 83
Great Britain, 60, 115, 298*n*
Greenberg, Rabbi Irving, 222, 257–58
Greenberger, Robert, 254
Greens (Germany), 45–46, 52, 54
Grossman, Vasily, 167
Grosz, Paul, 91–92
Gruber, Karl, 69
Guillaume, Pierre, 134
Gwosdz, Paul, 17
Gypsies, 9, 48, 54, 55, 171, 234, 279, 298*n*

Habermas, Jürgen, 33, 36, 50
Hacker, Oskar, 70
Hacker-Lederer, Ivan, 80

Haerfer, Christian, 89–90, 293*n*
Haffner, Sebastian, 53
Hain, Yaakov, 20
Halevy, Yechiam, 265
Halter, Marek, 128–29
Hamberger, Wolfgang, 15, 17, 18, 26–28, 31
Hapsburg empire, 63, 64, 65
Hartman, Geoffrey, 229, 268, 269, 272, 274, 279
Hassner, Pierre, 46, 49
Heavy Sand (Rybakov), 207
Hebrew, 168, 170, 218
Heimat, 41–42
Hertzberg, A. J., 103
Herzog, Chaim, 56
Hier, Rabbi Marvin, 237–51, 285–86
  Academy Award won by, 237
  attention-grabbing tactics of, 243–44
  background of, 239–40
  high-tech approach of, 248–49
  Holocaust imagery exploited by, 244–48
  political power base sought by, 246–48
  see also Simon Wiesenthal Center
Hilberg, Raul, 163, 222, 265
Hillgruber, Andreas, 34–35, 36
Himmler, Heinrich, 37
Histoire, L', 154
"historians' debate," 34–37, 48–49, 51
historical revisionism, 11–12, 255, 268
  through comparison, 34, 35, 41, 45–46; *see also* relativization
  in France, 134, 137–38, 149
  in Germany, 32–37, 41–51
  "historians' debate" and, 34–37, 48–49, 51
  inversion of perpetrators and victims in, 11, 42–44
  periphery vs. core of fascism in, 41–42
  Schlusstrich and, 11, 44–45, 47–50
history:
  learning from, 279, 283
  valuation of, 283
  writing and teaching of, 284
History of the Soviet Union, A (Hosking), 163–64
Hitler, Adolf, 17, 33, 34, 37, 39, 43, 50, 52, 53, 54, 59, 100, 135, 142, 246, 250, 260, 281
  Austria and, 61–62, 65, 67, 68
  Jewish declaration of war against, 35–36, 42
Hitler-Stalin Pact (1939), 151, 160, 163, 212, 213
Hitler Youth, 45, 74
Hoedl, Carl, 83
Hoffmann, Stanley, 142
Hofmann, Paul, 63, 65
Holocaust:
  denial of, 11, 32–33, 56, 144–45, 280
  effectively transmitting memory of, 284–87
  exploitation of, 224–25, 230, 232, 237, 244–48
  historical revisionism and, *see* historical revisionism
  "lessons" of, 279
  "marginalization" and "externalization" of, 39–41
  as quasi-religious event, 223
  rationalization of, 216, 280–82
  relativization of, 34, 35, 41, 45–46, 116, 120–21, 135, 280, 281–82
  shifting blame for, 280
  suppression of remembrance about, 279–82
  as term, 9, 10
  as tragedy for Western civilization, 278–79
  as unique event, 281
  as uniquely Jewish experience, 278
Holocaust, 43, 145, 273 ,284, 300*n*
Holocaust Memorial Council, U.S., 163, 226–27, 255, 258, 259–62, 302*n*–3*n*
  Bitburg affair and, 228–29, 301*n*
  competition for membership on, 263–264
  Germany's relationship with, 259–62, 263
  Wiesel's resignation from, 262, 263
homosexuals, 54, 55
Honecker, Eric, 59
Hosking, Geoffrey, 163–64
Huhn, Heinrich, 17
Hussein, King of Jordan, 85

Ignatavicius, Z., 179
Indelible Shadows (Insdorf), 303*n*
Indians, American, 280, 282
Institute for Conflict Resolution, 89
Institute for War Documentation, 109

Intifada, 229–30, 247–48
inversion of perpetrators and victims, 11, 42–44
Iran, 90, 91, 283
Israel, 10, 85, 144, 205, 221, 228, 231, 233, 234, 239, 240, 246, 247, 256, 259, 261, 266, 281, 300*n*
  American Jewry's support for, 11, 224–25, 226, 247–48
  Austrian students sent to, 87
  Austria's facilitation of immigration to, 90–91
  Eichmann trial in, 39, 118, 221–22
  German relations with, 54, 56
  Intifada in, 229–30, 247–48
  Six-Day War and, 183, 222–23, 224, 229, 230
  Soviet Jews and, 168, 169, 170
  student rebellions and, 40–41
Israel Bonds, 250
Italy, 64, 161
Izieu, raid on farmhouse in, 123, 126–28, 145
Izvestia, 204

Jackel, Eberhard, 36–37
Jackson, Jesse, 229
Japan, 41, 116, 212
Jenninger, Philipp, 52–54, 56–57, 279
Jewish Anti-Fascist Committee (JAC), 170, 204–6
Jewish Co-ordination Committee (Netherlands), 104
"Jewish Court of Honor," 104
Jewish Federation, 222, 239, 241, 242
Joffe, Joseph, 49, 289*n*
John Paul II, Pope, 243
Journal of Social Studies, 78
Jouvenel, Bertrand de, 296*n*
Juppé, Alain, 136
Justice Department, U.S., 245
  Office of Special Investigations in, 82, 210, 239, 300*n*

Kahane, Meir, 225
Kahn, Annette, 125–26
Kampelman, Max, 234
Katyn Forest massacre (1940), 214
Katzman, Abner, 96, 98–99
Keller, Bill, 172, 173, 184
Keller, Heinrich, 85
Kennedy, John F., 282
KGB, 175, 177, 189, 193, 196
Khatyn memorial, 213–14
Khrushchev, Nikita, 172, 201, 205, 218
  Babi Yar and, 188–89, 193
  Stalin attacked by, 165, 203, 211
Kiev, 185–98, 298*n*
  Memorial Complex in, 185–86
  see also Babi Yar
Kiev Encyclopedia, 187
Kirkland, Irene, 233
Kissinger, Henry, 232–33
Klarsfeld, Beate, 115, 145
Klarsfeld, Serge, 115, 120, 121, 126, 127, 133, 141, 145–46
Klebinder, Edith, 128
Knight, Robert, 66
Kohl, Helmut, 36, 44, 45, 46–50, 51, 55, 57, 244, 260, 261
Korean War, 40, 49
Korey, William, 167, 188
Korotich, Vitaly, 195, 196, 197–98, 214, 215–16, 217, 219
Kramer, Jane, 78
Kreisky, Bruno, 71–72, 73, 77, 81, 84
Kriegel, Blandine, 113, 114
Kristallnacht, 22, 52–54, 56, 57, 67, 289*n*

Lacombe, Lucien, 143
Lagrange, Simone, 121, 123–24
Langer, Lawrence L., 267
Lanzmann, Claude, 134, 138–39, 157, 284
Laqueur, Walter, 280
Larina, Anna Mikhailovna, 204
Latvia, 163, 178, 213
Laub, Dori, 273
Lauder, Ronald S., 83, 244
Lauenstein, 267
Lefèvre, Pierre, 112–13, 114
Lellouche, Pierre, 153
Lenin, V. I., 160, 168, 200, 216
Leningrad, siege of, 159, 210, 216
Le Pen, Jean-Marie, 113, 136, 137–38
Lesèvre, Lise, 119, 122, 124
Lévy, Bernard-Henri, 144, 147, 156
Levy, Lisa Wallach, 15, 19
Libération, 122, 134
Liechtenstein, 85
Lingens, Peter Michael, 71, 73, 80
Linz, 67, 70
Lipstadt, Deborah, 231, 232, 263, 264, 280–81

Literaturnaia Gazeta, 188, 200
Lithuania, 163, 169–70, 210, 213, 257
  collaboration battalion from, 178–80
Lottman, Herbert R., 147
Loumiauthr, Alexander, 75
Lowenberg, William J., 252, 262, 302*n*
Lozovsky, Solomon, 206
Luftwaffe, 42
Lump family, 21–24
Luza, Radomir, 66
Lyons:
  Barbie trial as viewed in, 130–33
  history of, 132–33

Maier, Charles S., 35
Malle, Louis, 143
Malzacher, Hans, 70
Maquis, 154
Marenches files, 149–50, 152
Markham, James, 42, 44
Markish, Peretz, 206
"martyrs," victims as 282
Martyrs Memorial and Museum of the Holocaust (Los Angeles), 238–39, 241–42
Marxism, 201, 203, 215–16
Mauthausen, 67, 97
Medvedev, Roy, 161, 165, 198–200, 203, 211
Meed, Ben, 231
Meissner-Blau, Freda, 91
Memoirs of Ivo Pannekoek, The (Dekking), 107
Mengele, Josef, 54–55, 252, 269
Mérindol, Pierre, 132, 133
Messerschmidt, Manfred, 84
Meyerhoff, Harvey ("Bud"), 252, 261, 263, 264, 302*n*
Mikhoels, Solomon, 170
Milton, Sybil, 57, 163, 243
Minguet, René, 150
Minsk, 171–85
  devastation of, 171–72
  Museum of Great Patriotic War in, 173–84, 208
  slaughter in ghetto of, 171, 210
Mitterrand, François, 47, 48, 113, 115, 142, 148, 149–50, 151–53
Mock, Alois, 90–91
mode rétro, 143
Modiano, Patrick, 143, 296*n*
Momjian, Set, 259
Mommsen, Hans, 32, 38, 42, 50
Monde, Le, 133–34, 135
Moscow News, 204
Moscow Radio, 170
Moulin, Jean, 115, 117, 138
Mubarak, Hosni, 85
Museum of Jewish Heritage—A Living Memorial to the Holocaust (New York), 254
Museum of Tolerance (Los Angeles), 238, 248–49, 254, 264
My Lai massacre, 280, 282

Nagasaki bombing, 116, 281
National Front party (France), 136, 137–38
National Public Radio, 239
National Socialism:
  Austrians' acceptance of, 65–66, 68, 76, 292*n*
  in Germany, 17, 33, 35, 37, 38, 42, 50, 260
  in Netherlands, 93, 94, 96–97
National Socialist party (NSB) (Netherlands), 93, 94, 96–97
Neither Right nor Left: Fascist Ideology in France (Sternhell), 147
Nekrich, Alexander, 164
neo-Nazis, 145, 245
Netherlands, 10, 64, 93–111
  anti-Semitism in, 99, 101, 109
  black widow's pension in, 93–95, 99, 109
  campaign against Jews in, 100, 101–4
  cooperation with Nazi occupiers in, 94, 97, 100, 102–4
  decimation of Jewish community in, 97–98
  German invasion of, 100
  history of Jewish community in, 100–101
  interest in war and Holocaust in, 108, 109–10
  Jews hidden by gentiles in, 95, 98
  National Socialism in, 93, 94, 96–97
  neutrality policy of, 99–100, 111
  pensions for Jews and resistance members in, 107–8
  persistent sensitivity about war years in, 94, 95, 98–99, 104–5
  resistance movement in, 96, 100, 102, 105, 107, 108, 109

return home of Jews and resistors to, 108–9
reverence for Frank in, 95–96
special registration in, 102–4
Waldheim scandal and, 286–87
Neue Kronen Zietung, 76, 88
Neumann, Moritz, 56, 288*n*
Neva, 298*n*
New Austria, 77
New Haven Farband, 273
New Yorker, 78
New York Times, 42, 46, 74, 83, 88–89, 169–70, 184, 256
Nicaragua, 49
Nimmerrichter, Richard, 88–89
Noir, Michel, 137
Nolte, Ernst, 35–37, 41, 42, 141
North Atlantic Treaty Organization (NATO), 32, 39, 46, 58, 153
nuclear weapons, 46, 47, 49, 116, 282, 283–84
Nuremberg Tribunal, 38, 75, 82, 116
Nutkiewicz, Michael, 222, 223, 241, 242

Office of Special Investigations, U.S. (OSI), 82, 210, 239, 300*n*
Ogonyok, 195, 197, 214
Operation Black, 75
Ophuls, Marcel, 143, 156, 157, 284
Oppenheimer, Henny, 13–14, 23–24
Ory, Pascal, 140, 147, 143–44
Ovchinnikov, B., 188
Ovsishcher, Lev, 175

Paape, A. Harry, 97, 98, 99, 100, 108, 109
Pain, The (Duras), 148
Palestine Liberation Organization (PLO), 40, 226, 256, 300*n*
Palestinians:
Intafada and, 229–30, 247–48
suffering of Jews compared to, 281
Pamyat, 168, 217–18
Paris, Erna, 123
Pasqua, Charles, 136–37, 150–51
Passover, 282–83
"Past That Will Not Pass Away, The" (Nolte), 35–37, 41, 42
Paxton, Robert O., 39, 141 ,142–43, 151, 152, 156, 284
People's party (Austria), 72, 77, 78, 81, 83, 90, 292*n*
perestroika, 166, 171, 172, 183, 202, 218–219
Perroux, Camille, 130–31
Pétain, Marshal Henri Philippe, 132, 141, 147, 153
attitudes of young people toward, 154–55
as father figure for nation, 143
Mitterrand's views on, 151–52
televised debate about, 150
Peter, Friedrich, 73
Peterson, Peter, 260–61
Peterson, Wolfgang, 44
Petrakova, Tanya, 186–87, 189, 190
Pius XII, Pope, 179
Playing for Time, 239
Poland, 15, 39, 40, 97, 159–60, 212, 214, 243, 266, 270–71
Pol Pot, 41, 116, 135, 281, 283
Pompidou, Georges, 142
Pravda, 204
President's Commission on the Holocaust, 227–28, 254, 257–59
Presser, Jacob, 97, 98, 100, 101, 102, 103, 109
Profil, 71, 73, 74, 76, 80, 84
Purge, The (Lottman), 147

Quaddafi, Muammar, 85

Radzinsky, Edward, 163–64
Rally for the Republic (RPR), 136–37
Rathkolb, Oliver, 65, 68, 69, 74
rationalization, 216, 280–82
see also relativization
Ravensbrück, 124
Reagan, Nancy, 244, 246
Reagan, Ronald, 82, 252
Bitburg affair and, 11, 47, 48, 49, 55, 228, 301*n*
honored by Hier, 244, 246
Red Army, 34, 72, 212, 213
Reder, Walter, 73
Redgrave, Vanessa, 239
Reifman, Léon, 128
Reiter, Else Baum, 20
Reiter, Ron, 20
Reitz, Edgar, 41
relativization, 34, 35, 41, 45–46, 280, 281–82
in Barbie trial, 116, 120–21, 135
Renn, Walter F., 55–56

resistance:
  Bruskina affair and, 174–85, 282, 298*n*
  in Netherlands, 96, 100, 102, 105, 107, 108, 109
Resistance, French, 143–43, 150, 152, 201, 282
  Barbie trial and, 113, 115, 116, 117, 119, 120, 121, 123, 124, 125–26, 131, 138
  collaborationists purged by, 140, 147
  Jews' bitterness toward, 121
  Marenches files and, 149–50
  myths about, 114, 132, 141, 148, 149, 154, 155
Resnik, Regina, 169–70
revisionism, *see* historical revisionism
Charles E. Revson Foundation, 273
Ringel, Erwin, 90
Ritschel, Elisabeth, 74
Roques, Henri, 148–49
Rosenbaum, Eli, 292*n*
Rosenblatt, Gary, 239, 244–45, 251
Rosensaft, Hadassah, 252, 255
Rosensaft, Menachem Z., 225–26, 244, 245–46, 247, 248, 250, 285, 300*n*
Rosenthal, A. M., 88–89
Rossner, Karl, 70
Rothschilds, 65, 198
Rousso, Henry, 139–40, 142, 147, 155
Helena Rubinstein Foundation, 263
Rudd, Mark, 223–24
Rudof, Joanne, 272, 273
Rushdie, Salman, 283
Russian nationalism, 217–18
Russian Orthodoxy, 161, 190
Russian Revolution (1917), 160, 161, 168
Rybakov, Anatoli, 207
Rykov, Aleksei, 207

Safire, William, 256
Salomon, Berta, 21–22, 23–24
Saudi Arabia, 56
Savitsky, Mikhail, 208–9
Schlayon, Alexander, 194–97, 198
Schlusstrich, 11, 44–45, 47–50
Schmidt, Anton, 17, 29
Schneider, Peter, 39, 40–41
Schuster, Frank Feist, 19
Sedar, Marianne, 144, 146
Seigneret, Jacques, 131
Seigneret, Lucette, 131–32
Senate, U.S., 255
Sharansky, Nathan (né Anatoly), 162
Shatrov, Mikhail F., 202, 207–8, 216
Shayevitch, Adolf, 170
Sher, Neal, 55, 82
Sherbatseyvich, Volodya, 174
Shoah, 134–35, 138, 284
Sichrovsky, Peter, 72
Siegel, Mark, 255–56, 257
Singer, Israel, 63, 81–82
Sinowatz, Fred, 77
Six-Day War (1967), 183, 222–23, 224, 229, 230
Slavs, 171, 191, 298*n*
Sobibor, 97
Socialist party (Austria), 72, 76–77, 82
Socialist party (France), 150–51
Soetendorp, Awraham, 97–98
Sokol, Yuri, 194
Solarz, Stephen J., 227
Sommer, Theo, 57
Sonn, Herbert Naftali, 17, 25–26
Sonnenfeldt, Helmut, 45, 46, 48, 54
Sorrow and the Pity, The, 143, 284
S.O.S. Racisme (Stop Racism), 129
Soulier, André, 133
Sound of Music, The, 61, 62
Soviet Union, 11, 34, 35, 37, 39, 40, 46, 57, 58, 60, 75, 142, 158–219, 225, 263, 279, 280, 281, 283, 284
  access to archives in, 163, 215, 299*n*–300*n*
  anti-Semitism in, 167–71, 173, 182, 183–84, 188–92, 194, 205, 217–18, 246
  art as a vehicle of memory in, 207–9
  Austria and, 69, 72, 85
  authoritarianism in, 164–65, 166, 201
  Babi Yar and, 186–98, 207, 210–11, 218, 299*n*
  Bruskina affair in, 174–85, 282, 298*n*
  casualties in, 161, 171, 185, 198, 297*n*
  centrality of World War II in history of, 160–62, 165
  collaboration in, 160, 163, 178–80, 184, 191, 210, 213
  commemorations in, 170, 194, 210–211, 242, 284, 301*n*
  denial of Jewry's disproportionate suffering in, 159–60, 167–68, 169, 187–88, 193–94, 216–17, 218

different attitudes toward war in, 199–200
emigration of Jews from, 168, 169, 171, 189, 218
family as vehicle of memory in, 206–207
forces working against memory in, 212–18
gender gap in, 200, 299*n*
historians subordinated to politicians in, 198, 215
historical reassessment in, 162–66, 171, 198, 200–204, 209–10, 215–216, 287
history of war distorted in, 212–14
improvements in status of Jews in, 169–71, 218
Jewish homeland in, 168–69, 205–6
Marxist ideology in, 201, 203, 215–216
nationalities issue in, 166–67, 168
oral tradition in, 204–5, 299*n*
"peace lesson" in, 158–59
plight of Jews in, 167–69
reemergence of memory in, 163, 204–211
resurgence of Russian nationalism in, 217–18
war-crimes trials in, 179, 210
war memorials in, 161–62, 171 ,185–186, 213–14

Soviet War Encyclopedia, 184
Speer, Albert, 250
Stahl, Lesley, 244
Stalin, Joseph, 37, 41, 167, 181, 200, 206, 218, 279, 280, 281, 299*n*
historical reassessment of, 162–63, 165, 201, 203-4, 211, 216
Hitler's pact with, 151, 160, 163, 212, 213
purges under, 160, 162–63, 169, 170, 191, 200, 207, 297*n*

State Department, U.S., 69, 227, 266
Stein & Day, 250
Steinberg, Elan, 80, 82, 292*n*
Steinberger, Martin, 19
Steinhage, Martin, 29
Stern, 40
Stern, Fritz, 32
Stern, Lee, 20
Sternhell, Zev, 147, 296*n*
Steyr-Daimler-Puch Works, 69–70
Steyrer, Kurt, 76, 78, 293*n*
Stobbe, Dietrich, 53–54
student rebellions:
in France, 39, 142, 144
in Germany, 39–41, 45
in United States, 39, 223–24

Sturmabteilung (Storm Troopers; SA), 74, 77
Stürmer, Michael, 46, 49
Suslov, Mikhail, 205–6
Sweet, Paul R., 69–71
Syndrome de Vichy, Le (Rousso), 147

Taibaudier, Mme., 127
Talisman, Mark E., 252–53, 264
Tas, Louis M., 101, 103
Tass, 210, 215
Taylor, Elizabeth, 244
Tazdait, Djida, 135–36
television, 41–44, 134–35, 145, 150, 156, 273, 284, 300*n*
Thatcher, Margaret, 239
Theresienstadt, 25, 97, 98, 104, 129
Thomas, Michel, 120
Tidl, Georg, 74
Tonningen, Florentine van, 93–95, 99
Tonningen, Meinoudt Rost van, 93, 95
Tovmasyan, Nonna, 172, 174, 214
Trash, the City and Death (Fassbinder), 44–45
Treblinka, 234, 247, 250
Trotsky, Leon, 163, 168, 180
Trud, 175
Trusk, Kirill, 174
Truth About Austria, The, 88
Turkey, 259, 281, 302*n*
Two Kinds of Destruction: The Shattering of the German Reich and the End of European Jewry (Hillgruber), 34–35, 36

UCLA, 267
Ukraine, 185–98, 217, 299*n*
anti-Semitism in, 190–92
Bandera's rebellion in, 212–13
collaboration in, 163, 178, 191
see also Babi Yar

Ukratelye Film, 195
United Kingdom, 161, 239
United Nations, 90, 169, 225, 256
Waldheim as Secretary-General of, 75, 78–79

United States, 11, 46, 57, 60, 69, 90, 131, 142, 154, 155, 161, 166, 210, 220–275
  anti-Semitism in, 224, 229, 233, 245, 250
  anti-war protestors in, 39, 223–24
  atrocities ascribed to, 40, 41, 49, 116, 120, 280, 282
  awakening of survivor consciousness in, 221–23, 224
  Bitburg affair and, 11, 45, 47–48, 49–50, 55, 228–29, 286, 301*n*
  commemorations in, 222, 226–44, 248–49, 251–66, 284, 300*n*–301*n*
  creative efforts at prompting memory in, 287
  education about Holocaust in, 286
  financial success of survivors in, 224
  Holocaust experience foreign to, 233–234, 235
  Holocaust imagery exploited in, 224–225, 230, 232, 237, 244–48
  Jewish activism in, 223–26
  Jewish anxiety in, 229–30
  obsession with Holocaust in, 230–232
  Soviet archival exchange with, 163, 215
  suppression of memory in, 220–21
  videotape projects in, 239, 266–75
  Waldheim affair and, 75, 82, 85
U.S. Holocaust Memorial Museum (Washington, D.C.), 227, 228, 238, 251–66, 273, 274
  debate over appropriateness of, 230–236
  displays and technology at, 264–66
  fund raising for, 258–59, 262, 302*n*
  genesis of, 255–57
  Germany and, 259–62, 263
  inclusion of Armenian tragedy in, 259, 302*n*
  personal tributes for donors to, 263
  universality issue and, 254–55, 257–258
  unveiling of cornerstone for, 251–53

Vasiliu, Tatyana Leonidovna, 158–59
Vatican, 85, 131, 179, 239, 243
Veil, Simone, 116–17, 137–38
Vergès, Jacques, 113, 116–17, 119, 120–121, 122, 134
Vichy government, 114, 139, 147, 153, 155, 156, 284
  anti-Jewish laws of, 132, 133–34, 151, 152
  Halter's plan for trial of, 128–29
  Mitterrand's views on, 151–52
  myths about, 140, 141, 152
  Paxton's thesis on, 142–43
  televised debate about, 150
videotaped oral histories, 239, 266–75, 285–86
Vienna, 63, 64–65
  Jewish community of, 65–66, 67, 79–80
Vietnam War, 40, 49, 116, 120, 223–24, 225, 233, 235, 280, 282
Vietnam War Memorial (Washington, D.C.), 227, 235, 258
Vinocur, John, 46
Vlasov, A. V., 188
Vranitzky, Franz, 84, 85

Waldheim, Kurt, 10, 11, 62–64, 67, 72, 73–92, 95, 164, 243, 279, 280, 286–287, 292*n*
  analyses of victory of, 77–79, 292*n*, 293*n*
  criticism of WJC's campaign against, 80–82, 86
  panel of historians' investigation of, 83–84
  pressure for resignation of, 84–85, 86
  surveys reflecting effect of, 87–88, 89–90
  as UN Secretary-General, 75, 78–79
  as vehicle of memory, 63, 86
  wartime record of, 74–75, 292*n*
  Wiesenthal's defense of, 81
Wallace, Bert, 19, 20
Wallach, Yehuda L., 84
War and Remembrance, 303*n*
war-crimes trials, 55, 285
  in Austria, 69, 88
  of Eichmann, 39, 118, 221–22
  at Nuremberg, 38, 75, 82, 116
  in Soviet Union, 179, 210
  "war crimes" vs. "crimes against humanity" in, 113, 116
  see also Barbie, Klaus
War of the Bombers, The, 42–43
Warsaw Ghetto, 250, 266
Warsaw Pact, 58

Washington Post, 168
Wehrmacht, 33, 34, 39, 72, 74, 82, 86
Weimar Republic, 50, 52
Weiss, Johanna Lump, 15
Weizmann, Chaim, 35–36, 42
Weizsäcker, Richard von, 37, 51, 52, 289*n*
Wertheimer, Samson, 65
Westerbork, 97, 98, 104
Wexler, Anne, 257
Wiesel, Elie, 220, 222, 241, 250, 282
 Bitburg affair and, 228–29, 301*n*
 national Holocaust museum and, 227, 253, 254, 257, 258, 260–63, 264, 302*n*
 Petersen's relationship with, 260–61
 in President's Commission, 227, 257, 258
 resignation of, 262, 263
Wieseltier, Leon, 221–22, 231–32, 242, 245, 246–47, 248, 249
Wiesenberg, Hermann, 20
Wiesenthal, Simon, 53, 67, 240–41, 243–44
 Peter investigated by, 73
 Waldheim affair and, 81, 84
Simon Wiesenthal Center (Los Angeles), 170, 237–51, 254, 264, 274
 accomplishments of, 242–43, 251
 bitterness between Martyrs Museum and, 240–42
 establishment of, 240–41
 facilities of, 238
 multifaceted activities of, 239
 Museum of Tolerance at, 238, 248–249, 254, 264
 see also Hier, Rabbi Marvin
Wilhelmina, Queen of Netherlands, 100
World Jewish Congress (WJC), 35–36, 73, 91
 Waldheim affair and, 74, 75, 76, 80–82, 83, 85, 86, 292*n*
World War I, 47, 64, 99, 143
Wouk, Herman, 303*n*
Wounded Knee, 280, 282
Wyman, David, 280

Yad Vashem (Jerusalem), 87, 96, 129, 233, 238, 287
Yale, Video Archive for Holocaust Testimonies at, 266–75, 285
Yashchenko, Viktor R., 163
"Year of Reflection" (Austria), 83, 85–86, 89, 91
Yevtushenko, Yevgeny, 188–89, 207
Yiddish, 168, 218
Young, Andrew, 256
Young, James, 254, 255, 269, 281
Young Arabs of Lyons and its Suburbs, 135–36
Young Pioneers, 176
Yugoslav War Crimes Commission, 75

Zeit, Die, 36, 37, 57
Zelman, Leon, 79–80, 82, 86–87
Zivs, Samuil, 194
Zlatin, Sabina, 128
Zweig, Stefan, 65